Consumption and Management

New Discovery and Applications

Bingxin Wu

CHARTRIDGE
BOOKS OXFORD

Chartridge Books Oxford
Hexagon House
Avenue 4
Station Lane
Witney
Oxford OX28 4BN, UK
Tel: +44 (0) 1865 59555; Fax: +44 (0) 1865 884448;
Email: info@biohealthcarepublishing.com
Website: www.biohealthcarepublishing.com
First published in 2011 by Chartridge Books Oxford
ISBN: 978 1 907568 07 7

British Library Cataloguing-in-Publication Data: a catalogue record for this book is available from the British Library.

Typeset by Domex, India
Printed in the UK and USA
Cover design by Hutchins Creative
English translation by Bang Jin

Contents

List of figures and tables

Figures

Tables

Preface

By Professor Yuanchen Dai

Mr. Bingxin Wu wrote a book called *Consumption and Management* when he was 70 years old. It is an honor for me to read it first. And I have many thoughts and feelings.

Last April, I heard his speech and read his paper about the theory of consumption at a proseminar on theory of consumption in Peking University. Then I read his book *Bingxin Wu Anthology*, published ten years ago, so he and his book left a deep impression on me. My field is the history of social development. I profoundly feel that people have been more thirsting for living better than in the past, which has led to the improvement of human society for thousands of years. The desire for and realization of increased consumption and higher living standards from one generation to another are motivation for society to create and accumulate more wealth. Human history is a history of creating. The rise of a society is the rise of creation. Therefore, I think that Mr. Wu's emphasis on the research of consumption theory has captured the fountain of power of social improvement. Upon such consensus, I encouraged him to publish *Consumption and Management*, and I offered to write the preface.

During communication with Mr. Wu, I learned that he is from Shandong Province with a legendary background. His father died when he was five years old and his mother died when he was six. He began to farm when he was seven. He liked learning when he was young, but he could not afford to buy books because of his poor family situation. He borrowed books from neighbors and studied in the open air. He knew well of the life direction indicated by Chinese culture and its established ambition for rendering service to the nation. At the call of country, he left his home to work on constructions in Baotou Iron and Steel Base at the age of 19. Then he was transferred to work in the Inner Mongolia Mining Bureau, Baotou Valvate Plant and so on. He successively assumed the office of accountant, section chief, chairman of the labor union, secretary of the party branch and president of technical school, and was rewarded for his contributions many times.

Mr. Wu retired from a state-owned enterprise 22 years ago. In the spirit of the saying 'As heaven maintains vigor through movements, a gentle man should constantly strive for self-perfection', he established his own enterprise from Baotou to Huainan and then settled in Jinan. His Sanzhu Group possessed health care products, medicine, medical equipment, and ecological cosmetics industries. It had fixed assets of billions of yuan, and its highest annual sales income reached 8.4 billion yuan with 820 million yuan in annual tax. It had been the biggest private enterprise in China, and was called an 'economic miracle' by domestic and foreign economists. In 1994, Sanzhu Group was confirmed to be a high-tech enterprise by the State Scientific and Technological Commission and Shandong Scientific and Technological Commission. In 1997, it was confirmed to be a key high-tech enterprise of a national torch plan by the State Scientific and Technological Commission. In the same year, it won the five star diamond award issued by the American High Quality Service Scientific Association. In December 1997, 'Sanzhu Trademark' was confirmed as a Shandong famous brand. The outstanding achievement of Sanzhu received many praises from the Party and state leaders.

In society, many people know Mr. Wu as a successful entrepreneur, but actually he is a hard- working scholar who likes learning theories and exploring thinking. He had been the president of a technical school. Nowadays, he has been invited as a visiting professor and special visiting researcher by many domestic and foreign universities and research institutes. He has continued writing articles. At the beginning of the Economic Reforms and Openness, he wrote with great sincerity to the State Council to propose his plan to manage the national affairs.

Mr. Wu is a brave and wise person indicated first by his cognition of market economy. For most people today, knowledge of a market economy is not a problem, but in the early 1980s, there were many debates about whether China should establish a market economy system. Under the condition that the central government did not confirm that our national economic system should be a market economy, Mr. Wu had proposed that the socialist economy should be a market economy in his paper 'Consumption and Economic Law'. He discussed this issue through origination and development of economic law in human economic life. He claims that our country must implement market economy and that consumption is a traction force for production competition. He firmly believes that consumption creates production and wealth and is the most important driving force for economic development. Therefore Mr. Wu defined consumption as his long-term research task 30 years ago.

Consumption is an important behavior and process in human social economic activities. Traditional classification of consumption divides it into production consumption and living consumption. Mr. Wu classifies consumption into three kinds: living consumption, production consumption and social consumption. Social consumption mainly means public consumption such as national administration consumption, national defense consumption, scientific research consumption, and education consumption. Compared with the old method, I think this classification is creative and advanced.

As is known to all, there are four stages for the general process of social production: production, distribution, exchange, and consumption. Production is a basic stage that not only determines distribution and exchange but also determines consumption. Types, quality, and quantity of products of social production objectively regulate consumption's object, structure, and patterns. No production, no consumption. However, consumption also has its significant position and effects in the process of production and reproduction. In a static view, consumption is the termination of the social production process, which is the final test for the economic benefits of reproduction. In a dynamic view, it is the precursor of the next production process, which provides targets, demands, and power for the new production process. In addition, it provides important feedback information for production and reproduction through commodity circulation and markets.

For this reason, consumption is the final target of social production and the stage of social reproduction process. Consumption is an indispensable condition for human existence and labor force recovery. Labor force recovery is a precondition to guarantee the continuity of the production process. The influence of production on consumption is that production provides objects for consumption, determines consumption patterns, and inspires new consumption needs. Consumption also affects production and improves or hinders the development of production. In the capitalist system, workers are exploited by capitalists. Economic crises as the consequence of overproduction are inevitable because of the antagonism and contradiction between great increases of production and the relative decrease of purchasing power of working people. In socialist society, material and cultural living levels of people improve with the development of production. The rise of people's consumption level, in turn, continuously promotes the development of socialist production.

It can be seen that consumption is a significant stage. To a certain extent, it has not only a huge effect on total economy, but also a key function. Consumption cannot be separated from research and production. They supplement and promote each other.

Generally speaking, entrepreneurs are interested in production and circulation, because the production process is basic. The most important things are what kind of modern equipment is to be used and what measures are to be taken in the production process to make sure that the products produced are suitable for the market's demand. The other one is circulation. Circulation mainly refers to the market, since the value of the products produced by enterprises is ultimately realized through the market. If products cannot win the market or be washed out from the market, there will be a crisis in the enterprise. General entrepreneurs always focus on market and production but give little attention to research on consumption, because consumption is the last stage of the whole social production process.

Mr. Wu suggests that consumption is not passive and negative, and it has determining effects compared with production. He has seen that consumption has a huge counteractive influence on production, circulation, and distribution, so he decided to research this question. Marx revealed the production secret of capitalist production, capitalist exploitation, and the trend of capital accumulation, starting from commodity. Mr. Wu discussed every aspect of consumption of the whole society starting from consumption, which included many economic problems such as production, research, revenue, finance, price, value, currency, credit and other economic issues. This book has taken him more than 30 years, and required his utmost effort. This book reveals his profound theoretical basis for exploring scientific truth and his novel method of studying economic problems.

I think that it took an academic insight for the author to set consumption as a breakthrough of economics research to carry out long-term special research. After reading the entire book, I think the author makes several points with a new perspective, in the following ways.

Key features of the book

Using subjects to study consumption problems

This is the first monograph that uses many subjects to systemically and wholly study consumption problems. It not only studies consumption from economics, management and marketing perspectives, but also from those of philosophy, sociology, culture, and history. In particular, the author utilizes systematic and scientific theories and methods to study consumption, as he recognizes that consumption is a complicated and dynamic system to research. He uses quantitative analysis in many aspects and describes the positions, influence, and significance of consumption in the entire economic field, even social life.

Studying consumption through history, reality and the future

The author studies origination, development, function, and continuous new change of consumption through history, reality, and the future. From the beginning of human society until modern times, Mr. Wu reveals a truth that the whole history of the development of human society, including the extension of human life and social development, is pushed by the power of consumption. The history of human economic development suggests that the ultimate target of each social cell's economic behavior depends on consumption, and the final direction of any product is consumption. Therefore, all important social activities take place around consumption. When the social machine starts to move, consumption begins. When people are born, consumption begins. From heroes to common people, from a macro view to a micro view, from part to whole, from individuals to colonies, the whole human society must be in the process of consumption and creating consumption as long as vigor exists.

Consumption is the eternal core topic in economics, which is always focused on by economists and economic theorists and is emphasized by national departments and decision-makers. The mechanism of consumption indicates that the circulation of consumption is vital for the whole circulation and effects of the national economy.

The position and function of consumption in the development of the national economy

In the macro view, and with thorough research on consumption from different angles, the book makes clear the position and function of consumption in the development of the whole national economy and the power of social development created by the continuous extension of consumption. He provides many policy-directed suggestions that can be the scientific basis for government to make a decision on consumption problems. Mr. Wu suggests that the main power of development of the national economy is not investment or trade but consumption. This view greatly accords with spirit of the Seventeenth National Congress of the Communist Party of China. When discussing the transition of the economic development mode, the report of the Seventeenth National Congress stated:

> We must keep to the new path of industrialization with Chinese characteristics, pursue the policy of boosting domestic demand, particularly the needs of consumption, and propel three transitions in the mode of economic growth: the transition from relying mainly on investment and export to relying on a well-coordinated combination of consumption, investment and export; the transition from secondary industry serving as the major driving force to primary, secondary and tertiary industries jointly driving economic growth; and the transition from relying heavily on increased consumption of material resources to relying mainly on advancement in science and technology, improvement in the quality of the workforce and innovation in management.

The Seventeenth National Congress emphasized expanding consumption to make it a pulling force for economic growth. Economic development in 2007 indicated that the power of consumption for promoting the national economy first exceeded investment and trade since reform and opening to be the leading power of economy. The development of history was completely in accordance with the conclusion of Mr. Wu's research.

New opinions about consumption

The book puts forwards many new opinions, concepts and thoughts about consumption, such as the structure of the consumption chain, the structure of the value chain, the law of value of consumption, the contribution of the nature of consumption, the investment nature of consumption, consumption as a force for expanding reproduction, and consumption as the direction of the money vote for consumers. These creative opinions not only help readers to recognize the value of consumption, but also broaden our horizons from a macro-economic perspective. Mr. Wu suggests that consumption is both the starting point and the end point of production.

Consumption–production–distribution–exchange–consumption is not only an operating law but also a logic course. Consumption is the motivation of production, but the production process also involves consumption. Production not only creates consumption products but also continuously creates new needs of consumption and patterns. These academic thoughts can give new inspiration for research about consumption.

Rational analysis of theories on consumption

The book does not copy theories about consumption at all times and all over the world, but rationally analyzes and critically absorbs these theories. The book profoundly analyzes consumption level theories of Confucius, the inaction consumption theory of Taoism, and the extravagant consumption of Guan Tzu. Although they are old problems, they make us feel new and fresh. For instance, for the consumption thinking of Lao Tzu and Taoism, the author considers that Lao Tzu and Taoism promoted inaction consumption that advocated being content with one's lot and taking things as they come. It denied the enjoyment of consumption and restrained people's consumption desires. Lao Tzu and Taoism demanded no desire in the mind, and being content with one's lot to restrain people's continuous needs of consumption. The author much admires the consumption thinking of Guan Tzu, including his extravagant consumption ideas. Guan Tzu had opinions about both abstention consumption and extravagant consumption. The principle of abstention consumption was a generally applicable foundation principle. The opinion of extravagant consumption was proposed in particular conditions to stimulate social production, which should be affirmed and admired. Mr. Wu thinks abstention consumption and extravagant consumption are the unification of realistic stability and social development.

In addition, the author brilliantly analyzes Adam Smith's An Inquiry into the Nature and Causes of the Wealth of Nations, Keynes's The General Theory of Employment, Interest and Money, and Samuelson's Economics, admiration, criticizing, abandoning and adopting them. The book provides a systematic account on consumption thinking in Marx's Capital. In Capital, there is no particular part about consumption, but many chapters have discussions about it. It is estimable for the author to connect with other works of Marx to draw a conclusion on Marx's consumption thinking. The author makes a relatively systematic generalization on Deng Xiaoping's consumption thinking including the strategic target of consumption, the strategic emphasis of consumption, and specific consumption policies. It not only makes us feel not only that the author has a profound theoretic basis, but also that Consumption and Management has been established on a solid theoretical basis.

Concluding remarks

Publication of *Consumption and Management* has external as well as internal motivations. In the macro view, it grew during the period of the economic reform and reflects the acclimated historical trend of reform. In a micro view, it is the result of Mr. Wu's elaborative research and continuous thoughts. The book derives essences of excellent scholarship from forefathers and the West. It develops through combining the economic thoughts of Marx and Deng Xiaoping and the author's practice. The book builds on reasonable factors of excellent traditional economic theories and explores, discusses, and concludes new economic theories from economic practices in new situations, which include new breakthroughs, opinions, and thinking modes. Great practice is produced by great theory. Today's achievement of Sanzhu benefits greatly from Mr. Wu's consumption theory.

Overall, it can be seen that *Consumption and Management* has been created through theory and practice. The author has worked in state-owned enterprises for more than 30 years, so he has abundant practice and experience with a planned economy and private economy nearly 30 years after the economic reform and openness. Things written on this basis are not only rich in substance but also have many unique opinions on comparative research. Mr. Wu has been an executive committee member of the National Business Association, vice director of China's Private Technical Industrialist Association, Shandong PPCC member, Jinan standing PPCC member, chairman of Shandong Private Economy Labor Union, and vice chairman of Jinan Business Union. These roles have offered him the opportunity to have contact with the decision-making administration of the country, which provides more bases in the macro view for his research.

As a part of his study, Mr. Wu's theory reflects an individual view, with many questions that need further research. As an individual view, if it can suggest research methods for everybody, it will contribute to the development of theories. In the scientific research field, there is no single person who can exhaust a truth or complete an entire theoretic system; they can only blaze a way in researching and exploring truth.

During my communication with Mr. Wu, I have come to admire his unremitting will deeply. Although he is nearly 70 years old, he leaves no stone unturned and finds every opportunity to continue his research diligently, as he deals with multifarious affairs. I expect that this book can be recognized and valued by elites from governments, enterprises, and academia after being published. Nowadays, the publication industry is flourishing and publishes thousands of books every year, but good books are scarce.

As an experienced economic theoretical researcher, I can say that *Consumption and Management* is a good book that is worth reading.

Professor Dai

Professor Yuanchen Dai was born in 1926. He is an honored academician of the Chinese Academy of Social Sciences, professor and researcher at the Economic Institute of the Chinese Academy of Social Sciences, as well as a famous economist. He was the eighth national committee member of CPPCC, committee member of Taikangaoqiao Sodality of CPPCC, special adviser of National Federation of Industry and Commerce, decision-making consultant of Municipal Party Committee of Beijing, expert consultant of Beijing Municipal Government. Professor Yuanchen Dai mainly engages in theoretic research of macro-economic management and Chinese economic system reform. He has written more than ten books such as *Socialist Macroeconomics*, *New Theory of Chinese Economy*, *Non-loose Reality and Loose Realization-Macroeconomic Management under Dual Systems*, *Exploration of Chinese Price Problem, and Researches on Chinese Economic System Reform Modes*, *Chinese Labor Market Cultivation and Wage Reform*, and *From Closed Economy to Opening Economy*, and hundreds of papers.

About the author

Bingxin Wu, born in 1938 in Rongcheng Shandong Province, is the Board Chairman of the Sanzhu Group Company, honorary professor of Beijing Genetic Engineering Research Institute and Beijing Nuozhou Institute of Biology, and director of Shizhen Institute of Biology. He is also an honorable professor at Shandong University, contract researcher for Shandong Academy of Social Sciences and the Oriental Institute, and guest professor at the Institute of Microecology of Dalian Medical University. He is an executive member of China Association of Industry and Commerce, vice president of Shandong Jinan Municipal Association of Industry and Commerce, director of Shandong Private Entrepreneurs Union, vice president of the Association of Chinese Professionals, and the deputy director of Chinese Private Scientific and Technological Association and the National Private Technology Entrepreneur Association, as well as the standing director of China Chinese Medicine Institute. He was given an award as 'China's meritorious figure in developing mart economy' by the China Seminar of Mart Economy and *China Mart Economy* newspaper and won the Global Diamond Award of the American Association of Sciences for outstanding service. He has invented nine personal patents, including an international one, and has published *Collected Works of Wu Bingxin* and *Passionate Poems of Wu Bingxin*, and more than 20 papers on management at home and abroad.

Fax: 0086-531-83532368
Tel: 0086-531-8353236
Email: haohai-feng@163.com

1

Introduction

Consumption is a holy power.

Consumption creates everything in human society. It deserves a high position in society because of its holiness.

Consumption is the permanent focus in economics which draws attention not only of the economic circle and of economists, but also of the national functional departments and decision-makers. The mechanism of consumption shows that the operation of consumption has decisive significance for a wholesome national economic operation and its efficiency.

Consumption is the beginning and end of the economic development cycle, as well as the sum of all human activities. It is the sum of awareness, understanding, thinking, thinking pattern, and consumption awareness acted upon human brains by three important consumption practices. It is not only a conclusion of academic theories but also a product of theory and practice. We can say that this is a new revolutionary systematic theory of consumption.

This book is about the systematic theory of consumption science. It is a comprehensive study of the origin, development, classification, principles, application, and other systematic theories of consumption; it researches the origin of natural science and social science and concerns a great number of subjects, for example, philosophy, history, economics, management, leadership science, marketing, and merchandising. It is a large-scale multidisciplinary and academic work of penetration and integration.

Consumption is the sum of all the human activities. There is no society without consumption, no economy without consumption, no human-nature relations without consumption. Therefore, to guide all the scientific research of human beings and direct the consuming practice with consumption is the base of academic theoretical research. It is the starting point, foothold, and destination.

Subject definition

Human consumption is the sum of the whole consumption process that is driven by the metabolism instinct to obtain material from nature, then to create new needs and desires by human knowledge, and further to create new material products (including the spiritual culture). It includes the definitions of narrow-sense and broad-sense consumption. *Consumption and Management* puts consumption in the broad background of human social science and natural science. It studies the social position, social roles, and function principles of consumption. It is a science that focuses on the practice and function principles of production, living and social consumption.

At the same time, *Consumption and Management* deals with the relations between human consumption and nature, human consumption and economic development, human consumption and social civilization and progress, human consumption and consumption practice, as well as human consumption and consumption awareness and action.

The ladder structure

These are the levels of the ladder structure:

- the systematic theory of structure consumption science;
- the three important consumptions of constitutional structure;
- the sub-system structure of each consumption system
- the detailed classification of the sub-systematic consumption system (the detailed classification is left out)
- the leadership management during the practice of three major consumptions.

Three important consumption systems

In the three important consumption systems, scientific research and production consumption are the premise of the realization of living consumption and social consumption. Scientific research and production consumption can be divided into three sub-systems:

- the scientific research and production consumption for the realization of living consumption – the scientific research and production

consumption which satisfies the increasing material and mental consumption needs of humans – the consumption realization of capital's commodity production and exchange management process
- the scientific research and production consumption for the realization of social consumption – the scientific research and production consumption which satisfies the increasing material and mental consumption needs of society
- the scientific research and production consumption of basic industry which bases itself on the first and second sub-systems.

The realization of a continuous increase in living consumption, social consumption, and research and production consumption requires the development of the country itself. Only with continuous growth in productivity can the country promise the three important consumptions to promote the natural cyclic development of economy. Research and production consumption derive from consumption; research consumption is the production consumption for new knowledge and new techniques which constantly creates new consumption needs and consumption desires. It creates new consumption commodities for living and social life, and new consumption patterns, and pushes the development of new consumption levels.

Object of study

The research subjects of *Consumption and Management* are three important consumption systems (shortened as three systems) of humanity's living consumption, scientific research and production consumption, and social consumption in light of human consumption.

Consumption and Management regards three systems as its main research objects and researches on the general rules and all the relations such as the relations between consumers; relations between consumption and demand; relations between consumption and commodity exchange; relations between consumption and distribution; relations between consumption and management; relations between consumption and nature; relations between consumption and the development of human beings; relations between consumption and human wealth; relations between consumption and productivity and production relations; relations between consumption and economic base and superstructure between the three systems and social activities in the perspective of human consumption. It tries to figure out the basic natural rules, market regulation rules, and macro-control rules of how consumption affects economic development, as well as the general and specific rules in developing the process of all kinds of economic relations.

Tasks of the subject

The basic research tasks of *Consumption and Management* are to use Marxist consumption theory to summarize the experience of consumption practice, to make clear the position and functions of consumption in social reproduction, to increase people's consciousness to know and use the consumption mechanism and rules, to put the understanding of the consumption on a systematic, theoretical, and scientific basis, to study and borrow the general doctrine on consumption at home and abroad, to better master and apply consumption rules, to supply the scientific foundation for development of the strategic goals of national economy and the consumption plan, principles, and measures for the realization of these goals, to propose a scientific basis for the rationalization of the industrial and product structure of national economy, to cultivate talents, and to push the development of productivity of consumption society and the development of social civilization.

By making clear the consumption mechanism and its movement principles, *Consumption and Management* attempts through:

- research on the internal connection between consumption, production, distribution, exchange and consumption by consumers, to discuss the nature of consumption and features of socialism with Chinese characteristics under the premise of a market-oriented economy, and its position and function in cyclic national economic development
- the internal connections and interactions of consumption and economic development, to discuss the decisive function of consumption in promoting economic growth as well as the internal connection between consumption and industrial structure adjustment
- research on the internal connections and interactions among the needs of consumption, consumption structure, consumption pattern, and consumption level, to discuss the movement, general principle and effect-evaluation standard of consumption
- research on the interactions among the needs of consumption, consumption structure, consumption pattern, consumption level and their changing trends with superstructure, to discuss the conditioning

and direction of national development strategies, principles, policies, plans and regulations for consumption

- comparative research on consumption theories and practice of China and foreign countries, to draw on the experience of domestic and foreign new research results on consumption and discuss the general mode and rules of consumption movement
- research on consumption activity and principles of consumption chain, to discuss the consumption psychology, consumption behavior of consumers and their families and their influence on social economic basis and superstructure
- research on the relations and rules among consumption and nature, scientific research and production consumption, distribution, exchange, consumer's consumption process.

Aims of the book

The researching aims of *Consumption and Management* were to meet the needs of increasing human material and mental consumption, scientific research and production consumption, and social consumption to build harmonious and peaceful social relations and living environments for human beings. At the same time, the book will help people to adapt to the natural rules during the economic development process and obtain the happiness of human beings and a harmonious coexistence with nature.

The research work in *Consumption and Management* is based on cross-cutting penetration, integration, promotion, and co-development of philosophy, sociology, economics, management, leadership science, marketing, finance, and other natural sciences. It researches the productivity of consumption society from the perspective of the consumption of human original basic need and proposes 15 factors of consumption society mechanics. Economy, society, culture, and the developing process of human beings all belong to the sphere of research.

The breakthrough point of the research is to divide human consumption into three systems – living consumption, social consumption, and scientific research and production consumption; it discovers that this three-fold system is the rule that promotes the cyclic development of economy and the natural rule of economic development – the production and exchange of commodity run through the needs of three important consumption systems and create market-free (natural) financial and economic laws (Adam Smith called it 'an 'invisible hand"). After research, we find that it is a visible hand and can be understood and controlled. It has great active and positive functions as well as negative ones. It is the natural solution for micro and macro supply–demand contradiction of the unity of opposites. The principal aspect of the contradiction is the great active functions in market-free (natural) financial and economic process. The secondary aspect is the negative functions. In times of financial or economic crises, the secondary aspect will become the principal aspect, which will greatly harm the economy.

The solution of the contradiction is to stick to nation-centered economy and the living consumption-oriented macro market regulation system (composed of six aims, three means, and twenty factors), to continuously exercise the regulatory loop of imbalance to balance and balance to imbalance in the process of the three important consumptions. It is also necessary to guarantee the smooth development and function of the natural principles of three important consumptions in the macro market regulation process so as to ensure the increasing material, mental, and cultural demands of people.

Research methods

The *Consumption and Management* employs scientific research methods. The most outstanding one is that the author combines his practical experience closely with his theory at all times, especially his revolutionary method of tracking down the origin of consumption. He inspires new ideas through continuous theoretical study and abundant practice for 60 years, and extracts the essence of his practice to build a theoretical concept, which is full of descriptive and explanatory features. The five concrete research methods in *Consumption and Management* are discussed below.

The philosophical method

This method includes dialectical materialism and historical materialism. The philosophical thinking runs through *Consumption and Management.* A great number of analyses of the economic and social problems are based on philosophical wisdom.

The qualitative and quantitative analysis method

The *Consumption and Management* uses both qualitative and quantitative analyses. Based on the statistical data, a mathematical model is set up to analyze the indexes and their values. The method judges the nature, features, and developing regulations of the object through the instinct and experience of the author, as well as the past and present conditions and the latest information of the objects. The two methods are used alternatively in *Consumption and Management.*

The systematic analysis method

Consumption and Management regards consumption as a system and gives integrated analysis to the systematic factors to figure out the applicable solution for the problems. It investigates and researches the human consumption process using the perspective of a system. In the research mentioned in *Consumption and Management*, it always regards consumption as a complete and complex system so as to avoid one-sidedness.

The investigation and research method

Many conclusions in *Consumption and Management* are based on on-the-spot investigations, the usage of basic theories and research on internal rules of consumption. Another feature of this book is that it pays great attention to sampling survey and typical investigation, so the data in the book are reliable and the conclusions are correct.

The comparative research method

Comparative research methods are used a lot in *Consumption and Management.* The methods include theoretical comparative research, management comparative research, marketing comparative research, cross-cultural and cross-discipline comparative research, and so on. The vertical comparison in *Consumption and Management* focuses on the comparative analysis of the same comparable subject – consumption in different situations with different characteristics in different periods, and the horizontal comparison in the book focuses on the comparative analysis of the different consumption conditions and characteristics in the same period. Through the vertical comparison and horizontal comparison, readers can understand consumption – the core topic in economic and social development – from different angles.

Research formula

The research formula in *Consumption and Management* is consumer consumption –> scientific research and production consumption –> distribution consumption –> exchange consumption –> consumer consumption:

1. Consumer consumption creates scientific research and production. The process of scientific research and production is a process of consumption. Commodities as well as the consumption pattern and level of consumptions are generated in production.
2. Science and technology is the capability which transfers into the productivity of a consumption society during the production process; it is also the valuable wealth of new technical products which are consumed by direct consumers and realize the productivity of a consumption society on the market exchange process.
3. Distribution consumption is a distribution policy decided by the social system and national law; it is a method deciding how the social members acquire social wealth and the amount of wealth they get. It decides the consumption power, the consumption and its level of the social members. Distribution includes the distribution of production output, salary or profit sharing, and the redistribution of social wealth after tax.
4. The exchange consumption process is one part of a product's value. The production exchange process is a consuming process. The dealer who takes part in the product exchange serves as the bridge between producer and consumer. Only through exchange can the final consumption of a commodity be realized. This is a rule that develops by consumption, which leads the cyclic development of economy. Its performance on the market is the free (natural) market financial and economic adjustment rule. The free (natural) market financial and economic adjustment rule has an important active function as well as a serious negative function. A national superstructure should control this rule on the macro level and ensure a continuous and orderly development of economy following the spiral loop of imbalance to balance and balance to imbalance.
5. Consumer consumption is the destiny of the production; a commodity is consumed by direct consumers so that the aims of scientific research and production and the value of productivity of a consumption society are realized. The consumption needs of consumers are developing and unlimited.

Theoretical references

Consumption and Management is a gathering of domestic and foreign theories about consumption. In order to write this book, the author studied and researched numerous Chinese and foreign economists' theories concerning consumption. He obtained penetrating statements and unique ideas of these economists and drew their essence from them, which is a very important basis for the formation of this book. We can say that the author could not have written this book without the work of these predecessors. These theories mainly include:

- consumption theories from the traditional Chinese culture, including the consumption thoughts of Confucius, Lao zi, Mo zi, and *Guanzi*
- references from Western economic theories, including Adam Smith's *An Inquiry into the Nature and Causes of the Wealth of Nations*, Keynes's *The General Theory of Employment, Interest and Money* and Samuelson's *Economics*
- references from Marx's consumption theory, such as *Capital*
- references from Deng Xiaoping's consumption thought, mainly including Deng Xiaoping's consumption strategic goal, the strategic focus of consumption and consumption policy and so on.

Major academic purposes of this book

To endow consumption with a lofty academic position

Discovering the value of consumption as well as endowing it with a lofty academic position is one contribution this book makes to Chinese economic theory research.

Consumption and Management is not only the first comprehensive treatise on consumption from the multi-disciplinary viewpoint in China, but also the first book regarding consumption as the basis of economic social research. The book researches consumption from the perspectives of economics, management, and marketing, as well as from the angles of philosophy, culture, and history. With systematic scientific theories, the book regards consumption as a complex dynamic system and uses the methods of qualitative analysis and quantitative analysis to describe the position, influence, and decisive significance of consumption in the economic field and whole of social life.

Consumption is the starting point as well as the end of production. Consumption –> scientific research and production –> distribution –> exchange –> consumption is a motion law as well as a logical process. Consumption is the motive of production; the scientific research and production process is also part of consumption, which produces commodities and creates new consumption needs and new consumption patterns. Consumption decides everything. We can say that these academic thoughts discover the essential characteristic of market-oriented economy from an academic viewpoint.

To propose new consumption classification

Traditional classification of consumption includes production consumption and living consumption (not including mental and cultural consumption). *Consumption and Management* divides consumption into three categories – living consumption, scientific research and production consumption, and social consumption (including mental and cultural consumption). Social consumption refers to public consumption in terms of state administration, national defense, research, education, public security, justice, aviation, aerospace, and scientific exploration. Compared with the traditional classification, the new one moves further and is creative.

Traditional economics divides the social production process into four sectors: production – distribution – exchange – consumption. Production is the most basic sector, which decides not only distribution and exchange, but also consumption. The variety, quality, and quantity of products which are produced by social production decide objectively the target, structure, and pattern of consumption. There is no consumption without production.

In fact, consumption is both motive and purpose in production and reproduction. Consumption decides production; the products which are produced in production are consumed in the commodity exchange process by consumers so as to realize the purpose of production. So consumption decides everything.

To discover and elaborate three rules

Consumption and Management discovers and elaborates three rules: natural economic law, market regulation law, and the law of macro-economic control.

Natural economic law refers to the natural rule (mother rule) that three important consumptions drive the cyclic development of economy. It means: consumption – market – demands (increasing consumption needs of desire – recognition – knowledge and inspiration – recognition) – scientific research – production – consumption of higher level. It is a natural economic law of spiral movement.

The market-adjusting rule says that currency appeared during the moving process of humanity's practice in three important consumptions systems and the commodity production and exchange process. The developing process of currency produces the economic law of financial enterprise and the law of natural (free) market economy. This rule is not an 'invisible hand' but a rule that can be recognized and controlled. Currency and its financial instrument decide the production and exchange of capital, and consumption produces the consumption chain (consumption value chain) – macro consumption value chain and micro consumption value chain – during the commodity production and exchange process of capital.

Natural (free) market economy rules and natural (free) rule of financial market are twin sisters who depend on each other but are not the same as each other.

The macro-market regulation rules of the state-led economy that centered on the living consumption refer to the idea that since the superstructure of national system and government are the representatives of the overall economic foundation, overall production relations, overall productivity, overall ideology, and rights and consumer's benefits of all the citizens. The responsibility and right of superstructure is to serve and protect the consumption benefits of all the citizens. Therefore, the nation should dominate the economy; the national macro-control market should be living-consumption-centered so as to give full play to the positive functions of the rule and prevent and overcome its serious negative functions.

To suggest a consumption-economy-centered macro-control adjustment system

According to *Consumption and Management*, market self-adjusting economic law is a tangible rule which should be recognized, researched, and controlled by the national government. The government should make full use of its positive effect and restrict its negative effect. So the macro-adjustment system of a nation is composed of three parts: economic measures, legal measures, and administrative measures.

The research in *Consumption and Management* begins from the origin of human consumption. It concludes with the experience and lessons of economic development in human society, especially the experience and lessons after the first financial economic crisis in the world. It also draws a conclusion on the experience and lessons during the social development process of planned economy and socialistic market-oriented economy with Chinese characteristics: 'National government should dominate the economy with a living-consumption-centered financial and economic macro adjustment rule.' It is composed of six aims, three measures, and 20 factors. The cycle of imbalance to balance and balance to a new imbalance will be focused in the systematic dynamic movement, and development of the consuming market economy rules will be macro adjusted continuously. This requires that the national leaders put their subjective initiative into full play in using the country elements, comprehensive national power, and the national management functions to realize scientific development in practice, prevent serious periodic financial and economic crises, and push the continuous development of social civilization.

To put forward the important statement of productivity of consumption society

Nobel Prize winner Robert Mundell (Professor of Columbia University in the United States, the winner of the Nobel Economics Prize in 1999) believed that productivity of consumption was the important statement in the 21st century, which had great influence on China and the world, as well as crucial theoretical and practical significance for promoting the virtuous cycle of China's national economy and establishing a harmonious society.

The productivity of a consumption society is an important branch science of *Consumption and Management*. It makes a statement on the practice process of the three important consumption activities from the point of view of consumption, from the level of macro to micro, from the level of the relations between consumption and nature, from the level of consumption and philosophy, from the level of consumption and society, from the level of economics, from the level of natural science, from the level of consumption and distribution, from the level of the commodity production and exchange of science and technology and capital, from the level of consumption and macro management (the level of enterprise marketing management), and from the level of consumption and micro management (the level of financial management of family consumption).

Consumption and Management points out that the pulling force of the productivity of a consumption society on the economic increase is embodied in the new production needed by consumption and supplies the impetus and purpose for production. New needs for related products are created during the consumption process, which supplies new requirements for production and impetus and purpose for reproduction, so there is no production without consumption demand, and the production should be processed according to the consumption needs, which is typical in a market-oriented economy. Taking consumption as the pulling force includes the creation of consumption and creation of consumers' new needs.

To point out the way of transferring economic increase

Consumption and Management points out that production is the foremost means and avenue for social life under a planned economic system, while consumption is the foremost avenue under a market-oriented economy. The shortage of commodities in a plan-oriented economy arises for artificial reasons, while the market-oriented economy can satisfy the changing needs of the three important consumptions. So, only by putting consumption first, and taking consumption as the most important driver of the national economy, can the market-oriented economy be realized.

In recent years, the scale of social consumption investment has become very large. If the scale keeps developing, then the scale of social consumption investment will continue to increase in the tenth Five Year Plan. Some experts estimate that if the present investment ratio adds 1%, the GDP of China will increase by 0.22 of a percentage point; if the citizens' consumption ratio adds 1%, the GDP of China will increase by 0.87 of a percentage point. From these data, we can see that the living consumption contributes much to the economic development, and we should pay more attention to the proportional relations of the three important consumptions.

History has given us an important signal that China has entered an era in which living consumption has become the main pulling force. From the national macro direction, we can say that China has entered the living-consumption-oriented economic developing era. This phenomenon will not change whether politicians, thinkers, and economists notice it or not. For how many years will China have the two-digit developing rate? In the book, the author does not consider that social consumption investment, import–export consumption and living consumption have the same importance. Living consumption is the most important, while the other two are of minor importance. If we can control living consumption, we grasp the key point. At the same time, the author points out that China has a potential investment environment and boosting domestic demand is the great impetus to the continuous development of China's economy. This is the academic direction of this book.

To deepen the labor value theory and new classification of labor

Labor value theory is the very foundation of Marxism as well as one of the basic theories of political economics. Value is created by abstract labor and living labor. Labor is the source of value. This is the basic content in labor value theory and is a scientific proposition:

- *Consumption and Management* deepens labor value theory and gives a new definition to productive labor.
- *Consumption and Management* endows the new concept of 'labor consumption value' to human labor and makes a new classification of it.

The classification in *Consumption and Management* breaks the simplification of traditional classification of labor. It sets a more concrete premise for studying the new socialistic concept of labor and proposes a standard for judging and weighing labor value. When we judge a kind of labor, we should notice whether it produces surplus value, whether it benefits people's health, and whether it plays a positive role on social life. This is the standard of labor value for producer's reference.

To inherit and develop the traditional philosophical theories

The definition of philosophy

Consumption and Management proposes for the first time a new concept of philosophy: philosophy is the highest level and method of human thinking in understanding and reforming nature, the wisdom crystallization of natural and social science, and the expression of awareness and wisdom at the highest level.

Philosophy originates from human practice process on relations of nature (matter), three important consumptions and nature, as well as the reaction process of human brain. Thinking, thinking process, cognition, consciousness, consumption awareness, and wisdom are created through the human brain's instinctive function (to discover and receive information, foster impressions, memorize, store, process, create thinking and thinking processes, and output information), and then act on three important consumptions of human beings. It is a process of discovering, creating, accumulating, inheriting, and developing, and also an infinite development process in circular spirals. Therefore, discovery, knowledge, and inspiration (creative thinking) recognition is the core of the philosophy.

Consumption consciousness

Driven by the instinctive consumption of metabolism, mankind obtains materials from the natural world, and then creates new needs and desires continuously with human intelligence, the total sum of the whole process of consuming material (including the spiritual and cultural) products and three important consumptions; this process makes mankind connect with nature. During the practice of three important consumptions, human beings constantly learn the relations of man and nature and of different individuals to understand themselves.

Consumption and Management proposes and demonstrates the regularity of ideology and the regularity of solving the contradictions in the developing process of ideology. It points out the differences between ideology and ideological methods, universality of effect of the seven ideological methods in common sense on three important consumptions activities, and the cyclic law of imbalanced to balanced, balanced to imbalanced in the development of unity of opposites.

The book perfects the motion relations of philosophy and three rules and regards unity of opposites as the common rule in the practicing process of all the things. It points out the motion law of partial qualitative change to total qualitative change and mutual transformation of quality and quantity. It believes that negation of negation should be changed into negation of affirmation because negation of affirmation is more scientific and practical. These two rules are the internal motion laws of unity of opposites and do not have equal position.

The spiral development law of cognition

The general law to perfect cognition refers to a development process of discovery – > feeling – > apperception – > impression – > knowledge – > knowledge (thinking and understanding) – > inspiration – > experience – > experimentation – > summarization – > abstraction – > reasoning. Knowledge exists throughout the process of cognition. Inspiration is the creative thinking while experience and experimentation are scientific means to learn about nature; there will be no innovation and creation without knowledge, inspiration, experience, and experimentation. Moreover, the spiral development law of cognition was put forward.

Consumption as the motive for the development of social civilization

Human consumption means the sum of consumption process. From birth, human beings are compelled by instinct to consume, and ask nature for consumption materials, and human wisdom produces new demands and desires to produce consumption materials. Over the long history of mankind, family, nation, tribe, private ownership society, and country came into being. And along with them is the consumption need which promotes three major industrial divisions in human history.

Family is the main body of living consumption and production consumption; after the detailed division of labor in production consumption, especially after the detailed market division of the production and exchange of capital products, family becomes the main body of living consumption while it is not the combined body of living consumption and production consumption. The smallest cell in society is family. Family is a social cell as well as the consuming cell. Society is made up of families (including the one-person family). Family is a family of consumption, so society is a society of consumption. There is no individual, family, nation, party, community or country without consumption.

Consumption creates human society and production. The production and consumption processes create class and class contradiction. The severe unfair distribution of consumption wealth leads to the class struggle in society.

Consumption leads to war because war is also a kind of consumption. War is regarded as the source of all evils, but it has the roles of building country and liberating the productivity of a consumption society, as well as pushing the development of social civilization.

Consumption creates new producing technology. New high-technology transfers into the productivity of the consumption society and produces products with new technology and high technology. Social civilization develops during the consumer's consumption process.

Thus, consumption is the power source for the development of social civilization.

To introduce knowledge and inspiration into epistemology

Epistemology is a long-discussed issue, the science of the initiation and development process of human cognition as well as its laws. It focuses on sources of people's consciousness, cognitive ability, cognitive form, cognitive nature, the structure of cognition, the relationship between objective truth and cognition, and so on. In modern philosophy, especially contemporary philosophy, epistemology gains more and more importance. In the development history of epistemological thought, every introduction of a new important concept is to initiate great academic change. Throughout the history of Western philosophy, in general there are three major philosophical revolutions caused by the introduction of new concepts:

- Plato introduced 'logos' into epistemology, which forms the first transcendentalism.
- Immanuel Kant introduced 'psyche' into epistemology, which causes great revolution in the history of philosophy.
- Marx introduced practice into epistemology, which brought another major change in the history of philosophy.

Fourth, *Consumption and Management* introduced knowledge and inspiration into epistemology.

'Consumption practice and consumption awareness' in *Consumption and Management* is summarized below.

The process through which people develop cognition can be divided into the following three stages:

- The first stage is to observe, discover, feel, apperceive and foster impression (presentation), namely the stage of perceptual knowledge.
- The second stage includes knowledge, inspiration, experimentation, thinking and judgment, which means to try the experience out and learn from the lesson, i.e. the first phase of rational knowledge. This is the basic stage of human practice, the foundation of the formation of rational knowledge.
- The third stage is to summarize and reason abstractly, i.e. the highest rational stage of thinking, concept, viewpoints and conclusion.

Theory of consumption introduces knowledge and inspiration into epistemology. It will be emphasized that the introduction made by the *Consumption and Management* is not a reference in a general sense but is regarded as an essential link of epistemology. Having knowledge and inspiration admitted to epistemology gives two aspects of significance. For one thing, knowledge is an important quality of modern people, needed by those who want to achieve something and which they must keep developing and improving. For another, it is imperative to cherish knowledge and respect inspiration from the point of society, and to realize that knowledge may bring a better and more special thinking process to individuals, organizations, or even the whole country, while inspiration perhaps implies one or several significant inventions.

To propose and enrich national factors, comprehensive national strength, national management function, enterprise management law, and management factor

Country elements: ① territory ② people ③ legal national ruling power system ④ superstructure system ⑤ legal system.

Comprehensive national strengths: ①national resources ② economic strengths ③ cohesive force of people's will ④ productivity level of consumption society ⑤ military power ⑥ degree of state development ⑦ diplomatic strength ⑧ control capability of government. The organizational and control capability is the core for organic combination of the government system as a whole. Without such capability, none of the strengths will be able to take effect.

The 18 elements of national management stand for the factors the national superstructure adopts for macro management with correct thinking and thinking methods, leadership approach and leadership art. The purpose is to improve the labor efficiency of the state managing officials, to realize the low consumption cost for macro consumption, so as to achieve a relatively high level of management objective.

Enterprise management is a systematic management. The outer environment of the enterprise is the living condition for an enterprise and the management of the outer living conditions is a kind of management of public relations. Management of enterprise connotes the inner part of the enterprise management. Only by linking the inner and outer managements together with systematic organic management can a lower scientific research and production consumption cost be achieved and more qualified products with use value be produced. The consumption cost is reduced during the marketing process, the preference of consumers can be acquired, scaled sales can be realized, the best profit effect and social effect can be achieved, and the best value of a narrow sense of productivity of consumption society can be realized.

To put forward leadership management theory

Leadership management science develops from general management, management science, operation research, and systematics. The research focus of general management and management science is on management, and seldom emphasizes the function of leadership in management; leadership science focuses on leaders and seldom emphasizes the management function in the systematic activity process of leaders. So, management science and leadership science are both one-sided. Leadership science combines the opposites of leaders and subordinates; both the leaders and the subordinates are management objects, and leadership management involves the coordination of the whole system; it studies the common target, united ideology and management in the striving movements of leaders and subordinates, as well as the general and specific rules of leader' power, authority, responsibility, benefits, functions, and the relations between leaders and subordinates in the systematic process.

There is no leadership without the management of three important consumption practices and no management without leadership in human history. There is no leader without subordinates, no leader without decisions and management under a common goal in certain conditions. Leaders and subordinates are all managing subjects, and leadership management activity is an undivided unity of opposites. The leader is the main contradiction and the main aspect of a contradiction, while the subordinate is the secondary contraction and secondary aspect of a contradiction. When the main contradiction cannot suit the secondary contradiction, the contradictions will interchange – a new leader will appear.

In the third chapter of *Consumption and Management*, more than 160,000 words are dedicated to the detailed description for leadership management.

To give a comprehensive research and study on the internal rules in consumption and management

Leadership management science can be divided into macro-consumption leadership management and micro-consumption leadership management.

Macro-consumption leadership management is the overall management of a national superstructure and government of three important consumption activities. Micro-consumption leadership management includes the marketing consumption management of enterprise production consumption marketing and exchange marketing process of market-consumption products, and the financial management of household living consumption.

Macro-consumption leadership management

National management law: the nature and scale of a country's system decides the national management mode.

National macro-consumption leadership management involves authorities with responsibility and national superstructures – comprehensive national strength and 18 factors of national management function – organically functioning by way of proper analytical logic, ideological, and leadership measures. Macro-consumption leadership management can increase the working efficiency of national managing officials and realize low consumption levels of macro consumption, so as to achieve high-level management.

Micro-consumption management

Enterprise management rule: production art decides the production mode; the production mode decides the management mode; the marketing mode decides the marketing management mode.

Enterprise is the economic cell of society. A new concept of enterprise management is proposed in this book. Enterprise management should be people-centered and adopt technical instruments, working methods, enterprise culture and management mode to serve enterprise scientific research, production and sale, make a systematic integration with a combined management of hard and soft management and relative low consumption cost to produce high-quality consumption commodity so as to achieve a good dual-beneficial goal.

Enterprise leadership management philosophy and ever-developing enterprise culture are the soul of an enterprise. Enterprise leadership management requires the clear understanding of the relations between enterprise management benefit and development benefit, macro benefit and micro benefit, and the strategy, tactic, and plan of the development of the enterprise. Suitable thoughts and ideological methods, leadership measures, and art should be adopted to employ the organic management of hard and soft management, to minimize consumption in the production and commodity exchange process, to increase production efficiency, and finally to achieve the best production and management goals.

The aims of household living consumption management are to increase consumption fund (income) and to improve consumption level.

Management of exchange and consumption of commodity

Management clarifies two problems: the concept and nature of commodity exchange marketing process, and the marketing factors in the commodity exchange process. There are similarities and differences between marketers and manufacturers. Commodity exchange marketing is a very important factor of the productivity of a consumption society, and the bridge between consuming the product of a manufacturer and the direct consumer, the bridge to the realization of production aim. Without it, the consumption of a direct consumer and the productivity of the consumption society will not be realized. So, merchants are also great laborers (labor combining intellectual labor and physical labor).

To put forward a new concept and mode of marketing

Consumption and Management puts forward the new concept of marketing in a revolutionary way. It points out that consumption and marketing management are the management of the process from commodity exchange to its consumption by consumers. The long history of human beings is a scientific research and production consumption process led by living consumption and social consumption. New needs of consumption are created during this process and the needs act on consumption. People's increasing needs of consumption for material and mental wealth lead to the cyclic development of economy. Therefore, marketing for target demands is called 'large systematic service marketing based on target needs of consumers', and to satisfy this means everything for an enterprise.

The new concept of 'large systematic service marketing based on target needs of consumers' is a continuous and evolving social marketing process and also a process of pursuing consumption satisfaction of target consumers. Systematic service marketing influences the organization of various aspects in society, participation of the people, the great market service structure and the increase of the marketing cost. The purpose of management is to control and direct the consumption during the social marketing process, carry out comprehensive budget-control management, achieve good enterprise marketing benefits – enterprise profit benefit and social benefit by relatively low consumption cost.

The author proposes six models on the marketing operation pattern and points out that the marketing mode and management mode will develop along with the development of time and consuming needs of consumers.

To demonstrate the general rules of 'consumption creates wealth' and surplus value

All social wealth is produced during the process of consumption. Consumption is the starting and end point of the motive and purpose of scientific research. Only by consumption of consumers, can value and surplus value of the products be realized.

Consumption and Management puts forward and demonstrates the wealth accumulation of surplus product value in socialistic society in consumption. During the market exchange, commodity has not only a common value exchange rule but also a specific rule. For example, a brand credit and realization rule of surplus product value, people's customs and realization rule of surplus product value, a regional adaptation and realization rule of surplus product value, a purchasing level and realization rule of surplus product value, a service quality and realization rule of surplus product value, a convenient and timely supply of commodity and realization rule of surplus product value, a supermarket and realization rule of surplus product value, production in investing period and realization rule of surplus product value and so on.

Enterprises in a socialistic country must produce surplus value for the improvement of people's living standards and the rapid development of the socialistic construction.

Academic and practical significance of this book

Consumption is the starting and end point of economic circulation. In the 30 years of research, the author aims to rebuild a systematic theory on consumption which suits the development of the time. The author understands that his theory may be a bold creation, a huge theoretical project, and a piece of tough work. But he believes that the promotion of this theory will reform the traditional economic structure and economic ecology. It will become a brand new strength for the development of China's economy and society and further establish the academic position for consumption in all the disciplines.

Consumption and Management is a huge systematic theoretical project. With his own invention and the practice and thinking of his life, the author makes an overall systematic statement for the recognition of the social developing process in human history in the light of consumption with a great number of breakthroughs. This theory has important practical significance, as well as academic and historic significance.

Consumption and Management is the output of the author's research for 30 years, and is a revolutionary theory. *Consumption and Management* opens a new age for the combination of scientific theory on consumption with practice, enlightens new thoughts in the academic field, has great practical significance for the integrated national operations and benefits for the national economy. The promotion of this book will definitely foster great people, push harmonious development of the theory on three important consumptions, satisfy the increasing consumption demands of people, benefit the development of human beings and the improvement of social civilization, and finally achieve the harmonious co-existence of people's happiness and nature.

2

The academic status and theoretical constitution of consumption

Consumption is a holy power. Consumption is endowed with exalted standing because it creates everything in human society.

Consumption is the eternal topic in economics, which is always emphasized by economic theorists and national functional departments and decision-makers. The mechanism of consumption indicates that the circulation of consumption is vital for the entire circulation and effects of the national economy.

Consumption is the beginning and end of the economic cycle, as well as the sum of all human activities. Three important consumption practices act on human beings to enable the human brain to generate awareness, thinking method, and consumption awareness. It is not only a conclusion of academic theories but also a product of theory and practice; this is a new revolutionary systematic theory of consumption.

Section 1 Scientific implications for human consumption

The concept 'human consumption' is different from the previous concept of 'consumption'. In traditional economics, consumption is considered just as a link in the social production process, but the concept of 'human consumption' considers consumption as a complex process of the whole of economic and social life. The overall task of the book is to interpret and research this process and explain the general law of economic and social development.

Human consumption is the whole process of human consumption, which can be divided into human consumption in a broad sense and human consumption in a narrow sense in concept. In a narrow sense it is the concept that consumers get ever-increasing material, spiritual, and cultural satisfaction while acquiring products, service, and experience; or it can be said that consumption is a behavior that consumers freely get at the cost of currency, referring to consumption during the processes of life and labor.

In a broad sense human consumption includes social consumption – social public consumption – mainly including social management, national defense, national security, research, education, health, environmental protection, social assistance, public welfare , international trade, and so on. In traditional studies, consumption in the broad sense is usually considered a secondary distribution of economic benefits; the research of consumption in the broad sense exists only in the field of distribution; in this book, the research of consumption is placed within the consumption field for study and the law of national macro control can only be obtained through this study method.

During the practice process of human beings, new consumption desires and cognition are continuously created as well as new consumption demand and products. Consumption is most directly dependent on the existence and sophistication level of human demand, and the whole process of consumption can be predicated according to the nature and diversity of requirements. In turn, only through consumption can people's requirements be satisfied; the more abundant the consumption content is, the more possible that the people's demand can be further developed. If the development of demand is the motivation and purpose of consumption, then consumption is the necessary prerequisite to maintain and continuously develop the demand.

In the area of commodity production, as a result of the existence of self-sufficient economic sectors, living consumption is closely related to labor consumption, and there is no obvious separation between the two. However, in the developed area of commodity production, living consumption is clearly separated from labor consumption and the separation is clear and strict.

Certainly, human consumption also comprises spiritual and cultural consumption. Traditional economics pays less attention to the spiritual and cultural consumption of human beings and does not consider it an economic variable in study; in contrast, this book regards spiritual and cultural consumption as an important economic variable. Scientific research and production, living consumption and social consumption include spiritual and cultural consumption, which is given as important a status as human material consumption. Although in the backward area of commodity consumption people's spiritual and cultural consumption does not play an important role in their economic life, along with social progress and economic development, and the improvement of people's consumption capacity, the amount of spiritual and cultural consumption continuously increases in quality and quantity. This point has been proved both in developed countries and in the ever-changing consumption structure in developed areas in China. Therefore, spiritual and cultural consumption will play more and more important roles in human consumption structure and in a growing proportion; if the spiritual and cultural consumption is neglected in study, it means the neglect of a series of economic phenomena related to spiritual and cultural consumption, including the economic phenomena involving labor, production and consumption pattern as well as social economic effects related to spiritual and cultural consumption. To identify spiritual and cultural consumption as the important aspect of human consumption is one of the features of this book.

The nature of human consumption activities is different from that of animal consumption activities. As Marx said in *Capital*, the nature of human consumption is a kind of 'subjective, and most essential nature of human beings' (1867), and this kind of subjectivity is formed through the labor process and social networks. Animal consumption is directly related to animals' activities, being a kind of instinctive and life activities. The consumption activities of human beings separate production and consumption in time and space, and it is that kind of separation that displays sociality of consumption and subjectivity of human beings and their social attributes. In this sense, human consumption becomes an integral part of the substantial existence of human beings.

Section 2 The academic status of consumption

Driven by the instinctive consumption of metabolism, mankind obtains materials from the natural world, creates new consumption desires and cognition, and then creates new materials, spiritual, and cultural products; this is regarded as the consumption process.

After a comprehensive analysis is conducted on the works of western classical and modern economics, it is easy to determine that western mainstream economics has always been centered on production and put consumption at a subordinate position. The system of neo-classic economics has serious defects on the issue of consumption; it lacks an abstract consumption concept in the production theory of value, the concept of consumption increment in the production theory of capital, and active consumption concept in production teleology. The production-centered trend appeared many times during the industrialization process and led to economic crises. In the transition from industrial economy to information economy, the customary overlook of consumption value has become the serious defect of western mainstream economics.

This book will rectify the status of consumption, restore the value of consumption in economic circulation, endow it with a deserved academic position, and call for the revolution of people's notion of consumption, since it is of great academic significance in the east and the west. Otherwise, it is impossible to realize the transition in consumption philosophy and the change in the pattern of economic development.

In the traditional consumption study, consumption is an important link of social reproduction. It is the process of meeting the needs of human beings by use of social products. Consumption can be divided into two categories: production consumption and living consumption. The former means the use and consumption of production materials and labor force in the course of production of physical materials. The latter means the behavior and course to use the produced physical materials and mental products to meet the needs of personal life and 'perform life function out of production course.' It is the indispensable condition for regaining and reproducing a labor force. Living consumption in its general sense means personal consumption.

In macro economics, consumption refers to a person's or a country's total expenditure for consumption within a certain period of time. Before the 1930s, the research on consumption theory was relatively simple; at that time, the dominant orthodox was Marwill's demand theory. The viewpoint of this kind of demand theory is to assume that consumers' income is constant; the commodity quantity obtained by consumers changes in the reverse direction with the fall and rise of prices. Engels' coefficient is an important factor to evaluate consumption level. In this light, consumption plays an important role in macro economics.

In micro economics consumption is studied by examining individual economic units – such as individual producers, individual consumers and the economic activity of individual markets – as research objects to analyze how an individual producer allocates limited resources for various commodity products to obtain maximum profit, and how individual consumers allocate their limited income on various commodities to acquire maximum satisfaction. Micro economics also analyzes how an individual producer determines the output, cost, quantity of production factors to be used, and profit; how the income of production factor suppliers is determined; and how to determine the effectiveness, supply volume, demand volume and price of an individual commodity. Consumption also plays an important role in micro consumption.

Micro economics studies the practice and consequences of individual participants in economic activities. Macroeconomics studies the overall economic behavior and consequences of society overall; it analyzes the overall economic operation, including social output, income, price level, and employment conditions.

Although many scholars have noticed the importance of consumption, the subject has not been given due attention. Karl Marx did not specifically discuss the theory of consumption and *Capital* has no chapter on it. In early economic works in China there was no theory of consumption; even at the end of the last century, when China had implemented economic reform and become more open, the problem of consumption was not considered, and the importance of consumption has never been established academically.

In the west and in China there is a tradition of overlooking, even suppressing, consumption. This has affected people's conception of consumption for a long time and become part of mainstream ideology. *Consumption and Management* believes that it is essential to restore the value of consumption in economic circulation, to endow it a deserved academic position, and to call for the revolution of people's notion of consumption; unless this is accomplished it will be impossible to realize the transition of the idea of consumption to the mode of economic development.

The historic mission of *Consumption and Management* is to establish correctly the academic status of consumption, which traces and studies the origin, development, classification, principles and application of consumption with comprehensive research methods to form a systematic theory. The study is involved with such disciplines as philosophy, history, economics, management, leadership science, marketing, and merchandising, which form an inter-disciplinary and inter-filtrating systematic theory on consumption.

Section 3 Classification of human consumption

The problem of classifying consumption is important in consumption study. If the classification is made inappropriately, many wrong conclusions will be drawn. Traditional and new methods of classifying human consumption are described below.

The traditional classification of human consumption

Traditionally consumption is divided into production consumption and living consumption (excluding cultural consumption).

Traditional economics divides the overall process of social production into four categories: production, distribution, exchange, and consumption. Production is a basic stage that determines not only distribution and exchange but also consumption. Types, quality and quantity of products of social production objectively regulate the consumption objects, structure, and patterns. No production, no consumption. It is concluded that production determines everything.

New classification of human consumption

The new classification of human consumption divides consumption into three major parts: living consumption, social consumption, and research and production consumption.

Living consumption

The first and most essential part of living consumption is the most fundamental material and mental consumption of an individual. This consumption is an endless pursuit of human beings from survival consumption to enjoyment consumption. The second part of living consumption is in the form of collective consumption. Generally speaking, it is the collective or an organization who pays the consumption fund (with little or no individual payment) which is applied within the group as consumption expenditure, for instance, the consumption of travel, conferences, and entertainment activities, and all living consumption such as food, clothing, housing, and transportation within the group.

Social consumption

Social consumption is the management consumption of state superstructure, consumption of national defense, consumption of education and scientific research, consumption of sports, consumption of national infrastructure investment, of urban infrastructure, of space flight and so on.

Scientific research and production consumption

Scientific research and production consumption is decided by living consumption and social consumption. Production consumption makes living consumption and social consumption, and then creates new consumption pattern and consumption level. Without needs of consumption, there is no production. And without scientific research and production consumption, it is impossible to realize new consumption desire and reality consumption. Scientific research and production consumption also include exploration, gathering, smelting metal, tool making, and so on, and are the foundation of the three important consumptions.

Consumption is both motive and purpose in production and reproduction. Consumption decides production; the products which are produced in production are consumed in the commodity exchange process by consumers so as to realize the purpose of production: consumption–scientific research, production–distribution–exchange–consumption, wherein consumption goes through the whole process; consumption decides everything.

Consumption determines production and scientific research; the production process is also consumption, where the pattern of consumption is produced. Consumers' consumption drives the production competition and development, for only in consumption can the products become commodities and new production requirements be created. The purpose of production is consumption, but meanwhile the producers will also generate social benefits and enterprise benefits, otherwise the enterprise will cease to exist. It is concluded that consumption decides everything.

Three levels of human consumption

1. The three levels of human living consumption are:
   - minimum survival consumption
   - well-being and enjoyment consumption
   - the pursuit of luxury consumption.
2. The three levels of social consumption are:
   - the consumption of maintaining all the minimum material and mental civilizations, such as the public order, security and living conditions for maintaining the co-existence of countries, areas, nations, and citizens with basic living conditions
   - higher level of enjoyment and technology, the consumption of material and spiritual civilizations of maintaining public orders and security of the country and area to ensure the co-existence and co-development of the citizens, and of living conditions, and so on
   - high and the higher levels of enjoyment and technology environment, the material, spiritual and cultural consumption for maintaining national and regional safety and security to ensure public order and the desired living environment for co-existence and co-development of all citizens.
3. The three levels of consumption of scientific research and production are:
   - the consumption of the scientific research and production tools, apparatus, and equipment that meet the basic need of human survival

- the premise of life enjoyment consumption and social consumption of higher levels is the consumption of higher levels of scientific research technology and production technology
- the preconditions of higher-level life consumables and social consumables: higher-level scientific research technology and production technology; higher-level living consumables and social consumables cannot be produced without higher-level scientific research technology and production technology.

Consumption pattern and consumption level standard

The study of consumption pattern in *Capital* starts from the commodity production and commodity exchange process, and there is an emphasis on capitalist production mode and production relation.

The formula of study of consumption pattern in *Consumption and Management* is consumption desire, cognition, and nature create scientific research; the production consumption pattern – scientific research and production consumption – create consumption products, and the consumption pattern – consumption products consumed by consumers – create consumption level and social civilization progress.

Consumption patterns and production relation

The superstructure government represents the overall production mode and production relations of society, the total productivity of the consumption society, and the fundamental interests of the people. The income mode of social members, the redistribution of social wealth and social security pattern of social members are settled with laws and policies. The directorate and operators of enterprises represent the mode of production, production relation and consumption society productivity in a narrow sense; they promulgate enterprise rules, regulations and bylaws based on national laws and policies, and constitute specific distribution policies and award policies on the basis of three driving forces (the material driving force, spiritual driving force and information driving force); and directly influence the awareness of household living consumption as well as consumption pattern. Therefore, the superstructure is of great importance for regulating the national micro consumption pattern.

Consumption classification and standard

The consumption pattern is divided into macro and micro consumption patterns. The macro consumption pattern is the pattern of three important consumptions during the progress of human society, which represents the consumption level and social civilization progress level during the overall process of development of human society. The consumption patterns in different historical periods of human development (Stone Age, Bronze Age, Iron Age, Age of Steam Engine and Internal Combustion Engine, and Electrical and Electronic Age to today) represents the consumption level and social development progress level of that age; nevertheless, if the products are not consumed by consumers, the discussion of consumption level or social civilization progress is out of the question.

The micro consumption pattern is the consumption level of specific consumption patterns in family living consumption and social consumption. The consumption level of individual families depends on the family's income and consumption awareness. Only corresponding consumption awareness can enable the realization of consumption pattern and level compatible with the income.

Four classifications of scientific research and production consumption

Scientific research and production consumption can be divided into four categories. First is basic scientific research and production consumption, such as consumption of mining, smelting, and manufacturing of raw materials scientific research. Second is consumption of the scientific research and manufacture of production tools, machines, and foods, which is living consumption and social consumption. Third is scientific research and production consumption for social consumption, including scientific research and production consumption of:

- social basic facilities such as city construction, railway, highway, flood control dykes and reservoirs
- national defense, such as consumption of weapons, facility operation tools, and space flight.

Fourth, scientific research and production consumption of living consumption (material and mental products included), including the production consumption of food, clothing, housing, transportation and entertainment books and so on. Each of the four categories forms systematic scientific research production consumption itself. The purpose of all these production consumptions is to meet the ever-increasing material and mental living consumption needs of human beings. The social needs of consumption promote the three important consumptions which are made up of scientific research production consumption according to the circular spiral development rule. This rule is the natural rule of economic development.

Section 4 The theoretical framework of consumption

Consumption is the sum of all the human activities. There is no society without consumption, no economy without consumption, no human-nature relations without consumption. Therefore, to guide all the scientific research of human beings and direct the consuming practice with consumption is the base of academic theoretical research, the starting point, foothold, and destination. Figure 2.1 provided the theoretical framework for consumption research in this book.

Subject definition

Human consumption is the sum of the whole consumption process that is driven by the metabolism instinct to obtain material from nature, then to create new needs and desires by human knowledge, and further to create new material products (including the spiritual culture). It includes the definitions of narrow-sense and broad-sense consumption.

Consumption and Management puts consumption in the broad background of human social science and natural science. It studies the social position, social roles, and function principles of consumption. It is a science that focuses on the practice and function principles of production, living, and social consumption.

At the same time, *Consumption and Management* deals with the relations between human consumption and nature, human consumption and economic development, human consumption and social civilization and progress, human consumption and consumption practice, as well as human consumption and consumption awareness and action, and so on.

The ladder structure

These are the levels of the ladder structure:

- the systematic theory of structure consumption science
- the three important consumptions of constitutional structure

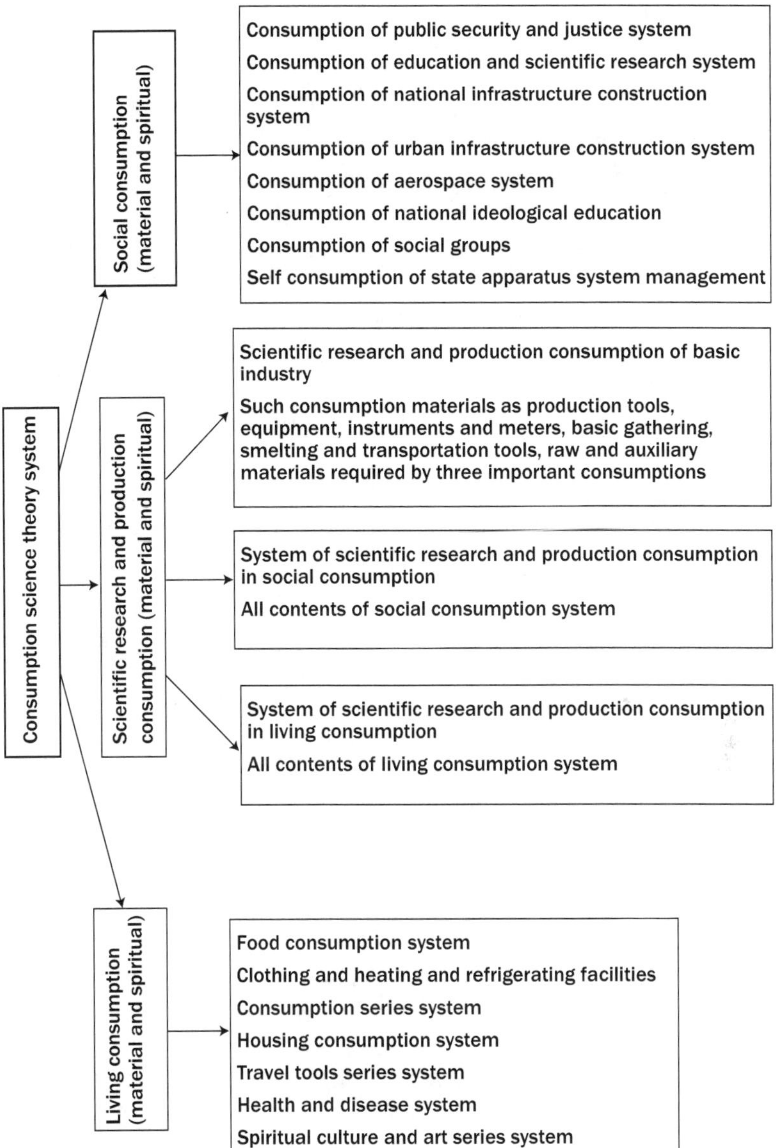

Figure 2.1 Consumption theory framework

- the sub-system structure of each consumption system
- the detailed classification of the sub-systematic consumption system (the detailed classification is left out)
- the leadership management during the practice of three major consumptions.

In the three important consumption systems, scientific research and production consumption is the premise of the realization of living consumption and social consumption. Scientific research and production consumption can be divided into three sub-systems – scientific research and production consumption:

- for the realization of living consumption – the scientific research and production consumption which satisfies the increasing material and mental consumption needs of humans, that is the consumption realization of capital's commodity production and exchange management process
- for the realization of social consumption – the scientific research and production consumption which satisfies the increasing material and mental consumption needs of society
- of basic industry, which is based on the first and second sub-systems.

The realization of the increasing scientific research and production consumption of living and society requires the development of the country itself. Only with the continuous development of productivity can it promise three important consumptions to promote the natural cyclic development of the economy. Scientific research and production consumption derive from consumption; scientific consumption is the production consumption for new knowledge and new techniques which constantly creates new consumption needs and consumption desires. It creates new consumption commodities for living and social life, creates new consumption patterns, and pushes the new development of consumption level.

The process of capital commodity production and capital commodity exchange further expands and promotes the development of consumption commodity channels and socialized exchange of commodities. Today, during the process of capital commodity production and socialization of capital commodity exchange in the overall human society, micro production relation, production relations involving enterprise behaviors and macro production relations of the whole society are also in process; the relationship between economic base and superstructure is in process; the relationship between human consumption and the natural world is in process; the interactions of these relations constitute the basic contradictions of society and form dissipative structures of society. Diverse and complex enterprises are cells of social economic foundation and such non-productive social organizations as social groups, political parties, and religious groups are integrated in the process of three important consumptions of the whole society. However, without three important consumptions, any individual, family, social group, party, religion, or nation cannot survive and there will also be no politics without consumption.

During the active process of three important consumptions, the contradiction between consumption society productivity and productive relation, between economic base and superstructure, and between three important consumptions and the natural world are also generated. The active process of three important contradictions also generates internal contradictions of society and external national contradictions (contradiction among states). Within a nation, the core of all these contradictions lies in the creation and distribution pattern of the wealth consumed by society, the legal form in which the social individual and social groups acquire social consumption wealth, and the proportion of wealth they get. Where people agree with the values and whether people consider the pattern as fair or unfair (absolute fairness does not exist). People's living consumption and enjoyment of consumption are determined by their share of social consumption wealth; their share of social consumption wealth determines their purchasing capacity, consumption awareness, consumption mode, and behavior as well as the mode and behavior of social activities.

All these are practical activities of three important consumptions, and the practical activities of three important consumptions are management object and management tasks of leadership management science.

The object of study

The research subjects of *Consumption and Management* are three important consumptions systems (shortened as three systems) of human's living consumption, scientific research and production consumption, and social consumption in the light of human consumption.

Consumption and Management regards three systems as its main research objects and researches the general rules and all the relations such as the relations between consumers and consumers, between consumption and demand, between consumption and commodity exchange, between consumption and distribution, between consumption and management, between consumption and nature, between consumption and development of human beings, between consumption and human wealth, between consumption productivity and production relations, between consumption and economic base and superstructure, and between the three systems and social activities in the perspective of human consumption. It tries to figure out the basic natural rules, market regulation rules, and macro-control rules of how consumption affects economic development, as well as the general and specific rules in the development process of all kinds of economic relations.

Tasks of the subject

The basic research tasks of *Consumption and Management* are:

- to use the Marxism consumption theory to summarize the experience in consumption practice
- to make clear the position and functions of consumption in social reproduction
- to increase the people's consciousness to know and use the consumption mechanism and rules
- to put the understanding of the consumption on a systematic, theoretical and scientific basis
- to study and borrow general doctrine on consumption at home and abroad
- to better master and apply consumption rules
- to supply the scientific foundation for the national economy development strategic goals and the consumption plan, principles, and measures for the realization of these goals
- to propose scientific basis for rationalization of industrial and product structure of national economy
- to cultivate talents
- to push development of productivity of consumption society and the development of social civilization.

Through making clear the consumption mechanism and its movement principles, *Consumption and Management* attempts:

- through research on the internal connection between consumption, production, distribution, exchange and consumption by consumers, to discuss the nature of consumption and features of socialism with Chinese characteristics under the premise of a market-oriented economy, and its position and function in cyclic national economic development
- through the internal connections and interactions of consumption and economic development, to discuss the decisive function of consumption

in promoting economic growth as well as the internal connection between consumption and industrial structure adjustment
- through research on the internal connections and interactions among the needs of consumption, consumption structure, consumption pattern, and consumption level, to discuss the movement, general principle and effect-evaluation standard of consumption
- through research on the interactions among the needs of consumption, consumption structure, consumption pattern, consumption level and their changing trends with superstructure, to discuss the conditioning and direction of national development strategies, principles, policies, plans and regulations for consumption
- through comparative research on consumption theories and practice of China and foreign countries, to draw on the experience of domestic and foreign new research results on consumption and discuss the general mode and rules of consumption movement
- through research on consumption activity and principles of consumption chain, to discuss the consumption psychology, consumption behavior of consumers and their families and their influence on social economic basis and superstructure
- through research on the relations and rules among consumption and nature, scientific research and production consumption, distribution, exchange, consumer's consumption process.

Aims of the subject

The researching aims of *Consumption and Management* lie in serving the needs of increasing human material and mental consumption, scientific research, production consumption, and social consumption so as to build harmonious and peaceful social relations and living environment for human beings. At the same time, the book will help people to adapt to the natural rules during the economic development process and obtain the happiness of human beings and harmonious coexistence with nature.

The research work in *Consumption and Management* is based on the multi-crossing, penetration, integration, promotion, and co-development of philosophy, sociology, economics, management, leadership science, marketing, finance, and other natural sciences. It researches the productivity of consumption society in the perspective of the consumption of human origin and proposes 15 factors of consumption society mechanics. Economy, society, culture, and developing process of human being all belong to the researching sphere.

The breakthrough point of the research is to divide human consumption into three systems – living consumption, social consumption, scientific research, and production consumption; it discovers that this tri-system approach is the rule that promotes the cyclic development of economy and the natural rule of economic development; the production and exchange of commodity run through the needs of the three important consumption systems and creates market-free (natural) financial and economic laws (Adam Smith called it an 'invisible hand'). After research, we find that it is a visible hand and can be understood and controlled. It has great active and positive functions as well as the negative ones. It is the natural solution for the micro and macro supply–demand contradiction of the unity of opposites. The principal aspect of the contradiction is the great active functions in market-free (natural) financial and economic process, the secondary aspect is the negative functions, but when financial or economic crises happen, the secondary aspect will become the principal aspect and will harm the economy.

The solution of the contradiction is: stick to nation-centered economy and living consumption-oriented macro market regulation system (composed by six aims, three means, and twenty factors), follow the regulation method of continuous prominent-balanced and balanced-prominent in the three important consumptions processes. Guarantee the smooth development and function of natural principles of three important consumptions in macro market regulation process so as to ensure the increasing material, mental, and cultural demands of people.

Research methods of consumption science

Consumption and Management employs scientific research methods. The most outstanding one is that with rich practical experience, the author is able to relate his own practice closely with his research all the time, especially his revolutionary method of tracking down the origin. He stimulates the new ideas through the way of deep thinking based on his theoretical study and abundant practice for 60 years, and extracts the essence of his practice to a theoretical height which is full of descriptive and explanatory features. Five specific research methods are used in *Consumption and Management*, which are discussed below.

The philosophical method

This method includes dialectical materialism and historical materialism. The philosophical thinking runs through the book of *Consumption and*

Management. A great number of analyses on economic and social problems are full of philosophical wisdom.

The method of qualitative analysis and quantitative analysis

Consumption and Management uses qualitative analyses and quantitative analyses. Based on statistical data, a mathematical model is set up to analyze the indexes and their values of the subject. The method judges the nature, features and developing regulations of the object through the instinct and experience of the author, as well as the past and present conditions and the latest information of the objects. The two methods are used alternatively in *Consumption and Management*.

The systematic analysis method

Consumption and Management regards consumption as a system and gives integrated analysis for the systematic factors to figure out the applicable solution for the problems. It investigates and researches human consumption processes from the system perspective. In the research mentioned in *Consumption and Management*, it always regards consumption as a complete and complex system so as to avoid one-sidedness.

The investigatory research method

Many conclusions in *Consumption and Management* are based on on-the-spot investigations and usage of basic theories and research on internal rules of consumption. Another feature of this book is that it pays great attention to sampling-based survey and case-based study, so the data in the book are reliable, and the conclusions are reasonable.

The comparative research method

Comparative research methods are used extensively in *Consumption and Management*. The methods include theoretical comparative research, management comparative research, marketing comparative research, cross-cultural and cross-discipline comparative research, and so on. The vertical comparison in *Consumption and Management* focuses on the comparative analysis of the same comparable subject – consumption in different situations with different characteristics in different periods, and the horizontal comparison in the book focuses on the comparative analysis of the different consumption conditions and characteristics in the same period. Through vertical comparison and horizontal comparison, readers can understand consumption – the core topic in economic and social development – from different angles.

The arrival of the consumption era in China

Economic development and consumption theory are mutually reinforced and supplementary; the study of consumption theory promotes economic development and social civilization and economic development also promotes the study of consumption theory; the relation of the two is inseparable and dialectically unified.

At present, in China, more and more scholars are beginning to take up consumption study. Although no systematic theory has formed, these studies raise people's awareness of consumption and promote economic development. Now, the systematic theory on consumption is being shaped, and the systematic theory will surely guide the economic development of China. It will not only guide the Chinese government's decision-making concerning the macro control of the national economy, but also will instruct the formation and sophistication of the modern consumption concepts of Chinese people. It is obvious that the role of theory cannot be ignored.

In addition, in today's China, consumption theory is ever-developing and becoming more sophisticated and a consumption theory with Chinese characteristics is gradually taking shape. The reason behind that is that during the economic development of China, the theorists gained clearer understanding that consumption plays a key role in promoting the national economic operation, and they also reasonably gained the knowledge that consumption also plays a decisive role in economic and social operation; consumption deserves very important academic status. The reality repeatedly proves that the author's perspective on consumption years ago was correct and scientific.

Here is an analysis of the current consumption characteristics in China.

First, the 17th CPC National Congress defines the strategic decision to transform the economic growth mode transformation, expanding domestic demand and transforming the investment-led growth model to a consumption-led growth model; this decision is fully based on the theoretical basis of modern consumption. The central authorities not only notice but also attach great importance to the significant role of living consumption in driving economic development.

In the 17th CPC National Congress, Hu Jintao, Party General Secretary, brought forward some new requirements for the goal of building a moderately prosperous society, including a number of new requirements for the consumption patterns in China. This was the first time that consumption patterns in China and related new requirements were issued in the Party Congress, and they have great guiding significance.

According to consumption economics theory and international experience, when GDP per capita reaches 1,000 dollars, the consumption structure of people begins to change from one of survival to one of enjoyment and development, and businesses like retail and automobile industries are stimulated; when the GDP per capita reaches 3,000 dollars, it will enter a full development period with the all-round development of housing, insurance, and tourism. At the time GDP per capita of China reaches 1,800 dollars; in some areas the number is even higher. It means China has entered a transition period of the new round of consumption structure updating; most areas have begun to enter enjoying type. Against that background, it is very possible for China to transition from an investment consumption and import and export trade consumption pulling type into a domestic living consumption pulling type and to comprehensively promote economic development via domestic market.

In addition, economic development is not necessarily at the cost of large investment. In recent years, the scale of social consumption investment has grown much bigger. If the scale keeps developing, then the scale of social consumption investment will continue to increase in the tenth Five Year Plan. Some experts estimate that if the present investment ratio adds 1%, the GDP of China will add 0.22 of a percentage point; if the citizens' consumption ratio adds 1%, the GDP of China will add 0.87 of a percentage point. From these data, we can see that the living consumption contributes a lot to the economic development, and we should pay more attention to the proportion relations of the three important consumptions.

Market economy is decided and driven by consumption demand. However, it must be centered on a living consumption under state-led economy; market macro control of the market refers to that during the commodity and commodity production exchange process, six purposes, three means and twenty factors are applied to achieve dynamic control of balance and imbalance; in that way, the sustainable economic development is achieved through continuous regulation.

In the next half year of 2007, most GDP growth in China comes from domestic demand: the dominance of investment consumption is converted into the dominance of living consumption. According to data from national statistics bureau of China, Mark Williams, economist of the London Research Institute, predicted that from July 2007, the growth contributed by living consumption would exceed the contribution of investment consumption. Governmental control on bank credit will enable the consumption growth rate to slow down.

According to the statistics of consumptive expenditure data in China, the actual expenditure of residents is significantly growing, especially in education, housing, and tourism, where sharp increase is witnessed. In 2007, the growth rate of urban disposable income per capita exceeded the growth of GDP for the first time in the past five years; it was an important stimulus factor and facilitated consumption to maintain rapid and sustainable growth.

Most developed countries, America included, hope that China's growth rate depends mostly on domestic demand living consumption, less on export consumption and investment consumption, and this is also internationally constructive for China. If China's trade surplus no longer expands, domestic consumption demand will play a more important role in economic growth, and then the tensional situation of international trade will be eased.

Next, we will notice that at present China is converting from an export consumption country to a domestic consumption country to promote economic growth and development.

It is undoubtedly a highlight under the background of the global recession that China has been converted from an export consumption country into a country where economic development is driven by domestic consumption.

It can be seen that in 2007 such domestic demands as road and railway construction, automobile and clothing production were a powerful driving force of the economy.

The international balance of payments of China of regular items broke a new growth record in 2007, accounting for 10% of gross domestic output value. It means that China's output greatly exceeds consumption volume, and it is urgent to export surplus products. It is the trade surplus variable, not the absolute value, that influences a country's GDP growth. The growth of China's net export (export volume minus import volume) has never become the main factor of economic growth. From 2005 to 2007, the net export of China only contributed 2–3 percentage points to China's GDP growth, and, oppositely, the contribution of domestic demand reached 8–9 percentage points. The recent data indicates that although export contributes to the economic growth, for the export products, some consumers tend to be more rational and economize and some consumers tend to pursue vogue and fashion and prefer to enjoy the exquisite life and consumption style.

Individualism and convergence coexist in the consumption market and internationalization is as important as regionalization. On one hand, people will only focus on limited brands in purchasing electrical appliances, packaged food, and soft drinks; one the other hand, few brands are powerful enough to occupy a large market share, such as clothing, cosmetics, and cigarettes and drinking brands. In addition, people tend to select international brands for laundry products and audio and video products, and tend to select regional products for seasoning products and deepfreeze products.

Physical consumption and service consumption are classified into several grades. People will search for appropriate places according to their own income status. High-grade leisure places like villas, high-grade marketplaces and high-grade recreation places are impossible for those on a low income. Places like storage-type marketplaces, convenience stores, and consumption cooperation marketplaces are popular with those on a low income. The appearance of various retailing places, such as shopping centers, large-scale marketplaces, supermarkets, convenience stores and special stores, meet the requirement of different consumers. Places like beauty and hair salons, night clubs, bathing centers, and bowling gyms will become the spiritual and cultural homes of people with higher incomes.

The situation of consumption saturation or lack of consumption among high-income people continues to co-exist with the situation of high consumption demand but low consumption capacity among low-income people. High-income people have purchased houses and cars and have their houses well-furnished. However, although low-income people want to consume 10,000 or 100,000 Yuan each year, they do not have enough money at hand, which inevitably promotes the development of credit consumption and lease consumption.

In summary, in the first 15 years of the 21st century, basic living consumption tends to continuously upgrade. People's living consumption is becoming more high-grade and the focus of the overall consumption of residents is gradually converting from living consumption to focus on improvement of life quality and converting from the pursuit of material consumption to the pursuit of spiritual and cultural consumption, and converting from satisfying the basic living consumption to aspiring for people's overall development. People will pay more attention to famous brand consumption, environmental protection, and energy conservation; spiritual and cultural products will become popular, and intelligent, convenient, beautified, individualized, and green consumption will become the main trend.

Finally, savings of Chinese residents have great consumption energy. At the end of 2007, the household deposit balance of financial institutions had reached 17,600 billion Yuan.

For the first half year of 2008, various Renmingbi deposits had increased by 496.49 million Yuan, realizing a year-on-year increase of 157.74 million

Yuan. At the first half year, the household savings deposits increased by 2207 billion Yuan, realizing an year-on-year increase of 1379.8 billion Yuan. According to the statistics, among the newly increased deposits in the first half year, over 44% of deposits are contributed by household savings deposit. In June, RMB deposits increased by 771.5 billion Yuan, household savings reached 371.1 billion Yuan, and the household contribution rate for the newly increased deposits reached 48.36%. In addition, the deposits of non-financial companies increased by 1625.6 billion Yuan, which is a year-on-year decrease of 27 billion Yuan. This huge sum of deposits will be converted into a kind of great consumption energy along with the advent of the consumption era.

China is promoting the transformation of savings to consumption, which is obviously one of China's focuses in stimulating domestic demand. Along with the growth of income and savings of Chinese people, the yearly consumption level of some of the high-income residents in China has increased from 10,000 Yuan to 100,000 Yuan and to hundreds of thousands of Yuan. To achieve this transformation, the self-accumulation of residents will require a long time, and the development of consumption credit will promote the consumption demand of residents. Therefore, the state will reinforce its management for emerging hot consumption markets and establish a standardized credit system as soon as possible to promote the rapid development of consumption credit and provide an excellent consumption environment for consumers.

In summary, through 30 years of opening up and reform, China is gradually transforming from a planned economy to a market economy and has made world-renowned achievements. Chinese people are 'fumbling through the river' in practice and explore the road of development. At present, China has implemented an economic development pattern which centered on living consumption under the guidance of macro control of the state-led economy. During the great development of the economy, society, culture, and civilization over 30 years, the government and entrepreneurs of China have acquired valuable experience; however, because they continue to lack substantial experience, there are also lessons to be drawn in future practice. In the rapid development of world economy and in the big trend of transforming towards economic globalization, the road taken by China is worthy to be noticed by international communities.

3

Classical theories of consumption

Consumption and Management is a gathering of the essence of domestic and foreign theories about consumption.

This comprehensive book refers to almost all the famous Chinese and foreign economists' theories concerning consumption. The author integrated the penetrating statements and unique ideas of these economists and drew out their essence to form the theoretical basis of this book. We can say that the author won't reach the research level without the research work of these predecessors.

Section 1 Consumption theory in Chinese traditional culture

The consumption concept of Confucius

The main trend of the traditional Chinese concept of consumption is the hierarchy consumption thinking of Confucianism; the representative is Confucius. The core of Confucius' consumption thinking is to regulate the consumption concept, behaviors, and modes by the hierarchy of 'Rite'.

Confucius thinks that consumption behaviors should follow the idea of economy of expenditure and simplicity. Rite, asks for simplicity rather than luxury in the eyes of Confucius. Luxury is not only a category of expenditure, but also a consuming desire of people that will make them lose moral control of their consumption behavior so as to destroy the hierarchy consumption regulation of 'Rite'. On the other hand, 'simplicity' looks shabby but it represents the moral control of consumption behavior and is suitable for the hierarchy consumption regulation of 'Rite'.

The consumption concept of Laozi

The consumption concept of 'letting things take their own course' is important in Taoism; the representative of Taoism is Lao zi, the founder of Taoism. He advocated morality, adaptation to nature, governing by doing nothing and having a small territory with small population. As for consumption thinking, he promoted giving up luxury and coming to simplicity, purifying one's heart, and restricting one's desires, and experiencing happiness to lead to contentment.

Laozi proposed the contentment rule for how to satisfy the needs of consumption on the basis of 'few desires' and simplicity: 'There is no guilt greater than to sanction ambition; no calamity greater than to be discontented with one's lot.' He thought the standard of satisfaction did not lie in material goods, but in the contentment of one's heart. If the person couldn't be content with what he had, that would be the greatest calamity. Contentment represented the spirit of Tao.

The consumption idea of 'letting things take their own course' in Taoism denies the enjoyment of consumption and advocates having few desires, simplicity, and contentment. His contentment asks for stability in one's present condition, which objectively suppresses people's consuming desire. Laozi and Taoism require few desires and contentment to suppress the increasing human needs of consumption. We can say that contentment is full of philosophical meaning and has positive significance to the harmony of one's body and soul, as well as the adjustment of the contradiction between consumption needs and consumption power.

It is worth noting that Confucius (and Confucianism) and Lao zi (and Taoism) have different academic interests and values, but they both focus on the simplicity trend of consumption thinking. And their different consumption thinking features are presented under this similar trend.

The consumption concept of Mozi

The consumption concept of Mozi is unique in Chinese economic consumption thinking history. His concept regards economy of expenditures as the center of consumption. He proposed the general consumption standard which broke the hierarchy system; he asserted that consumption could be ensured by developing production; he claimed that the consumption level should increase with the growth of production: 'The pursuit of beauty comes after the satisfaction of one's hunger; the pursuit of elegance comes after having a warm coat; the pursuit of happiness comes after stable living.'

Mozi pointed out the real causes of 'three miseries' were that there was no basic consumption guarantee for common people. 'No food for hungers, no clothes for people who feel cold, no rest for labors', and 'these three phenomena are the great miseries for common people'. For these, Mozi cried out: 'We must supply food for the hungry, clothes for the cold, and rest for labors.' There are points which can be referenced in Mozi's ideas:

- *To repress the consumption polarization.* Mozi proposed the general consumption standard, which broke the hierarchy system to satisfy most people's consumption needs; and only this standard could ensure the stability of society and the development of society.
- *To increase the consumption level should be based on the development of production.* Mozi realized the relations between production and consumption; he asserted that the consumption level should be based on the development of production. He emphasized that social consumption should be based on the development of production and the consumption level should correspond to production conditions. 'Wei' and 'Shi' are the production relations and consumption. If 'producers are sick and there are a great number of consumers, then there will not be a harvest year.' So, if we want to ensure and improve consumption, we should try our best to develop production.
- *To practice thrift from top to bottom and to condemn waste.* The purpose of Mo zi's economy of expenditures is upward not downward, and is to restrain the parasitic consumption of the upper ruling class. Mo zi put forward that all the kings, vassals and officials should 'be thrifty to themselves and then become examples for the common people' so as to realize an economy of expenditure in the whole society, to form a good social atmosphere, and to benefit the country and people.

The consumption concept of Guanzi

The consumption concept of *Guanzi*, a philosophical work by the 7th-century author Guan Zhong, opened the author's mind. *Guanzi*'s consumption concept is unique and has incomparable academic significance.

In the book *Guanzi* there are consumption ideas of thrift as well as ideas of advocating luxury. The thrift consumption rule is generally in use while the luxurious consumption rule is proposed under special social conditions to stimulate social production. The two consumption ideas form a unity of present stability and social development. The consumption thinking in *Guanzi* shows an idea that in daily life, we cannot simply judge the importance of thrift and luxury and absolutely treat them as 'suitable' or 'unsuitable'. Timely appropriate practice of thrift and luxury is crucial.

There is an article in *Guanzi* entitled 'Luxury' that focuses on the luxurious consumption which had unique significance in ancient China. This article emphasizes the policy influence and practical significance of luxurious consumption and does not regard it as the basic rule of social consumption behavior. This point of view shows the characteristics of dialectical thinking. Luxurious consumption in *Guanzi* is outstanding with foresightedness because there is no school that has a similar idea in pre-Qin period. It adds new color to the traditional thrift consumption thinking.

The idea of advocating thrift and suppressing luxury runs through the book of *Guanzi*; we can see it in the chapters 'Jin Du', 'Fa Fa', and 'Qing Zhong'. Thrift is the main aspect of consumption thinking in *Guanzi*, while the luxury thinking draws most attention. *Guanzi* pointed out that if the country was too frugal, it would be harmful for the infrastructure projects, while if the country was too luxurious, it would be harmful to commodity resources. It means there are negative factors for production in thrift, and luxury will lead to wealth being wasted. Of course, this is from the perspective of consumption's influence on wealth production. From the theoretical point of view, thrift consumption thinking and luxurious consumption thinking are put forward as ways of overcoming these two harmful trends, and they become each other's cause so as to conform to the Taoist tradition of *Guanzi*.

Guanzi also discloses that consumption's stimulation to production is not unlimited, and luxury should have a 'degree'. 'Be strict to oneself, conform to the regulations and be thrifty, then disaster will not come even if happiness is lacking; be luxurious, break the law and offend the regulations, then happiness will never come even without disaster.' A clear understanding and judgment of the degree of luxury is the important rule and standard for its value. Excessive luxury will not promote economic development and causes the contradiction of production and consumption so as to waste resources and hinder the development of production and social progress. On the other hand, excessive luxury will foster hedonism and the one-sided pursuit of material enjoyment so as to cause various corruptions and a declining social moral.

Section 2 Consumption theory in Western economics

In Britain, classic economics began with William Petty and David Ricardo; in France, it began with Boisguillebert and Sismondi; Adam Smith and Quesnay were also among them. After 150 years of research, these economists demonstrated the factors, conditions, and approaches for increasing capitalistic wealth and the systems and principles of capitalistic economic operation. They set up the foundation of labor value theory, with a focus on contradictions between salary and profit, and profit and land rent. They did not mention to a significant degree. The author of this book draws more from the theories of the economists discussed below.

The consumption thoughts of William Petty

English classical political economics is considered to be the beginning of Western economics. Classical political economics reflects the age and class characteristics of capitalism during its inception and development period; it emphasizes capital accumulation and advocates consumption frugality. It affirms the status and role of consumption compared with mercantilism.

The core of Petty's consumption thought insists on less consumption and more accumulation. He thinks that abundance of products for consumption leads to over-consumption, and over-consumption can make people become lazier. Workers are satisfied with a minimum living standard, so he thinks that law should only ensure that the workers can get the most necessary life materials. If the life materials extended to the workers are doubled, then, what the workers do will be halved compared with what they are capable of completing when their wages are not doubled. For society, that is tantamount to losing the products created by the same amount of labor. He also classifies capital expenditure according to the degree to which the expenditure is favorable to production; they are eating and drinking, purchasing clothing and furniture, building houses, improving land, mining and fishing as well as the enterprise of importing gold and silver from abroad in turns. It indicates that his thought is also heavily marked by mercantilism. He insists on using taxation to change the proportional relation between consumption and accumulation: 'Through imposing taxation on people who indulge in eating and drinking, the fund accumulated can be used for useful practice, such as improving land, fishing, mining and opening factories. It is obvious that this kind of taxation is beneficial for the country where these people are located' (Petty, 1662).

Adam Smith's The Wealth of Nations

Just like William Petty, Adam Smith also puts capital accumulation in first place and advocates frugality in consumption. His understanding of consumption thought lies in his genuine recognition of the role and status of consumption for the first time in history. He initiated the proposition that the sole purpose of production is consumption, and the essence of consumption power (what he actually refers to is purchase power) is the consumption value obtained by income, but not the currency or gold, which is the negation of the concept of the wealth of mercantilism.

Adam Smith argued that in the mercantile system the interest of consumers is almost constantly sacrificed for that of producers, and that it seems to consider that production rather than consumption is the ultimate end and object of all industries and commerce (Smith, 1776). He suggested that consumption is the sole end and purpose of all production; the interest of producers ought to be attended to only as needed for promoting that consumers. Smith used abstract general production instead of capitalistic production, regarding satisfying consumers' interests directly instead of chasing profit as the sole end of this kind of production. We should note that Smith thought the realization of the purpose of production required a division of labor to develop production, a laissez-faire approach at home and free commerce abroad, so as to supply more commodities to satisfy people's consumption demands. Adam Smith held that consumption was the ultimate end of demands. The theory proposed by Adam Smith and other classic economists didn't mean that consumption was a key element for demands, but the single production of commodity. If there was no consumption, then the demands of production would be meaningless.

Keynes' The General Theory of Employment, Interest and Money

In the 1930s, the great economic crisis and great depression brought unprecedented shock to traditional economic doctrine; in *The General Theory of Employment, Interest and Money*, Keynes (1936) proposed that the root of the capitalist economic crisis lies in inadequate effective demand, which results from people's psychological state – 'diminishing consumption propensity', 'diminishing capital marginal efficiency' and 'flexible preference'. He makes use of marginal consumption propensity to illustrate the condition for maintaining the stability of the multiplier principle and the capitalist economic system. When marginal propensity declines, the multiplier principle can amplify investment amounts, which can reduce the gross income and gross employment, cause dramatic shock to the economy, and, thereby expand effective demand through demand management. Starting from expanding demand, he approves expenditure for personal squandering as well as for public squandering and agrees with the viewpoints illustrated in Mandeville's *The Fable of the Bees* (1714). He thinks that, in the long run, because of the decrease in the interest rate (the marginal efficiency of capital will also decrease), high-income people will tend to reduce their savings and raise their consumption propensity. Seen from the pattern of income distribution, with the decline of the consumption propensity among high-income people, assuming that society adopts the mode which is in favor of eliminating the inequitable situation to redistribute wealth and income, then considered from the perspective of promoting propensity to consume, it is beneficial for capitalist economic growth. Keynes invented the concept of consumption function and absolute income hypothesis. Both became the foundations for successive research studies. Thereafter, research on the consumption function became an enduring hot topic in economics.

Keynes (1936) also considered that employment was decided by effective demand (including consumption needs and investment needs), and effective demand was affected by three basic psychological factors – 'consumption tendency', 'expectation for asset's future earnings', and 'liquidity preference' for currency and volume of money. His advice was to extend government's power of intervention in the economy – taking financial measures, adding public expense, lowering the interest rate, stimulating consumption, increasing investment so as to improve effective demand and realize the full employment balance of economy.

Samuelson's Economics

Samuelson's *Economics* (Samuelson 1948) also gives great enlightenment to the study of consumption science systematic theory. Samuelson was the first American economist who won the Nobel Prize. He was a universal genius in economy who researched in economics, statistics, mathematics, and other fields. He combined Keynesianism and traditional micro economy and founded the 'neo-classical synthesis' – the modern framework of western economics in which all schools were given clear explanation and just evaluation. In 1970 he was given the Nobel Prize by the Royal Swedish Academy for developing mathematics and dynamic economic theory, and his research concerns in all the fields of economy.

Samuelson combined Keynes's macro-economic theory with a new classical micro economic theory to form the new classical synthetic school. From the first edition in 1948 to the current 19th edition, the school continuously absorbs new research results of modern economists and the book *Economics* became the most influential schoolbook of the second half of the 20th century. Its consumption theory integrates the thoughts of various schools. Using the perspective of the micro consumer behavior theory, the marginal analysis utility theory of Jevons and Pangbaweike and the theory of demand by Hicks are inherited and absorbed. Ordinal utility theory is used to replace cardinal utility theory and homogeneous curve concavity; relative diminishing marginal utility and revenue budget line are adopted to illustrate the marginal principles rational consumers abide by. Price change generates an earning effect and substitution effect for consumers and enables the demand law to take effect. Demand elasticity and supply elasticity decide the proportion of interest gained by consumers and producers, respectively. In this way, consumption theory has become the starting point of research for all modern micro economics. As to its macro part, analysis is conducted for the consumption rate for both the long term and short term. In *Economics*, Samuelson (1948) argued that seen from the perspective of the long term, a low consumption rate or low consumption propensity is beneficial for economic growth: 'Higher consumption relative to income can decrease investment and slow down economic growth; lower consumption relative to income can generate high investment and rapid economic growth'. Within short periods of time, its relation is uncertain:

> The interactive relation between consumption and income plays different roles within short periods of time, especially during the expansion or contraction period of the economic cycle; when the economic situation promotes the rapid development of consumption and investment, the overall expenditure or overall demand will increase, short-term output and employment rate will improve. However, when high taxation rates or low consumption confidence leads to the decrease of consumption, the overall consumption will decrease and the economy will probably enter into a recession period.

All in all, Samuelson's consumption theory is the combination of classical thought and Keynesianism.

In the sixth chapter of *Economics*, Samuelson gave a wonderful statement of consumption. The choice and utility theories, diminishing marginal utility theory, substitution effect, individual demand, market demand theory, and consumer surplus theory in the book have greatly enlightened the author of this book. For example, the choice and utility theories tell us that selective consumption means consumers tend to choose the goods and services which they consider as the most valuable. Utility means how the consumer arranges the order of different goods and services. Marginal utility theory is about the new and extra utility produced when the consumer uses up one unit of commodity, while diminishing marginal utility theory tells us that accompanying the consuming of certain goods, the new or extra marginal utility is decreasing – when the consuming amount of certain goods is increasing, the marginal utility is decreasing. All these theories gave great edification to the author's research and management.

The consumption thoughts of Say and Malthus

Jean Baptiste Say (1803) formally introduced consumption into the theoretical system of political economics. He considers that consumption means the extinction of utility and the things whose value cannot be diminished cannot be consumed; the phenomenon of houses catching fire is also consumption, for the utility is extinguished. In this way, he thinks that the sole research subject of consumption is the degree to which consuming behavior generates satisfaction, and the sole purpose lies in the comparison between the loss incurred by or the satisfaction provided by consumers' consumption. Thereby, the gain and loss estimation made by consumers decides the appropriateness of consumption. Say indicated that production can create self-demand and avoid inadequate demand. Malthus, Sismondi, Marx, and others objected to his law. However, before the revolution conducted by Keynes, Say's viewpoint had always been considered as the mainstream thought.

Thomas Robert Malthus brings forward the concept 'effective consumption' for the first time in the history of consumption theory. He points out that effective consumption believes that people are capable and willing to pay a price to purchase products to the effect that this kind of price can sustain the continuous supply of the products without reducing the profit margin. He thinks that the consumption of the landlord is essential for avoiding the economic stagnation caused by the surplus supply of the market; the special function of a group of non-productive consumers is to protect the balance between products and consumers and enable the hardworking people nationwide to gain maximum exchange value and promote the growth of wealth. Although Malthus approves the consumption behavior of the landlord employing a large number of employees but objects to the transfer payment made to poor people to increase consumption demand, for this practice can increase population; meanwhile, he objects to providing funds for excessive non-productive consumption.

Section 3 The consumption theory of Karl Marx

In Marx's *Capital* and his other famous works there is no specific chapter on consumption, but there are many statements about consumption. The consumption thinking of Marx is discussed below, based on the statements he made.

The scientific definition of consumption

Marx believes consumption includes scientific research and production consumption, as well as personal consumption. The process of production consumes materials like raw materials, fuel, workshop, and equipment, and consumes the physical and mental labor of the producer. Material products are produced through consumption. This kind of consumption and production is united directly – 'production is directly consumption'; 'from all the concerned factors, production itself is a consumption activity'. Another kind of consumption refers to personal consumption, that is, living consumption. It is the destination or the final purpose of social reproduction. Living consumption also has active significance to the whole social reproduction sector.

The inherent unity of consumption and production

Marx regarded consumption as a concept relative to production, which was one of the basic sectors of social reproduction such as production, circulation, distribution, consumption, and so on. Seen from the operation mechanism of the social economic system, consumption has interdependent, inter-connectional, and inter-creation relations with production. In Marx's preface of the famous *Capital*, he stated the dialectical relation of the unity of opposites between production and consumption. 'Production is direct consumption'; 'consumption is direct production'; 'there is no consumption without production', and vice versa. In terms of all production factors, the production process is also a consumption process, – the consumption of production materials.

The decisive role of consumption on production

Marx emphasizes the decisive role of consumption on production from three aspects:

- Consumption makes production become realistic production. Products become realistic goods only in consumption, and consumption is the final checking of production.
- Consumption creates new demand and supplies motive and purpose for production.
- The realization of new production modes requires that the guidance of production should be the extended range and appearance of new production modes.

When discussing the production and consumption of relative surplus value, Marx uses three key terms of consumption – volume, range, and new needs – to emphasize that only by extending the present consumption volume to a larger range can new needs be created. Only as new needs appear, can the new use value be discovered or created so as to produce new consumption. If there is no new consumption (including increasing the consumption amount, enlarging the consumption range, creating new consumption patterns, and so on), the use value produced by new production departments which are different from those produced by original departments will not be acknowledged by society.

Consumption power and consumption level

Marx brought forward the theory of consumption power for the first time. Consumption power refers to the consumption capacity of consumers within a certain period of time, which includes consumption power in two senses:

- knowledge, know-how obtained from learning
- payment capacity obtained from distribution.

Therefore, in *Capital*, Marx (1867) indicated that consumption capacity is the precondition of consumption and the first means of consumption; this capacity is the development of one person's talent and the development of one kind of productivity. Marx establishes a correspondent relationship between consumption power and productivity and points out their connection. He said:

> Economy is also the economy of labor time... and this kind of economy is equal to developing productivity. It is obvious that, the purpose of economy is not to be abstinent but to develop productivity; the development of productivity is not only the development of consumption capacity but also the development of consumption materials.

Marx clearly illustrates the internal relation between consumption power and productivity. To develop productivity also means to develop the capacity of production, which leads to the development of consumption power and consumption materials? Consumption materials are objective factors of consumption; consumption capacity is a subjective condition of consumption. Consumption capacity not only realizes consumption, but also expands the market for production and provides a conceptual 'internal motive' for production, becoming the precondition of production; meanwhile, consumption also gives back producers for production, and producers are decisive factors of the development of production. The producer quality is to some extent decided by the consumption capacity. If people have high purchase capacity, they will acquire richer knowledge, higher technique, and high consumption quality and, thereby, high self-quality. Consumption knowledge and technique are cultivated during learning and spare time, being a talent of human beings. People's talent is also a production capacity, and thereby, the development consumption capacity is 'the development of a kind of personal talent', also 'the development of a kind of productivity,' and it can 'act upon the labor productivity as the more powerful productivity' (Marx, 1867).

Marx's consumption theory holds that consumption is established on an integral base where production, exchange, distribution, and consumption are mutually acted upon and organically related, being both dialectic and systematic. Production, exchange, distribution, and consumption are mutually related and inseparable important factors within the same system. The recognition and understanding of exchange, distribution, and consumption are essential for the recognition and understanding of production.

Section 4 The consumption thought of Deng Xiaoping

Deng Xiaoping's consumption idea is an important part of his theory system. At the same time as China's reform and openness period, Deng boldly proposed his consumption idea and pointed out that the improvement of consumption level is the essential requirement of socialism. He asserted that 'poverty is not socialism' and pointed out that enhancing comprehensive national power should regard the improvement of people's living standard as its premise, the increasing of gross national product (GDP) had laid a solid foundation for the improvement of people's living standard.

The strategic aim of consumption

The consumption strategic aim of Deng's theory was in three steps: adequate food and clothing, being well-off, common prosperity. The first step was to double China's GDP in the 1980s and in the base year of 1980, the GDP per capita was only 250 dollars; doubling it meant we should reach the GDP per capita of 500 dollars; the second step was doubling the GDP per capita of 500 dollars at the end of this century to 1,000 dollars. The realization of this aim would mean we have become a well-off society; we have transformed a poor China into a well-off China, and, at that time, our GDP would be over 1,000 billion dollars. Though we still have a low per capita number, the national power would be greatly strengthened; the aim still has the third step: in 30 to 50 years of the 21st century, the GDP per capita will quadruple the rate of 1,000 dollars and reach 4,000 dollars. If we realize this step, China will achieve the level of a moderately developed country, and this is our ambition.

The strategic emphasis of consumption

The first step of Deng's strategic aim for consumption is to solve the problem of adequate food and clothing; the second step is to reach the well-off level and finally to achieve common prosperity. In the entire strategic plan, he regards the second step – well-off – as the one to emphasize: 'When we reach the well-off level, people's mental outlook will be different.' The so-called well-off level is not only an aim for level of living, but also an integrated aim for consumption. This is the first time Deng used statistical indicators to quantify the strategic aim of consumption.

Consumption policy

Deng's consumption idea can be divided into three aspects:

- *The policy about agricultural development.* He said, 'In 2000, the problem of grain should be solved' (Deng, 2006). The aim of this policy is to satisfy the people's demands for crops; and the increase of peasants' consumption level will bring an extremely large demand for industrial products so as to push the development of industry.
- *The policy of common prosperity.* This requires us to try our best to increase the consumption level of all citizens. But common prosperity is the ultimate aim; during the realization process, we allow part of the people to get rich first and some areas to become prosperous first, because common prosperity doesn't mean average prosperity; nor does it mean prosperity at the same pace.
- *The policy of moderate consumption.* Deng stresses many times the need to strengthen the policy guidance for human consumption: 'moderate' is the key.

The author has a deep understanding that Deng's strategic idea of consumption is a scientific and systematic theory, the inheritance and development of Marx's thinking about consumption in the new situation. His theory not only outlines the ambitious objectives of the China's development of consumption which can be achieved through effort, but also puts forward the theoretical basis for the road of sustainable consumption. The author has made a thorough study of Deng's consumption idea that develops Marx's consumption thinking and acknowledges its great instructive influence on *Consumption and Management.*

From the above analysis, we can see that this book systematizes and refers to the consumption theories in China's traditional culture and Western economics as well as the consumption theory of Deng Xiaoping, which has unique Chinese characteristics and is the important feature of this work. In this light, the academic point of view expressed by this book is not groundless but the inheritance, development, and innovation of ancient and modern ideas and theories on consumption.

The exploration of truth is eternal and we are continuously pioneering the road leading to truth. The academic innovation of this book is to some extent based on the research achievements of predecessors and the book contains an understanding of the laws behind social phenomena as well as the conclusions produced by the author through years of laborious study and research.

4

Consumption and economic law

This chapter aims to study the rule that consumption leads to the circular spiraling development of the economy on a macro level from the angle of consumption itself, including the role played by consumption in the development process of human beings and its inherent overall relation with economic activities. In order to further understand economic law, the way economic law emerges during the developing process of human society should be made clear. That means to clarify the conditions of emergence and the developing process of economic law, its power and relations with the subjective will of human beings must be revealed. It can be generalized as follows:

1. Economic laws concerning natural consumption and free market control are created through three important types of consumption. In other words, the law of natural economy is created through living consumption, social consumption, and production consumption (which together are called consumption, in short). It is created during the spiral development process of the economy, which is driven by increasingly high materialistic, spiritual, and cultural consumption needs of human beings.
2. In human society, it is consumption that creates the economic foundation of private ownership, creates the production combining productivity of a consumption society and production relations, and creates a nation and the superstructure. The country and superstructure represent and act for economic foundation, productivity, and production relations, as well as the interests of citizens. The economic foundation determines the objectives of production which generate basic economic law. It has influences on natural (free) market finance and economic law. Free-market economic law, generated from the exchange process of commodities, has both positive and negative effects.

3. Interventions to mitigate the negative effects of free market control finance and economics from the state superstructure during the process of commodity production, exchange, and consumption of capital are called state dominant macro-control economic laws, which create the market economy rules of macro control. Economic law is objective and independent of man's will. When people's subjective will conforms to objective economic law, the economy develops rapidly; when people's subjective will violates objective economic law, people will be punished, and the economy will experience slow development, stagnation or regression or even economic crises (serious proportional imbalance). When people can understand and master economic law, adapt to it, intervene in it, and control it, there will be sustainable development of the economy. In this way, acting upon the economic law will show people's subjective initiative.

It can be seen that with people's understanding, grasping and application of the natural economic law, the law of free market control and the economic law of macro control will play the role of promoting or influencing economic development.

Section 1 Law of three important consumptions leading to the circular spiral development of economy

The law of consumption and the circular spiral development of economy

Consumption pulls the development of scientific research and production. New desire and consumption demand continuously come into being during the whole course of the practice of living consumption, scientific research, and production consumption, and constantly lead scientific research and production to much newer and higher consumption stages. Accordingly, through scientific research, and production, human beings again produce new commodities and markets for consumption and reach new consumption levels. New desires of consumption and demand are the motive for consumption. A corresponding consumption power is required to realize consumption. Consumption is the result, and once the desired result is obtained through consumption, new consumption needs will emerge.

Consumption creates new demand desire, scientific research and production, new consumption markets and the special commodity – currency. Consumption promotes the constant advancement and development of productivity; and it creates the economic base and its superstructures, the whole of social wealth, and the development of culture and civilization of society. While consumption develops itself, it also creates its own rule of economic development – the rule that consumption leads to the circular, spiral development of the economy – 'consumption – market – demand (desire, knowledge, and inspiration of ever-increasing consumption demand) – scientific research – production – higher level consumption.

Endless development is realized based on the natural law of circular, spiral development, which incurs various laws of economic development as well as the general law and adjustment law related to this development. All these laws ensure the circular, spiral development of the economy and provoke the economy to develop from a low level to a higher level.

Generation of economic law

A more thorough understanding can be gained for the operation of the law of consumption in creating the spiral development of finance and economy by combining the historic process. In his *The Origin of the Family, Private Property and the State* (1972), Engels discussed the generation and development of family, private ownership and the state, and the relations between the state and private ownership and so on. From that, we can see how human beings live, produce, distribute, and exchange, or in other words, possess and acquire social wealth. From the development of this process, we shall study the generation and development of economic law and how it acts upon the economy.

With the appearance of surplus products, private ownership emerged. Meanwhile, mutual exchange emerged to meet people's diverse demands. Along with the development of the economy, especially the three divisions of labor in social production, human beings were divided into different classes. In the primary stage, there was only barter exchange. With socialization of production, barter could not meet the demand of social production and different classes. Then currency, a special commodity, was invented, which dominated all other commodities, played an extremely energetic role, and brought everything in society under its control. Since the producers were not capable of great numbers of exchanges, people who were specialized in commodity dealing – merchants – appeared.

Commodities showed great vitality through currency, which promoted widespread and rapid exchange of commodities as well as the expansion of exchange from home to foreign countries.

Originally, the exchange of commodities was an economic activity aimed at meeting the needs of living consumption, production consumption, and social consumption. However, the purpose of merchants' economic activity is to gain profits. Therefore, they spare no efforts to study types of commodities needed at different times and at different festivals, by the upper and lower classes in each region, departments, and groups, so as to invest maximum capital and energy to seek profits. Merchants keenly look for sales markets from every corner. As a result, and always control production groups.

When certain commodities exceed people's living, productive, or social demands, or in other words, when supply exceeds demand, commodities will become overstocked, prices will fall, production will halt or fall back, and economic crises will break out. When certain commodities cannot meet people's needs of living consumption, production consumption or social consumption, supply falls short of demand. Therefore, it is a natural law of economic development in human society that living consumption, production consumption and social consumption drive the development of the economy.

When there were surplus products in clans, prairies, and tribes in a primitive society, private ownership and then classes appeared. With the development of production, human beings have been developing from lower stages to higher stages: the slave trade replaced primitive society; feudal society replaced the slave trade; capitalist society replaced feudal society; socialist society replaced capitalist society. However, the development of the social system is very unbalanced. The superstructure of government can realize great forward development, but not its economic foundation. A superstructure government can enter into a new socialist system within a short period of time, but the economic foundation of capital is insurmountable, and it must undergo a development process; therefore, any new social system must vigorously promote economic development or it will be confronted with crisis.

An economy with capitalistic private ownership as its economic foundation should develop according to the interests and needs of capitalists. Working exclusively for profits is the purpose of the capitalist. They have no social responsibilities. All economic plans of capitalists are aimed at seeking profits. There are positive effects, however, for profits can transform into productive capital and promote social and economic development.

Because capitalists compete for profits, the capital transfers without clear purpose among the departments, which results in anarchy of social production. In an anarchical market economy, when a certain commodity falls short and its price rises, capitalists will quickly invest in the department producing this kind of commodity. Then the commodity originally in short supply quickly becomes a commodity in excessive supply. Free market financing and economic law can regulate the supply relationship, and this is a great contribution; meanwhile, it can also result in financial and economic crisis, which is the negative effect of (free) financial and economic law.

The process in which three important consumptions push the spiral development of the economy creates and generates the free control law on the market of commodity exchange. The economic foundation determines productive objectives and generates basic economic law. The state's intervention in the free control law on the market of commodity exchange generates the market economy rules of macro control; the intervention of a socialist state-owned economic foundation on the market of commodity exchange generates socialist market economy rules of macro control. The basic economic law is determined by the economic foundation, the level of productivity in a certain historical period and the nature of living consumption needs. The basic economic law is subject to the needs of the economic foundation and superstructure and also acts upon economic law.

If the superstructure is suitable for the economic foundation, the production relations will be suitable for the productivity. The development of three important consumptions acts upon development of the natural economic law.

Circular spiral development law of consumption and market

Consumption and the market follow the circular, spiral development law of consumption and market – demand (desire and knowledge inspire understanding of a new commodity) – research – production – consumption and market.

The first cycle of the circular law

The first cycle of the circular law starts from consumption and the operative drive toward scientific research, production consumption, and the consumption of market consumers:

1. The objects of science and technology research and experimentation are consumption and market. Before setting up a project, scientific

research should in the first place survey the supply and demand information of the three important consumptions and their respective three levels on the market.

2. On the basis of the capacity of the unit, one kind of research project that is proportional to the capacity of the unit should be selected; the product should integrate new and higher technology. After the product is successfully developed, an analysis for its social and enterprise benefits should be conducted and then it should be decided whether to establish the project.

Scientific research

After mastering the large quantity of information on the market consumption, the unit should make objective comparisons and selection according to its labor, material, and financial resources, make decisions to set up projects, organize scientific research staff to jointly solve the key problems, strive to archive new results with the fastest possible speed within the shortest possible time, and carry out pilot tests in time to make good preparation for all the technological experiments for large-scale production. What should be noted from this is that the scientific research institutions of the production units or the professional scientific research units must set up market consumption information departments which are responsible for doing the preparation work for scientific research. Reasonable scientific research projects derive from precise and valuable information. Otherwise, significant waste or even crimes may occur.

Production

These are the principles of production:

1. The capital for production should not be invested unless the new scientific achievements have been demonstrated and the supply of the products indeed has been shown to fall short of demand. The capital for the reform of new technology should not be invested unless the commodity has been demonstrated to meet the market consumption need. Blind investment will cause loss and waste to the enterprise or even to the country, and could be regarded as a sort of crime.
2. Produced commodities should be new-tech or high- and new-tech products – the products with competitive power on the market.
3. Produced commodities should have a certain volume of social consumption demand and strive for the maximum market shares.

4. The produced commodity quality should be in a leading position among the same category of commodities in quality and satisfy consumers in respect of such standards as technological content, modeling, and taste.

The produced commodity quality should be in a leading position among the same category of commodities in quality and meet consumers' standards for technological content, modeling, and taste.

Now the enterprise should promptly organize labor, material and financial resources to ensure that the new products are promoted in the market. Then the enterprise should accumulate the experience of serving consumers to expand market shares and obtain consumer preferences to the largest extent, striving for big social and enterprise benefits.

The first cycle ends; the second and third cycles circulate forward endlessly

These are the principles of the cycles:

1. If the unit does not work hard to surpass itself, others will surpass it, even if the unit has leading science and technology results or inventions. Therefore, the unit should dare to deny the laggard things of it and confront new things so as to make constant creation and development.
2. In the process of collecting information about the consumption situations of consumers, an enterprise should constantly find out new problems, movements and results, and promptly organize the collecting of information, striving for better commodities.
3. Scientific research should closely follow in the steps of consumers on the market. The development of scientific research should constantly supply new and higher scientific achievements or new-tech achievements for production. Scientific research is the motive for the development and production of the enterprise.

The rule circulates around the consumption market

The cycle starts from the information of the consumption market, and returns to the consumption market. This return is not the end point; rather, it is a circular, spiral development which promotes economic development and the progress of social material civilizations and mental civilizations.

Section 2 Market financial and economic law

Financial monetary rules govern the whole process of capital commodity production, exchange, and consumer consumption; it is essential to study the financial monetary law and general and special economic laws.

Relations between consumption and market

Consumption and demand are contradictory and unified. They are contradictory because the prices of commodities, which consumers buy directly from producers, are generally lower than those they buy from the market. Sometimes this price gap may be large. The use value of this commodity does not increase with the value increase in the circulating process. In contrast, its use value may decease because of the improper storage and damage during circulating process. Therefore, consumption and demand are contradictory.

However, consumption and demand are also unified. First, the exchange of commodities is realized on the market. The supply–demand relation of commodities is displayed through the market. Second, commodities sometimes can be consumed without realizing the exchange values. For commodities with identical use value, this is particularly prominent in the societies and countries whose capital and commodity production is underdeveloped. Besides, the consumption market plays a service role for consumers, which is realized by offering services to consumers. A perfect consumption market guarantees the realization of the rights and interests of consumers, and only a developed consumption market can satisfy the selection demands of consumers. A consumption market can play a certain rule of guidance; it plays an active role in increasing the consumption benefits and validity of consumers. This is the benefit function of the market. With the production and development of commodities, the industry division of labor will be finer, and commodities will be merchandised gradually or completely.

These are the relations between consumption and market:

1. The case that commodities do not enter the field of circulation, when they are consumed by individuals instead of being circulated commodities in the marketplace, happens under self-producing and self-selling conditions. The commodity realization of the capital is realized in the exchange process, so self-producing and self-selling goods do not

display themselves as commodities. However, its actual use value does not disappear because it does not participate in commodity exchange. The same consumption value still exists.

2. The exchange of commodities on the market can be realized through various channels such as big-market, small-market or direct exchange between manufacturers and consumers. Under the condition that they have the same use value, their prices may have great difference. Therefore, the simpler the circulations of commodities on the market, the lower their prices are, and the better it is for consumers.
3. Manufacturers can gain big social benefits and enterprise benefits in certain ways. In order to let more commodities meet consumers directly, to decrease the increment price in the exchange process, to increase the production of commodities and to gain big social benefits and enterprise benefits, the manufacturers confront the monopoly of the sellers of commodities, strive for the internalization of production and selling, sell commodities directly to consumers, or to the largest extent, reduce the links of the circulation process and greatly increase the production and market share of their commodities.
4. The commodity exchange between manufacturers. In order to reduce costs, the final product manufacturer realizes the contract commodity exchange with the manufacturer of raw material commodities needed in his production process. This plays a great role in speeding up the capital circulation, reducing the cost of his commodity, and increasing the competitive power of his commodity on the market exchange.
5. The fluctuation of the commodity price. The price of the commodity purchased on the market by the direct consumers is under direct influence of the supply–demand relation. When supply exceeds demand, the price rises; when supply falls short of demand, the price goes down. The birth of the information market and information value will gradually reduce or relieve the blind market monopoly, competition crisis, and repetitive production, which is beneficial for the macro regulation of the country. Meanwhile, the information market and information value greatly assists commodity socialization.

Relations between consumption demand and consumption credit

On the market economy, consumption demand is the only everlasting driving force of economic development. The government emphasizes investment need as well, but ultimately, investment demand is determined by consumption, and mainly determined by social consumption.

The social and economic significance of consumption credit and consumption demand

The needs of consumption are consumers' current payment capacity for market commodities and the kinds of commodity services in a fixed period. Consumption demand determines consumption credit; the content, nature, and method of consumption need to determine the kind, purpose, and scale of consumption credit. Consumption credit can ensure the realization of the demand for consumption, promote the demand for consumption to realize consumption development, and then consumers' consumption of developed consumption demand will resort to consumption credit once again, so the two promote each other. The direct purpose of developing consumption credit in commercial banks is to stimulate consumption, expand domestic demand, and promote economic growth.

Law of consumption credit promoting demand for consumption

These are the laws of consumption credit for promoting demand for consumption:

1. When supply generally exceeds demand on the market, and the development of the entire economy is affected, measures such as banks' increasing low-interest loans to consumers, lowering deposit rates and compressing deposit amounts can be taken so as to raise purchasing power on the market, boost purchasing power, and promote economic development, using the growth in consumption as a driver for production of commodities.
2. When supply falls short of demand, the banks (usually in the case of inflation) can take measures such as raising the deposit ratio, enlarging deposit amounts, reducing current flows on the market, and issuing more loans to commodity production projects, so as to increase the whole production of commodities, promote consumption, and spur the development of the national economy.
3. When supply exceeds demand in a certain industry on the market, measures such as low interest credit or low interest loans can be offered to direct life consumers to promote consumption and commodity production.
4. When supply falls short of demand in a certain industry, measures can be taken such as paying in advance or making down payments, or increasing credit quantity or the number of low-interest loans to this industry, to increase investment in reproduction, and promote consumption and rapid development of economic development.

5. When there is too much social liquidity for consumption, banks can increase the number of enterprises with promising economic benefits to list on the stock market, lead consumption capital to production, increase investment in reproduction, use the form of bank loans and bank bonds, and issue enterprise stocks to society by banks, to adjust consumption and promote the whole national economy. These are the usual types of consumption credit.

Changing the traditional lagged consumption pattern and promoting implementation of credit consumption

For many years, influenced by the traditional culture, Chinese residents' consumption has mostly been based on self-accumulation. China must rapidly develop consumption credit, and transform the lagged consumption based on people's self-accumulation into proper advance consumption supported by credit, thus to enable consumption to play an active role in driving economic development.

From the perspective of the bank, credit can advance the operating effectiveness of commercial banks. Presently, competition between banks is fierce. Traditional deposits and loans bring less benefit, which forces banks to find new benefit points. Enlarging consumption credit is one of the most important measures for banks. From the perspective of consumers, credit can promote people's material and cultural quality of life. Finance is the centre of the modern economy; developing consumption credit can meet the habitants' consumption demand. Raising people's quality of life promotes the realization of the purpose of socialist production.

Policies to establish and promote a robust consumption credit market

Restricted by consumption patterns and people's inadequate purchasing power, the consumption credit market develops slowly. The following measures should be taken:

1. Change the traditional consumption pattern. From the perspective of changing people's concept of consumption, we must raise people's consciousness of using various financial offerings of banks, of credit consumption, and all kinds of consumption. We will change people's traditional consumption pattern of accumulation through various propaganda and education methods, and encourage them to enjoy services provided by the bank.

2. Put forth powerful policies to stimulate consumption. From the perspective of policy, the policies for stimulating consumption should be further strengthened. Positive financial and currency policies should be taken to increase domestic demand, stimulate consumption, and strengthen the policies for stimulating consumption. On the one hand, we must adjust policies on income distribution and increase the urban and rural income level. On the other hand, we must adjust or cancel all policies that restrict consumption.
3. Cultivate new consumption points. From the perspective of benefit, new growth points of economy and consumption should be positively cultivated. We must positively develop service consumption, such as telecommunication, tourism, entertainment, health, and sport; we must rapidly and healthily develop real estate, spurring a large number of people into the commercial house market. Meanwhile we must start the secondary market and have new houses, old houses, and houses of different price levels all enter the consumption domain. We must especially develop higher education, and cultivate specialized talents for the country.
4. Build good financial environment for consumption credit. At present, the government has issued some regulations, rules, and advice on consumption credit, but there is no law fully stipulating the behaviors of parties to acquire and distribute consumption credit, so we must, as quickly as possible, constitute a consumption credit law to regulate market behaviors and ensure the healthy development of the consumption credit market. In addition, the commercial banks must change their management concepts, see the prospects of the consumption market and consumption credit strategically, improve their knowledge of the importance of consumption credit, and take consumption credit as an important method of improving assets structure, improve the quality of assets, cultivating new business growth points and benefit growth points. The emphasis on production credit should be turned to consumption credit, raising the proportion of consumption credit in the credit assets of commercial banks.

The relationship between consumption and currency appreciation and depreciation

The impact of currency appreciation on consumption

Taking China as an example, appreciation of the RMB can make consumers' money more valuable. Seen from the narrow angle, appreciation benefits consumers, while seen from the angle of the entire state's economic development; appreciation of the RMB can bring uncertainties for national macro-economic regulation and bring difficulties to employment. Personal income decreases. At the same time, because of appreciation, overseas tourists will find reduced expenses when they visit China, which will also have great impact on our service industry, tourism, and so on, and then employment in these areas of the economy will also be affected.

The appreciation of the RMB will also promote increased import commodities coming into the domestic market, which will allow partial shares of the domestic market to be seized by oversea enterprises. These two aspects can have one result: parts of domestic enterprises need to be readjusted and many people will possibly become unemployed. Moreover, appreciation of the RMB will also have many effects in the domestic professional areas. For instance, it is profitable to aviation, trade, and so on. Part of these professions' international service is paid through foreign exchange (mainly the US dollar), therefore, appreciation of the RMB will bring exchange gains or losses to these professions. However, the traditional sectors advantageous in export business are directly impacted, which include textile clothing, electrical appliances, machinery, and so on. Cost increases that are brought by appreciation of the RMB can cause the drop of these professions' profit margin.

The impact of currency depreciation on consumption

These are the possible impacts of currency depreciation on consumption:

1. Depreciation may enhance people's expectation of inflation, and domestic consumption will be stimulated. In future economic development of China, domestic consumption has the most potential, and the depreciation of currency can actually stimulate consumption and impel economic growth.
2. Depreciation may maintain the competitive power of Chinese commodities in the international market. Meanwhile, if government can promptly promote a policy that cancels or reduces the tax reimbursement for exports, it may not only relax the pressure that foreign countries exert on appreciation of the RMB, but also can achieve the purpose of financial deregulation; however, all these possibilities depend on the overall economic situation.
3. Depreciation can adjust the division of different domestic social stratums' income structure and increase minority groups' income.

Appreciation of the RMB may improve the competitiveness of Chinese agricultural and labor-intensive products in the international market, increase minority groups' employment opportunity and income, and withstand the impact that entry to the World Trade Organization brings to Chinese agriculture.

4. Depreciation will open broader operating space to financial policy. Compared with deflation, moderate inflation can not only provide more effective use space for the Central Bank's monetary policy tools, but may also expand the utilization space of financial policy.

Treating the dual functions of currency appreciation and depreciation seriously

To consumers, both appreciation and depreciation have dual functions: it could truly bring benefit to some consumers; it will also do harm to other consumers. Therefore, when considering appreciation or depreciation, we must certainly analyze dialectically and treat it based on the general national situation, analyze it scientifically and treat it seriously. We should adjust properly according to the situation of Chinese and international economic development. The Chinese government has reiterated that China's exchange rate reform is mainly a question of time, and the Chinese government will not yield to foreign pressure; I greatly appreciate this kind of national demeanor shown by the Chinese government, but it must be based on the whole economic situation.

Relations between money created by consumption commodities exchanged and amount of money issued

During the course of consumption commodity exchange, original commodity exchange at the primary took the form of commodity barters; the special commodity currency was created during the development, representing equivalent value of commodities for exchange for all types of consumption goods. During the development of currency as a special commodity, the currency trading enterprises were created (the primitive exchange shops, money houses, and then banks). Banks and the financial markets, in turn, invented many financial tools; thereby the financial institutions began to dominate the entire course of the capital exchange, commodity production, and consumption.

The function of currency and characteristics of the amount of issued currency

Currency has five functions: the measure of value, means of circulation, means of hoarding, means of payment, and world currency. Among them, the measure of value and means of circulation are the basic functions.

Currency is issued under the name of the state using the national coercive power. In real life, it is the ratio tool used to weigh 'the value created by humans'. Private banks are strictly forbidden to issue currency or it will be the delinquency and crime committed by the national superstructure government committed to the people in the country; for the whole process of the production capital commodity, exchange and consumption is ruled by currency finance, which is the most important but not the sole tool of the state's macro control.

Because the currency is issued imperatively by the state, 'the supply' of currency becomes an important tool for the state to regulate the economy. Generally speaking, there are three characteristics of the amount of issued currency: profitability, balance, and destructiveness. Profit means that the country can increase the 'available' amount of money and payout through issuing more currency. Stability is the maintenance of a balanced development of the economy through scientifically maintaining a stable amount of issued currency. Destructiveness means that unscientific and excessive amounts of issued currency will initiate inflation and destroy normal economic development.

The amount of issued currency is determined by the total value of a country's commodity in circulation; if the amount of issued currency is lower than the total value of commodities in circulation, the market will slump and economic development will slow down. If it is higher than the total value of commodities in circulation, the prices will rise, and there will be inflation. In fact, one cannot estimate the number of commodities in circulation precisely; various commercial banks will deposit a portion of their funds in the People's Bank of China, to guarantee stable prices and avoid inflation. The People's Bank of China decides the size of the portion; this is the ratio of deposits.

Determination of the amount of currency to issue

How to determine the amount of currency (paper money) to issue? (New financial instruments may substitute the issuance and circulation of the paper currency.)

What first needs to be explained is that the amount of issued currency in circulation is a matter for the Central Bank; it cannot be achieved by any concrete bank. The amount of issued currency in circulation is decided by three factors: the quantity of commodities that are waiting to be circulated, the price level of commodities, and the velocity of circulation (the volume of alternative financial instruments must also be calculated).

The amount of required currency in a society is decided by many factors. It is mainly determined by the entire society's overall consumption power. Specifically, it is determined by four factors:

- the supply of social commodities
- the supply that service may provide
- the investment scale of enterprises
- individual consumption power.

In the commodity exchange, currency is the medium of exchange; therefore, the total price of commodities for sale decides the total amount of needed currency. But one unit (Yuan) of currency may serve as the medium of commodity several times; therefore, it is the flow but not the stock of money that is determined by the total price of commodities; in addition, pay attention to deduct the amount settled by the alternative financial instruments instead of paper currency in circulation.

If **M** stands for the amount of required currency, Q indicates the amount of commodities on sale, P expresses the average price of commodity, V is the velocity of circulation, and then the above formula may be indicated as follows:

$$M = \frac{PQ}{V} + A + B$$

This currency requirement formula by Marx has important theoretical significance. However, it is necessary to add the currency in the hands of consumers and the currency in savings, the amount of currency used in circulation by the enterprises, and the overhead provision of supplement currency (expressed by A); in addition, the stock portion of enterprise ownership is a particular commodity generated by increasing the amount of enterprise capital in the stock market; the total amount of exchange transaction in such particular stock market (expressed by B) should also be added to the formula. Thus, the overall currency requirement formula should look as follows:

$$M = \frac{PQ}{V} + A + B$$

It reflects the basic principle that circulation of commodities determines the circulation of money. Currency is created to suit the demand of commodity exchange, because commodity exchange must enter circulation and adjust the amount on the market according to the demand of exchange. Whether this kind of change on amount is carried on spontaneously or artificially by the government department, it must enter the circulation domain. This kind of analysis has an important guiding sense for us to understand the developing money credit relations and the inherent relations between the circulation of commodities and money.

Based on the Marx's amount of required currency formula, using the perspective of the relations between consumption and currency, I propose the following analysis:

- When the general market consumption level (the total price of commodities for sale) surpasses people's demand, we should expand the issuance of consumption fund and the issuance of construction fund in the case of constant velocity of circulation.
- When the market is inflating, we must correspondingly reduce the amount of issued currency.
- In order to maximize the foreign market, we should reduce the storage of domestic foreign exchange and simultaneously increase the amount of issued currency in the domestic market.

Attention to three relations in issuing currency

China is a developing country and should pay attention to the relations between the amount of issued currency, price, and people's consumption level and correctly understand Chinese positive monetary policies. It involves three dialectical relations:

- the relationship between the amount of issued currency and price
- the relationship between price and living standards
- the relationship between the amount of issued currency and people's consumption levels.

We can draw these conclusions:

- Under the premise of an invariable commodity supply, an increased amount of issued currency will cause a rise in prices.
- Under the premise that people's incomes are static; a rise in prices will inevitably lead to a drop of living standard.
- If the amount of issued currency increases and the incomes of people have not been increased correspondingly, then the drop of money's purchasing power will lead to a drop in living standards. However, if the additional issued currency turned out to be in people's real incomes, at this time, to increase purchasing power, the living standard will be improved.

About paper money and credit money

Paper money is the mark of value issued and circulated forcedly by the state. It is the representative of metallic currency. Paper money itself does not have value; it only executes the functions of circulation and payment means by replacing metallic currency. It can be exchanged according to the exchange rate, and it can also be deposited, but it cannot act as a store of value. Paper money is created from currency's function as a means of circulation. With the increasing development of the banking industry, while paper money serves its widespread function and circulates massively, credit money is created. Credit money has many forms, such as bank notes, checks, promissory notes, bank drafts, and so on. Credit money manifests credit relations between the creditor and debtor.

There are two kinds of phenomena that have direct relations with the amount of issued currency: inflation and deflation. Inflation and deflation harm the normal development of the economy.

The dialectical relations between society's general consumer power and the amount of issued currency

Here, society's overall consumption power includes people's consumption power. This kind of consumption power is a paying capacity and has close dialectical relations with the amount of issued currency.

The amount of currency that the general consumer power of society demands immediately influences the motion of social economy. In the situation of sufficient currency supply, the stronger the currency demand, the more positive its influence on economy and society will be. Because huge currency demand needs huge supply, huge supply needs the acceleration of production, the acceleration of production inevitably brings the growth of output value, the material wealth of society will be richer. Otherwise, in the case of sufficient money supply, the smaller the demand, the more negative the influence on economy and society will be, since the serious insufficiency in currency demand will cause massive backlogs of products, block production, even resort to deceleration of production to maintain its vigor.

Moreover, in the case of an insufficient currency supply, the stronger the demand for currency is, the more negative the influence on economy and society is, since the insufficient supply will affect the growth of economy. Otherwise, under the situation of insufficient currency supply, controlling the corresponding needs of consumption can have a positive influence on social economy, because it can maintain an orderly and accelerated environment.

According to the proportional relations between general consumptions' paying capacity and currency demand, we can know that if we can control general consumption's paying capacity, we can control the currency demand. The goal of controlling currency demand is to maintain the balanced and fast development of the social economy. Because paying capacity is expressed by the payment function of currency, the size of the paying capacity is symbolized by the measure value of currency. Therefore, if we can control the amount of currency in circulation, then we can control the paying capacity. Increasing of the amount of issued currency can increase the payment capacity.

Relations between consumption, law of value, and price

The price of all consumer goods on the market is under the control of the law of value; without the law of value, the price of all consumer goods would not exist. Simultaneously, without price, value would not exist. The price of commodities fluctuates around value:

1. The price of consumer goods deviates from their value. If such deviation is bigger, to the enterprise, the profits and taxes it creates will be higher. The higher the accumulation, the higher income the employees will receive.
2. The price of a commodity deviates from its value. If this deviation is low to the enterprise, its surplus value is low. The lower the accumulation, the lower the relative income the staff receives, the development speed of this industry or enterprise will be slow.

3. When the price of some or some kinds of consumer goods is lower than their value, through strengthening the internal management of enterprises and reducing costs, we can try to make up the deficits and get surpluses. From the balance between price and the actual value to the imbalance where the price is somehow higher than the actual value, the enterprises could still survive and develop.
4. If the price of some or some kinds of consumer goods are lower than their value, it is impossible to make their price enhance to the balanced level or higher than the value level; the enterprises should claim bankruptcy immediately, change the line of production, or be annexed by highly efficient enterprises.
5. The price of commodities fluctuates around value.
6. In the process of consumption, the price of commodities is influenced by not only the supply–demand relation but also the season and holiday.
7. In the consumption process of a commodity, certain places will set prices according to seasons in order to stimulate consumers' psychological desire to purchase.
8. The bargain price of a commodity. In the exchange of commodities in free market, the bargain may happen in various times or places. The fluctuations between the commodity price and its value may be extremely large; therefore, on the market exchange, the bargain is everywhere and intense, and the success of a transaction is often the result that both sides compromise.
9. Agreement price. In the exchange of bulk commodities, in order to ensure benefits for both sides, a price based on agreement is always adopted. The prices of commodities are thus influenced greatly by the supply–demand relation in this kind of transactions.
10. The price of brands. Under ordinary circumstances, the prices of well-known brands are higher than those of similar commodities and form psychological prestige values and psychological desire values of commodities. Therefore, brand commodities appear whose prices are artificially higher than their values.
11. The high-expense consumption in special places of entertainment. In special places of entertainment, the prices of material and spiritual commodities are often higher than their values. Furthermore, the high facility value and high service value enable the formation of high-income, high-profit, and quickly accumulated industries, such as high-quality nightclubs, restaurants, and so on.

Relations between consumption and savings

Keynes' absolute income theory

The income discussed by Keynes is the absolute actual income of the current period. The 'current period' is the present period without considering past and future; 'absolute' is the absolute level of income without considering the relative level of income; the 'actual' is the income calculated according to the currency's purchasing power without considering the nominal income calculated according to currency. These restrictions serve as an important distinction between Keynes' income theory and other income theories.

Duesenberry's relative income theory

Duesenberry believes that consumption is not decided by the absolute income level of the current period, but by the relative income level – the highest income level compared with others' income level and personal historical income level. In modern society, highly qualified commodities enter the consumption area, which stimulates consumers' consumption desire, and at the same time keeps their dignity through consumption. Once the income and consumption level of high-income earners are considered as the symbol of social status and success, their consumption pattern will become the object of others. Then, because of the preference of consumers, high-income earners set an example for low-income earners.

Modiglianli's life cycle theory

Modiglianli's research (1970, 1975, 1976) on life cycle mainly focuses on this assumption: everybody arranges their consumption according to all the expected income of their life, namely each family's decision on consumption and savings at any time more or less shows the family's attempt at an ideal distribution of consumption in its whole life cycle, while every family's consumption is restricted by the total income of the family in its entire life cycle.

All economists agree that consumption is decided by disposable income, but they disagree on what disposable income is. Keynes defines disposable income as the level of absolute income; American economist Duesenberry defines it as the level of relative income, and in the permanent income hypothesis it is defined as permanent income (Duesenberry, 1949).

Friedman's permanent income theory

Friedman holds that the consumer's income consists of temporary income and permanent income, whose influences on consumption behavior and savings behavior are different. The permanent income hypothesis is put forward in his *A Theory of the Consumption Function* (1957), and this theory is considered one of Friedman's significant contributions to economics. He believes that people plan their consumption level according to long-term and permanent income rather than temporary income. Affected by many accidental factors, temporary disposable income varies, but people's consumption would not go up and down with it.

In order to realize maximization of utility, the consumer actually consumes according to the level of income that can be gained in the long term. Temporary and short-term income affects the consumption level only when its variation affects the expectation of permanent income. Thus, we conclude that people's income consists of two parts: temporary income and permanent income; only the permanent income affects people's consumption, so consumption is the steady function of permanent income. Temporary income is the income acquired in a short period; it is accidental income, and can be plus (e.g. an unexpected bonus) or minus (e.g. it is stolen). Friedman believes that only permanent income affects people's consumption.

Features of Chinese residents' savings

As a result of the lag in financial system reform in China, the bond and share market is relatively small, so bank savings are the sole important investment type available to most Chinese inhabitants. With the reform of the financial system and the development of banking, especially, the reform and development of currency policy and the capital market, the people's savings have become more varied. The sole savings deposit has developed into various modes including savings deposit, investment in securities, and establishing private enterprises; the savings of the inhabitants show many new features.

There are several reasons for the great increase in the amount that Chinese people save:

1. Since the reform and opening-up people have had more money; Keynes' general rule on people's disposable income applies in China, and growth of income is the key factor determining how much people save.
2. System reform, especially the initiation and implementation of reform measures on medical treatment, housing, employment, and pensions,

makes people less confident about their income in future, and this encourages them to save.

3. Changes in interest rates influence the amount people save savings. Deposit interest rates have two effects on people's savings: an income effect and a substitution effect. When there is inflation, people can correctly anticipate it, so they can make decisions on savings according to changes in the interest rates. The opinion of the classical school is that when interest rates rise, savings grow; when interest rates drop, savings decrease. However, in reality, the effect of interest rates on savings is uncertain; the information is always incomplete or out of date, and when it is impossible to form a correct anticipation on inflation, the level of a nominal interest rate may exert actual effect on savings.
4. The anticipation of inflation affects people's savings behavior. After the reform, China's economic system introduced market mechanism, the original fixed price system was broken, the price level kept rising, and inflation occurred. Generally speaking, other things being equal, inflation would reduce people's actual income, and then savings would decrease. When people anticipate that the inflation rate will rise in the near future, they will consume more before prices rise or advance their consumption that was originally planned for the future, and meanwhile increase their substance savings. These would all decrease people's savings in the current period, and if consumption is critical, the bank deposit will be used, and the 'buying spree' occurs.

The variation in people's savings

Since the economic system reform in China, the variation in people's savings has been the result of many factors. There are effects of short-term factors and of long-term factors, and there are effects of non-economic factors like system reform and of economic factors, so it is hard to explain the change in savings based on a single factor. Short-term savings are the result of mutual effects of economic factors including economic growth, interest rates, inflation, and the unemployment rate, and system factors including medical treatment, endowment insurance, education and tax reform, and the government's macro-control policies.

Savings are connected with people's income, general prices, and consumption, and have a deep influence on national macro-control policies on currency and investment, so it is of significance to analyze the inner mechanism of savings and their growth law.

In China's new period, the connotation and function of savings has changed. Since the reform and opening-up, the function of savings has been extended considerably. Savings can absorb various funds besides the individual balance of income and expense, for these reasons:

- *Absorbing savings with high interest.* Some financial institutions raise the interest rate for savings without official permission or raise it in indirect ways; the rate is thus much higher than the legal interest rate, and consequently various public funds from enterprises, institutions, and government agencies are absorbed into their savings.
- *The deposit competition among banks.* In order to absorb savings, the financial institutions continuously improve their hard and soft facilities, and take various measures to add new services, improve service attitudes, and streamline service procedures.
- *Extending the function of savings.* Savings is made to be a comprehensive financial service, and has obvious effects.
- *The main trend of savings in China.* Under the new circumstances of initial development of a market economy, the variation of people's income, consumption, and savings has turned out to be complicated. The main trend can be generalized as the growth of income, which spurred the harmonious growth of consumption and savings, and led to corresponding structural changes, such as the rise of consumption level, the growth of disparity, and short-term savings. Also, the savings intentions of people with different income levels vary. The immediate consumption of people on a high income increases and their relative saving is decreased while people on low incomes, with limited purchasing power, decrease consumption and increases the amount they save to some extent.

Analysis of countermeasures to consumption and savings

In recent years, the rapid growth of Chinese residents' savings has been consistent with the speed of economic growth. The relations between savings rates and economic growth can be explained with Modiglianli's life cycle theory (1970). However, the change in savings structure and the increase in non-performing loans in banks in recent years also reveal some critical problem to which importance must be attached. Therefore, the following suggestions are proposed to the national and regional financial sectors:

1. *Diversify financial services.* The main form of Chinese people's monetary assets is savings deposits; they use fewer other forms such as securities and cash. The habitants should be led to build risk consciousness and strengthen their investment consciousness and risk consciousness. As for the government, when making financial policies, it should reflect the principle of coexistence of risk and profit: the higher the risk, the higher the profit.
2. *Increase investment channels and eliminate financial risks.* The reform of the financial system in China lags behind its economic growth, and the people's investment channels are comparatively limited. Under the conditions of having few investment channels, Chinese people have had to put most of their savings into banks in the form of bank deposits. The increasing savings of urban and rural inhabitants must now be moved through direct financing. We must develop a shareholding system, capital funds, and capital markets such as stocks, to guide the savings of urban and rural residents to direct financing, and thus lower the risk to the banking system and ensure the steadiness of the national banking system.
3. *Encourage and guide inhabitants to commit to healthy consumption.* In order to encourage Chinese people to consume, the government should have a well-integrated consumption policy for them, make in-time adjustment to merchandise tax rates, restrict consumption fund control within government's behavior, let them consume as per the principle of individual utility maximization, and reduce the prices of high-grade commodities.
4. *Lessen citizens' worry and eliminate psychological obstacles to consumption.* At present, many citizens, especially laid-off workers, unemployed personnel, retired employees with low incomes, and so on dare not consume; when they acquire money, they save it, because the social security system is not perfect. Accordingly, the urgent thing to be done now is to solve problems such as the living security of laid-off workers before they get another job, the low income of and medical treatment insurance for retired employees, and so on.
5. *Use the regulation of the height of interest ratio to guide and control the trend of savings.* When there is an excess of social commodities, the government should lower the interest rate to compress the deposit amount of banks, increase the fund of consumption in market and promote consumption. When social commodity supply falls short of demand, the government should raise the deposit interest rate to absorb social consumption fund, lower social purchasing power, increase fund

investment in production consumption, increase reproduction and ensure the rapid development of economy.

Section 3 State intervention in market financial and economic law

In October 1929, the first world economic crisis broke out. The Wall Street Crash is probably the most severe disaster ever suffered by the financial world. Starting with the closing of the first bank, the crisis gradually spread across the whole of Europe. The crisis was caused by the monopoly management of capitalist society. At that time, in his *The General Theory of Employment, Interest and Money* (1936), Keynes proposed that the country should intervene in the economy and adopt proactive fiscal policies and legal means to regulate it; based on this theory, Roosevelt proposed the National New Deal and promulgated a series of policies and laws that were successful in America. By drawing on this experience, some countries, including European countries, rapidly rectified the negative effects of the market economy (an 'invisible hand') and prevented the disasters that had emerged during the development process of capitalist society, enabling the economy to march towards sustainable development. Keynes's theoretical guidance on state intervention in the economy created new life and progress in capitalist society.

In July 1944, headed by America and England, 44 countries convened a conference in America's Bretton Woods. It was agreed to establish the World Bank and the International Monetary Fund with the world currencies pegged to US dollars. On December 27th, 1945, the signature content was double pegging – the US dollar being pegged to gold, and world currencies being pegged to the US dollar.

In August 1971, when American gold could no longer sustain the increasingly depreciating US dollars, the Nixon government was compelled to give up the 'gold standard system' with the exchange rate at one ounce of gold for $35 dollars. Free floating exchange was implemented.

Since the US dollar was de-linked from gold and the world currencies were de-linked from US dollars, the financial market became a free market. Financial currency enterprises – banks and free financial markets – continuously created derivative products (which are also called new financial tools), which gained rapid development. Large-scale capital operation enterprises emerged, such as financial companies, insurance companies, security companies, investment companies, and trust funds, and they all managed the special product – currency – but the operation did not increase physical wealth for society.

Derivative products in the financial market promoted the production, exchange, and development of industrial goods on one hand and also generated severe false bubbles – economic indexes – on the other. The World Bank and the International Currency Fund already detected the existence of this kind of severe crisis but had not established any supervising organizations or safeguarding measures.

At the end of 1987, the Cook Commission of the Bank of International Settlements brought forward the international standard of appropriate bank capital, which acquired official approval of 12 countries in 1988, the famous Basel Protocol, which was formally implemented in 1990. The purpose was to exert the active effects of the financial market and financial tools to overcome negative risks and crisis.

It is obvious that under the existing financial system it is no longer possible to fully depend on the market to regulate the economy, and that the state will inevitably intervene to regulate the direction of its economic development as well as its decision-making.

The intervention on the market and the financial law in western countries

The primary stage of the capitalist social system

When the economic foundation of capitalist society had just developed out of feudal society, its main part was commodity production and the exchange of private capital (there was little state-owned capital). The primary stage of private capitalist economy was the stage for the primitive accumulation of capital and for the bourgeoisie's ruthless exploitation of the proletariat.

Monopoly capitalism in capitalist society

This was the stage of commodity production and the exchange of monopolistic capital, and commodity production, and the exchange of private capital developed into commodity production and the exchange of monopolistic capital. The nature of the capitalist social system had changed from an economic foundation of private capital to an economic foundation of monopolistic capital.

The economic foundation of monopolistic capitalism damaged the economic law of free market finance economic law and resulted in global economic crises, such as the global economic crisis which was originated from America in October 1929. This was the revenge of the law of market economy, which was broken by the social economic foundation of monopolism developed from capitalism.

The growth stage of capital as economic foundation in capitalist society

In capitalist society, as the productivity of consumption society rapidly developed, capitalists' capital accumulated at a faster speed in the primary stage of private capitalism as economic foundation. Such capital accumulation was soon converted into social reproduction. In order to expand and raise capital for reproduction, capitalists appraise their fixed assets (including intangible assets) and transform a small or large part of them into a special commodity of capital for transactions in a specific capital market – the stock market. The price of the stock always fluctuates with the enterprise's operating profits and is also affected by the supply–demand relation. Conversion to this special commodity rapidly increases the value of business capital. It is a two-edged sword: it actively accelerates the development of the national economy and promotes productivity of a consumption society inspired by consumption, while the economic base monopolizes the pricing of market commodities, the market, and the prices of raw materials, resulting in a monopoly in economic industries. On one hand, it benefits the enterprise with high profits. On the other, it seriously breaks the natural law – regulation law in the free market; the three important consumptions drive economic development. In consequence, severe economic crises will take place.

Every coin has two sides. The superstructure of capitalist countries intervenes in the economy with national power, for instance, in establishing antimonopoly and other laws and rules, which is economic intervention by administration. In this way, the economic foundation is converted from capitalists' monopoly capital into social capital. For example, GM in America and Siemens in Germany are enterprises whose capital has become social capital. The economic base of capitalist society changes from private capitalists' capital to capitalists' monopoly capital, and finally to social capital, which can also be called a social system based on social capitalism.

In the period that the economy in capitalist society was mainly based on social and national capital, the democratic political system (separation of powers) was implemented, and the state compulsively regulated reallocation of social wealth according to the taxation law so as to solve the class contradiction between the poor and the rich. This reflects the socialist nature in the capitalist regime and is a great progress in the development of capitalist society.

In the economy of developed capitalist countries such as Germany, the state-owned capital plus social capital is the major economic base, while in America, France, Britain, and Japan social capital is the main basis of the economy.

Under the social system in which the economy is mainly based on state-owned capital and social capital, the government scientifically intervenes in the law that the three important consumptions drive the development of the economy. That can be referred to as the economic law of 'state intervention' or 'state intervention in economic law', by which the 'law of macro adjustment of the market economy' is generated to control the world economy to develop continuously in a relatively good condition. If the law is violated, the economy will surely be punished.

The phase of state intervention in the economic law of free market regulation in capitalist society

The economy in capitalist society was mainly based on social and national capital; the democratic political system (separation of powers) was implemented, and the state compulsively regulated reallocation of social wealth according to taxation law so as to solve the class contradiction between the poor and the rich. This reflects the socialist nature in the capitalist regime and is a great progress in the development of capitalist society. It will be noticed that the 'invisible hand' of free economic adjustment has always been playing a significant role. Keynes's theory has important realistic significance and has received excellent results; however, he does not recognize the precondition for the generation of free financial and economic law or its functions – the essence of positive and negative effects; nor does he realize that free market adjustment law is also a 'visible hand', which has both general law and special law. He tried to solve the problem objectively and the measures he adopted could only solve the extremely urgent problems and could hardly solve the fundamental problems that occurred during the changing process of the economy. Therefore, financial and economic negative effects are inevitable; the occurrence cycle can be prolonged, but the occurrence is unpreventable, and the problem is not solved fundamentally. For example, in 2007, a worldwide financial and economic crisis broke out again.

The economic base of the former Soviet Union is national capital monopoly

In the former Soviet Union most economic bases of agriculture and private capitalism were converted into national capital through revolution. In the economic recovery period, Lenin carried out production and exchange on the basis of national capital. Planned economy was implemented in the former Soviet Union, and state-led economy comprehensively intervened in natural economic law and made great achievements in economic development. Meanwhile, the former Soviet Union attached such importance to culture and education that it allocated a large sum of funds from its limited financial expenditure to invest in education.

During the economic construction led by Stalin, the economic base was completely national capital. As for the production and exchange of means of production, capital commodities did not exchange inside the country but transferred among internal enterprises. Only consumer goods exercised exchange, and the government set the prices. At that time the former Soviet Union was short of funds for economic construction, so where did the money come from? The answer was people's accumulation. The prices of industrial consumer goods were relatively higher while that of grain was lower, and workers' incomes were lower, too. As production was totally planned, farmers' motivation could not be made best use of for a long time.

At the beginning of the first five-year plan of the former Soviet Union, according to the national economic plan, priority was given to heavy industry and light industry was delayed. Thus consumer goods were deficient for a long time. Despite the high GNP, people's living consumption level was very low. The fundamental economic law in socialist countries was: 'Socialist production should be increased and perfected with the help of high-technology, so as to meet the growing material and cultural demands of the whole social economy.' This is the integration of the law of planned economy with the law of natural economy – the government employed plans to intervene with the natural law and financial and economic laws of free market, which governed the three important consumptions. Plans were hardly realized, partly because of the state monopoly and intervention in natural economic law, partly because of the complexity and diversity of the development and the increase of demands on the three important consumptions, especially on consumer goods. The former Soviet Union's state-led economy was not centered on living consumption, but on social consumption. Though the national economy kept developing at a high speed, the ratio of the three important consumptions was seriously unbalanced. The long period of imbalance reflected the economic base of national capital. As the superstructure failed to meet the needs of economic development, serious contradictions arose.

On the positive side, the Soviet Union was very successful as national power dominated economic development. It was in favor of the development of natural economic law, but was influenced by the three important consumptions. Principal leaders in the Soviet Union held to the way of thinking that subjective initiative was omnipotent, which badly destroyed the positive effects of the financial and economic laws of a free market. Thus contradictions could not be solved for a long time and a national political crisis was doomed to break out. Therefore, the overall disintegration of the Soviet Union was inevitable because the superstructure was no longer adaptable to the economic base, and the related production was not adaptable to the productivity of consumption society for a long time; the superstructure and production relation violated the basic economic law of a socialist country and violated the internal law of economic development applicable to various societies, which led to a serious economic crisis and ultimately the disintegration of the Soviet Union.

The economic law of market finance under the adjustment of a planned economy and the economic law of market finance under the adjustment of high macro control

The economic law of a consumption market under planned economy regulation

In the days when productivity was very low, the national economy lagged behind, and there was difficulty for the national income to meet the minimum standard of living, or when the economy was blockaded by special foreign economy, performing the planned economic regulation of a consumption market could help to ensure the existence and development of the nation, and at the same time, the financial resources and the physical resources could be maximally planned and centralized to put in the project which is crucial for fast development of the national economy to promote the improvement and development of the whole national economy. It is also critical to establish the distribution policy and consumption ratios of the gross national income and gross national expense in a planned way and in reasonable proportions.

Shortly after the establishment of the People's Republic of China, the population of China increased quickly, but the development of production could not meet the consumption needs of the increasing population. Under a planned economy, the country carried out a state monopoly on purchasing and marketing of grains and supplied commodities such as clothing to the population. At the time, the country implemented the distribution principle of low income and more employment, thus guaranteeing certain capital accumulation in the country. With further development of the economy, the original planned equalitarianism of distribution and consumption policies hampered the development of productivity. The policies had to be adjusted to adapt production relations to the change of the economic base. In 1984, the Central Committee of CPC decided that the socialist economy was the planned commodity economy on the basis of public ownership; reforms with market orientation began. The implementation of the new policy dramatically promoted the development of Chinese productivity and increased the living standard and consumption power of people.

According to Marxism Leninism, in the advanced stage and the communist stage, agaon the market economy will inevitably turn to consumption market economic rules under planned regulation.

Consumption market economic law under a high degree of macro regulation

Since the 1990s, the leadership level of China has decided to implement a market economy – to develop the economy according to the market economy rules. This decision accorded with the overall national economic base and system constituted by many economic factors in the primary stage, the constant and fast development of the standard of productivity. These are the main features of the market economy in China:

1. The economic sectors of the primary stage of market economy – the dominant economic sectors of the state-owned economy and national economy, collective economic sector (basically belonging to local state-owned sector), private joint stock economic sector, social economic sector (stock market enterprises), individual economic sector, and foreign and single proprietorship and joint economic sectors – constitute the economic base of the primary stage of market economy in China.
2. The competitive developments of a market economy under planned economy and market economy are both identical and different. They are identical in that:

- the competitive development of the market economy is to follow the most basic natural economic law
- both participate in the production, operation or services of society, either as independent institutions or as individuals, and both strive for good social and economic benefits according to consumers
- both strive to collect the information about consumption development to better use it
- both apply new or high and new technologies to improve their productivity level in order to increase their powers in market competition
- both strive to increase the quality and decrease the costs of their products to the utmost extent so as to strengthen their competitive powers
- both enforce, to the utmost extent, the interior planning, regulation, division, system, and control management of the enterprise, the dynamic competitive management, and the diagnosis and decision management in order to obtain the best operation benefits. The interior planning and management of an enterprise organizes production in full correspondence with the consumption demand of the market.

3. There are two main differences between a planned economy and a market economy:
   - under a planned economy, the laborers are all masters of the country; the relations between individuals and the country, between individuals and the collectivity, and between collectivities and the country were those of infinite liability
   - under a planned economy, a contest system was implemented; the initiatives of the people were mobilized through labor contests, while they were organized through competition under a market economy; contests and competitions appear identical, but have essential differences.

4. The planned economy and market economy are different in that the socialist economic base determines the products that meet people's ever-increasing material and mental needs. This is also the production purpose of planned economy. The national capital of planned economy is the capital of the whole people, the main body of the economic base. The representative who masters the capital is the communist party. However, enterprises are also entities of the market economy, the entities that assume independent calculation and sole responsibility for their own profits or losses. They are in fierce competition with any

enterprises of other economic factors. Therefore, the Party and government's control of state-owned enterprises must be direct control. For enterprise entities of other economic factors, the control methods are different. For national economic basic factors, the smaller the private capitals are, the bigger the socialized factors will be, and the more intense macro regulation will be needed to regulate the economic development using banks, tax levers, distribution policy, the price rule of value, and the adjustment of investment orientation, and to interfere and support the economic development by using all administrative means, laws, and regulations.

China and the market economy under national macro control of the economy

To adhere to healthy economic development, China must uphold the market economy law under macro control. We must study earnestly and learn how to manipulate the movement law of the six economic patterns:

- The circular and spiral law of economic development is stimulated by the three important consumptions. That is the natural law of economic development.
- The economic law of free-market regulation (an 'invisible hand', but modern research has found that it is not only visible but also operable and controllable), which comes from the sale process when consumers' needs are looked into in the commodity exchange.
- The basic economic law. This arises from the rule that economic bases decide the purpose of producing.
- Monopolistic economic basis seriously interferes with the natural law of economic development, and breaks the law of free-market regulation.
- The state interferes with the economy, and this produces the law of a macro-control market economy.
- At the early stage of the reform and opening-up, China was changing from a planned economy to a socialist economy; as there was no available experience, we had to adopt the method of 'fumbling through the river' to explore a suitable road of development. Through the 30-year development process of the reform and opening-up, rich experience and great lessons have been obtained concerning the socialist market economy and it gradually marches towards sophistication.

The Chinese government begins to lead the economy and intervene in finance and the economy: 'financial and economic law that is centered on living consumption under the macro control of state-led economy'. This law is gradually being recognized by the state superstructure, and meanwhile, this kind of macro-control law creates the economic development pattern of China.

The practice of China featured construction powerfully proves the demand that the basic economic law needs to be realized. Chinese economic construction has achieved a lot and gradually set up an independent and more complete industrial system and national economic system according to the economic laws adopted by our economic operation mechanism at that time, which takes the planned economy as primary and the market economy as auxiliary (different from the overall planned economy implemented by Russia). But it should also be realized that economic law was often violated because of a lack of understanding of the economic law. Especially because of the lack of an understanding of the auxiliary role played by the market finance and economy and of its action, national economic development was damaged and stagnated, even fell back. So at a certain historical stage, the market economy must exist; it is the objective reality.

On the other hand, people's needs are the most complicated and fragmentary objective reality. People's cognition always falls behind the objective reality. Under the current conditions of science and technology it is impossible to completely satisfy the needs of people only by depending on the unified plan. This is because the planned economy is made according to the needs of objective conditions and reality, and people's subjective cognition of problems cannot be 100% correct, which violates the economic law, the socialist economic development will be affected.

Some people still believe that China is economically backward, with low socialization of production, so there are not the conditions to carry out a planned economy. The planned economy could only be carried out after productivity had achieved full development. Some people even think that carrying out a planned economy is a fantasy in China, and it is man-made enforcement, which is against the objective law.

That argument doesn't hold water. First, these people don't know where the economic law comes from, whether the law comes into existence automatically or is imagined by people without any facts as its basis, whether the law comes from an economic basis or from the needs of life consumption, production consumption, and social consumption. Second, they don't know the nature of a market economy. What they have seen is that the market economy has developed highly and freely in the capitalist world and made the capitalist economy develop accordingly. They have seen the extravagant feast and revelry and market prosperity of the capitalist world, so they are eager to implement capitalism in China. There are still many people who don't know that capitalist countries have adopted the measures of market economy that involve macro control and regulation by the state, nor do they study economics, progress, and changes in the developed countries. Third, if it is correct that after the economy is in an advanced state and the level of socialization of production is high, the planned economy could inevitably be realized, the first economically advanced country, Great Britain, and subsequently the United States and Japan, would have become socialist. This did not conform to Marxism-Leninism.

Some would argue that the former Yugoslavia once abolished the planned economy for a period of time, and its national economy had developed quickly. Though the former Yugoslavia adopted a market economy, it created a system of socialist autonomy union and made production relations adapt better to the development of productivity. At the same time social plans were carried out harmoniously throughout society, and made up for the passive aspect of the market economy. Despite all these measures, inflation still could not be totally avoided. China should learn from its successes and from its failures.

To sum up, important consumptions are the natural law of economic development, and the economic basis determines the basic law of the economy. The state interferes with the law of free-market regulation of economic spiral development, which is the requirement of the needs of three important consumptions, and thus brings the law of macro-controlled market finance and economy into existence. The economic basis of the state-owned capital of the socialist Soviet Union belongs to the economic basis of state-monopoly, which was an overall planned economy, using planned economy to interfere with the regulation law of natural market economy upon which the three important consumptions rely. The problems it could not solve were the complicated preferences and needs of people's living consumption and the increasingly complicated varieties and needs of people's consumptions. As the conditions lasted for a long time, it was inevitable to that people would complain and there would be a political crisis.

The economic basis of socialist China basically belongs to the economic basis of national capitalism, and also belongs to the natural economic law of the state-monopoly interfering with the three important consumptions.

But unlike the Soviet Union, China insists on carrying on the law of a developing economy, which makes the planned economy primary and the market economy supplementary at the beginning of the reform and opening-up. The measures make use of the natural economic law of the three important consumptions, and enable the superstructure to adapt to the economic basis and the production relations adapt to the growth of productivity. But it is not perfect. So it is necessary to free our thinking and carry out opening up and reform and the natural economic law of the three important consumptions interfered with by the state. It would be macro control to interfere with the law of economic development to develop the economy. This is objective and will not be subject to people's will.

The economic basis of advanced capitalist countries has moved into the stage of an economic basis of social and national capital. The state superstructure has improved from democracy based on the capitalist economy to the democracy representing the social capital and partially national capital. The economic laws which emerged on the basis of social capital and partially national capital and intervene with natural economic law must be the market economic rules as the state macro control.

The natural law of economic development stimulated by the three important consumptions is independent and not subject to people's will. The market financial and economic law of macro control or macro regulation does not mean the end of the crisis and contradictions between supply and demand. The relations between supply and demand are a unity of opposites. Just because the process of supply and demand is a unity of opposites, its law needs to be regulated, which is a law, too. Just because it is a law of a unity of opposites, it is important for the state to interfere with the economy and regulate the development of the law of a free market economy in order to better satisfy the development needs of the three important consumptions, and the consumption needs of people's increasing material and spiritual civilization.

5

The macro-control system on the consumption market

Early economic theory emphasized that market regulation and control is performed by an 'invisible hand'. The 'invisible hand' was proposed by Adam Smith (1723–1790), the 18th century English economist, in his book *The Theory of Moral Sentiments*. Initially the phrase meant that individuals consider only their own interests in their economic lives and are driven by an 'invisible hand': only through labor division and market effect can the purpose of national prosperity be achieved. Later on, it was interpreted as meaning that the government should not interfere with national economic development, which should depend on social demand. This kind of social demand is considered an 'invisible hand' for regulating the market.

The successors of Adam Smith conducted precise analysis to uncover the perfect competitive market mechanism in the form of equilibrium theory. Under the condition of perfect competition, the production scale is small and all the enterprises are managed by business owners. Independent producers do not influence the product market price, and consumers use currency as ballots to decide the quantity and quality of products. Producers aspire to maximize profit, and consumers aspire to maximize utilities. Price freely reflects the changes in supply and demand, and its function is to allocate scarce resources on one hand and distribute commodity and labor services on the other. Through the 'invisible hand', entrepreneurs earn profit, workers obtain wages that are decided by competitive labor force supply, and landowners acquire rent fees. Supply automatically creates demand and savings and maintains equilibrium with investment. Through free competition, the whole economic system reaches general equilibrium. In dealing with international economic relation, free and unrestrained principles are followed. Government does not regulate foreign trade. The 'invisible hand' reflects the economic reality of free competition at the primary stage of capitalism.

Under normal conditions, the market will maintain healthy operations with its internal mechanisms, wherein the main foundation is the rationality principle of economic man and rational selection under the control of the rationality principle of economic man in market economic activities. These selections gradually form the price mechanism, supply mechanism, and competition mechanism of the market economy. These mechanisms are just like an 'invisible hand', which governs how individuals practice market law.

Market mechanisms operate on the basis of the rationality principle of economic man. In the economic mechanism of the market economy, consumers make purchase decisions based on the principle of maximization of utility and producers make marketing decisions on the principle of maximization of profit. Between demand and supply, the market guides resources to allocate resources effectively according to the natural fluctuation of prices. The market is just like an 'invisible hand', which drives producers and consumers to make their respective decisions under the mutual interaction of the price mechanism, supply and demand mechanism, and the competitive mechanism.

Is what Smith said true?

The 'invisible hand' emphasizes the free regulation of economic development, but in the first worldwide economic crisis, it's just this 'invisible hand' that leads the capitalist private economy into a capitalist monopoly and ultimately a destructive world economic crisis. In 2007, a sub-credit crisis broke out in America, which also resulted from the negative effects of the 'invisible hand'. This phenomenon proves the severe historical limitations of Adam Smith's theory.

The theoretical study of all the economists from Adam Smith to Marx, Keynes, and Samuelson unanimously start from production research and their research chain is production – distribution – exchange – consumption; the research shows that production decides everything. However, this kind of theory inevitably leads the economy into recession when used to guide economic development. Therefore, the construction of a macro-control system must be reinforced; so it is with the management of the consumption market.

Section 1 Macro consumption and regulation and management of living consumption-centered macro market under state-led economy

The formula chain adopted in the general theory on consumption in the study of political economics is consumption – scientific research – production – distribution – exchange – consumption; the research on gross social consumption starts from the origin of human living consumption and involves study on a series of contradictory relations and laws of overall scientific research, production, distribution of gross social wealth, and consumption during the commodity exchange, as well as the ultimate realization of the consumption process. The conclusion is that human living consumption is the origin and power source of any economic system. The state-led economy centers on living consumption, which is the responsibility of state superstructure.

The relationship between scientific research and production consumption of living consumption and social consumption

Scientific research and production consumption of living consumption are among the most important consumptions, and their core, because food, clothing, housing, and travel are the most basic human consumptions. During the development process of the demand of living consumption, self-contradiction is also generated: the natural contradiction of demand exceeding supply and supply exceeding demand; during the development process, the contradiction between the development of social consumption (including public living consumption and the consumption of the superstructure itself) and development of living consumption also emerges. The reason is that the improvement of the level of human living consumption depends on the development of productivity of a consuming society and the development of productivity of the consuming society will give priority to the development of secondary industry, which consumes production; this is the basis of development of productivity of a consuming society. In this way, the production consumption of living consumption and social consumption can gain rapid development and human beings' ever-increasing demand on living consumption and social consumption can be satisfied; that is the contradiction existing in the development process. The state will also implement living consumption-centered macro control under a state-led economy for the financial market and economic law so as to give play to the advantages of the financial market and natural (free) economic laws and avoid the destruction of their negative effects.

In order to achieve a strategy centering on living consumption, import and export trade will also be vigorously promoted so different countries can exchange the needed products and supplement one another's preference and demand so as to jointly develop the level of living consumption. Meanwhile, social consumption must be vigorously developed to ensure people live and work in peace and contentment and continuously satisfy their ever-increasing material, spiritual, and cultural consumption demands. It is required that the superstructure will coordinate and solve the contradictions among three important consumptions, develop productivity in a consumption society, and promote overall financial and economic development and progress in social civilization.

Establish centers for collecting market information

Market information collection and research centers must be established for the three important consumptions of the state to provide valuable and accurate information for decision-making at the state level.

Information content (comprehensive domestic and international information) includes:

- living consumption and its classification information, scientific research, and production investment information of living consumption as well as the proportional relation between the two
- the proportional relation between high-grade enjoyment living consumption and scientific research and production consumption, and its development predication
- the status quo of the development of the new scientific research technology and potential information
- information of fundamental scientific research combined with production
- technological property rights during the technological protection period, invalidity time, and market status quo information
- the proportional relations between the scientific research and production consumption investment in basic industries of a society, scientific research, and production consumption investment in social consumption and scientific research, and production consumption investment in living consumption
- the status quo of overall proportional relation between direct living consumption and household income proportion between basic social construction investment and people's living consumption and investment in social consumption
- the proportion between investment in social infrastructure and investment in research and production of basic raw materials, as well as its influence on living consumption

- the proportion of imports and exports that account for the investment and production of three important domestic consumptions
- international market classified competition status, including:
    - market demand status of developed countries
    - demand status of developing countries
    - potential market expectation
    - strategy to enter international market
- the allocation and competition status of resource consumption market
- the development status and development potential of the high-tech level
- proportional demand and supply relation market predication of living consumption and scientific research and production consumption
- proportional demand and supply relation market predication of social consumption and scientific research and production consumption
- a prediction of the equilibrium between the improvement of people's living consumption level and scientific research and production consumption capacity
- a prediction of the influence of an improvement of people's living consumption level on social consumption
- a prediction of the influence on living consumption of the state's excessive investment in scientific research and production consumption and basic construction and production consumption as the basis of social consumption.

Grasp, guide, control and adjust production consumption investment at the macro level

Means of macro control and management include:

- taxation policy control
- financial control of production consumption and investment
- administrative control of production consumption and investment
- control of means of resource allocation
- market management and control
- legal management and control, such as antimonopoly laws.

The macro control of the market that centers on social consumption under the state-led economy can also serve the purpose of promoting rapid development of the economy; however, this inevitably leads to the occurrence of political, financial, and economic crisis, and even war, which can endanger the safety of other countries and people in other countries as well as the interests of the nation and its people. For example, the recessions in pre-World War I Germany, Japan and the Czarist Russia Empire and pre-World War II Germany and Japan were all caused by economic regulation and control, which was centered on social consumption under a state-led economy.

If a government can focus on living consumption, the rapid economic development can continuously improve people's material, spiritual, cultural, and civilization consumption level and cannot endanger the safety of the country and other countries, or the interests of the people.

Section 2 Purpose, means, and factors of national macro control of market financial and economic law

The three important consumptions affect the economic development in a circular and spiral way and create the law of market finance and economy regulated by nature, which is referred to as a free market regulation economic law. It has gigantic force, and promotes human cultural development and continuous progress. But it has some embedded contradiction, generating negative effects. Who is going to influence regulation and control? It is the state. The state intervenes by using its power in the law of natural market regulation, referred to as the 'law of national intervention in the economy', resulting in the 'law of macro control of the market economy'.

The national superstructure represents the economic foundation, the productivity of a consumption society and the production relations, and also the fundamental interests of all citizens in a nation. Therefore the government must adjust and control the development of the market economy in accordance with economic law.

So what is the purpose of state regulation? The author holds that there are six main purposes:

- price stability
- full employment
- developing productivity of a consumption society to enhance economic growth
- the balance of international payments

- constant improvement of people's living consumption level (material and spiritual)
- constant improvement of the comprehensive national strength.

The national economic macro control, from a historical point of view, generally falls into three types of situations:

- *Classical economic control.* The classical economics and the new-classical economics are of the view that market itself is the best way to regulate economic activities. Through this 'invisible hand' the 'Pareto optimality' of resource allocation can be achieved.
- *Keynesian regulation.* In the 1930s, after the second world financial crisis, Keynesian economics stressed government means and government behaviors as an important means to regulate economic activities, and government intervention became a major policy of the mainstream economics. From the beginning of the US government's intervention in the economy, the economic developed Western capitalistic countries began to follow suit.
- *The variation of the market conditions and economic activities.* This occurred in the 1970s, under the influence of a series of economic events, especially the failure to control. The United States first introduced a series of measures such as deregulation. Before reform and opening up in China – when implementing the planned economy – macro control was realized mainly by means of executive orders. Though some success had been achieved, the negative effect was overwhelming.

After years of constructing a socialist market economy in China, the macro-control system improved daily, and the macro-control system with the Chinese characteristics has taken form, and mainly applies economic and legal measures as means of macro control, supplemented by necessary administrative means. In the early 1990s the successful realization of a 'soft landing' for China's national economy, and in 1997 China's success in overcoming the difficulties and challenges of the Asian financial crisis, helped China acquire precious experience, and also helped its macro-control system gradually mature.

The author believes that this macro-control system mainly consists of six purposes, three means and 20 factors (which will be explained below). The three means are economic, legal, and means. The economic means are the economic policies formulated by the government. The legal means are the economic regulations established by the government. And the administrative means are the economic orders issued by the government.

With the economic means the government carries out macro control of the national economy by way of regulating the economic lever of consciously depending on and applying the law of value. The economic lever is the form and tool of value, which controls the social economic activities, including price, tax, credit, and wages at the macro level. As the economic means, the financial policies mainly include such tools as budgeting, taxation, bonding, and payment transfer to adjust economic structure and social distribution. Financial policy mainly means that the central bank and supervision departments reinforce supervision of the financial industry via implementing currency policy and comprehensively such means as interest rates, exchange rates, discount rates, reserves against deposit, and public market businesses to regulate the currency supply, stabilize the currency value, and promote economic growth. The overall objective and requirement of the macro control planned and promulgated by the state are the basis for constituting fiscal policy and currency policy. State planning is an important means for macro control, which is comprehensive, predicative, and strategic.

The legal means are the use of legal forces, through economic legislation and justice and the application of economic law, whereby the government regulates the economic relations and economic activities to achieve the goal of macro control. In a sophisticated market economy system, generally speaking, basic national policies are fixed by law at first; then the medium and long-term development plans and specific policies are promulgated on the basis of law. The means of macro control are mutually coordinated to achieve the macro-control task and goal, wherein, the legal means act as the basic mode of macro control and other control means are carriers. Legal means adopt legal measures to fix and standardize the economic means and administrative means to ensure the legality of various means of macro control.

Legal means of macro control have safeguard functions and guidance functions, which are non-substitutable by other control means. The specific embodiments are as follows:

- First, the legality of the forms adopted by macro control is assured by adopting legal forms to convert macro-economic decisions into realistic economic orders and putting the macro control into the legal track so as to provide legal guarantee for realizing macro control and standardizing the national macro-control behaviors.
- Second, the economic efficiency of macro controls is guaranteed

because the legal means adopted by macro control aim at the market economy and it will abide by the requirements of the law of value on the market economy to obtain internal rationality.

- Third, the compulsoriness, stableness and directness of macro control are guaranteed. Law has compulsory effectiveness; any company or individual will abide by the law or be punished. In addition, there are many regulatory stipulations, which are fixed in the form of law, and the relatively more stable and formal legal acts will not be changed frequently.

During the process of developing a market economy, legal means will play more and more important roles in macro control, and macro control has become the main means of government in performing economic management functions, and the law which has the property of macro control has become the core of the economic law system.

One of the important characteristics of the development of a world economy lays in the strategic nature of economic development, which should be further reinforced, and contemporary countries place very important emphasis on macro control in the regulation of the national economic activities. Just as some economists analyze, the macro control of Western countries has changed from the previous 'making up market deficiencies' to 'building the future of the country', which greatly improves the status of laws and legal means for macro control. In China, government investment and management system is gradually giving place to a macro-control legal system. The law of macro control is becoming the core of the economic law in China. Related macro-control legal means are also becoming the core means during the implementation of economic law in China.

In China, along with the establishment of a socialist market economic system and further deepening of the economic system reform, the mode of direct state intervention in the micro market with forcible means is gradually converted into the mode that the state adopts economic and legal means to regulate the aggregate relation of macro-economic activities. At present, China has stipulated a Budget Law, an Individual Income Tax Law, a Law on the Management of Tax Revenue Collection, a Land Management Law, a Government Procurement Act, a Banking Act, a Commercial Banking Law, an Audit Law, a Price Law, a Foreign Trade Law, a Security Act, a Statistics Act, and so on. The promulgation of these laws and regulations provides legal guarantees for the national macro control and promotes the effective allocation of resources.

Administrative measures make use of compulsory orders, directions, regulations, and other administrative measures to adjust economic activities through administrative organs to achieve the goal of macro adjustment. The administrative measure has authoritative, vertical, free, and fast characteristics.

The main elements of macro control performed by the state are discussed below.

Fiscal policy

Fiscal policy has four elements: tax policy, the profits of state-owned enterprises, other revenues, and government expenditure policies. The state influences the level of the national output primarily by controlling tax revenue and expenditures, but the methods for doing each is different.

In China, a proactive fiscal policy has been implemented for many years, and the effects are excellent. Relevant departments have clearly claimed that proactive fiscal policy will gradually fade out in the next few years. The author thinks there is still long-term room for development in China and other developing countries. The problem right now is that national saving is mainly centralized in banks, which are the main channel to transfer savings into investment. However, in recent years because of a high rate of non-performing loans, in order to guard against financial risks, they cannot greatly expand loans. Therefore, the pace of investment and financing system reform should be accelerated, the methods and tools for transferring savings to investment should be expanded, and the proportion of direct financing should also be expanded in order to solve China's problem of a slow increase in social investment.

Monetary and financial policy

This policy plays an equally important role in macro-economic policy, belonging to the basic means of government regulation. The implementation of monetary and financial policy is mainly achieved indirectly by the central bank's control of monetary supply. In China, the official capital bank and main securities and financial companies have made great adjustments. The financial companies should be dominated by the official capital in any country; otherwise, it would be irresponsible for the whole national.

Revenue policy

Income policy is primarily the policy used to control the increase in wages and prices, including consultative and mandatory implementation. Revenue policy is the most controversial of all the measures. Some economists are critical of this policy, holding that revenue policy cannot settle substantial problems, but can undermine the automatic regulation mechanisms of the market, and even distort economic relations and do harm to the efficiency of the market. The scholars who cling to this policy believe that even though there are flaws in revenue policy, it can be used to satisfy temporary, momentary needs without paying a heavy price. Here, we should clarify a basic point that the people's living consumption is the core of the three important consumptions; living consumption power is decided by comprehensive income and consumption consciousness. To improve the capability of living consumption thus bring about consumption is the source power of economic development.

Foreign trade policy

The foreign policies applied by the countries that insist on the implementation of trade protectionism are mainly tariff barriers, exchange rates, foreign exchange controls, and foreign trade controls; however, those that adhere to freedom of trade, to a varying degree, apply these policies too, but mainly by the government's proper to intervene in the foreign trade market, and even joint intervention. The purpose is to maintain the balance between import and export trade and the stability of the foreign exchange market as well as the balance of payments.

In addition to the factors discussed above, there are some other indispensable factors:

- to control and allocate land territory, marine territory, and airspace resources
- to decide the direction of capital flow
- to use labor resources reasonably and formulate allocation policy
- to use national resources reasonably
- to collect corporate profit tax reasonably
- to develop productivity of consumption society vigorously
- to guarantee the monetary supply

- to establish sound law and regulations for managing economic activities
- to reallocate social wealth reasonably
- to establish a reasonable security system for all kinds of funds
- to vigorously develop education and scientific research
- to greatly improve the people's consumption power
- to formulate social welfare and security policy in a reasonable way
- to develop import and export trade vigorously
- to formulate a reasonable employment policy
- to formulate reasonable population and fertility policies.

Only by applying these factors accurately can the productivity of a consumption society be better developed, human living consumption and social consumption be guaranteed, and people's increasing needs of consumption for material and spiritual culture be satisfied. The three important consumptions affect economy dynamically to develop in a circular and spinal way; the 20 factors of the state-led macro-control market economy rules are also dynamic. They highlight balance – the regulations and laws highlighting balance are going forward in the course of movement. This kind of law is not at people's will. Only through good use of these 20 factors and conformity to these kinds of regulations and laws can economic development be controlled.

6

Consumption, the fundamental driving force of economic development

During the development of human society, the tremendous driving force of consumption should never be underestimated. Consumption is the primary and original driving force of human development, being the ultimate reason of the social division of labor and also the driving force of scientific research and production. In order to satisfy the desire to consume, people will devote more enthusiasm to developing productivity and progress towards a newer and higher consumption level. It can be said that consumption promotes the progress of social civilization, and consumption creates everything.

Section 1 On research formula of consumption

The research formula in *Consumption and Management* is consumer consumption – scientific research and production consumption – distribution consumption – exchange consumption – consumer consumption:

1. Consumer consumption creates scientific research and production. The very process of scientific research and production is also a process of consumption. Commodity as well as the consumption pattern and level are created in production.
2. Science and technology is the capability which transfers into the productivity of a consumption society during the production process; it is also the valuable wealth of new technical products which are consumed by direct consumers and which realizes the productivity of a consumption society on the market exchange process.

3. Distribution consumption is a distribution policy decided by the social system and national law; it is a method for deciding how social members acquire social wealth and the amount of wealth they get. It decides the consumption power, the level of consumption for the social members. The distribution includes the distribution of production output; the salary or the interest bonus, and the sub-distribution of social wealth from national revenue.
4. Consumption in the exchange process is one part of a product's value. The production exchange process is a consuming process. The dealer who takes part in the product exchange serves as the bridge between producer and consumer. Only through exchange can the final consumption of a commodity be realized. This is a rule that develops by consumption, which leads the cyclic development of the economy. Its performance on the market is the free (natural) market financial and economic adjustment rule. The free (natural) market financial and economic adjustment rule has a great active function as well as a serious negative function. The national superstructure should control this rule at the macro level and ensure the continuous and orderly development of economy according to the imbalanced – balanced, balanced – imbalanced spiral law.
5. Consumer consumption is the final goal of the production; commodity is consumed by direct consumers so that the aims of scientific research and production and the value wealth of the productivity of a consumption society are realized. The consumption needs of consumers are developing and unlimited.

The conclusion is that consumption determines everything: consumption decides scientific research and production; the consumption of direct consumers realizes the purpose of scientific research and production. If the produced products are not consumed by consumers, there will be production suspension and factory closedown.

Section 2 Consumption creates demand

Human beings have the natural instinct to use consumption materials impelled by metabolism. They have low-level characteristics of memory, cognition, knowledge, and inspiration and primary-level characteristics of group-dependence. During the long course of development and the increase in consumption, human beings create intermediate and high-level characteristics of material and mental cultural satisfaction and enjoyment, intermediate and high-level social characteristics, and high-level thinking characteristics.

The consumption of food, clothing, housing, and transportation

The consumptions of food, clothing, housing, and transportation are the results of the natural characteristics of human beings. Only if the materials are consumed can the actual use value and social surplus value of materials be produced and measures of wealth come into being.

Human beings feed on milk the moment they are born. This is a physical intuitive characteristic. A mother generates milk for the baby the moment she gives birth, and this is her physical intuitive property. Therefore, eating food is an inborn characteristic of human beings. In the process of eating food, they are consuming these foods. Consumption is the intuitive natural property of human beings. With the growth of human population, the amount of food is not sufficient, and human beings generate new consumption needs and desires. They begin to capture animals and plant grains. Hominids suddenly found that hard stones and sharpened bamboos were strong enough to damage things, but there were not many such stones and bamboos. Therefore, new consumption needs, desire perception and knowledge, and inspiration perception were generated and hominids began to look for hard stones, wood, and bamboo and make them into stone swords and axes with which to make tools and weapons. In this way, they increased their ability (namely, new productivity) to prey on foods.

In human history, with the discovery of iron ore and copper and the success of smelting technology, human beings produced such tools and weapons as iron swords and iron spears, which brought productivity to a new level. Therefore, it is in the process of consumption that human beings generate new consumption needs, desire perceptions and knowledge, and inspiration perceptions, thus producing new consumables and consumption tools. Hence a circular spiral development is generated.

The evolution of material consumption of human beings

At the very beginning, human beings ate grains and raw animal meat, and wore animal furs. In a natural conflagration, many animals were burnt to death and some grains were burned. After eating burned animal meat and grains, human beings found that burned animal meat and grains were more delicious than the unburned. Therefore, they generated a new consumption demand desire perception and knowledge inspiration perception. Was it possible to preserve kindling so that they could often have cooked foods? Then they began to study the method to preserve kindling. In this process, they increased the level of consuming foods. While preserving kindling, human beings encountered wind and rain, and later found that certain stones could generate sparks through friction. In this way they generated consumption demand, desire perception, and knowledge to produce fire. Then they began to look for certain kind of stones and got fire through friction by drilling into wood. This brought the human standard of life up to a new stage.

In the long history of human life, humans constantly increased their abilities to adapt to nature, found and generated new consumption demand, desire perception, and knowledge inspiration perception, and promoted the unceasing development of scientific research and production. Therefore, stone houses, brick houses and storied houses were built gradually.

In the whole process of humanity's material consumption and of their observation, discovery and thought, they generated new consumption demand, desire perception, and knowledge inspiration perception, and thus promoted the redevelopment of scientific research and production, and then new consumptive commodities were produced. This process never ceased developing forward according to the circular spiral rule.

Section 3 Consumption promotes three major divisions of labor

In the book *The Origin of the Family, Private Property and the State*, Engels proposes three major social divisions of labor at the later period of primitive society where there were respectively hordes being separated from barbarians, handicraft being separated from agriculture, and the appearance of the class of businessmen. At the primary period of human society, social productivity was very low, the natural division of labor, which is based on gender and age, existed among primitive men and there was no social division of labor in any form. Driven by the continuous development of productivity, three major social divisions of labor appeared and it was just the continuous demand of consumption that promoted the three major social divisions of labor; each major division of labor greatly promoted the development of production and commodity exchange.

The first social division of labor occurred at the end of primitive society; the agricultural tribes and hordes were separated from hunters and collectors, and agriculture came into being.

For the consumption need of existence at the early stage of primitive society, human beings applied such simple production tools as wood sticks and stones to engage in gathering, hunting, and fishing on the basis of the natural division of labor to sustain minimum subsistence. Gradually human beings were informed of the growth laws of some plants and began to cultivate them beside their houses; under these conditions, primitive agriculture came into being. Animal husbandry developed from hunting with the invention of bows and arrows and with the accumulation and improvement of hunting experiences and techniques. People begin to hunt more and more animals, some of which were kept for breeding, and animal husbandry came into being. At the stage of gathering and hunting, the primitive agriculture and primitive animal husbandry was underdeveloped; gathering was a more reliable way to provide substances than hunting, which constituted the basis of a matriarchal society.

After the appearance of primitive agriculture and animal husbandry, animal husbandry developed rapidly. Livestock not only provides meat for eating, but also skin for clothing and bone for tools. Compared with hunting and gathering, animal husbandry not only can provide people with reliable material of living consumption but also economize the labor force; in addition, compared with primitive hoeing and harrowing agriculture, the harvest is more abundant and guaranteed. With this background, animal husbandry became a more important sector for production than agriculture in some areas. In some grassland areas, such as Middle Asia, Western Asia and South Europe, some tribes gave up agriculture and engaged in animal husbandry; in this way, the first major social division of labor in human history came into being.

The first major social division of labor

The first major social division of labor promoted commodity exchange; before that, because there were different productions conditions, several accidental exchanges occurred among the clans and tribes to acquire necessary products. Since animal husbandry became an independent production sector, production efficiency improved, surplus products were produced, and frequent exchange occurred. Along with the development of agriculture and animal husbandry after the first major social division of labor, mankind could produce more products than necessary for sustaining the labor force, which made exploitation possible. More and more wealth was accumulated in the hands of patriarchal families; they were gradually detached from labor and become exploiters. Meanwhile, along with the development of production, more and more labor force was required and the prisoners of war were no longer slaughtered, but were converted to be slaves for the labor force. In this way, the slavery system developed in a scattered way. Therefore, the first major social division of labor resulted in the first major social disintegration. Society was disintegrated into two classes: masters and slaves, exploiters and exploitees; and private ownership came into being at the same time. The first major social division of labor also caused revolution in family relations; males began to dominate animal husbandry; the matriarchal clan was on the wane; and the patriarchal clan was gradually established and transitioned towards individual families.

The second major social division of labor

The second major social division of labor was the separation between handicrafts and agriculture, when the handicraft industry came into being. This further promoted the development of productivity, and more abundant living consumption materials were produced. Along with the application of copper wares, bronze wares, and iron wares, there began to be widespread cultivation of farmland and reclamation of forestry and land. The expansion of the scale of agriculture diversified business varieties. Besides the planting of grain, gardening and various economic crops were cultivated and the economic crops were processed into oil and wine, etc. Along with the increase in the scale of operation and diversification of the operational activities, various manual operations, such as metal processing, textiles, ceramics, brewing, oil squeezing, ship building, metallurgy, and casting, developed; the variety in the handicraft industry increased, with increasingly complicated production technology. Individual people were more and more incapable of taking up such diversified activities as farming, animal husbandry, and various handicrafts; under this condition, some people were detached from agriculture or animal husbandry and engaged in the specialized undertaking of the handicraft industry. More and more professional handicraftsmen appeared and finally handicraftsmen were separated from agricultural activities, becoming an independent production sector.

The second major social division of labor promoted the expansion of the scale of production and the improvement of production efficiency. The increase of surplus products further promoted the development of the slavery system, which was no longer a scattered phenomenon but had become an integral part of the social system. Slaves became the main labor force. Batches of slaves were driven to the field or workshop to labor. At that time, besides the difference between free man and slave, the difference between rich people and poor people also appeared. Private ownership gains further development.

The third major social division of labor

The third major social division of labor occurred when commerce was separated from agriculture and handcraft industries; commerce came into being.

During the period of the disintegration of primitive society and the formation of a slavery society, after the second major social division of labor, more and more surplus products were produced; commodity exchange was more frequent, and the exchange zone continuously expanded. Under such circumstances, some people were needed to specialize in the commodity exchange business, consequently becoming the essential intermediaries between producers and commodities; businessmen appeared along with the sector that was specially engaged in commodity exchange – commerce.

Through the two major social divisions of labor, the commodity exchange gained full development. The continuous development and expansion of exchange enabled commodities to be produced as consumption goods, which in turn promoted the further development of exchange. Along with the expansion of the scale of exchange and the increase in the variety of exchange, the direction of commodity exchange between producers and consumers became more and more inconvenient; under such circumstances, intermediaries who were specially engaged in exchange appeared, and they were the primary businessmen. The uninterrupted business activities enabled some businessmen to be separated from production and to live on commodity exchange.

The third major social division of labor first appeared in the areas most active in commodity exchange – the development of business and the appearance of businessmen further promoted the development of commodity economy. However, although the commodity economy in slavery society has gained certain development, it basically belonged to the natural economy, which was mainly decided by the productivity level at that time. Many slave-owner manors combined agriculture and the handcraft industry, and their main purpose of production was to satisfy the slave-owners' demand for luxury consumption, not for the sales of the products. Products were converted into commodities and human beings did not often act as commodity producers. Along with the development of industry and commerce, cities gradually appeared in slavery society, and urban and rural opposition emerged; cities served as the center of business and commerce, and as the center of slavery rule; more and more wealth was accumulated in cities and slave-owners began to build palaces, mansions, magnificent temples, and altars, and carry out artistic and scientific research. Meanwhile, the opposition between brainwork and physical labor appeared.

From the above analysis, we can easily conclude that it is consumption which is the motive power of subsistence that promoted the three major social divisions of labor. The three major divisions of labor laid the foundation for the basic pattern of the future social division of labor and exerted great influence on social economic development. The emergence and development of commerce generated a comprehensive influence on the economic, political, and cultural development of society.

Section 4 Consumer demand and consumption

The driving effect of demand on consumption

Consumption creates demand, and demand in turn promotes consumption; it reacts to consumption. This reaction is forceful. Consumption needs and desires belong to the mental sphere; consumption is the action in reality, to satisfy consumption needs and desires depends on consumption capability and condition. The demands and desires of consumption act on consumption, which pushes consumption to realize and develop, which is the contradiction of dialectic relations of opposition and unity. In economic activities, scientific researchers, producers, and sellers of commodities all try their best to identify new consumption demands, research and produce commodities demanded, and identify new consumption patterns to meet the new consumption demands, so as to pursue new economic and social profits and maximize them. All these economic development activities satisfy consumers' demand and realize new consumption and profits. In this way consumption creates economic and social profits.

Unbalanced consumption supply and demand and business opportunities

In the process of economic development, consumption is extremely unbalanced. Differences, even great differences, in consumption needs, taste, faith, and custom exist between different individuals, families, areas, nations, and continents. Differences also exist between the poor and the rich and their respective purchasing powers.

In the process of economic development, there are three general differences of social consumption commodities; some living consumption and social consumption commodities and scientific and production commodities are general commodities in one area while enjoyment commodities are common in another. This is the difference between the poor and the rich and their purchasing powers; the difference between the poor and the rich and their respective purchasing powers also exists in living consumption between individuals and families. In the development process of economic activities, there also exists such a phenomenon that in one area supply exceeds demand for certain commodities, while in another area supply falls short of demand. For the latter situation, consumers are eager to buy these commodities, but they cannot obtain them. This is a very important business opportunity for economic development.

Producers and sellers all try their best to discern such business opportunities. They seize them and promptly organize production or the sale of certain commodities, thus not only satisfying the consumption demand of consumers but also gaining great profits. In this development of the social economy, producers and sellers find business opportunities in time to satisfy consumption demand. Even common commodities can create big economic profits. At the same time, relations between supply and demand constantly adjust, and the economy is regularly and rapidly developed. These business opportunities are derived from an unbalanced supply and demand, and they promote the rapid economic development.

New-tech commodities created by scientific research and production

New-tech commodities created by scientific research and production require new consumption patterns to meet new consumption demand.

Create new consumption patterns corresponding to new consumption demands

After new-tech commodities are produced, China should first carry out suitable marketing and promotion to inform consumers about the characteristics and functions of the new-tech commodities and then organize people or units of consumption demand to carry out a pilot study to reveal consumption patterns. When the pilot study succeeds, and is approved by people or units who are willing to purchase such commodities, we should extend the propaganda of such new-tech commodities to the relative people or units, provide detailed services, and extend the promotion sale of such commodities.

Create diversified demands and consumptions

From the common popular consumption commodities, select those whose functions are approved by consumers, make creation on their techniques and packing – develop and produce newer consumption commodities – and conduct timely and appropriate marketing campaigns. By following the above procedures, you can promptly attract potential consumers and create better operational effect.

Section 5 Promotion of consumption and production

The relations between consumption and production are like those between fish and water. Consumption demand promotes the constant development of scientific research and production, which constantly creates new commodities, demand desire, and consumption patterns, so production determines the quantity and quality of commodities and the level of advancement of social culture and civilization. Those whom the producers are pursuing all the way are consumers. Pursuing the market is a way, but not a purpose; the purpose is the direct consumption of commodities. The direct objects of competition between producers are direct consumers, but not dealers. The direct objects of competition between dealers who possess commodities are also direct consumers. At this point, producers and dealers are a pair in a contradiction which is both opposite and unified. On the one hand, they depend on each other, and on the other, they are contradictory because of their different interests. However, their ultimate goals are the same.

The mutual promotion of consumption and production is mainly embodied in the following two aspects: consumption creates production. In turn, production (including the production of new-tech commodities and the reproduction of general commodities) creates consumptive commodities, new consumption patterns, levels, and results.

The whole process of production is the process of consuming commodities. This consumption process is also the process of creating new commodity-value.

It is also in this process that consumption creates production. No consumption, no production, and no motives for production. It is in the process of production that consumption creates new consumptive commodities (products) (this point has been discussed in detail previously in Chapter 4).

The produced commodity will be consumed in the consumption process and be transferred into the wealth of practical value. If this commodity (product) cannot realize its proper use value or whole value in the consumption process, it will be a commodity with no use value, namely, a waste product.

Wealth is realized in the commodity needs of the consumption process. The products (commodities), which have not realized the needs of consumption cannot increase wealth, but will reduce the original wealth. Therefore, wealth is created in the commodity consumption demand process.

Section 6 Consumption promotes scientific research and production competition

Consumption drives the development of production competition

Human beings' living consumption and social consumption determine the consumption of scientific research and production. The consumption of scientific research and production creates consumption products and create consumption patterns and levels. The aim of consuming scientific research and production is ultimately to meet people's increasing material, spiritual, and cultural demands as well as the social needs of consumption. In the process of being consumed, the product created in the process of consuming scientific research and production realizes its value-in-use. This process of development is also the one through which consumption draws the enterprises to produce benefits (social benefits and corporate profits).

From beginning to end, producers pursue consumers of commodities. Commodity producers should spare no effort to give satisfactory service to consumers. The producer who gains direct consumers will acquire the market initiative. The direct consumers are the most authoritative evaluators and judges of the commodity, so producers and dealers of the commodity should unconditionally accept their evaluation and suggestions, and constantly improve the quality of their commodities.

All the scientific researchers, producers, and dealers of goods are deeply committed to finding new consumers and to doing research to produce commodities for the new needs of consumption, and new forms of consumption to meet the needs of new consumers in order to track the new economic and social benefits and maximize them. This economic development activity meets the needs of consumers so as to achieve new consumption and benefit. Such is the way that consumption creates economic and social benefits. This process of consumption development affects the development of production competition.

Possessors of the means of production develop in the mutual exclusion and competition in order to pursue the highest profit. In management skills, the level of technology, product variety, product quality, management efficiency, and so on can all be improved, updated, increased, and raised constantly in the competition for production, as the mode of production changes constantly, while the consumption and cost of raw materials are constantly on the decline.

This shows that consumption is 'the biggest traction in production competition'. New modes of consumption are constantly created in the production competition, and raised to new levels constantly. The whole practice of economic development has fully proved Marx's wise words in *Capital* (1867):

> As consumption creates new production needs, thus creating intrinsic motivation of the concept of the production, and the latter is the precondition of the production. Consumption creates a driving force for production; it also creates the object those functions as the decisive element in the production. Without needs, there will be no production. Then consumption reproduces the needs.

Consumption will always be the traction of the competition for production, and consumption of different forms, natures, and levels is bound to create different production modes. And production, in turn, creates consumption styles.

Competition and economic crisis

When there is competition for profits as the purpose, competition law enables domestic wealth to be highly concentrated in the hands of the minority, and the relative majority are in poverty, ensuring the maximum profits of capitalism by way of continually enslaving and plundering the people of other countries, especially underdeveloped countries, and also through war that aims to ensure the highest profits and by militarizing the national economy or plundering the wealth or consumption resources of other nations.

The combination of the basic law of economy and the most common internal natural laws of the economic development gives rise to the economic law of market regulation. The market law of capitalism flows like the tide with its direction alternating in this kind of production competition, which forms the law of the cyclical economic crisis. On the other hand, it promotes the development of productivity in a consumption society, but also gives rise to monopoly, which is the origin of evil.

Competition is necessary in China market economy

At present, the economic foundation of China has six economic forms: state ownership of capital (plays the dominant role in national economics), collective ownership, social capital (stock market capital), foreign-owned capital, joint venture capital, and individual ownership capital. The later three economic forms belong to the capitalist economy under the leadership of a socialist market economy, which play an important role in the socialist economy.

The six economic forms that determine socialist economic law base production on a higher degree of technology that grows and improves constantly, to ensure maximum satisfaction of the needs of material and cultural consumption. With its combination with the most basic innate natural law in the process of economic development, the financial economic operational mechanism of macro control and market regulation is generated.

The socialist market economy and capitalist market economy are essentially different. However, considering the competition of consumption, they are consistent. Varieties of economic forms in the development of commodity production in China inevitably form competition for commodity production, though this kind of competition is under the guidance of national macro control, rather than blind free production competition. Even under a market economy, the competition should be carried out under the guidance of the national macro control; otherwise it will contravene the basic socialist economic law. Social commodity production also develops in competition, but national macro control is very important for the competition. Competition must be guided and regulated under macro control. No competition, no progress; at the same time it can be seen that the socialist macro control is necessary to the whole socialist construction. The more serious mistakes in the regulation, the greater waste will be caused, and the greater the risk is. Macro control is of vital importance.

One of the relations between the market economy and the planned economy is that the market economy in China develops under the guidance of national macro control, which means that it does not develop blindly. On the one hand, it develops in competition regulated by the market. At the same time, banks control capital. In addition, there are tax and interest control and the necessary administrative intervention to prevent some serious overproduction of certain commodities and ensuing heavy losses. The market economy always follows its own law and moves ahead in the competition. It has a positive side and a negative side. The socialist economic and financial law also has contradictions within the opposite and united movement process, which requires the development of financial and economic law under macro control; on the other hand, the socialist economy in China itself should be the market economy under the implement of macro control.

The so-called inadequacy of a planned economy mainly lies in people's subjective understanding of the plan. In some cases changes that lag behind the objective reality appear, especially the plan with regard to people's daily necessities, and it is difficult to achieve a balance between supply and demand to meet the demand for diverse products in a timely manner. In this aspect, there is nothing to do but totally depend on the self-regulation of the natural economic law of the market in order to reflect, in a timely manner, on the new changes and to provide information as the foundation of amending and adjusting the enterprise production plan.

The market economy in China develops in the competition under the implementation of the macro control of the state. Moreover, in the process of commodity production, the systematic production of the micro-economic enterprise itself is very strict, as the planned production law of commodity and the economic profits of enterprises are closely connected. If the internal production plan of the enterprise violates the most general, inherent natural law of economic development, the economic profits of enterprises will sensitively decline, and soon restrict the normal implementation of the production plan. This will force the leaders to make, modify, and implement their production plan according to the needs of the market, and to strictly follow the plan to organize production. At the same time, enterprise leaders will be forced to do research to predict the market requirements in a timely manner, and to sign the sales contracts and the supply contracts for raw and auxiliary materials based on the mandatory plans and the needs of the market, and to organize production. Only in such ways can enterprises be ensured of better economic profits.

If the whole national economy is included in the contract-based production, the development of national economy will be on the way of legal economic production. In that case, the loss caused by the bureaucracy and irresponsibility in the economic work will be much less, and at the same time the accumulated socialist surplus product value will increase, and socialist construction will greatly speed up.

I take the system of organizing production based on the contract as a specific way in the general sense, in which the socialist plan for control and market control regulate the relations between production and consumption. It is a law of social and legal regulations, so is called the law of contract-based commodity production.

The third relation between the market economy and planned economy is that in the development of the socialist economy, an enterprise that wants to be profit-oriented and rid itself of the control of the national plan will certainly be punished. The national plan's control and guidance of the market's financial and economic law lies in limiting the blind development of the production of commodities; the state provides information about market supply and demand for enterprise producing the commodity to guide the production unit to compete and develop according to the needs of the market. What is more, through adoption of the law of value, the lever action played by banks, administrative measures, and tax measures, the government should support enterprises to compete in some short-term commodity production and restrict the development speed of long-term production.

To sum up, the socialist economy is developing in the competition. Without competition, there will be no progress, and long live the competition! Some scholars used to attack the socialist theory with this kind of viewpoint: 'With the eradication of private ownership, the wind of laziness will spring up.' This is a question posed by some scholars on whether the socialist economy has the momentum to develop. Introducing the competition mechanism to the socialist economic system is sure to provide a strong driving force for economic development. Of course, when introducing the mechanism of competition, we must at the same time strictly follow the financial and economic law of market regulation under the state macro control and give full play to the function of the competition in the most general inherent natural law in the process of economic development. This requires our government and planning departments to organize a strong information institute, adopting modern information statistical means to carry out the statistical summary data on supply and demand and dynamic development trends in a timely yet accurate way to analyze and forecast economic development trends in order to provide accurate information, according to which the state planning and regulation departments can amend and complement the regulation plan in a timely manner. On this basis, the macro-control departments of the state can continuously regulate the dynamic prominent – balance, balance – prominent process during the macro-control process. Only in this way, can the socialist market economy develop quickly via competition, while following the objective economic law all the way through.

Section 7 Consumption is the fundamental driving force of economic development

Consumption is the purpose of human production. In the re-production of society, production must be conducted around consumption demand, and consumption must guide the production. Production and consumption are mutually dependent, restricted, and supplementary. Consumption determines production and production creates the products for consumption; production is only the means, and consumption is the ultimate purpose. The quantity, scale, grade, and speed of consumption determine the quantity, scale, grade, and speed of production; whether consumption can be successfully realized determines whether the production cycle can be successfully completed. It can be said that whether the products and number of products can be accepted by consumers determines the prosperity or decline of the producers.

If we consider investment as a kind of social consumption (exhaustion), then we can consider living consumption as the ultimate consumption. In this way, consumption can be classified into ultimate product consumption, investment consumption, and export consumption. Intermediate product consumption and export consumption are basically conducted around ultimate product consumption.

Living consumption is at the core of three important consumptions, being the origin and power source of economy. Social consumption is consumed for living consumption; the purpose of social consumption is to ensure the people in the country live and work in peace and contentment and to achieve social harmony and national security. Social consumption drives the continuous innovation and development of the consumption of scientific research and production and drives the development of productivity in a consuming society. It provides guarantees and preconditions for living consumption and social consumption. There will be no progress in the modes of living consumption and social consumption without the development of scientific research and production consumption; their relation is contradictory, unified, and mutually supplementary.

Investment consumption comprises living investment consumption, social investment consumption, and reproduction investment consumption. Real estate investment belongs to the production of the real estate commodity; the worldwide real estate price greatly departs from the law of value and in no way reflects the actual demand and supply relation of housing consumption and it is the result of speculation activities of the interest community. In the failure of macro control, investment consumption problems take the form of wasteful investment covering repetitive investment in production, investment in supply-exceeding-demand, and investment in image projects. On one hand, investment consumption is inadequate, and on the other, serious waste and irrational investment exist.

The social consumption of China has a great demand for public consumption, such as workshops, machinery, and so on, for production consumption, and all the consumption is preparation for the production of end products. To a certain extent, investment consumption is the guarantee for living and social consumption requirements. Investment consumption creates the condition for increasing the total social supply on the one hand and drives the consumption demand for raw materials on the other, and it also increases the purchase capacity of consumers via increasing employment.

According to investigation, about 40% of investment in fixed assets is used for end product consumption. Every increased percentage point of investment contributes a 0.44 percentage point of growth to gross domestic product. Before the 1990s, China was basically at the stage of aggregate demand exceeding aggregate supply, and investment had become the important driving force of economic growth. During this period, aggregate demand was essentially driven by the expansion of the aggregate supply. Afterwards, China's economy gradually marched out of the shadow of scarcity, and it became more urgent to coordinate the ratio between investment and consumption better. The unbalanced ratio between the investment rate and the consumption rate influences the normal operation of the economy. If the investment rate is too low, the aggregate supply will be lower than the aggregate demand on the market; product demand will exceed supply and commodity price will rise. If the consumption rate is too low, the aggregate supply will be higher than the aggregate demand; surplus products will be produced; the demand will be inadequate and even deflation can occur. At present, China's investment rate is more than one time higher than the world average level, being one of the countries in the world with the highest investment rates. Although this may result from China's special national conditions, over-capacity and low investment efficiency are indisputable facts.

Increasing export consumption by expanding foreign trade is one of the important ways to promote economic development. Domestic aggregate supply and aggregate demand are closely related to import and export of foreign trade. When the supply of certain domestic products exceeds demand, corresponding imports will be reduced, and exports will be increased to the international market; when certain domestic products run low, corresponding imports will be increased to satisfy the demand of the domestic market. However, the growth of foreign trade export will ultimately fall on domestic demand, because seen from a long term perspective, exports are generally balanced with imports, or a series of problems will occur. If the increase in the consumption of final domestic products slows down, it is hard for the export trade to maintain long-term speedy growth.

It is obvious that investment consumption and export consumption are ultimately determined by the consumption of end products. If the consumption of living consumption is inadequate, it will be meaningless to expand investment consumption and hard to sustain the continuous expansion of export consumption. Therefore, it is the consumption of end products – consumption of living products – that is the fundamental driving force of economic development.

In addition, consumption demand plays an important role in driving national economy and promoting productivity growth.

The development of the national economy is mainly driven by consumption demand, investment demand, and export demand. As a result of different conditions in various countries, these three kinds of demands account for different proportions in driving the GDP. According to the general law, consumption demand is the most fundamental force, usually accounting for 70% to 80% of GDP. China is a developing country; the consumption rate (the proportion of ultimate consumption accounting for GDP) is relatively low at about 60%; economic development is mainly driven by domestic demand – consumption demand and investment demand. World economic integration also requires us to expand export demand; while fully utilizing the foreign market, we must strive to develop the domestic market, especially the rural market, which is the basic touchstone of China's economic development. In 1998, influenced by the Asian financial crisis, export demand was checked; the income growth of urban and rural residents slowed down, and consumption demand was relatively inadequate. In order to raise the growth rate of the national economy, China adopted proactive fiscal policies to boost the investment demand of fixed assets, which greatly facilitated the realization of the 7.8% growth rate of the national economy in 1998.

The measures of consumption level include mainly the ability to pay and the actual purchasing power of a currency, the consumption structure, and especially Engels' coefficient (the proportion of food expenditure accounting for overall expenditure). The factors influencing residential consumption in China are income level or consumption capacity, the consumption system and consumption policy, the consumption environment, and the consumption concept.

During the long-term development of the national economy, production, distribution, exchange, and consumption are four factors that decide everything. Under the planned economic system, various corresponding systems are formed; ever since the Third Plenary Session of the 11th Central Committee of the CCP, the economic system has undergone significant reform but reform of the consumption system still lags behind. Over the previous long period of time, China implemented a low wage welfare-type consumption system, and the country suffered from more and more burdens and problems. Therefore, the consumption system and consumption policy became the important factors impeding the development of productivity, so reform of a consumption system and adjustment of consumption policy have become imperative.

The following work must be conducted:

1. China must gradually form a consumption system which combines the state, collective, and individual capacity, and is dominated by individual expenditure.
2. China must speed up the reform of housing, health care, education, social insurance, and public transportation. It must promote commercialization of residential housing and rental housing for economically disadvantaged groups, and jump start the secondary market. For the reform, which involves an increase in personal expenditure and the expectation of personal expenditure, timing must be well managed to avoid doing everything at the same time.
3. China must start consumer credit and promote credit-based consumption. There should be emphasis on installment payment on

real house mortgage, car, large-piece home electric appliances, large-piece farm machinery, and so on. For this, an evaluation system for personal credit consumption will be established to form a national network. The bank deposit will implement real name system and the consumption credit of bank will avert risks via securitization.

4. The government should encourage the urban and rural residents to have service consumption according to the personal capacity to pay, such as education and training, medical and health care, psychological health consultation, books and newspaper subscriptions, domestic and overseas tourism, catering services, entertainment and housekeeping services. Meanwhile, standards for these industries should be reinforced.
5. The government should adjust and reform taxation and charges, which restrict consumption. The government should also cancel unnecessary additional taxes and auxiliary charges. For example, in the past, when the household electricity use exceeds a certain amount, an extra electricity charge was imposed; now, it should be reversed: when electricity use exceeds a certain amount, the electricity charge should be reduced. Also, costs involved in the purchase of commercial housing can be further reduced or cancelled.
6. The government should develop policies and regulation on renting. In 1995, the turnover of leasing trade all over the world had reached US$550 billion and was increasing at an annual average speed of 20%; however, at present, the turnover of the leasing trade in China is less than US$1 billion. The purchase of commodity use rights will be encouraged by consumption policies. The commodities appropriate for leasing are equipment needed by production and construction; transportation tools, especially cars; household goods, especially electrical appliances, furniture, children's supplies, and medical and health care appliances; agricultural machines, residences, office buildings, and so on. Reformation of the consumption system, adjustment of consumption policy, expansion of consumption fields and enlargement of consumption demand are urgent problems to be handled by China; whether these problems can be settled is of great significance for expanding domestic demand and ensuring stable national economic growth.

7

Consumption, distribution and taxation

Many factors affect the state of consumption, among which scientific research and production are the most powerful internal drives; national redistribution policies – particularly taxes – also significantly affect the state of consumption and determine the level and direction of consumption. The reasonableness of the distribution system and tax policy could even affect scientific research and production, and determine whether social development is dynamic or not.

Section 1 Relations between distribution, consumption and superstructure

Distribution, consumption, and superstructure are three interlinks, whose relationship is like fish and water. The superstructure determines the gross revenue, expenditures, and overall distribution policies of the country and regulates overall consumption levels, while the distribution proportions and consumption level are fixed according to the overall development level of the country's productivity and the overall national revenue and expenditure levels. Right and good distribution policies and consumption proportions in turn promote the development of productivity, an increase in consumption level, and the development of the whole national economic base; and it further solidifies the superstructure. In his speech in 1957 'On the Correct Handling of the Contradictions among the People', Chairman Mao Zedong stated:

> The socialist production relation, which adapts to the development of productivity, has been established. However, it is not perfect yet. These

imperfect aspects are contradicted to the development of productivity. Besides the case of adaptation and contradiction between production relations and productivity, there also exists the adaptation and contradiction between superstructure and economic base.

Thus socialist economic development should constantly resolve the imperfect aspects of the superstructure and economic base, and constantly solve the imperfect aspects of production in relation to the development of productivity.

State of the development of an economic base and productivity

The development of an economic base and productivity is in a constant dynamic state. The development of economic base depends on the development of productivity. Owing to the increase in the cultural, scientific, and technological quality of human beings, science and technology are developed at a higher speed than ever before. This in turn increases productivity. Such an increase in productivity demands that production relations quickly adapt to its development.

Rapid development of productivity

The fast development of productivity inevitably promotes the development of the whole national economy and promptly increases the basic capital of the whole national economy and economic power. Thus, the superstructure – the country – will be stronger, safer, and more stable. The security and prosperity of the country will enrich and strengthen citizens.

Overall distribution of social wealth

Thanks to the fast development of productivity and the increase in the strength of a national economic base, the proportion and relative value of the country's overall distribution of social wealth are increasing in the following ways:

- Pay is directly based on work and more payment for more work.
- Surplus value increases in the social capital of each individual citizen.

- The increase of subsidies for low-income citizens keeps up with the status quo of living standards in the process of state wealth redistribution
- The input in social undertakings increases.
- The capital input increases in the modernization of the entire state apparatus.

Unbalanced proportions of the total social wealth distribution lead to unbalanced development of industrial structures, and therefore may affect the development of the entire economy. Thus, management and control must be strengthened especially over distribution and use of total social wealth for various social consumption needs. Severe waste must be reduced or eliminated. Investment efficiency and labor efficiency must be enhanced. Those are major responsibilities of the government. Or, it will be a case of obvious malfeasance.

Section 2 The contradiction between consumption and consumers

At the primary stage of socialism, we have to practice the production of commodities and exchange of capital. The people at this stage are inevitably in a position to produce capital commodities and manage the relationship between production relations and productivity. In the process of commodity exchange and consumption, society has to conform to the distribution principle of more pay for more work and the principle of repeated redistributions of social wealth based on macro regulation. However, there are inevitable contradictions because of the differences between consumers and consumer groups. If not resolved well, these contradictions may lead to conflicts and become causes of instability in society, therefore:

1. The enterprise should emphasise regulation to ensure the interests of the lowest consumers. This is the need of reproduction.
2. The enterprise should implement macro regulations on the redistribution of regional interests to satisfy the minimum consumption needs of the social public.
3. The enterprise should implement macro regulations on the redistribution of overall state interests to meet minimum consumption needs, for the purpose of mitigating various types of contradictions and achieving the wealth of the nation, wellbeing of people, and the long-term stability of the country.

4. The policy on obtaining and redistributing social wealth by the government is the basis for resolving conflicts between consumers; it is a meaningful and yet difficult event to liberate the productive forces, constantly adjust production relations to productive forces, eliminate social consumption waste, corruption, and crime, and promote the harmonious development of society. Making progress for the benefit of the country and people in spite of difficulties and possible criticisms will finally win understanding from others and prove to be valuable.

Section 3 Consumption and distribution

Economic relations under socialism serve the consumption of the whole nation

The superstructure, which represents the interests of the people and masters the national machinery, completely serves citizens' consumption and the whole country. Its purpose is to strive and struggle for an increase in human living consumption, social undertakings, and national defense. All the policies and strategies of the country and all its distribution policies and modes are based on the preconditions that they should accord with basic social and economic conditions, ensure the productivity initiative, ensure the stability and security of the country, and promote the comprehensive development of society. Distribution is an important element of state government to develop production and make production relations suit the development of productivity.

Social consumption depends on superstructures and production relations

Superstructures and production relations determine the proportion of individual living consumption to the social consumption of social undertakings, the proportion of defense to the entire national machinery, and the proportion of all levels of consumption. The primary stage of socialism is still the stage for capital commodity production and value exchange. At this stage, the basic principles are more pay for more work, sharing of surplus wealth of social capital, as well as distribution of means of production and constant redistribution of overall social wealth.

Redistribute the social wealth repeatedly to reduce distinctions

The premise of redistributing social wealth many times is to narrow down distribution differences and ensure there is a minimum level of social consumption. We adhere to the distribution principle of more pay for more work, and pay attention to the difference between complex labor value and simple labor value, and to the quantitative difference between simple labor value and that of large, dirty, and hard labor. The difference in distribution should be substantial. Generally speaking, labor value can be divided into complex labor value and simple labor value. The pay for these two kinds of labor cannot be the same. Engels once said that many kinds of labor contain the techniques and knowledge obtained through use of more or less labor, time, and money. Does complex labor produce the same commodity value as simple labor, at the cost of pure simple labor? Apparently not. Therefore, complex laborers should get more pay. Otherwise, it is unfair. Unreasonable distribution proportions may influence the development of productivity.

Reasonable distribution principles promote the development of consumption

The rational development of the whole consumption society is tied to productivity development of the whole consumption society, while unreasonable distribution principles restrain the development of productivity and react on the development of consumption. The slow development of consumption will affect the development of productivity and the advancement of social and cultural progress. Therefore, the relationship between consumption and distribution is like that between fish and water; consumption and distribution can also be compared to twin sisters who depend on each other, promote each other, and restrain each other. The relationship between consumption and distribution is the basic relation and a basic element of the entire political economics.

Section 4 Distribution, consumption, production and production relations

An individual's consumption level is determined by his or her labor value spent in the process of his social production and labor. The latter also determines the way and quantity of the pay that can be claimed, the amount of capital surplus value in the process of his or her capital commodity production, and exchange. The individual's consumption level is also determined by the policy of repeated redistributions of the national macro interests.

Proper labor distribution principles and methods

Correct labor distribution principles and methods can directly promote the development of productivity and consumption. In contrast, erroneous distribution principles and methods will restrict and affect the development of productivity and consumption. The slow development of consumption will in turn influence the development of productivity. It is a three-link relationship, in which distribution is the main contradiction as well as the main aspect of contradiction.

Reasonable distributions in enterprises will motivate the enthusiasm of the personnel

Reasonable allocation of the leaders of a factory such as managers or directors, researchers, and workers will mobilize the initiatives of the personnel of the factory to the maximum. Human resources are the most active factor of productivity. Only if employee initiatives are mobilized can their talent be fully used to reduce costs to the utmost. Meanwhile, they will produce the best products on the basis of certain material production capability, to better satisfy the consumption needs of society.

Faster development of social consumption will bring development of scientific research

In the working process of the laborers, the more pay they get, the more and faster their social consumption will be developed, and the more the development of scientific research and production will be promoted.

Enterprises are a main part of the foundation of the national economy

The economic benefits of the enterprise are directly related to the income distribution of the personnel and their purchasing power for consumer goods. Therefore, at certain times, in certain places, and in certain spaces, the principals of the enterprise determine the development speed of the enterprise's productivity, the entire consumption level of the enterprise, and the income of the personnel and their purchasing power. The economic benefits of the enterprise are mainly determined by the principals of the enterprise aside from the policies of the country.

Section 5 Consumption and scientific research

The innovation and creation as the result of scientific and technological research is the crystal of knowledge inspiration and wisdom. It is always the most direct goal of consumers as well. The consumer of commodities is the impetus for scientific and technological research, invention, and creation, and promotes the improvement of consumer goods from primitive to sophistication.

The purpose of scientific experimentation is constantly to create new consumption demand and desire; any scientific experiments without a consideration for consumption are purposeless and blind, and hard to transfer into productivity in a consumption society. What should be noted here is that goal-oriented fundamental scientific experimentation and applied research should be unified. The former is the premise for the later.

To ensure the realization of the above-mentioned purpose, basic scientific research should be undertaken by national scientific research institutions, research oriented universities, and competent science laboratories of large business groups. Once there is a breakthrough in basic scientific experimentation, we should promptly turn to applied research, so as to transfer such a breakthrough into productivity as soon as possible, to promote economic development and prevent the split between basic scientific experimentation and applied science and technology research.

Universities, research institutions, and competent manufacturers should all establish information organizations to get information about the consumer market, research results of science and technology research institutions, and all the information about the trends in science and technology. These organizations should collect and study the information in time, establish updated research projects, and, standing in the forefront of the profession or the world, promptly organize labor and material resources to carry out relevant experiments, to produce results and secure market share as soon as possible.

Organize the unification of science, industry, and trade for the purpose of achieving internalization of domestic market and internalization of international market, to the largest extent and at the fastest speed, in market share, transfer of science, and technology innovation into productivity, and creation of maximum social and enterprise benefits. The success of Sanzhu Group serves as a good example.

Section 6 Consumption and taxation

Tax revenue is the main source of Chinese national income, the economic lever to regulate and adjust national economic development, the main method of adjusting income, distribution, and redistribution, and the main economic lever to adjust consumption funds and ration and ensure the steady and balanced development of society. The government carries out the following actions:

- It uses different ratios of individual income tax to adjust and control individual consumption funds in society so as to reduce the high consumption disparity between social members.
- It uses different tax rates to adjust and control social consumption, for example collecting sales taxes on top-grade non-producer commodities and devices and collecting TV tax, car tax, banquet tax in order to regulate consumption.
- By raising the commodity tax rate for high consumption and non-producer commodities, it increases the overall social wealth to reduce or resolve the conflicts between consumers.
- On living necessaries and urgent living consumption and social welfare, it adopts low tax rates, tax cuts, or tax free policies to cut down merchandise cost, promote consumption and economy, and spur the entire economic development.

Section 7 The relationship between consumption, taxation and scientific research

New technological achievements and high scientific achievements should be tax free. At a certain production stage, not collecting tax or reducing it to a certain amount will spur the rapid transform of scientific achievements and encourage rapid transformation into productivity of a consumption society. This process of transformation is one of reorganization, acceptance, and consumption of high and new technological achievements in society.

Once high and new scientific achievements are transformed into productivity, a good economic situation with high tech, high consumption, high taxes, high accumulation, and high speed will come into being in the process of market consumption; it is supported by tax cuts and tax waivers, and has high added value. After a short period of tax reduction or tax waivers, the process is formed of accumulating and cultivating the tax source. Developing high and new technology is highly profitable; the consequential high consumption brings the enterprises high accumulation and rapid development, which in turn promotes the development of high and new technology, creates high tax income, and spurs rapid development of national economy.

Section 8 The relationship between taxation, consumption and production

Tax rates are also an important lever to regulate relations between consumption and production.

The ultimate purpose of taxation is to ensure the development of production and a reasonable national economic structure. Taxation is an important method to perform regulation and adjustment besides bank credit control. It is common to reduce the tax payments of supporting enterprises and businesses and collect additional adjustment tax from industries and businesses that are not in favor of regulation. When expenses and the cost of production become higher than the commodity price, the entity enterprise has to claim bankruptcy and close down. New consumption needs drive emerging and competent enterprises to grow and expand through merging and acquiring the bankrupt enterprises, which activates the change in industrial structure and development of reasonable consumption, and promotes economic development.

Section 9 The relationship between consumption and donation

This has the following features:

1. *Consumption and donation are the opposites of a unity.* Consumption is the need for human survival; human beings unceasingly explore high

and new technology to improve productivity, to obtain better consumer goods, and to raise their own consumption level. With the development of material civilization, spiritual civilization also develops and makes great progress; thus, the great spirit of donation is produced, which is for other people's happiness, for the development of national happiness, for the security of country, and for the safety and happiness of the people. This great dedication reacts to the progress of all society, and promotes the development of human material civilization and spiritual and cultural civilization. At the same time, it promotes the development of productivity, social consumption, and the progress of the entire social culture.

2. *Voluntary donation.* A person lives not only for food, clothing, housing, transportation and security. Making contributions to the happiness of others and the entire social consumption is always regarded higher than demands on society and material enjoyment. Because of this, millions of ambitious people's spirit of donation also react on the progress of world science, technology, and material civilization, which promotes the progress of social spirit and culture, and the human consumption level will develop unceasingly from the preliminary to a higher phase.
3. *At the historical stage of exchanging commodities through money, people are aware or unaware of being the producer and consumer of commodities.* Though people have not realized they contribute to society, in fact, in society exchange, their surplus products also have made contributions to others.
4. *The spirit of self-sacrifice.* For common happiness and safety in life, people need to develop the spirit of self-sacrifice for collective and national interests. They need to take the individual or a small number of people's sacrifice as the price for ensuring most people's happiness and safety.
5. *The spirit of donation for other people's happiness despite one's own hardness.* The progress of humanity and society inevitably create a great spirit of donation. Someone who endlessly enjoys other people's happiness will always think about other people and seldom care only about him or herself. After being brought to a great height of development, this great spirit of donation also educates people and enhances their enthusiasm for constructing spiritual and moral civilization.
6. *The great spirit of devotion of educationalists and scientists.* Teachers and educationalists are the engineers of the human soul, like gardeners.

> They develop people's talents and devote themselves silently. Scientists work selflessly for the progress and development of humanity's material and spiritual consumption. Scientists are very great; their inventions impel the higher development of social material and spiritual civilization consumption levels.

If we say that the diligence and frugality of 'saving each penny for revolution' is a kind of devotion, then from the viewpoint of economy, consumption creates and devotes everything. First, general consumption, the basic living consumption of consumers, can complete the ultimate goal of production. If general consumption has the function of capital appreciation, it may develop simple social reproductions and use the saved fund in reproduction consumption, which may increase social consumption in expanded reproduction. Therefore, to be economic in consumption increases the need for consumption and speeds up economic development.

Second, high-class consumption may promote the development of scientific research and production. With the development of scientific research and improvements in people's purchasing power, past needs for enjoyment transform unceasingly into primary needs. This kind of unceasing pursuit, the unceasing improvement of consumption levels, stimulates scientific research and products, thus scientific research and production develop unceasingly from one stage to another, new one.

Third, consumption can accumulate capital for country and enterprise. From the macroscopic societal angle, through tax revenue, the country may nationalize a part of the fund that consumers provide for producers through purchasing. This kind of unceasing accumulation of state-owned funds may improve social welfare and perfect the services of culture, education, health, and so on. All wealth in society is created by consumption.

Therefore, consumption is a kind of devotion to enterprises, scientific research, production, and society. Consumers' earned income is a kind of devotion to society. It is not only a consumption power, but also a devotion to society through consumption. This kind of consumption devotion is an endless chain of economic development.

Here, we should explain that consumption is different from luxury and waste; waste is a kind of criminality. Making the best use of things is the full use of social resources. It is not contrary to our traditional virtue of 'diligence and frugality'. People of our time should inherit the glorious traditions of the Chinese nation – diligence and frugality. The spirit of diligence and frugality is still needed to be brought to a great height of development.

Section 10 Scientific and reasonable taxation policies to promote continuous growth of three important consumptions

Studying China's economic development, we find that the major problem in China now is deficiency in effective demand. To solve this problem, the central government has to adopt a proactive fiscal policy, integrate various economic means, start investment, guide and encourage consumption, use every conceivable means to explore international markets, and ensure the sustained, rapid and healthy development of the national economy. Only in this way can we promote investment demand, consumption demand, and export consumption demand.

Some tax policies in China are unfavorable to the growth of total social demand, for example, the heavy burden of taxes and fees reduces the yield of investment; various and overabundant government charges greatly increase the burden on investors; besides, the heavy burden of some kinds of taxes increases the burden on investors and consumers.

VAT threshold is too low, yet the tax rate is too high. The preferential treatment of key industries, especially new high-tech industry encouraged by the state for development, is not enough and the preferential approach is rather simplistic. The tax levy on fixed asset investment is too wide and the tax rate is too high (up to 30%), which does not encourage private investment. In addition, the current preferential treatment does not guide investment orientation, optimize industrial structure, and stabilize capital resources. Besides the above-mentioned burdens of taxes and fees, a more important reason for the lack of enthusiasm in private investment is the lack of stable capital resources and policy guidance from the government.

Therefore, the government should take more scientific and reasonable tax policies to promote the effective growth of aggregate demand:

1. It should reduce the tax burden. In VAT, increase the threshold for small-scale taxpayers and reduce the tax rate appropriately. Reduce the rate of some tax items, such as cosmetics. For corporate income tax, it should strengthen preferential treatment for new high-tech industry and basic industries like infrastructure and agriculture and increase the preferential approaches.
2. It should reform preferential tax policies; change the regional-based tax preference to industry-based tax preference with special attention to backward areas. In investment direction, it should make full use of tax policies, and guide state-owned and private capital (including foreign capital) to invest in much-needed industry, products, technology, and

backward areas, and encourage companies to invest in technological advancement and structure upgrading, including investment in research and development, technological transformation, and the introduction and innovation of equipment. Give utmost preferential treatment to these investments, regardless of domestic or foreign ownership.

3. It should clear extra burdens like unreasonable fees, levies, and fines, and cut off the 'evil power hands' reaching out toward companies.
4. It should enhance residents' consumption capacity. Increase the income of medium and low-income residents and reduce their burdens by adjusting taxation and promoting distributive justice. It should support agricultural industrialization and rural urbanization; encourage the development of township enterprises to increase the income of farmers and reduce their burdens; and encourage domestic and foreign investments in towns and villages. It should give tax preferences to companies investing in agriculture (especially high-tech agriculture) and rural infrastructure; and cancel numerous unreasonable charges in rural areas, levy taxes for public welfare undertakings, but reduce the amount of tax in general.
5. It should expand support for laid-off and unemployed workers in taxation, encouraging them to start work again. Laid-off and unemployed workers who engage in community services should be exempt from personal income taxes; the preferential policies for business tax, extra charges on education funds, and city planning taxes should be expanded to other industries and taxes, including not only community services, but also other industries and trades encouraged by the state and including not only the above-mentioned local taxes, but also national taxes like VAT.
6. It should improve personal income tax, start estate tax, and gift tax; promote justified income distribution; increase the threshold of personal income tax and the top marginal federal tax rate; and strengthen the monitoring of tax sources.
7. It should refine and improve the import and export tax rebate policy. Apart from further raising the rate of export tax rebate, improving the 'exemption, offset and refund' policy, handling work related to export tax refunds in time and implementing the principle of 'how much to be levied, how much to be refunded', we should also strongly support foreign economic cooperation, make full use of China's abundant labor resources and unused, surplus technology and equipment, and encourage labor services, overseas project contracts, and foreign investment. Therefore, a systemic preferential tax policy should be issued early to

improve the business tax policy in cooperation with foreign enterprises. Enterprises that invest in foreign countries and at the same time lead product and service exports should get as much preferential tax policy support as possible.

8. It should develop policies to keep down inflation, starting by controlling the prices of main production factors. Because of the constant increase in costs under the current inflation, industries and factors that involve the interests of the state and people, like food, oil, coal, electricity, water, liquid gas, and natural gas, still have expected price rises. Ineffective regulation and control would lead to a runaway economy, severely reduce residents' income, hurt consumer confidence and expectation, and then inhibit consumption. In response to the rise in prices for production factors, especially for energy products, to put a cap on price cannot be a permanent solution. The government should study the reasons for the rise in prices, find a way to deal with it, and then relieve it.

China is a developing country with great potential for consumption demand, which is an important attraction for the sustainable development of China's economy. At the same time, the government should examine the effectiveness of social spending to reduce waste. Eliminating ineffective investment consumption is an important task in macro-leadership management and things that are extremely urgent should be solved first. Social consumption definitely promotes, guarantees, and develops personal consumption.

8

The consumption chain

Human living consumption and social consumption lead to scientific and research consumption and then create new consumption products. This process runs through the whole development of human society. As a complete process, it is not separated or isolated. Each part of the process is connected so as to form a complete chain. The consumption process promotes commodity production as well as the development of commodity exchange, which is realized by the dissipative structure, so as to create the consumption chain. The consumption chain is a structural intangible chain in the consumption system. Both the lateral and longitudinal consumption chains start with a certain consumption form and end with another consumption form, and then develop into a higher level dialectically and spirally.

The study of the consumption chain must begin with the relations between consumption and production, between consumption and exchange. It will never succeed if attention is only paid to consumption. Without commodity production and exchange, consumption is just like water without a source or a tree without root, and will not form a consumption chain.

The consumption chain can be divided into the macro-consumption chain and the micro-consumption chain. The macro-consumption chain is the summary of millions of micro-consumption chains, and the micro-consumption chains are the cells and foundation stones of the macro-consumption chain. To study the macro-consumption chain will help us recognize the general development trends and laws of the economy and human society; to study the micro-consumption chain will help us seize chances and critical points in competition and promote favorable factors and avoid the unfavorable, so as to remain invincible.

Section 1 Consumption and the consumption chain

It is human instinct to make use of consumption materials. Consumption creates demand, and demand leads to consumption, so demand has a strong influence on consumption. In the process of economic activity, all the researchers, producers, and distributors are seeking the new demander and researching and producing the new commodities that are in demand as well as the new consumption forms so as to satisfy the new demanders, and finally to pursue new economic and social benefits and then maximize them. Consumption leads the development of scientific research and production, and the consumption and exchange of commodities as well. As a result, the consumption chain comes into being.

The consumption chain is the 'chain' of the consumption system. Consumption is both the start and end of the consumption chain. It is the spiral and dialectic development of affirmation and negation. It is a repeated systemic and holistic movement in dissipative structure.

Commodity exchange originally is an economic activity between a producer and a consumer, aiming to satisfy living consumption demands, scientific research and production consumption demands, and social consumption demands. But producers' business operations are for the purpose of pursuing benefits. Therefore, they spare no pains to find out when and what commodities are demanded according to the higher and lower classes in each area, department, country, and group, so as to input capital and energy as much as possible and finally realize profit. Developing the commodity exchange channel actively is the trigger to develop the consumption chain, which propels the development of economy.

Scientific research and production create consumables (or commodities) (production is consumption, consumption is production as well) needed by human beings and consumption patterns. The evolutionary process of human being is the dialectical development process of affirmation and negation and the consumption chain in which consumption triggers economic development in an interlinking development process. It is also the process of affirmation and negation.

The chain link and development of the consumption chain during the development process of the three major consumptions have their laws including macro-consumption chain law and micro-consumption chain law. The macro-consumption chain is represented in the motion of the micro-consumption chain; the micro-consumption chain is the embodiment of the macro-consumption chain.

Analyzing from the macro perspective, the motion of the macro-consumption chain and the 'three major consumptions' lead the rapid development of commodity exchange and circulation channels as well as commodity exchange. For the purpose of chasing profit, merchants freely trace the need of 'three major consumptions' in order to exchange commodities. The process of exchange has a double-edged effect: on one hand it greatly propels the development of 'three major consumptions'; on the other hand it exerts negative effect caused by the situation that the scientific research and production consumption determines the forms and consumption levels of living consumption and social consumption. However, during the whole process of extracting natural resources, blind development of scientific research and production consumption sometimes finds expression in demand over supply or supply over demand on the market exchange of commodities. If the oversupply of production consumption is severe, there might be an economic crisis.

The state superstructure plays a dynamic role of a subjective state machinery, using the administrative means, economic lever, and legal channels to strengthen the understanding of the regulation law of a free market of economic development activities so as to manage it, to implement the macro plan to regulate the market economic rules in order to exert positive effect and limit the negative effect of the natural law in regulating the economic activities on the market. In this way, economic crises can be relieved and prevented; at the same time the imbalance of the macro-consumption chain can be avoided and the formal operation of the consumption chain can be ensured artificially. It is the outcome of the state superstructure acting on market regulation law.

Section 2 The macro-consumption chain

The emergence of the macro-consumption chain

The macro-consumption chain arises in the process of commodity production and exchange in the form of money and monetary instruments among different areas and countries. Especially after the first and second industrial revolution, with the rapid development of international trade, the three major consumptions relations of different areas, nations, and enterprises grows interdependently and promotionally, and the macro-consumption chain comes into being.

The First Industrial Revolution prompted trans-regional and trans-national commodity production and exchange, and internationalized trade. This kind of international trade was very powerful, for it not only changed the degree of wealth accumulation, but also changed the social structure and knowledge components. In a similar way, where international trade develops the macro-consumption chain develops, as a result, the law of the development of macro-consumption chain formed. The Second Industrial Revolution made the relations between developed countries such as America, France, German, and Britain closer, so their consumption chains were connected closely macroscopically. The consumption chain assumed the inevitable responsibility of commodity production and exchange in international trade, and made economic development more interdependent and interrelated.

The function of the macro-consumption chain

The macro-consumption chain is the natural law deriving from the objective commodity consumption trade and cannot be changed by human will. In the process of commodity exchange in macro trade, it acts on the development of commodity exchange and propels the natural law of the three major consumptions. Its negative effect goes like this: trans-regional and trans-national international trade are closely related; an economic crisis occurring in a certain region or country (financial, economic) would lead to economic crisis in other countries or regions within the whole chain, thus resulting in international crisis.

The financial and economic crisis

A financial and economic crisis followed damage to the macro-consumption chain by the monopoly economy. The macro-consumption chain is the natural law deriving from the macro commodity economic trade. It leads the economy to develop spirally by the natural laws of the three major consumptions. In the process of economic development, large-scale industrial monopolized enterprises emerged, which carried out capital commodity production and commodity exchange with the purpose of infinitely seeking profit, thus damaging the natural development laws of the three major consumptions. Commodity production and exchange are highly concentrated and the market price of the commodity is monopolized as well. The law that the value rule fluctuates depending on the supply–demand relation does not regulate it. This is a serious consequence of monopolies merely focusing on exploiting profits. The rise of monopoly capitalism does not mean doomsday; even in such circumstances, human society will go on developing rapidly, but it leads to the overall progress (fairness, justice) of society.

National regulation and control of three major consumptions

There is national regulation and control of three major consumptions to ensure close and coordinated operation of the macro-consumption chain. In developed capitalist countries, during the process of commodity production and exchange of capital, the positive and negative effects of the natural law of three major consumptions can be found constantly, and the destructiveness of capital moving towards monopoly is found as well. The experience and lessons of the United States from the first economic crisis had positive effects on the natural law of three major consumptions and inhibited the negative effects at the same time; the state began to intervene in economic development and formulated various intervention laws such as the anti-monopoly law, using the economic lever and administrative means to intervene in economic development so as to promote economic recovery and sustainable development in the United States, and at the same time propel the progress of the whole American society. The various measures taken by American government to intervene in the economy were also adopted by France, Germany and other European countries, which also promoted the stable and interdependent development of macro-consumption chains and social progress in these countries.

Coordinated and close operations of the consumption chain boost the economy

In the early days of the foundation of PRC, Mao Zedong believed that heavy industry was the key to China's reconstruction. He thought that priority should be given to the production of means of production. It is correct beyond any doubts. However, we can never neglect the production of means of livelihood, and especially the product of grains for this reason. In 1962, Mao Zedong summarized the laws of development of the national economy and put forward the ideas of developing the national economy based on agriculture. These ideas formed a fundamental policy, 'based on agriculture, oriented in industry', for developing the national economy.

Now our question is how to regulate the proportion of investment in heavy industry, agriculture, and light industry appropriately, and the investment proportions in agriculture and in light industry should be increased. Now we have two options to develop heavy industry: one is to develop agriculture and light industry on a smaller scale; the other is to develop agriculture and light industry on a larger scale. In the long run, the former will make heavy industry develop less and slowly; at least the foundation is not so stable. Several decades later, the outcome shows that this method is not worthwhile. The latter will make heavy industry develop more and faster, and the foundation of development will be steadier as it provides for people's needs.

Coordinated operation of the macro-consumption chain and scientific development concept

Economic development has its own rules. Once people know the natural law of economic development, the state has its countermeasures towards economic development. First is to conform to the natural development laws of economy and bring its positive functions into play; second is to conquer its negative effects through national power. This is because the superstructure of a country stands for the total economic base of the whole society, gross productivity and gross production relations, so it has the responsibility to do so. Therefore, the country is the only force which can coordinate the macro-consumption chain (the value chain) and ensure the coordinated and scientific development of close interlinks of the consumption chain. On the other hand, we should also know that when a country cannot scientifically intervene in the natural law of economy, the consumption chain must be out of balance and economic crisis must occur.

Section 3 The micro-consumption chain

The macro-consumption chain is the concentrated expression of the micro-consumption chain while the micro-consumption chain is the concrete manifestation of the macro-consumption chain (the consumption chain develops in the form of interlinks). The consumption chain of economic movement operates in a dissipative structure system, which unconsciously influences living consumption (including spiritual and cultural consumption), social consumption, and scientific research and production consumption, and incessantly controls consumption ideas and consumption behaviors.

The emergence of the micro-consumption chain

Following the appearance of surplus consumption goods, barter comes into being; for example, nomadic people exchange cows, sheep, and horses for inland porcelain, foodstuffs, silk, and other commodities. During this primary product-exchange period, although there are interdependent relations, they are simple, territorial, linear and spontaneous, without the socialized interlinking relations of consumption.

With the development of the Stone Age, and then the Bronze Age and Iron Age, as a result of the development of smelting technology, processing industry, and productivity, human beings began the phase of family and handicraft industry workshop production. After the precise labor division between different industries, in the process of exchanging surplus products of equal value with money as a special commodity, consumption exchange occurred between individuals first, and was followed by consumption exchange between different collectivities or groups, which gradually formed into a preliminary micro-socialized consumption chain. This micro-socialized consumption chain promoted commodity exchange and the development of consumption economy. In the earlier period of commodity production and exchange, although a micro-consumption chain had formed, economic crises did not occur because the production and exchange of commodities had not developed.

Along with the development of scientific and technological productivity, the scope of commodity exchange expanded to trans-regional and trans-national trade, after society began to produce and consume capital goods, and exchange them. That is how the micro-consumption chain has gradually formed and developed.

Manifestations of consumption and the micro-consumption chain

Individual production, consumption and household consumption

Individual production, consumption and household consumption drive the consumption chain and influence consumption. For instance, a peasant cultivates farmland of 30 acres, and buys one tractor equipped with the facility to plow, plant, harvest, and thresh. After making a profit in the first year, he buys a house; in the second year, he decorates his house and purchases a color TV, a refrigerator, and a mobile phone; in the third year, he purchases a low-grade car; in the fourth year, he goes out traveling and sightseeing, which again drives consumption. It can be seen that he has made a great contribution towards the economic development of the whole society, and it is easy to understand how the micro-consumption chain forms in the process of such operations and its manifestation in the process of economic development.

Individual consumption and the consumption chain boost consumption

Labor rewards, wages, and bonuses through personal work are used for direct personal living consumption or purchasing appliances and other living consumption, which boost comprehensive consumption through the operation of the consumption chain.

In the process of commodity production and commodity exchange of capital, because of the extreme particular division of labor in production and society, no matter what one thinks subjectively, all consumption behaviors are in the process of making a contribution to social and economic development. This really embodies social relations featuring one in all, all in one and all for one, and one for all.

Automatic regulation of supply–demand

Automatic regulation of supply–demand is reflected by the micro-consumption chain and production consumption. When purchasing consumption goods on the market, price fluctuations of some consumption goods appear from time to time. The price of some commodities rises in times of short supply, but cyclically, the price falls again. This is the common reflection of the micro-consumption chain in relations between supply and demand. Businessmen instantly seize business information and then purchase and transport this kind of commodity from locations where supply exceeds demand to where demand exceeds supply to gain higher benefits. When over-demand in the area eases, the fast increase in supply results in a reduced price for this kind of commodity.

Another example is that increases in production consumption adjust temporary imbalance in the micro-consumption chain. For instance, if watermelons are undersupplied in one area, peasants will increase the output next year to meet the demands of the market, and thus the supply–demand relation will be automatically adjusted.

The micro-consumption chain adjusts the rise and decline of enterprises

The consumption chain and new enterprises

Consumption is the pull of production competition. All production consumptions compete in production with a focus on consumption. How to decide the investment in production consumption depends on investigation and research as well as decision-making about the consumption market. The consumption market investigation and research are the preparation of an enterprise for investment. Studying the current conditions of the supply–demand relationship is to learn how the consumption chain operates in an industry. If an unbalanced consumption chain results in demand exceeding supply in industry, or other external elements make it stand out with a huge consumption market, investors will invest in production consumption in this industry immediately. This process is part of the feasibility analysis before an enterprise makes any investment.

The process of producing common and regular consumables, promoting products' quality, and reducing costs through the use of new technology results in the outstanding development of the consumption chain and affects competition in the consumer market.

In another case where the marketer chooses the right market for a certain industry, appears to be more competent, and selects competitive products for consumption, with an excellent marketing mode, the marketer can set up an enterprise immediately, engage in the competition of the consumption market, and thus is able to drive an outstanding development of the consumption chain.

Consumption drives the continuous development of all consumptions such as scientific research and product consumption, living consumption, and social consumption. Demand exceeding supply is reflected in the consumption chain, providing opportunities for newly established enterprises and enterprise development, as well as for increasing employment.

The consumption chain and business failure

Consumption is the pull of production competition. In the process of competition some enterprises succeed and some fail; failures also exist in the process of market competition. Those failures take the form of supply exceeding demand, excessive costs, outdated technology, and poor services or services unable to meet the consumption mode of consumers in the operation of the consumption chain. The enterprise that doesn't have a deep understanding of the operation of the consumption chain or cannot grasp the operating principles of the consumption chain will cause gigantic losses or be eliminated by the market and even go bankrupt.

The consumption chain of the consumption mode structure and consumption

The macro and micro-consumption chain structure

The macro-consumption chain structure is a proportional relations structure among the three major consumptions of society; scientific research and production consumption must adapt to the demands of living consumption and social consumption. The macro-consumption chain demands that scientific research and production consumption must go ahead of social consumption and living consumption and keep in a certain proportion, because the material productivity of the scientific research consumption level and quality determines the productivity level of the living consumption level and quality. The development of scientific research productivity should drive the consumption chain structure of living consumption and social consumption to ensure a dependent and coordinated development. If imbalances exist among living consumption chains, social consumption chains and scientific research development chains, consumption capacity cannot meet the requirements of production consumption; a surplus of production would appear, resulting in an economic crisis.

But a boom in the living consumption chain and social consumption chain will definitely drive the development of scientific and production consumption. Therefore, in the process of production consumption, the production consumption cost in the form of laborer income, consumer purchasing power, consumption costs of scientific research, and the income for performing social consumption must rise simultaneously. The profits in the process of production and operation should be reduced. This can ensure the development of new productivity and make living consumption and social consumption drive the development of production consumption, to guarantee the close and harmonious operation of the consumption chain of the three major consumptions.

Micro-consumption mode and consumption chain structure

The structure of the micro-living consumption chain is decided by the consumption capacity and its proportional law is Engels' Law. Engels' coefficient, a proportional number derived from Engels' Law, is an indicator showing the living standard. Its computational formula is:

Engel coefficient expenditure in purchasing food/ total expenditure

Besides expenditure on purchasing food, the proportion of expenditure on clothing, housing, and daily necessities will slowly be reduced because of a continuous increase of people in a family.

There are different patterns of consumption structure in clothes, food, housing, and transportation of people. Individual income, living consumption mode, consumption structure, and consumption mode of the consumption chain by industrial structure determine the macro living consumption mode. Individual and household living consumption mode and structure depend on the consumption capacity of the total income of the family and individual, and at the same time are restricted by consumption consciousness. Families or citizens with the same consumption capacity may have different consumption modes because of differences in their consumption consciousness.

Factors such as social environment, culture, and custom also have great influence on consumption mode and structure. Studying people's consumption mode and structure, guiding people's new consumption consciousness, and creating new consumption modes and structures are the top priority of scientific research, production, and consumption operators as well as their important responsibility in observing, analyzing, studying, and driving the development of the natural law of economy from the perspective of the micro consumption chain.

Price change of one point in the micro-consumption chain affects the overall situation. Price changes in the micro-consumption chain lead to a chain reaction on the market. A price change of one point in the micro-consumption chain affects the overall situation. For instance, an increase in food prices makes a chain fluctuation in industries, domains, and people's living consumption related to food production.

If the range of the price rise is limited to about 6~7%, it is beneficial to economic development and will promote production consumption, increase the employment rate, and drive the integrated development of the economy. But an increase in price by a large margin leads to serious imbalance of the macro-economic chain; under such circumstances, government should take various immediate measures to prevent this.

These are some characteristics of the micro consumption chain and consumption at different levels:

1. *Performance rules of the consumption chain.* Satisfaction of the three major consumption demands in the process of capital goods production and exchange must be reflected in the prices and value chains of public commodities as well as the consumption modes and consumptive levels

of common working class and ordinary laborers in the process of commodity exchange on the market. Differences in economic development levels and living consumption levels among various countries and regions would lead to differentiation in general consumption levels and value. But a common characteristic is that the price differentiation between the costs of production and the market price of ordinary consumer goods is very small.

Reflected on the market are ordinary consumer goods taking 70~80% of the total goods on the market, luxurious living consumption goods taking about 20~30% of the total, with 20% profit margins for common living consumption goods – the highest could reach up to 30%. The market share of exclusive living consumption goods is 20~30% and the profit margin reaches 70~80 , thus making a significant contribution in driving high-speed economic development, high revenue, high accumulation, high science and technology, and high consumption. Although with a relatively low profit margin, common living consumption goods have made great and fundamental contributions to social stability. Ordinary living consumer goods, from the orientation of production consumption to direct public consumption, forms their own law of consumption chain, called Law 2/8, also called the performance law of the common consumption chain, including that exclusive living consumption goods drive the 'five highs'. We should study this law to guarantee the normal performance development of the consumption chain, embodying it to make it develop from a low level to a middle level then to a high level, driving rapid economic development.

2. *Consumption and a low living consumption chain.* The low living consumption chain belongs to the scope of the ordinary consumption chain, but reflects the performance rule of the consumption chain at a lower living consumption level, for instance, disadvantaged groups with too low an income from the performance rule of the consumption chain that food consumption takes 60~70% of the total income and other living consumption only takes 30~40%. The state should help disadvantaged groups to raise their consumption productivity level, increase their income and life assurance, eliminate poverty, and help them catch up with the living standards of other people, so as to drive domestic economic development.
3. *Consumption and a high consumption chain.* Human beings have entered a new stage of historical civilization in which science and technology change with each passing day. Consumer goods produced

using high and new technology and production consumption have continuously promoted the improvement and rapid development of consumption-based economic society. The consumption of high consumer goods produced by high technology and a high consumption chain drives rapid economic development. High consumption creates high revenue and high accumulation, while fast development in turn drives the development of high and new technology. Advanced science and technology productivity creates the chain development law of a high consumption chain.

At the same time as a high consumption chain drives fast economic development, we should understand that the group that consumes a high level of consumption is only 15~20% of the total consumption group. If the high consumption of a society and production are divorced from the living consumption of 80% of consumers, it will cause an imbalance in the macro-consumption chain and can lead to economic crisis. So the state should pay adequate attention to the consumption development of low and public consumption groups, and also consider how to resolve the conflicts between these groups and the high consumption group. Only in this way can we maintain rapid and continuous development of the economy.

The three major consumption operations are interdependent and closely connected, thus forming the macro-consumption chain.

Living consumption and social consumption drive the development of scientific research and production consumption, and production consumption decides the level and consumption mode of living consumption and social consumption. Social consumption also includes living consumption of public accommodation such as railways, highways, subways, marine transportation, and public gardens.

If production of living consumables cannot meet the consuming capacity of living consumption, the phenomenon of demand exceeding supply would occur. If the production of living consumables exceeds the consuming capacity of living consumption (products that are necessary for product turnover should be taken out of consideration), the phenomenon of supply exceeding demand would occur. It is the inevitable phenomenon of the natural economic law on the market. With the force of its power, the state would bring the positive effects of natural economic law into play based on respect for it and intervene in its negative effects at the same time.

In the practical process of economic activity, the influence of the three major consumptions in driving economic development is extremely complex, but its rule is invariable. For instance, wages and rewards change monthly and yearly; wages and rewards in the process of production consumption and operation increase continuously; prices change every day; the proportion of development for different economic fields varies all the time. All the above-mentioned factors are changing, however, with certain rules. Our research goal is to find out the rules.

China is a rapidly developing country and has great consumption needs, which is the motive driving the long-term and continuous development of China's economy. Living consumption and social consumption of the population of 1.3 billion in China provide the whole world with a huge consumption market, driving not only the rapid economic development in China but also the economic development of the world. It is an objective law independent of human will. China's economic development will make a great contribution to the whole world.

Section 4 The research consumption chain to change the marketing mode

Tracking the manifestation of a commodity in the operational process of the consumption chain and different customer demands for consumption has created different consumption chains. From the perspective of an enterprise, most productions are independent of each other; however, when observed from the perspective of the living pattern of customers, productions are related in the process of market commodity exchange, thus constructing dispersal and different consumption chains among productions as well as industries. An Australian entrepreneur's original idea of printing a newspaper on the packaging paper from a fast-food restaurant triggered a consumption revolution in the media. For him, to buy fast food and read news on the packaging paper at the same time was a kind of new living consumption, which was also an inspiration for marketing innovation.

From industry-based value chain to a consumption chain

The traditional concept of production determining everything has led to the orientation of operation and management – production–market–customers – with the belief that so long as quality productions are produced, customers would certainly purchase them. However, nowadays consumers hold the supreme position: their consumption decides scientific research and production. New technology products would not sell without recognition of their target consumers, so the primary task of marketing planners is how to make consumers recognize, accept and prefer new technological products, thus realizing the social consumption productivity of new technology products.

As consumption consciousness are more and more mature today, customers' recognition of quality products is more important than the products themselves, so 'brand' is more important than 'product' – the special rule for brand consumption chain based on credit value.

For instance, the decision to purchase a car for leisure travel represents a series of recessive consumption demands. It indicates:

- the appearance of the matching service of a 'service station'; otherwise, the car would not move
- the emergence of the car service industry; otherwise, the car could not be repaired when it broke down
- the appearance of facility catering for drinking and dining during travel, without which travel would be inconvenient.

In other words, purchasing a car would trigger a series of consumption behaviors and connect formerly irrelevant industries or products – such as service stations, maintenance industry, mineral water, and instant noodles – together. Their combination is based on customer demands instead of enterprise designs. Obviously, this kind of consumption relevance could only occur from the perspective of the 'customers'. From the perspective of the enterprises, service stations, maintenance industries, mineral water, and instant noodles are irrelevant products; however, under the lead of cars, or the lead of the living pattern of the customers, they form a consumption chain.

People learn from the consumption chain that products of enterprises cannot control customers' behavior. When products don't conform to the living demands and patterns of the customers, customers may not welcome the so-called quality products propagated from the single aspect of the enterprises. Seen from the perspective of customers' consumption, customers never pay attention to independent products or industrial classification; instead, they only focus on living consumption demands and patterns to make their choice.

Thus, a micro living consumption chain is created in the process of commodity exchange by the living pattern of living consumers. What kind of new consumption chain is formed among different products, industries or domains? The answer is that customers' living consumption and living patterns create the consumption chain. It is a pattern created by free selection of the customers, just as pearls scattered on the ground are constructed as a pearl chain by living consumption demands and production consumption process. The market is not controlled by enterprises or products but by the living patterns of customers.

A primitive viewpoint comes from the birth of enterprises: the task of enterprises is to produce quality products and sell them to customers, in which the administrative logic of 'production decides customers' is concealed. However, as a matter of fact, there's a consumption chain outside the individual enterprise or the industrial chain on the market. This recessive consumption chain connects together formerly irrelevant products, thus forming a new consumption landscape.

In daily life, this kind of 'consumption chain' can be found everywhere. For instance, the CD player forms the industrial chain relationship among composers, singers, CD producers, wholesalers, and retailers from the perspective of the industrial chain; however, from the perspective of the consumption chain, if CD players are placed in KTV rooms, new service products of the recreation industry are created by compartments, beers, beverages, and waitresses.

The transition from industrial chain to consumption chain represents the process of our re-recognition of the consumption market, which also represents the gradual change from understanding the market from the perspective of enterprises to the perspective of customers.

Enterprises nowadays are always complaining that customer consumption is more and more fastidious, more and more difficult to grasp. In fact, the consumption chain of the customers is not hard to grasp, instead, it can be traced through the living consumption demands of customers and the corresponding consumption demands.

A living consumption chain is the dissipation consumption chain of the upstream and downstream driven by customer consumption and consumption patterns. The market is not controlled by enterprises or products, but by consumption and consumption patterns of the customers. From the perspective of the industrial chain, the enterprises of the same domains are competitors in life-and-death combat; however, from the perspective of the consumption chain, enterprises of different industries may be competitors as well, but it's also absolutely possible that they would become partners indispensable to each other.

When a new consumption chain comes into being, it would surely break the traditional concept of centering on products or quality. In the traditional concept, 'quality products would surely sell well'. This concept implies that quality products are defined by enterprises, not by the customers; however, in a new consumption chain, quality products are defined by consumers and their living patterns and decided by customer preference and satisfaction. Only through setting in reasonable and correct living consumption mode could products win acceptance of the customers. Otherwise, with the homogeneous trend in product quality, differentiations between products are smaller and smaller; therefore, the final selection of the products should be based on preference and satisfaction of the customers.

Marketing enterprises should study the demands of respective new consumption targets based on manifestations in the operational process of the industrial chain, social consumption chain, and living consumption chain of the three major consumptions, so as to meet their preference and satisfaction, continuously create new marketing and management modes, to achieve better marketing effectiveness.

9

Consumption and surplus value

The theory of surplus value, which had been discussed by Marx, can be analyzed through the formula of static digital design in order to help people understand this law clearly. At the same time, this designed production value can be consumed completely and realize surplus value. Marx's design is very scientific, as he designed this surplus value according to the consumption of the overall production process, the advanced capital of capital production, and the amount of surplus value which is designed according to the supply–demand relation of market commodity, science and technology, and the content of knowledge. All these are constantly in flux at any moment in the operation activities of a market economy, and the quantity of surplus value is displayed in the consumption process. Therefore, without consumption, there would be no surplus value. But people cannot see or understand how the surplus value is produced; what the relationship between surplus value and people is; and what the relationship between surplus value, workers, and capitalist is, so he discussed it with static digital analysis.

Discussion herein is also based on a static analysis of surplus value, the designed commodity value quantity, and the commodity, which are finally consumed in the circulation process, so that the surplus value of designing is realized – the reference and re-understanding of the capitalist production and circulation law; the explanation of the law of special surplus product value in circulation; the accumulation law of socialist surplus product value, and so on.

The discussion aims to prove that Marx's theory of surplus value is still applicable in the development of socialist commodities in a market economy, which would never disappear as well. The only problems lie in deciding to whom the surplus value belongs, how the superstructure allocates it, and how to use the law of surplus value to solve social problems with the expectation of promoting the progress of material civilization, spiritual civilization, and human beings in general. However, the law of surplus value reaches consumers in the whole process of production, circulation, and consumption, and at last it is realized by consumption. Since the law of surplus value is realized through commodity production and exchange in final consumption, so it is a universal economic law, and a great natural law. It just depends on whether or not it is recognized, mastered, used, and controlled. In the discussion, the author does not refer to consumption everywhere, but would like to say that the accumulation of surplus value wealth can only be realized in the process of consumption. At the same time, the law of surplus value is not only the inherent law of value in which consumption creates wealth, but also the law in which consumption creates surplus value and surplus product value.

Section 1 Recognition and reference of capitalist production and circulation law

The law of surplus value and socialist surplus product value

Marx's theory of surplus value plays a significant role in China's socialist economic construction. It is the cornerstone for us to carry on research in the accumulation law of socialist surplus product value. The history of the emergence and development of this theory can give us a better understanding of the value of the theory of surplus value.

Through critical inheritance of the value theories of physiocrats, Smith and Ricardo as well as the criticisms of vulgar economics from the 1930s to 1950s of the 19th century, Marx established his own theory of surplus value. This is the core issue in the capitalist part of Marxist political economics. The theory of surplus value is an important and indispensable component of the political economics in *Capital*, which is also the classical work about the history of political economics. Marx's theory and methods are still of great guiding significance. The author's thoughts on the law of surplus value and the theory of surplus product value are guided by the Marxist theory of surplus value.

In capitalist society, the means of production belongs to the private realm; surplus value belongs to capitalists and stands for their interests. Eventually, the superstructure it serves possesses it and decides the ratio of allocation. (Especially during the period when the capitalist economy grew up to a higher social level, such as in Japan and other developed capitalist countries.)

The means of production in socialist society belongs to the laboring people at large as well as to countries and groups that stand for their interest. There is an essential difference between surplus product value in a socialist society and surplus value in a capitalist society. Surplus product value in socialist society belongs to laborers, the collective, and the state, while in a capitalist society, laborers create the surplus value but do not own it. On the contrary, the capitalists own it and have the right to the distribution, consumption, and accumulation of surplus value, all of which is carried out by governments and collectives that represent the interests of capitalists.

We also see clearly that commodity production is still going on in the historical stage of socialism, during which the law on the use value of production and productive value has not changed. The law of necessary labor and surplus labor condensed in commodity value has not changed, either. However, there is a qualitative difference compared with the value of the necessary labor and surplus labor as condensed in the commodity value in a capitalist society. It is a kind of value determined by the rulers of countries and collectives, who use this value to meet the increasing material and cultural needs of people according to the overall benefit of socialist economic development. The manifestations of the value of this necessary labor time are wages, bonus, and the labor insurance fund.

In socialist society, the M in commodity value is the value, which is created by laborers for social labor, which is the surplus product value when the value of necessary labor time is deducted from the total value of the new creation. (The reason why it is called surplus product value is that it belongs to laborers as well as to the countries and collectives that stand for their interest. So it can be more strictly distinguished from the nature of the surplus value in capitalist society that represents interests of capitalists.)

Marx's theory of surplus value reveals the law of surplus value production and the secrets that the capitalists exploit surplus labor value created by workers, which is of guiding significance in recognizing the commodity economy under the condition of socialized mass production. Here I would mainly talk about the law of necessary labor time for the commodity production as well as surplus labor time.

These are the differences between socialist society and capitalist society at the historical stage:

1. There is public ownership of the means of production in a socialist society.
2. The ownership of surplus product value belongs to laborers as well as countries and collectives that represent their interests.

3. Laborers get a certain part of social product value through enjoying public social welfare besides the income obtained according to the principle of distribution according to work.
4. Communist ideological and moral standards and the superstructure of national legal systems are created by the socialist economic base and production relations are to protect the interests of the broad masses and to serve people.
5. Capitalists' production aims to extract surplus value, while the purpose of socialist production is to ensure the laborer's increasing demands on material and cultural life.

The law of value and surplus value production

Karl Max indicated that we know that the value of each commodity is determined by the amount of labor materialized in use value. As a value, a certain commodity is only a certain portion of labor time. The second period of labor process refers to the time that is beyond the limits of necessary labor time. Although it costs the workers' labor and labor force, it does not create any value for workers. I call this part of time in the working day surplus labor time, and the consuming labor surplus labor. Here Marx has clearly and accurately discussed the form of value and surplus value and exploitation that the bourgeoisie extracts as surplus value. When we study this theory, we should also understand the development law of surplus value in the competition of commodity production and find out its guiding significance and relations with socialist commodity production as well as those with the accumulation of wealth in socialist society. These are our main reasons for studying and researching this theory.

The law of change of cost value, value, and exchange value of commodity

Capitalists' main production purpose is not only to produce use value, but also to produce use value in order to produce surplus value. However, under the condition of an unchanged price for a certain product, the greater the commodity's rate of surplus value is, the less the corresponding ratio of cost value in production is. On the contrary, the greater the corresponding competition of use value is, the faster the development of commodity production is; the less the commodity's rate of surplus value is, the greater the corresponding ratio of cost value in production is; the less the corresponding competition of use value is, the slower the development of commodity production is. Therefore, capitalists endeavor to improving technology and management as well as boost labor productivity in order to survive and grow in the competition, thus breaking the situation of lower rate of surplus value and developing towards a higher surplus value rate.

When commodities are exchanged on the market, the exchange is based on the market price, which is affected by the fluctuation of the supply–demand relation. However, when commodities are exchanged on the market, the exchange value – the market price – is not equal to the value formed by the commodity itself. Therefore, the truly realized surplus value of the commodity is the amount of relative surplus value in the exchanged commodity prices.

Although the commodity price is not equal to the value of the commodity, it has always fluctuated around the commodity value in commodity exchange. For example, if the market price is P, when $P - C = 0$, the market price is equal to its value; when $P - C < 0$, the market price is lower than the value; when $P - C > 0$, the market price is higher than the value.

What we have mentioned above is the general law of production value, surplus value, and use value to exchange value. However, the commodity should get through several exchanges before reaching the hands of direct consumers on the market and value increment does not exist in circulation. The price is bound to increase when commodities are in circulation. The longer the transportation distance of the commodity, the greater the value increment of the price; the fewer the number of transportations the commodity takes and the shorter the distance is, the less the value increment of the price is. Smooth commodity exchange is conducive to the rapid development of production and too many circulation links are a kind of waste, as they result in extra value increments on price, thus consumers pay more money and lower their living standards.

Developing productivity and law of surplus value (surplus product value)

The higher the level of productivity is, the shorter the consuming time of the necessary labor; the more surplus labor time and surplus value, the higher the surplus value rate will be. On the contrary, the lower the level of productivity, the longer the consuming time of the necessary labor; the less surplus labor time there is, the less surplus value and the lower rate of surplus value will be.

The law of surplus value, which is used to develop productivity and work material productivity, must adapt to the law of materialization labor productivity surplus value. The surplus value law of intellectual materialization productivity also applies to the historical stage of socialist production. In socialist society, the owners of the means of production are the state and the people. The surplus value generated from the above-mentioned laws becomes the surplus product value of the people, which belongs to the state, the collectives, and the people.

Capital monopoly competition and law of surplus value

In capitalist society, when commodity production develops to a certain stage, strong competitors must achieve the commodity's exchange value with less or no surplus value at first in order to defeat their opponents and kick them out of the market so they can dominate the market and get a higher surplus value. Then they will win back the lost surplus value in the competition with a higher rate of surplus value than before.

This is the characteristic law when the free production competition of capitalism develops to the capital monopoly stage. However, it is the most general law in the capitalist commodity world. The law promotes capital to develop toward monopoly in the world and results in the outbreak of economic crisis. It triggers new reform and development as well.

Production of investment and the law of surplus product value

In capitalist society, any investment project or factory investment aims to obtain surplus value, while in socialist countries, the investment aims to expand reproduction and increase the accumulation of surplus product value so as to meet people's increasing demands for material, spiritual, and cultural living consumption. However, before deciding to invest, any investor must first consider the necessity for investment, the source and capacity of the investment fund, the maximum and minimum benefit of the investment process, surplus product value after investment, and the overall benefit of total investment.

I put the laws regarding the saved or wasted amount of investment, the shortened or extended project time, over production or under production of surplus product value as the law of production of surplus product value in the stage of investment. Understanding this law is very useful for socialist investment and construction.

In the same investment, the higher the use efficiency of investment funds is, the more the surplus product value after investment will be; the shorter the investment period is, the earlier the commodity production will achieve the surplus product value, which means the reduction of the investment amount, so the more rapid the economic development will be. On the other hand, we can see that the means of investment is the determining factor of investment returns. The person under pressure has a strong sense of responsibility. On the contrary, the person without pressure doesn't have as much sense of responsibility. So pressure can promote commodity production speed and enhance efficiency. Therefore, there is a close internal relationship between investment benefit and production efficiency after investment.

The production of surplus product value is the production of surplus labor, and the capital of expanded reproduction mainly comes from the accumulation of surplus product value and transforms into capital. The realization of relative surplus product not only has ordinary law, but also has special law, which is produced from special conditions encountered in the exchange of commodities. The benefit of the special law differs from the ordinary law of surplus product value, but it is also included in the general law of surplus value. At the same time, we can also see that the higher the level of science and technology, the higher labor's skill and technique quality, the more the surplus product value will be, and the higher the accumulation of capital transferred into funds.

Section 2 Special surplus product value realization law in commodity circulation

In the process of market exchange, the commodity not only has the general law of value exchange, but also a special law. The ordinary law dwells on this special law, but the special law has its own particularity and forms its own inherent natural law.

Brand reputation and implementing the law of surplus product value

A commodity uses the brand to represent the reputation of its use value in the process of exchange and consumption. At the same time, producers attract customers by the reputation status of their products.

Generally speaking, commodities with higher reputations have more users; the higher the reputation value of the use value formed in the process of market exchange and consumption, the higher the market price will be;

the fewer the users, the lower the product's reputation on the market and the lower its price. The higher the brand reputation of a commodity, the higher its exchange value will be on the market, and the greater the surplus product value that will be realized. The lower the brand reputation of the commodity, the lower the amount of exchange value that is formed on the market; the less the surplus product value amount will be. I call the price difference formed by the difference in reputation as credibility surplus product value (a). In socialist society, the price difference is called the amount of credibility surplus product value (a). The formula is:

$$B - C = M \text{ or } B - C = -M$$

I call the difference of the volume of business caused by the reputation of two sides as the reputation value amount:

> Reputation value × proportion of surplus product value in the exchange value = credibility surplus product value

Reputation generates value for users through:

- durability
- decoration
- novelty
- practical functionality and quality
- conceptual spirit.

These five elements constitute the complex reputation surplus product value of labor. In development of commodity production and competition they play an important role in realizing surplus value, especially in how much relative surplus product value would be realized.

People's living customs and the law of realizing surplus product value

In the process of market exchange, the consuming demand and market value of the use value of the commodity are also affected by people's living customs and time, wherein lie special rules. If one can understand the law as well as organize commodity production and sales which adapt to this law, one can get more surplus product value. On the contrary, if production and sales are not well organized, the realized surplus product value is reduced.

The law of surplus product value for people's living customs has three basic elements: people's living manners and customs, people's purchasing power, and timeliness of supply. If producers or managers of the commodity violate one of these elements, the law will punish them.

Regional adaptability of commodity and the law of realizing surplus product value

In the process of exchange and consumption on the market, the commodity's value forms the exchange value or price, which is also affected by regional adaptability. The surplus product value, which is realized in the process of distribution, is also affected by this feature and formed by certain rules.

For example, if a Phoenix bicycle and a Defense bicycle are put on the market at the same time in the same city, the exchange value of the Phoenix bicycle increases to 200 Yuan from 170 Yuan and is sold out quickly. The exchange value of the Defense bicycle decreases to 145 Yuan from the original 150 Yuan in order to be sold out. Now a Phoenix bicycle and a Defense bicycle are sold on the trade market of a mountainous area. The exchange value of the Defense bicycle increases to 180 Yuan from 150 Yuan and is sold out quickly, while the exchange value of the Phoenix bicycle decreases to 165 from 170 Yuan in order to be sold out. The reason for the change in their exchange values is that the adaptability of the Defense bicycle is worse than that of the Phoenix bicycle in the city. But, the adaptability of the Phoenix bicycle is worse than that of the Defense bicycle in the mountain area.

Commodities of the same value may have a different exchange value on the market due to the regional adaptability of a commodity, and the amount of surplus product value to be realized can be different as well. With a fixed unit price, the volume of sale can differ, and the amount of surplus product value to be realized can differ, due to regional adaptability or inadaptability of a commodity. Overstock of a commodity can be caused by weak regional adaptability. I name the law governing the above situations the law of realizing surplus product value based on the regional adaptability of a commodity.

Purchasing power level and the law of realizing surplus product value

As we know, the reason for the realization of surplus product value is that a commodity has use value, which can be realized in the process of exchange and consumption on the market. If the commodity exchange stops, the surplus product value cannot be realized. As for commodity with use value, the higher the exchange volume is, the larger the amount of surplus product value that will be realized. The less the exchange value is, the smaller the amount of implemented surplus product value will be.

Commodity production is oriented towards consumers' demand. However, demand is not necessarily equal to consumers' purchasing power, but they affect each other. The improvement of social purchasing power will certainly promote the development of demand for commodities. On the other hand, although people have a purchasing need for a certain commodity, if the purchasing power cannot reach the desired level for the commodity, there will be no demand for the commodity, which will result in surplus, overstock, and loss. At this time, in the process of commodity exchange and consumption, the surplus product value of a commodity value would decrease, become zero, or lose the prepaid value of the commodity.

The greater the consumption of a high-grade commodity, the faster the high-grade commodity will develop; then the surplus product value of sectors that manufacture its means of production will improve.

Capital turnover speed and the law of realizing surplus product value

The speed of capital turnover reflects the management level of an enterprise or a business as well as the amount of benefits. To a certain extent, the shorter the time of capital turnover, the higher the return on investment will be, and the greater the surplus product value.

I call the surplus product value realized by shortened capital turnover the law of surplus product value of realizing better capital turnover. I call the surplus product value realized by extended capital turnover the law of realizing surplus product value of poor capital turnover. I call the above-mentioned law, which makes the surplus product value more or less because of the days of capital turnover being shortened or extended, the law of realizing surplus product value of the capital turnover rate.

Service quality and the law of realizing surplus product value

How does service quality form the value of surplus labor time? Because working quality is included in the labor, the level of labor's technical quality and service quality reflects the productivity level to a certain degree. The plant workers' technical quality and the law of realizing surplus product value will be discussed in the section on developing productivity and the law of realizing surplus product value. It is necessary to represent the law of surplus product value of service quality separately, so businessmen can be better aware of the importance of improving service quality.

Generally speaking, the higher the service quality is, the larger the sale amount of the commodity will be, and the more surplus product value will be realized; the lower the service quality, the lower the sale amount and the surplus product value will be realized, or there may even be no surplus product value. I call the difference (the surplus product value which is realized due to the level of service quality minus the surplus product value which is realized by ordinary service quality) the implementing law of surplus product value of service quality.

Supermarkets and the law of realizing surplus product value

The law of realizing relative surplus product value formed by the supply–demand relation in the supermarket relates to gathering commodities from different regions, of stronger adaptability, more novelty, different standards, and more varieties, to ensure meeting highly varied customer needs of different commodities and forming a three-dimensional sales market. The management feature of this kind of market is that commodities are purchased through batch delivery or directly from the manufacturer, thus reducing the time to wholesale and transportation and decreasing costs. Another characteristic is that if the operating time is long, the sales value of the commodity is lower than that in the ordinary market, the turnover of circulating funds is faster, the quality of service is higher, and the type and specification of commodities managed by an individual will be greater.

In supermarkets, because commodities are purchased directly from the manufacturer, the exchange increment value of transportation is reduced; on the other hand, as the speed of capital turnover is fast, the prepayment as a circulation fund is used less, and less loan interest is paid. Therefore, the cost value is lower than that in the ordinary market; the surplus product value is higher than that in the corresponding ordinary market. I call this law the law of realizing surplus product value of the supermarket. This law of the supermarket differs from the economic law of the international and domestic supermarket (high-grade commodity shopping malls and monopoly stores and shops). A supermarket is distinguished from other markets by the unique characteristics of its commodities, so this market generally is oriented towards users with higher purchasing power. The management method and commodities of the supermarket adapt to users with ordinary purchasing power as well as to users with relatively higher purchasing power.

The convenient and timely supply of commodities

The increase or decrease of the commodity's surplus product value is not just because the supply exceeds demand or the demand exceeds supply in the process of value exchange. Generally speaking, whether the commodity can be supplied timely and conveniently plays an important role in the realization of surplus product value, and it is also an important issue in the nature of socialist commerce service. Socialist commerce serves people and users, so it is inevitable to consider the convenience of users and the timely supply of the commodity. The objective is realized according to economic law or by administrative means. Usually the economic benefits of the latter method are far fewer than those of the former one.

Section 3 Socialist surplus product value accumulation law

Putting aside the unique production relations in capitalist society and compared with the general and special laws of developed commercial economy, Marx's surplus value theory still cannot be violated in the development of a socialist commodity economy. However, this law has been changed qualitatively into the law of surplus product value under a socialist system. So the accumulation of socialist capital should first follow the law of surplus product value; second, be self reliant and work hard; and third, realize the surplus product value of the consumption distribution according to work. It mainly refers to the consumption distribution among non-production employees, as employees involved in production take part in the distribution of 'V' (the variable capital) according to work. This will promote people to compete for the realization of 'four modernizations' and to create more surplus product value.

The accumulation law of socialism and particular surplus product value

As mentioned above, in capitalist society, the competition of capitalists for surplus value production produces the law of capital monopoly surplus value, which is special and unique to capitalist society. In socialist society, various production groups compete for surplus product value and result in the production and accumulation law of surplus product value, which is characteristic of socialist societies – the production and accumulation law, by which the national economy produced and competed for the surplus product value in a planned and proportional way. It is beneficial that production management groups and sale service groups compete with each other in a brotherly way for the production and accumulation of surplus product value. They feel great honor in accumulating the surplus product value they produced; the workers of a socialist society create their own surplus product value. At the same time, they also create expanded reproduction, which is used to consume and accumulate their own surplus product value in proportion, and distribute consumer goods on the basis of the law of 'distribution according to work'. This law also promotes the production and accumulation of surplus product value.

The unique law of capital monopoly competition for surplus value in capitalist society leads to periodic economic crises in the economy, resulting in recession, unemployment of workers, poverty, reform, rejuvenation, and new development.

The unique law of the accumulation of surplus product value of production in a socialist society promotes the rapid economic development of socialism as well as the ceaseless improvement of the material, spiritual, and cultural living standards of the people. The reason why socialist society could produce its own law of surplus product value production and accumulation is decided by the advanced superstructure and production relations of socialism, and the nature of the economic base of public ownership; similarly, the reason why capitalist society produces its unique law of capital monopoly competition for surplus value is that the superstructure, production relations, and productivity could not stay in harmony with one another and could not exert strong force upon the economic base.

The accumulation law of surplus product value of labor material in planned economic society

There are six economic forms in China's economic base: state-owned firms, collective firms, firms of individual small commodity production, Chinese and foreign joint firms, individual proprietorship capital firms, and social capital firms. Among these six economic forms, commodities of labor materials are exchanged mutually; on the other hand, the distribution principle of labor material in the historical stage of socialism is distribution according to work and the more you work, the more you are paid and the more is distributed and exchanged by monetary means. The state-owned enterprises are charged by relatively independent economic groups of production, management groups of sales service, and groups of transportation. They take charge of the production, exchange, and circulation of commodities. They are not only the master of the country, but also the master of their enterprises. They have the host duty to the management of means of labor and the management benefits. There is a close relation with their groups' common benefits. All commodity exchange between group A and group B of state enterprises are the exchange of commodities' use value.

I name the superfluous accumulation fund realized by the commodity production of means of labor the accumulation law of surplus product value of commodity production of socialist means of labor. I call it the accumulation law of surplus product value instead of the law of surplus product value because it includes the prolonged service life value after the means of labor are put into use. The prolonged service life value is the benefit of management originally. However, as we have not regarded means of labor as commodity production, but as allocation use in the past, the phenomenon of bad maintenance of equipment is common in enterprises, thus leading to serious damage and discarding of equipment as well as great waste. Only through this kind of calculation can we explain the essence and nature of the problem.

Organizing the production of commodities

During commodity production, which is mainly controlled by a planned economy and assisted by the market economy in socialist society, commodity production should be carefully carried out according to contract. This method can prevent the mass overstock of commodities and the waste of resources, which is caused by prolonged production, due to untimely supply of production consumption means and delays in transportation, thus improving the accumulation of surplus product value to the maximum.

Organizing the production of commodity according to contract is a system developed gradually after the commodity production of capitalist society developed into the stage of productive surplus and was restrained by economic crisis. To some extent, it plays an active role in helping capitalists reduce serious losses of surplus product value caused by blind production, provides legal protection of economic responsibility for capitalists to accelerate capital turnover, reduces over-production and cost, exploits surplus product value, and plays an important role in capitalists' scientific management of enterprise.

Organizing commodity production according to contract is a great capitalist contribution. In order to produce more surplus product value, capitalists unconsciously create an organic law of production and consumption for society. This law adapts to socialist commodity production and plays an important role in guiding the socialist production purpose and the development of the national economy in a planned, proportional way. If the whole national economy is brought into the state of organizing production according to contract, it means the development of the whole national economy is brought into the legal path of production. At that time, the economic loss caused by bureaucracy and irresponsible behavior would decrease greatly, the accumulation of socialist surplus product value would increase greatly, and socialist development would be accelerated.

I regard organizing the production system according to the contract as a concrete and universal method to carry out giving first place to a planned economy and taking market regulation as an auxiliary measure to regulate production and consumption. It is a law with social and legal normality. So I call it the law of production based on commodity contract. Because of carrying out the production system of commodity by contract, the factory reduces excessive production and ensures proper production. It also decreases product cost and realizes more accumulation of surplus product value and capital. I call this law the accumulation law of surplus product value due to contract-based production.

The law of value and price inversion of commodity in socialist society

On the whole, the price of a commodity in China still fluctuates around the value, with the price of certain commodities slightly higher than the commodity's value and the price of certain commodities slightly lower than the commodity's value, so price inversion is formed. This is because China constructed socialism on the basis of poverty and blankness; people's average living standard and social wealth were far from being abundant. In order to ensure meeting people's living needs, the price of the necessities of life, such as grain and cotton, must be slightly lower and this kind of commodity must carry out the policy of unified purchase and sale. If the country doesn't do this, people's lives cannot be stable. The price inversion of some commodities plays an active role in promoting the development of productivity and commercial production in the first 30 years of China's socialist construction. However, we should also see that with the improvement of people's living standards, the price inversion of commodities has hindered some products' further development. Therefore, under the new and changed situation, only a few commodities which have close relations with the national welfare and people's livelihood still receive state subsidy; all the other products should be treated according to the normal value law of the commodity, which can further promote the development of commercial production.

Some commodities are automatically and totally regulated by the law of value, which will affect people's living level; not following the value law of commodity will affect the production development of the commodity. If the state can further increase the living subsidy for city residents and follow the value law of some products, it will play an active role in the accumulation of socialist surplus product value and the rapid development of economic construction.

Some people worry that the regulation of some commodities by following the law of value will make the price go up and down greatly, which will affect people's living standard. Actually this is not so. The endurance factors for socialist price stability are that socialist commodities are produced under macro regulation of the national economy and the competition for surplus product value, and price fluctuates up and down around the commodity's value in a planned way. Quantity differences of demand and supply are controlled within a certain range by macro regulation and guidance planning (or it may be more proper to call it guidance controlled planning), so the phenomenon of long-term shortage and surplus crisis won't occur. (If surplus crisis occurs, it proves that we violated the law that the national economy develops under macro regulation and also shows that our work deviates from the socialist economic way. It should be noted that the economic crisis here does not refer to the situation in which some commodities exceed social demand for some valid reason. The appearance of demand exceeding supply and supply exceeding demand within a certain range is an inevitable normal law in commodity production and development.) The phenomenon in capitalist society in which the law of capital monopolizes competition for surplus value, the price fluctuates greatly, and people's lives become poorer would not occur.

Science and technology and the law of accumulation of surplus product value

We have already shown that surplus product value is the value of surplus labor time. What then are the relations between surplus product value and science and technology? Let's take Xiangfan city as an example.

Recently, this city successfully developed some energy-saving technology innovations such as low energy consumption cement, fast formed glazed tiles at low temperature, and so on. In two years, the power saved only through compensation technology was equal to an increase of one-fifth of the power for the whole city or an income of 300,000 Yuan. From this we can see that the higher the level of application of science and technology in production, the greater the commodity's surplus product value and the greater the accumulation; the lower the level application of science and technology in production, the lower the commodity's surplus product value, and the lower the accumulation.

Scientific management and the law of accumulation of surplus product value

The method and purpose of scientific management is to give full play to the highest benefit of the prepayment fund on the basis of certain material technology – to produce more commodities demanded by society with more service value and more surplus product value by using less consumption. In order to achieve this purpose, scientific management must carry out management of operations and products through the management of people; the management of people must be carried out through the management of labor organization; the development of people's minds and the distribution of material benefits to stimulate production (work) enthusiasm, thus promoting the management of matters. Therefore, socialist enterprise management must be a combination of political and economic means.

Strengthening scientific management can increase surplus product value without an increase in annual production value. I call the law of surplus product value created totally by scientific management the law of surplus product value of scientific management. The features of scientific management are:

- to make the productivity level of materialization of labor adapt further to the demand of the materialization of productivity
- to save the consumption of raw material and further increase the utilization ratio
- to further improve the qualified rate and optimization rate of products
- to shorten the days of turnover of circulation fund

- to acquire information about social demand and adjust production in order to meet the market demand quickly
- to ensure the timely meeting of users' demand and deliver the commodity in good shape in order to satisfy customers' demand.

The management methods and measures are different according to the specific productivity level and production formula. Therefore, the higher the management level, the more the surplus product value will be created; the lower the management level, the greater the loss will be. But there may be the phenomenon of a full load in the surplus product value, which is created by scientific management. When it becomes a full load, enterprises must develop new science and technology productivity if they want to improve the rate of surplus product value. I call the sum of product value, which is created by management, and the circulation fund saved by strengthening management the accumulation fund of scientific management, and its law the accumulation law of surplus product value of scientific management.

Comprehensive utilization and the law of accumulation of surplus product value

Comprehensive utilization is an important way to increase surplus product value. All enterprises have the potential to recover and use waste materials. The key problem is whether the enterprise pays attention to it or not. If all enterprise leaders and employees pay attention to the use of waste material, there would be a great quantity of surplus product value accumulation.

Distribution according to work in socialism and the law of accumulation of surplus product value

The distribution of surplus product value in socialist society is in accordance with Marx's distribution law. One part is used for living consumption; the other is transferred into the accumulation fund to expand reproduction and then to produce more surplus product value. If the accumulation part is too large, it will affect the improvement of material and cultural living standards and the enthusiasm for production; if the living consumption is too large, it will affect the accumulation and expanded reproduction and also greatly affect the increasing speed of material and cultural living standards in the future. Therefore, the distribution proportion should be arranged according to China's situation and the principle 'first for living and then for construction', which was put forward by Chen Yun.

On the other hand, we should carry out the socialist distribution principle of distribution according to work, and the more one works, the more one is paid. The basic meaning of this principle is to reward the diligent and punish the idle; in the historical stage of socialism, the productivity level was low, people's ideological consciousness was low, and labor was still a means of life, so the distribution method of equalitarianism discouraged the enthusiasm of workers, affecting the development of productivity and the accumulation of surplus product value. So we must carry out the principle of distribution according to work and the more one works, the more one is paid in the primary stage of socialism.

I call the difference that the amount of surplus product value realized according to the distribution principle according to work minus the amount of surplus product value realized by the distribution of equalitarianism surplus product value of distribution according to work and also call the law the law of surplus product value of distribution according to work.

Equalitarianism cannot reward the diligent and punish the idle in the primary stage of socialist society nor stimulate the enthusiasm of labor. It affects the development of productivity and the accumulation of surplus product value to be realized; it affects the speed of economic development and the improvement of broad labor's material and cultural living standard.

The implementation of the principle of distribution according to work fully stimulates the enthusiasm of labor; makes the means of production more adaptable to the development of productivity; and improves production efficiency, accumulation of surplus product value, and material and cultural living standards. Therefore, in the primary stage of a socialist society, the principle of distribution according to work – the law of surplus product value of distribution according to work – cannot be violated. If this law is violated, there would be punishment.

Distribution methods such as flexible wages, management contracts, and quota and capital carried out at present are in accordance with the law of surplus product value of distribution according to work. Distribution proportion is determined by relevant national regulations and the specific conditions of an organization. If the unit contracts blindly or does not improve the proportion of labor income accordingly – if the proportion of labor income is too high – it will affect the accumulation of the state and the enterprise as well as expanded reproduction and the speed of economic development; if the proportion of accumulation is too high and the proportion of labor distribution is too small, the enthusiasm of labor will be low, thus affecting the speed of economic development.

Technology transfer of joint venture enterprise and the law of accumulation of surplus product value

At present many people object to the joint venture enterprises. We would analyze the significance of joint venture enterprises for socialist construction by using the formula G - W - G.

Marx told us that the direct form of commodity circulation is W – G – W: a commodity is transformed into money, the money is converted into capital, and the behavior of selling is for the purpose of purchasing. As well as this pattern, we see another pattern with different characteristics, G - W - G: money is transformed into capital, the capital is converted back into money, and the behavior of purchasing is for selling. Money is transformed into capital through the later commodity circulation operation. Once it changes into capital, it is capital based on its mission. It moves close to the absolute value through the increase in volume. Indeed, there is a difference between the original prepayment value of 100 pounds and the value-added surplus value of 10 pounds in circulation, but this difference disappears quickly. The original prepayment value of 100 and the value-added surplus value of 10 pounds are not independent of each other at the end of the process. The result is that we get the value of 110 pounds, which is the same as the original 100 pounds, and it is also suitable to start a value-added process. Money at the end of the operation takes the same form as it did at the beginning of the operation.

From this law we can see that the surplus product value as the result of the socialist commodity production also comes from the added value of capital itself through commodity production. Through purchasing commodity, it enables new products to be produced and surplus product value to be generated, which are sold out again later. This is the law of G – W – G. However, if one wants to get this surplus product value, one should get money at the beginning as new capital. Without this new capital monetary, you cannot get new surplus product value to acquire wealth.

Suppose the monetary capital of China through the past accumulation itself is 1,000. After investing new capital, the production of surplus product value is 200:

1,200C' (1,000C + 200M = 1,200C')

If there is no new added capital, the proportion and rate of becoming rich can only increase constantly on this basis:

2,000C + 400M = 2400C'

If we want to obtain more surplus product value to acquire wealth more rapidly, or we want to get the surplus product value of 400, which is two times the original, we must get the new added monetary capital of 1000 at first – the original monetary capital of 1,000 and the new added monetary capital of 1,000 is 2,000:

2,000C + 400M = 2,400C'.

Then, how do we get this new monetary capital? The first method is to issue a certain amount of treasury bonds, but the amount should not be too large. Because if the amount is too large, it will affect the improvement of people's living standard and make people dissatisfied with the government. The second method is to take a loan from a foreign bank. It is also feasible if we can get a certain amount of preferential loan. The third method is to draw in foreign capital and run a joint venture enterprise through the policy of opening up. Suppose the joint venture capital is 1,000, with 500 from the Chinese side and 500 from the foreign side. Then 800 of the capital is used to introduce advanced equipment and the other 200 could be used as variable capital. The value of the products at the end of the yearly production process is:

1,200C' (800C + 200V + 200M = 1,200C')

The two sides of Sino-Foreign joint ventures regulate that this enterprise gets back the investment in five years and transfers in ten years, and the service life is 30 years. The operational result is that this enterprise realizes the surplus value in five years (the surplus value, not the surplus product value) of 1,000 in five years, and both sides get 500 (the surplus value after handing in income tax). If adding the income tax of 35%, which has been handed in, the surplus value is not 1,000, but 1,538.

The Chinese side gets the surplus value of 500 and the income tax of 538, and the sum of these two items is 1,038; the foreign capital side gets the surplus value of 500. If the surplus value is remitted out of China, it should be additionally levied at the foreign exchange tax rate.

The business result of ten years is that this enterprise realizes the surplus value of 2,000.The Chinese side gets the surplus value of 1,000 and the foreign side gets 1,000. The Chinese side levies the income tax of 1,076, so the total income is 2,076. The Chinese side pays the transfer fee of 333 to the foreign side, so this enterprise is transformed into a Chinese state-run factory after ten years. This factory can realize the surplus product value (not surplus value) of 6,152(including tax income) in the following 20 years:

6,000 + 2,076 + 6,152 = 14,228

Now we invest the monetary capital of 1,000 which China did not put in the joint venture, and the surplus product value (profit and tax which is generated by the joint venture) is 4,076 (2,000 + 2,076) together in ten years. If we calculate them to the limited time of the joint venture enterprise, the result is as follows:

$$6{,}000 + 2{,}076 + 6{,}152 = 14{,}228$$

From this law we can see that the foreign side invests one Yuan in China and takes away three Yuan and China gives the foreign side 2 Yuan, and gets 4 Yuan in ten years. China gives the foreign side 2 Yuan and gets 16 Yuan during 30 years if the time duration is 30 years. In order to explain this problem, we suppose this is an unchangeable example. However, it changes greatly in reality. But this law still does not change.

Thus we can seek unity in thinking. The Communist Party of China's important decision about the policy of opening up is a guideline and beneficial policy to the nation and people as well as an inevitable choice to construct socialism on the basis of backward economy and technology. In order to develop their own resources, the proletariats who have controlled their own fate must understand the special law of economic operation. Certainly, when we decide the direction of a joint venture, we have to consider the economic benefit in the transitional period or out of the transitional period and during the limit time of investment. We should not only consider the benefit of production ability, especially, but we must also consider and predict the benefit of the commodity's competitive ability after the transitional period. What's more important, we should consider that this product does not exclude the competition and development of a similar commodity in China and has the ability of excluding the competition and development of a similar commodity in the international market; this is the most important question when we formulate the plan for a Sino-foreign joint venture project. We should not commit suicide through the introduction of the 'knife', but make ourselves stronger and richer through using the 'knife', and this is our main purpose.

Conclusion

In a socialist society, absolute surplus product value is still produced by workers in surplus labor time. The value of a commodity is the content and basic of the exchange value (price), but it is not equal to the exchange value of the commodity. The surplus product value, which is realized in the process of exchanging use value, is the relative surplus product value which is realized through the commodity's price fluctuating up and down around the commodity's value.

The realization of the relative surplus product value is because when commodities are exchanged, various special conditions, characteristics, and factors make the price inevitably deviate from the value. For example, if supply exceeds demand or demand exceeds supply, the difference of a favorable climate, geographical position and environment, living customs, and so on would make the price inevitably deviate up or down from the value. Another situation is that one can't directly see the relativity of surplus product value from its appearance, but it also realizes the surplus product value relatively. Such as the law of surplus product value of service quality, the law of surplus product value of capital turnover and so on, the main feature as shown is not the price fluctuations up and down around value, but the constant changes in surplus product value in line with the changes in sales volume.

Another situation is the law of surplus product value in the supermarket. Its exchange value (price) is seemingly low, as if it deviates from value. This is not because supply exceeds demand, and in many people's opinion it looks like quick turnover and more return with small profits. In fact, this is not small profit, but the law of quick turnover and more return with large profits.

Under the socialist system, the state stopped the practice of 'big rice pot' and streamlined the production relations during the commodity production process, so that it can conform to the development level of productivity in a certain stage and build a direct relation between surplus product value, which is realized by the enterprise, and the benefit of the workers. Therefore, productivity would develop rapidly and the benefit could increase sharply.

After implementation of contracted responsibility linking remuneration to output in rural areas and coalition of industry, agriculture and business, the farmers (originally the people's community members) become the real subject in socialist production relations and the source of productivity. At the same time, it builds a direct relation between the benefits of management production and the benefits of members and gives full play to the potential of productivity to increase the surplus product value exponentially.

The law of surplus product value in socialist society has gradually been mastered and applied by more and more people. It will surely manifest its vigor and prompt the capital accumulation as well as economic development in the construction of socialism. The speed of the socialist construction in China will surprise the world for sure.

To conclude, the surplus value theory of Marx is still applicable in the development of a socialist market economy and will never lose its efficacy. What we should reconsider are just to whom should the surplus value belong, how the superstructure allots it, and how to utilize it to solve a series of social problems so as to promote the material and spiritual civilization as well as human progress. However, the surplus value must be realized through a process including production, circulation, and consumption before the surplus value comes to the consumer and is consumed by them at last. If consumers in the process of exchange could not consume the commodity, the wealth value and certain surplus value of the products will not be realized. Instead, it will lead to reduction or loss of interest or even bankruptcy of the enterprises. This law is not only a universal economic law and a great natural law, but also an eternal law. It is only a problem whether the people have realized, handled, and applied the law or not. The author did not mention consumption many times in this discourse. It is only necessary to reveal the law that the accumulation of surplus value can only be achieved through consumption at the same time; the regulation of surplus value is also an intrinsic law that consumption creates wealth and the law that consumption creates surplus value and surplus product value.

10

Consumption and the progress of social civilization

Consumption creates consumption demand, the process of consumption based on relevant social productivity and production relations, production, economic foundation and superstructure as well, which makes human society constantly move towards civilization and gain progress.

The process of scientific research and production creates consumer goods, consumption patterns, and consumption levels. In the development process of creating production, consumption has also created commodity exchange consumption. In the process of driving commodity production and exchange, consumption has also created currency, a special commodity that dominates the whole consumption process of the production of capital commodity and commodity exchange.

Consumption creates the process of production consumption and the division of industries and the further division of production processes. During the production process, class, hierarchy and superstructure, which represent the economic foundation, gross productivity of the consumption society, and gross social production relations, are created.

However, the basic contradiction of any society is the contradiction between superstructure and economic foundation as well as that between productivity and production relations. Once superstructure suits the development of the economic foundation and production relations suits the development of the productivity of a consumption society, scientific research and production, social economy, and social civilization would develop rapidly.

If superstructure does not adapt itself to the development of the economic foundation and production relations does not suit the development of productivity, the development of productivity, the development of the economic foundation, and the development of social civilization all would be hindered. And if the development of productivity is seriously hindered, social change or even a drastic class struggle is sure to be triggered. However, class struggle and class revolution result from the serious lack of adaptation of production relations to the development of productivity and the serious lack of adaptation of the superstructure to the economic foundation. Change and revolution mean liberating productivity, developing the productivity of a consumption society, developing the economic foundation, and developing social civilization and progress. Therefore, consumption is the power source of social civilization and progress.

Section 1 Generation of consumption and society

Human consumption and progress in primitive societies

Chinese scientists have excavated many fossils of primates' remaining bones and relics in our motherland, which indicates that the earliest primitives within China lived here more than one million years ago. Lantian Ape Men unearthed in Shanxi Province have a history of about 800,000 years or longer, while Peking Ape Men, unearthed in Zhoukoudian, Beijing, lived 400,000 to 500,000 years ago.

It is human instinct to demand consumption materials from nature and to create consumption materials. Peking Ape Men had more developed arms and legs, so they could work intelligently and create tools by their hands and the consumption materials from nature with these tools.

In the Stone Age Peking Ape Men used stone tools including stone axes, stone saws, and stone knives and took consumables from nature with these tools. In the time of Peking Ape Men, as consumption productivity improved, and laboring began to be divided by gender and age, human wisdom also developed. Due to the demand of the living consumption and production consumption of primitive people and the demands of human development, ancient people began to forbid direct intermarriage with relatives and began to marry people outside their immediate families. This kind of exogamy was the direct cause of the formation of clans. Consanguineous marriage was an important link in the transition from primitive clans to gentile community. From then on, the gentile community system with blood bonds began to develop. In different historic periods and under different social systems, the intimacy level and function of blood relationships vary. In primitive societies, blood relationships were fundamental, and the basis of social organization, playing a decisive role in social production and individual living. The confirmation of blood relationships facilitated the steady development of human society progress, the advancement of mankind, and the development of living consumption. Each leader, leading organization, or group in clan communities was responsible for distributing hunted consumption materials and protecting group safety.

Lewis Henry Morgan (1877) divides the creation of ancient social systems into seven phases:

1 *Low obscuration society*. This period began from the first period of mankind and ended when knowledge of fishing and using fire were obtained. During that time, mankind lived and consumed in their primitive and limited environment and fed mainly on fruits and nuts. Language with distinct syllables began in this phrase. No example of human tribes of this kind of social state has been found to date.
2 *Intermediate obscuration society*. This period began with the consumption of fish for food and the acquisition of fire and ended when the bow and arrow were invented. Mankind under this state spread outward from its primitive environment to most parts of the earth. Therefore, existing tribes, which belong to the intermediate obscuration society, include Australians aborigines and most Polynesians, who were in this state when they were found.
3 *Advanced obscuration society*. This period began with the invention of the bow and arrow and ended with the invention of ceramics, which resulted in epoch-making progress to the consumption pattern.
4 *Low barbarous society*. It seems a little arbitrary to divide obscuration societies and barbarous societies with the invention of the ceramics or the prevalence of ceramics industry as the boundary. However, considered from various aspects, there is not any dividing standard more appropriate than this. The first stage of the barbarous phase began with making pottery, no matter whether ceramics were invented by them or learnt from other tribes. After all, mankind had entered a new age of the consumption of technical ceramics products.
5 *Intermediate barbarous society*. For the eastern hemisphere, this period began with raising animals; for the western hemisphere, this period began with irrigation farming and building houses with adobe and stones. The invention of smelting can be decided as the end point.
6 *Advanced barbarous society*. This period began with the production of ironware and ended with the invention of the phonemic alphabet and writing with characters. Civilization began in this period.

7 *Civilized society*. This period began with the use of the phonemic alphabet and the appearance of documents. Civilized society is divided into ancient civilized society and modern civilized society. Pictographs engraved on stones can be viewed as a standard equal to the phonemic alphabet. According to Morgan's dividing standard of ancient advanced barbarous society, China entered the consumption age of ancient civilized society when Cang Jie invented characters in the time of the Yellow Emperor.

Since the power of the group is needed for creating consumables and consumption materials, the family was created. The generation of social marriage and family probably can be divided into several long phases. When human culture was in the low level of obscuration society, the system of communal marriage existed within prescribed scopes. Along with the advancement and development of ancient humans, as the range of cohabitation system gradually shrank, kinship forms developed from the low phase to high phase. Matrilineal kinship form started from blood kinships, based on collective intermarriage between brothers and sisters. The second form, the partnership family, replaced the first marriage system with a collective marriage that brothers shared wives, sisters, and husbands. Later, human society developed and advanced, and clans were formed on the basis of kinship, with matrilineal blood relationship prevailing. Since men were engaged on the outside while women were in charge of the inside in production labor, human society then developed into the consanguineous family with men dominating. Marriage has developed from polyandry and polygamy family marriage, to polygamy family, and then to the exclusive spouse system, monogamy, which is the modern civilized marriage family system.

The generation and development of ancient human society varied in the eastern and western hemispheres. Even in the same hemisphere, the social advancement levels among developed and advanced areas and clan tribes in remote islands and forests are quite different. In the 1940s, Tibet in China was still a slave society, and the minority living in the forest in northeastern China was still in the primitive clan tribe phase; hence, the development of human society has been imbalanced.

Peking Upper Cave Men in China in 400,000 B.C. should belong to the obscuration-forming phrase of Chinese primitive ancient society. In this period, they learnt to make tools with stones, to make needles with bones, and to make animal skins into clothes, creating their own living consumption materials. It may be the earliest evidence of human society. China is one of the oldest countries in human society, and it is also a country with the most complete continuous development of culture. There are more than 5,000 years that can be studied, which provides valuable proof for the progress of human society.

Consumption and progress of primitive people in the age of clan tribe

About 5,000 years ago in the Age of Teras there were many clans and tribes along the Yellow River basin and the Yangtze basin in China. Owing to the consumption needs for survival and reproduction, they migrated, allied, battled – disputes and fights frequently took place between tribes and clans (just like animals fighting and killing to survive and protect their own domains). Through the time of Youchaoshi (a nest made in trees for living) and the time of Suirenshi, productivity had significantly improved, and humans' ability to create consumption had been greatly developed, and the development of humanity, population and wisdom had been significantly advanced.

At that time, there were two most powerful tribes: the tribe headed by Shen Nong, the Yan Emperor, and the tribe headed by the Huang Emperor. Meanwhile, a Jiuli tribe with a valiant captain called Chiyou appeared. Combining all the tribes, the Huang Emperor held a life-and-death fight against the tribe of Chiyou in the suburb of Zhuolu and killed Chiyou in the end, thus protecting the consumption interest and safe living of the Yan Emperor and his tribe, so he gained devout support from tribes and was recommended as the leader of the tribal alliance. The battle in Zhuolu promoted the development of the living consumption, social consumption, and production consumption of mankind at that time, leading primitive humans to develop into the alliance of a clan tribal community. The alliance leader was decided by the system of recommending and selecting a successor upon death. In the primitive social system, three major consumptions created the community system of clan alliance.

Meanwhile Huang Emperor was recommended as the leader of various Chinese clan tribes, the remote clan tribal alliance community of mankind entered a new epoch of consumption progress. Suirenshi inherited and carried forward the progress of a consumption society; for example, he invented the method of knotting ropes to record events and the method of drilling wood to make fire, and he taught people how to eat cooked food, constructed high platforms for preaching and teaching, established markets for trading at noon, and built roads for business. As a result, there was a harmonious atmosphere then with a good authority function and compliant people. Hence, Suirenshi was also called the Sui Emperor. Then Cang Jie created pictographic characters, leading mankind develop into the time of characters – the consumption period of ancient civilization.

During mankind's long process of living consumption by fishing and hunting, they had kept lots of hunted animals for food. In this way, people gradually learnt how to raise animals and animal husbandry developed. It is said that survival skills such as netting and feeding were taught to people by a man called Fuxishi.

This kind of survival consumption and consumption patterns lasted for a long time, then a second, bigger leap in consumption driving the development of human cultural history occurred. That was the development of agriculture. According to the legend, Shennongshi not only led people to carry out land reclamation and planting but also invented a wooden tool to plough – Leisi (a wooden shovel with a handle), which facilitated laboring for people. In the primitive societies of mankind, due to the demand of humans, consumption drove the development of productivity and productions, and society constantly developed.

It is said that several very famous tribe leaders appeared successively after the Huang Emperor, who were called Yao, Shun, and Yu. The time of Yao and Shun has been considered by later generations as the heyday of the Chinese primitive clan tribal alliance community. After replacing Yao as the leader of the tribal alliance, Shun inspected water controlling sites in person, and when he found that Gun had failed to do his job, he killed Gun and assigned Yu, the son of Gun, to control the water. Finally, Yu succeeded in controlling the water. When Shun was old, he began to look for his successor as Yao had done. Because of Yu's contribution in water control, he was recommended to be the leader of the tribal alliance.

Section 2 Generation of slave society and the progress and development of three major consumptions

Qi founded the Xia Dynasty and China became a slave society

Yu became the leader of the tribal alliance with the dynastic tile of Xia. Yu cast nine dings (vessels), which stand for nine parts of China. Later the nine dings became the symbol of state power. After the nine dings were cast, Xiayu began to exercise supreme power and sometimes he even sanctified his power on purpose, thus preventing it from being violated.

When Yu died, he passed his throne to his son Qi, who began the family governing system. It meant that the clan community system of primitive society was thoroughly destroyed, and private ownership was officially established; the embryonic form of nationhood began to develop and slave society grew. This was an epoch-making progress in the history of mankind. It was also the essential consequence of the development of productivity of a consumption society from a primitive to a more advanced stage. Former clan tribe leaders became slaveholders and accumulated social surplus wealth. At that time, there had been labor divisions between agriculture and cottage industry, between animal husbandry, agriculture, and the handicraft industry. Mankind had developed from the Stone Age, the Wood Age to the Bronze Age. The productivity of a consumption society had been greatly developed. In other words, in the later years of the primitive clan community system, due to the appearance of surplus product, the appearance of private ownership, the major factors of slave society had grown and developed into a clan tribe community. When Xia Qi inherited the throne of his father and carried out the hereditary system of father passing inheritance to son, tribal leaders immediately followed him. Slave society came into being, and a new social system came into being.

In the slave society, private ownership was legalized; agriculture and the handicraft industry were developed further with more specific divisions of labor; the productivity of the consumption society was greatly enhanced; production was greatly developed; and the living and social consumption of people improved significantly. It also paved the way for the flourishing of culture; therefore, it was historic progress.

From the later tribal community system of primitive mankind to the establishment of the slave society of the Xia Dynasty, the consumption of mankind had developed from the original direct and simple living consumption to the three major consumptions modes including living consumption, social consumption, and production consumption. For example, the governing and administrative consumption of the tribal alliance leaders and the army and weapon production consumption for protecting tribe safety both belonged to the social consumption of that time. There had been copper mining, iron smelting, tool making, and the production of various production tools. Consumables and surplus products required by people were created with tools; it also developed into the phase of bartering.

From the foundation of the Xia Dynasty to 221 B.C. when the First Emperor of the Qin Dynasty extinguished six countries and unified China, the beginning of feudal society, the slave society in China lasted for about 1,800 years. With the development in productivity of a consumption society in slavery era, mankind went beyond the Bronze Age to the consumption phase of the Iron Age.

Dynasty replacement in slave society

Jie, the last monarch of the Xia Dynasty, was a famous tyrant in Chinese history. In the middle and lower reaches of the Yellow River, Shangqiu, in the Henan Province nowadays, there was a tribe called Shang with Shang Tang as the leader. Shang was powerful and was supported by many vassal states in the east who hoped Shang Tang would lead them to fight against the brutal reign of Xia Jie. Finally, the Xia Dynasty was replaced by Shang with the leadership of Tang. The Xia dynasty had ruled for about 500 years from the 21st century B.C. to the 16th century B.C.

There were, altogether, 24 monarchs in the Shang Dynasty, which was overthrown by King Wen of Zhou and his son King Wu of Zhou because of the tyranny of King Zhou of Shang. After his success and the establishment of the Zhou Dynasty, King Wu divided the country territory into hundreds of vassal states. By the Spring and Autumn Period, fewer than 100 vassal states were left, with only a dozen bigger ones such as Qi, Jin, Chu, Qin, Lu, Wei, Yan, Song, Chen, Cai, Zheng, Cao, Wu, and Yue. Every vassal state dreamed of becoming an overlord, so bigger states' striving for supremacy was an important characteristic of the Spring and Autumn Periods. A dozen bigger states contested intensely, resulting in five overlords who appeared successively, and who had been named the Five Overlords in the Spring and Autumn Periods in historic records. They were Earl Huan of Qi, Earl Wen of Jin, Earl Xiang of Song, Earl Mu of Qi, and King Zhuang of Chu, another way of saying that these men were the first overlords. The reason why Qi had become the earliest champion is directly related to the assistance of Guan Tzu. As the prime minister of Qi, Guan Tzu (about 725–645 B.C.) was a famous politician, militarist, ideologist, and economist in the Spring and Autumn Periods.

Guan Tzu, Shang Yang, and the First Emperor of Qin

Guan Tzu

Guan Tzu was named as Yiwu, with the alias Zhong. While he was prime minister of Qi for more than 40 years, Guan Tzu carried out a series of reforms in the economy, politics, and military. He paid much attention to economic development. To develop the economy, he first broke the restriction of the nine-square field system and took the advanced measure reviewing fields and taxing them. He suggested that the tax be levied according to the grade of the fields, which enhanced the use of poor fields and facilitated the development of production. Guan Tzu actively advocated the fishing and salt industry. He encouraged fish and salt trade by allowing fish and salt to be exported without taxation. He appointed fishing and salt officials and iron officials, developing the salt and iron industries with the strength of government. He minted and managed coins, emphasizing the development of commerce and the handicraft industry. He also set a 'light and heavy nine prefectures' system, collecting and distributing commodities according to the harvest and needs of the people in order to adjust prices. In this way, state wealth increased greatly, thus laying the economic foundation for the hegemony of Qi over other states.

In politics, Guan Zhong carried out the policy of 'three categories of labor in state and five Bi in rural area'. He restructured the original administration organization, setting 21 divisions of labor in the state, in three categories – three for industry, three for commerce, and 15 for civil service. He set five bi (regions or rural areas outside the capital city), each with officials to manage them. He also designated living areas for scholars and farmers, manufacturers and businessmen, and managed citizens by the household system. People were forbidden to migrate freely, which strengthened domestic governance.

Guan Zhong further carried out military reform, following the principle of 'doing domestic affairs with military command'. He expected peasants to combine the roles of soldier and farmer, and in so doing unified military organization and administration, so they were engaged in production in peacetime and could fight in wartime. He also invented the method of expiating crime by handing in weapons as well as copper and iron, so as to enrich state armaments. Guan Zhong also established a system to identify and select talents, prescribing those talents should be recommended from every fen, or they would be punished for the crime of 'shielding wisdom' or 'shielding talents'. A scholar could be promoted as a Shang, a zhizan (assistant), after three examinations and selection processes, giving some common people a chance to rise in status.

Guan Tzu assisted Prince Huan of Qi in promoting the rapid development of living consumption, social consumption, and production consumption of Qi with the power of the state, which indicated that the feudal social system had been established in the vassal state of Qi and slave society had been abolished.

Shang Yang

In 359 B.C., Shang Yang carried out reforms for the first time under the support of Prince Xiao of Qin by:

- abolishing the crown prince and the system of inheriting rank and property
- implementing a household organizing system and the practice of guilt by association
- awarding military achievement and prohibiting private fights
- encouraging farming and weaving
- encouraging an individual peasant economy.

It was prescribed that any family with more than two sons should break up the family and live apart when the sons became adults. They should make a living on their own without dependence on others, or double taxation should be paid.

In 350 B.C., Qin moved its capital to Xianyang and Shang Yang began to carry out reforms for the second time:

- He implemented the county system, whereby villages and towns were combined into counties. With unified planning, 31 counties were set in the state, each with a county magistrate and minister who were appointed and dismissed by the king of the state.
- He abolished the nine-square system, the field system of slave society, and opened crisscross crisscross boundaries between squares. He encouraged the cultivation of wild fields, acknowledging the private ownership of fields, allowing the selling and purchasing of fields, and levying taxes according to the space of the land.
- He unified the system of weights and measures, promoting domestic economic contact.
- The laws of Qin were formulated according to Law Sutra of Li Kui, and followed nationwide.
- Poetry books were burned.
- Tourism for the purpose of study was prohibited.

The two reforms of Shangyang were great a shock to slave holders. They strengthened the newly born landlord, developed the feudal economy, enhanced military power, intensified the control over people, and stabilized the social order. Qin, once poor and backward, became the most advanced, powerful, and prosperous state among various vassal states at that time, enabling the First Emperor of Qin to unify six states later.

The First Emperor of Qin

The First Emperor of Qin unified China, marking the success of the feudal society revolution. Ying Zheng, the king of Qin, extinguished the six vassal states and became the emperor of the first feudal country in Chinese history. He divided the country into 36 regions, each of which had counties. Three officials who were directly appointed by the central government administered every region. The central government consisted of several important official positions, including the prime minister, grand censor, military official, court official, and interior official, who assisted the emperor in ruling the country. All these officials were appointed, dismissed, and transferred by the emperor. They were paid by the national treasury and the positions could not be inherited.

The First Emperor of Qin had reunified currencies, weights and measures, 'copper tracks', and characters, all of which were beneficial for reinforcing national unification and the further development of society, economy, and culture. It was the greatest contribution made by the First Emperor of Qin.

After the First Emperor of Qin founded the first dynasty of the feudal social system in China, Chinese feudal dynasties lasted for nearly 2,100 years from 221 B.C. to August 1905. The Chinese bourgeois revolution led by Sun Yat-sen pulled the Qing Dynasty down, resulting in the ending of the Chinese feudal social system. It was the result of class revolution, which was caused by the obstruction of the superstructure of the Qing Dynasty to the development of the three major consumptions, the serious lack of adaptation of production relations to the development of productivity of a consumption society and the serious lack of adaptation of the superstructure to the development of the economic foundation. During 2,100 years of feudal society and dynasty replacement, the major factors of Chinese capitalist society had developed constantly. In the end, the feudal social system collapsed by means of revolution and a bourgeois democratic state was founded. Finally, the task of Chinese democratic revolution was finished under the leadership of the Chinese Communist Party. China then developed into a socialist system.

Japan and Britain in western society entered capitalist society through changes in feudal society, while the United States entered the capitalist social system through the war of revolution and the Civil War against the slavery system. Other countries such as the Netherlands, France, and Germany entered capitalist social system by revolutionary war against the feudal system.

To sum up, during the long process of historic development and advancement since primitive people began to create consumables, the social system of primitive clans and tribes was created at first, and then slave society was created following the development of living consumption, social consumption, and production consumption. During the development process of three major consumptions in slave society, feudal society was created. And during the long development process of three major consumptions in feudal society, capitalist society was created. However, the development process of three major consumptions in capitalist society would surely give rise to capitalist–socialist society. The development of the three major consumptions in capitalist–socialist society is sure to create a more advanced social system (Marxists believe it should be socialism).

However, during the process of creating a social system, the three major consumptions also created countries and their superstructure. At the same time, the superstructure represents the gross economic foundation of society, the gross production relations, and the gross productivity of a consumption society, and it influences and acts on the three major consumptions.

The process of the three major consumptions' creating the progress of civilization and the social system is a movement of the contradictory unity of opposites. The very process moves from partial quantitative change to qualitative change. Meanwhile, the process is a development of the cycle of affirmation and negation.

On one hand, the process of the three major consumptions initiating and driving the development of social civilization progress is attributed to the positive impact of superstructure, and the superstructure can exert a negative impact at the same time. On the other hand, the development process of the three major consumptions' creating and driving the process of social civilization is filled with the contradiction of social opposites and unity. During the development and movement process of the contradiction of social opposites and unity, there are laws of partial quantitative change to qualitative change and of the cycle of affirmation and negation. Because of this, society has been driven by consumption to develop and advance for over 5,000 years (maybe nearly 10,000 years) from the primitive society of clan tribal community to slave society. It took more than 2,100 years for civilization to advance from a slave society to a feudal society, and more than 2,000 years to develop from a feudal society to a capitalist society. Therefore, the cultural advancement and development of a society is slow.

Since mankind entered the period of capitalist society and socialism, owing to the development and never-ending change of science and technology and the productivity of a consumption society; democracy in politics and market competition in the economy; the relative justice and equality of the development of social legalization; respect for humanism; and the increased ability to acknowledge and understand various rules, the three major consumptions of mankind have developed rapidly. The gross social wealth created by the productivity of consumption society in the last 300 years is much more than the summation of wealth created in the history of mankind before feudal society ended.

Section 3 Generation of production consumption and class

After mankind entered the later period of tribal society, because of the needs of consumption, industrial division began to develop, such as agricultural crop planting, livestock raising and animal husbandry, and the cottage handicraft industry. Captives of war were not killed but preserved as slaves, while tribal chieftains became slaveholders. In other words, the primary social factors of slave society had appeared and grown up in the long period of the later tribal community. Later, mankind entered the slave society period through reform or revolution, and slaveholder class and the slave class developed.

During the long development period of slave society, production consumption division was grew further. With the development of private ownership, in the process the exchange of labor surplus consumption product, the production and exchange of consumption commodity appeared and industrial divisions became further delineated. The development of farming promoted the generation of a rising landlord class and farming slaves. As livestock feeding and animal husbandry developed, slave holders and slaves in animal husbandry appeared. As the production consumption in handicraft mills and workshops developed, workshop owners and the working class developed. In other words, the social factors of feudal society were generated and grew in slave society.

In the later period of slave society, along with the development of the three major consumptions of mankind, the further division of production consumption industries and the further division of production, the landlord class developed. Members of an employee class were employed to specialize in agriculture and the workshop owner and working classes also grew in number. During the exchange of surplus products, the production of industrial commodity and commodity exchange, the production owner class, the working class, and the commerce class developed. Thus the elements of feudal society developed from a slave society and mankind entered the feudal society through social change and revolution.

During the long development process of a feudal society, especially during its later period, development of new technical productivity resulted from the development of productivity in general consumption society. Thanks to the convenience of currency, there was rapid development of special commodities. In turn, currency controlled the production of consumption commodity and the exchange of consumption commodity exchange; industrial production division was clearer and more detailed.

The invention and wide application of the steam engine caused the first industrial revolution. After intensive production, consumption in industry was created, the commodity production consumption of capital and the consumption commodity exchange of capital began a new historic stage, with new bourgeois and working classes. Capitalist society was generated through social reform and revolution, the renewed civilized and advanced historical phase.

The capital production process disclosed by Marx brought about the law of surplus value, which was a great discovery; however, it is not only applicable to capitalists' exploiting workers. The law of surplus value exists during the development process of every developing and advancing society. A society cannot advance and develop without surplus value.

To sum up, classes emerged as the consequence of the development of the productivity of the consumption society, of the division and further division of production, the production mode, production type, and industrial division of the possessors of means of production, the appearance of property owners and proletarians. Because of the difference in the mode of acquiring social wealth of mankind between social groups, as well as the difference in social living consumption status, groups of people gradually form various classes.

Every class or social stratum formed by society possesses social wealth by different modes. The amounts of their wealth vary, leading to unfairness and severe unfairness, and eventually resulting in class contradiction. The settlement of these contradictions depends on national policies and laws for wealth distribution. Unfairness must be solved on the basis of policies and laws. When serious unfairness threatens the survival and living consumption of those without property, intense class contradiction and struggle is engendered and the national regime would be endangered. Therefore, adjusting the distribution of social wealth is not only an economic problem, but also a political issue.

Section 4 The origin of consumption, family, private ownership, and state

Consumption and family

Ever since the emergence of mankind is the process of mankind's desire and demand for consumables, and creating consumables requires group strength and the strength of certain social organizations. Clans, the group that formed in the beginning on the basis of blood, were divided and developed into tribes. Family developed later based on blood relationships. Due to the development of livestock husbandry, agriculture, and the development of the cottage handicraft industry, the labor division within the family further developed. Men began to shoulder heavy physical tasks and social responsibility, so men held the dominant positions in the family, and the patriarchal blood kin was generated. That was how the earliest social kin, the matrilineal family, was replaced by the patriarchal blood family, which has lasted until now.

Engels (1972) once discussed the development of the family system as follows:

> The development of family in primitive history lay in the process of constantly narrowing the range. In the beginning, sexual mutual marriage was popular within the whole tribe, then exclusion began from close relatives to remote relatives, and in the end, any group marriage form with only affinity relation became impossible in practice, leaving only a loosely connected couple whose marriage would cease when disconnected. This point has been proved by the practice of every nation in this development stage.

We have had a clearer understanding of the development of mankind from the influence of living consumption and production consumption on the generation and development of the family as well as the development and advancement of sexual marriage.

Consumption, private ownership, and nations

In *The Origin of the Family, Private Property and the State*, Engels penetratingly discussed the origin and development of sexual life and family in clans and tribes, the origin and development of clans or tribes, the generation and development of private ownership, the generation of surplus products and commodity exchange, and the generation of country in the time of the western clan tribe. In his discussion, Engels stated that the generations of Greek and Roman states grew from the development and advancement of slave society, and countries of slave societies were created via social changes. This was identical to the generation of family and the generation and development of private ownership in the social system of the clan or tribe community in primitive China. However, this was not true for Germany. Germans had a large population and little consumption resource in the area they occupied. The rapidly increasing population could not meet the requirement of their three major consumptions. Most of them had once served as mercenaries and were good at fighting. Their clans were constantly expanding their regional consumption resources by destroying consumption wealth and consumption resources of other regions during long-term wars. They robbed the Romans of two-thirds of all the Roman fields and dominated when the Roman state was decaying. Thus the country of the Germans was born.

Comparing China and the western world, we have seen that during the long period of the development from the living consumption of ape men, production consumption to social consumption, blood-related family, clan or tribe developed. Private ownership developed with the generation and production of surplus products. A large number of captives of war became slaves, making the chieftains of clans or tribes slave holders. The production and consumption patterns in slave society also came into being. The generation and more rapid development of private ownership inevitably resulted in commodity exchange and production consumption. In the beginning, bartering was carried out between individuals and between groups, exchanging surplus and desired consumption commodities. During the consumption exchange process of bartering, a special form of commodity, currency, was created. From then on, all the ordinary commodities have been exchanged by using currency as an exchangeable equivalent. Mankind entered a new stage of civilization at that time.

During this development process, production consumption and communal social consumption in the clan were created. Owing to the unbalanced development between clans or tribes, some clans or tribes became strong; with an increase in their consumption needs, they began to start wars of aggression to destroy the consumption wealth and consumption resource of weak clans or tribes so as to expand their own territory and satisfy their own consumption demand. Therefore, aggression and anti-aggression wars between clans or tribes occurred continually. Because of the wars, some clans or tribes either were extinguished or became new members, slaves, of another clan or tribe. As the three major consumptions drove the development and advancement of primitive society, clans and tribes were created with slave holders as an exploiting class. Slaves, as an exploited class, were also created, and countries based on a slave society developed at the same time.

In the countries of slave societies, kings were selected from slave holders within a family inheritance system, while the non-hereditary system or recommendation-election system in the stage of the tribal commune had been abolished. Reviewing several thousand years' history of slave society and feudal society, the fundamental and basic contradiction between the opposing class and the opposed class had never changed, because economic foundation is the private ownership of the means of production. The nature of society could not be fundamentally changed before the economic foundation of the means of production developed into social capital and public capital. All these were completed by the development and progress of the three major consumptions in human society and the constant change and revolution of society.

The nature of state power has developed and advanced into the democratic election system from the hereditary monarchy system in slave society and feudal society. Countries with developed capital and economic foundations such as the United States, German, Japan, Britain, and France had democratic election systems featuring a separation of executive, legislative, and judicial powers. The leadership in a socialist country represents the interests of people, the advanced national productivity of a consumption society, production relations of a consumer society, and the advanced culture of the people. It does not have any private interest apart from these (no economic foundation of means of production). It has been so far the most advanced social stage in the historical development of mankind.

The United Nations was founded on October 24, 1945. Though it has not been able to represent the real interests of people in various countries, it symbolizes the progress of human society.

In conclusion, the history of mankind is the history of the development and progress of the three major consumptions of mankind. In order to survive, mankind needs living consumption materials and must constantly create production consumption material. During the process of asking for living consumption material and creating production consumption materials, production consumption of new living consumption and of social consumption has been created. The three major consumptions have promoted and enhanced the progress of living consumables. The new consumables and consumption patterns constantly created in scientific research, production, and consumption are the development and progress of human consumption, which has created human society. When a country represents the interests of people, protects and promotes the constant and rapid development of its economic foundation, liberates productivity of the consumption society constantly, promotes its development, and makes production relations suit the development of the productivity of the consumption society, the three major consumptions develop rapidly in the country's economy, driving the national economy, politics, culture, and civilization progress to develop rapidly. The country flourishes and people live in peace. There is prosperity and powerfulness.

Section 5 National distribution, and the contradiction between consumers and social harmony

The cause for consumption unfairness and inequality

Since the generation of private ownership when mankind implemented a slave society, there has been unfairness in people's consumption and inequality in living. The three major consumptions drove private ownership society to develop from the slave society to the feudal society and then to capitalist society. Though mankind had developed from barbarous times to civilized times, private ownership has not changed. Even though socialism was established in socialist countries, including China, the social private ownership system has not been thoroughly destroyed. Therefore, a consumption contradiction between people still exists. Currently, we are still in the primary stage of socialist society; the commodity production of capital and the commodity exchange of capital must be allowed to exist. The whole of society is involuntarily related to capital commodity production and the productivity of a consumption society. At this stage, society has to carry out the principle of distribution according to work and production factors, and the principle of macro control on repeated redistribution of social wealth. However, due to the differences between consumers and between individual consumers and consumption groups, contradictions and conflicts are sure to emerge.

Extreme inequality and unfairness between people has always existed, and this is reflected in the living consumption of people in society as a difference in purchasing power. This difference depends on the level of social wealth acquired by people during the process of social labor. People gain social wealth in different modes and possess different amounts of social wealth, resulting in different consumption levels – often serious unfairness and inequality. This is the reason for the unfairness of social class.

Serious consumption unfairness and class struggle

In the development process of the three major consumptions, a few slaveholders, landlords, and state superstructures that represented their interests possessed the social wealth created. The superstructure of a country represents gross social economy, gross social consumption, social productivity, and gross social production relations. It should redistribute state-possessed social wealth among laboring people, so as to protect the elevation of the living consumption level of all laboring people and to stimulate the enthusiasm of laboring people to create the three major consumptions. If the superstructure of the country does this properly, laborers will be enthusiastic about their work, and there will be rapid development in the civilized progress of the three major consumptions in society. If not, there will be serious social consumption inequality. The people are the foundation of the superstructure of the country. The regime cannot be stable if the foundation is damaged and shaken.

Building a harmonious society

The way for a state superstructure to adjust the contradiction between consumers is to build a harmonious society. It is the responsibility of the country to manage the gross social wealth with its power, to control and adjust the collection of social wealth and the relative wealth of people through taxation, administration, and various economic means, to solve the living consumption security of vulnerable groups through the second and third redistribution of gross social wealth, and to support poor people to shake off poverty and become rich through the means of policy and poverty alleviation. It is a huge task, which cannot be solved by theoretical concepts but by social practice. It is a matter of moving from practice to theory with the theory directing the practice. It is an important process of social advancement and development requiring constant practice.

Building a harmonious society in China

As a socialist country with Chinese characteristics, the way for China to adjust the contradiction between consumers is to build a harmonious society. Since the implementation of the policy of reform and opening up in 1978, China has followed one focus and two basic points and followed the theory, line, and principle of allowing some people to become rich first and then driving the whole nation to become rich. China has followed the socialist market economy with Chinese characteristics. With the reaction of state power, the three major consumptions have been pushed to develop rapidly. The development of the three major consumptions drives the rapid development of the entire social economy and the process of social civilization. However, imbalances of development have also occurred, which is natural and inevitable. It is totally different from the egalitarian distribution policy in a planned economy. The country of a communist party that represents the interests of the people has realized these problems and has been solving them reasonably and scientifically step by step:

1. For the collection, management, and distribution of gross social wealth, China has established comprehensive and systematic tax policies, which are being designed and developed.
2. A minimum income is guaranteed for laborers. According to the provisions of laws and regulation, the country has enhanced laborers' status during the process of production consumption and the labor process in management and service industries according to the laws and regulations. A system has been established for a regular minimum wage standard, which is developing.
3. There is compulsory education. Among 1.3 billion Chinese people, a free education system has been implemented in primary schools and junior schools. As for vocational secondary schools, high schools, colleges, and universities, the basic expense for educational consumption and the allowances for poverty stricken students are implemented and guaranteed by the central government.
4. For national university research and education and major scientific research units, the country has increased investment with the charge of social consumption.
5. For consumption on utility and public welfare projects, the country has provided allowances.
6. For regions of lower living consumption, the country has allocated special funds from national finance to provide help for the alleviation and elimination of poverty. The country has also formulated relevant policies, such as free training in labor skills, scientific support, and poverty elimination.
7. For poor urban residents, the country has allocated salvation funds to guarantee their minimum living consumption.
8. Every year, the country allocates considerable relief funds for border areas, helping them shake off poverty and guaranteeing a certain living consumption level for them.
9. The country advocates charity, mobilizing social power to help poor and vulnerable groups.

The country adjusts the contradiction between social consumers and consumption through various tax policies and administrative means. Meanwhile, the country carries out civilization and cultural education in society, advocates mutual respect and love to solve contradictions, and creates social harmony.

Germany adjusts the contradiction between consumers through tax policy

Germany is a capitalist country with a developed economy, which implements a system of high taxation and high welfare. Every individual or enterprise in Germany with income pays tax. Germany taxes many items and there are high tax rates with comprehensive coverage. Meanwhile, many policies have been formulated specific to the objective of domestic economic and social development to adjust interest relations. Payroll tax is the main source of taxation in Germany.

It is reasonable for Germany to take individual income as the main source of national taxation revenue for these reasons:

- Levying tax on individuals is helpful to enhance the tax consciousness of citizens.
- Because of the rigidity of wages, fiscal revenue of the government has a stable and reliable foundation with a certain degree of increase.
- The contradiction between consumers' wealth can be adjusted effectively.
- People can supervise and encourage government public servants. All the expenses of the civil servants and the governments – social consumption – are met by taxpayers. It is thus natural for taxpayers to supervise the behavior and consumption of governments and civil servants.

The taxation system in Germany plays a decisive role in economic development and social harmony. However, it also has great negative influences:

- High taxation causes the high cost of production consumption cost and relatively slow development of technology, resulting in the reduction of the competitive capacity of production consumption. The exporting of industrial products is affected, which is unfavorable for Germany, which has been relying on exporting industrial products export for a long time.
- It is not favorable to attract foreign investment.
- The social welfare system provided by the German government for citizens has played an important role in narrowing the wealth gap and guaranteeing civil rights, but it has reduced the reemployment enthusiasm of the unemployed to a certain extent, sometimes they even pick and choose jobs.

The United States adjusts the contradiction between consumers through tax laws

The tax revenue administration system in the United States can be specifically divided into federal tax, state tax, and local tax. The three levels of taxes are levied according to the laws agreed by the state assembly; counties and cities can levy taxes according to the legislation of the assembly under the precondition of satisfying the state constitution. Since taxation is related to everyone's interest, laws related to taxation are usually strict. The legislation can only be passed with the agreement of a majority; sometimes the decision is made by a general vote of citizens.

Federal tax and social security tax make up the main body of American taxation. In the United States few items are taxed but there are complex levels of taxation. Besides, as for sales tax in circulation, tax payment is added to the sales payment at a given rate, which is a clear characteristic of consumer direct contribution. Therefore, individuals pay tax directly in the United States and tax in the United States is mainly paid directly by individuals. No wonder that American citizens are proud of their contribution as taxpayers to the states. The inheritance tax rate in the United States is 55%, and tax has to be paid before inheritance.

There are several aspects in American taxation that reduce the differences in wealth between consumers. One important method is that the tax rate goes up as income increases, so as to reduce the burden on low-income earners and to control the too rapid increase of the income of high-income earners. The most basic principle is that people with more income pay more tax and that people with low income get a rebate on the tax they pay. Individual income tax rates vary depending on other family members, especially the number of children.

Japan adjusts wealth inequalities between consumers through tax laws

In Japan central tax and local tax are divided clearly, and the legislative levying right is concentrated in the center. Based on the organizational structure of the Japanese government, the taxation system is accordingly divided into central taxes and local taxes, wherein local taxes are divided into county taxes and village taxes. The taxation by the central government mainly comprises income tax in direct taxes, corporation tax and consumption tax in direct tax, and these three taxes add up to about 70% of the central tax.

The tax in counties mainly comprises the main tax items of county tax and utility tax, and these two taxes occupy 65% of the total revenue. The main tax items in village government are villager tax and fixed assets tax, and these two add up to 80% of the taxation revenue of the village. At present, within the total amount of Japanese fiscal revenue, the revenue actually controlled by central government has fallen from 60% in the past to about 30%, while the total revenue actually controlled by local government has increased from 30% to 60%. With the expansion of Japanese local government, taxation domination and usage incline towards local government.

Taxation in Germany, the United States, and Japan

We have listed the above situations in Germany, the United States, and Japan, which are capitalist countries with developed economies in the current world. The superstructure of the three countries make use of state power and tax laws to levy and redistribute social wealth, to develop national economy and social civilization, to adjust the serious unfairness, irrationality, social non-harmony and instability between citizens and between consumers caused by income, so as to reduce serious inequality in wealth among consumers. Tax laws have played a very important role in adjusting social wealth distribution. Fundamental change has taken place in the social situation in capitalist democratic politics and pure private ownership in society when capitalist society developed just 300 years ago:

1. Capitalist society is advancing and developing constantly. The difference between it and the slave and feudal society in the past several thousand years is that political democracy with a tenure system has replaced the former absolute monarchy in politics. The democratic regime is widely supervised by all the citizens to a certain extent, and supervision can influence the regime, which makes the state regime better represent diverse interests of various classes and strata of citizens. Moreover, national laws can be modified and perfected constantly during the process of social development and progress. All these could not have happened in the early period of capitalist society.
2. The countries have been hurt by economic crisis in the process of the development of capitalism and have been able to realize that the three major consumptions are natural rules to drive economic development (unconscious realization). They adjust to it and master it with state power, so as to bring the positive effect of natural economic rules into play and overcome its negative effect at the same time. Laws, economic

levers, and administrative means are used as macro adjustment or macro planning, to supplement the development of market financial and economic rules.

3. The social difference between the rich and the poor is adjusted by the policy and means of social wealth redistribution, reducing the difference in wealth among consumers and classes, so as to guarantee social stability.
4. During citizens' working process, minimum wage income of every laborer per month is guaranteed and prescribed by law, so as to ensure a minimum living consumption level.
5. The countries guarantee the minimum living consumption level of citizens by providing living consumption security for unemployment.
6. The countries develop public welfare services to guarantee the increase of living consumption level of citizens with lower income.
7. Private enterprises transfer to commodity production and exchange consumption of social capital. For example, Siemens in Germany has transferred from private shares to social capital, and the family share of Siemens hardly existed. This symbolized the entrance into social capitalization in that country.

All the policies and measures taken by the countries to increase the living consumption levels of citizens with the lowest income are helpful to the harmony and stability of society. Even though the policies of various developed capitalist countries are different, they have a common ground: to protect the minimum living consumption level of citizens with the lowest income, so as to stabilize social order. The above-mentioned three countries have the same goal on this point.

All these changes are advancements made during the process of the development of capitalist society and are essential in the generation and development of socialist social factors in capitalist society.

Consumption creates scientific research and science and technology

The consumption development process creates new technology constantly; while new technology is constantly transformed into productivity, the production process, production relations and productivity combine and create production, product, consumption pattern, and consumption level. The levels of the three major consumptions are reflected as civilization progress in that time, as shown in Figure 10.1.

	Representative technology	Type of civilization
Stone Age	Technology in the primitive age of mankind	Early civilization
Ceramics Age	Technical progress in the primitive age of mankind	The age of early civilization
Bronze Age	Mining and smelting technologies	The age of bronze civilization
Iron Age	New technical progress had been achieved in mining and smelting of mankind	The age of iron civilization
Age of the steam engine	Human technology had developed into the time of mechanical and industrial production	The age of modern civilization
Electric appliances, telephone, telegraph, diesel engines such as internal combustion engines, steel making technology, and atom technology	Modern agriculture, industry, national defense, and social life with modern technologies	The age of higher civilization and progress
Age of electronic information	High and new technology entered the age of intelligent of production, living, and social consumptions	The age of advanced high civilization and progress

Figure 10.1 Technology and civilization from the Stone Age to the age of electrical information

Figure 10.1 shows the process of technology creating social civilization progress from the historical development process of human consumption creating technology. The technology of each age represents the degree of civilization progress of that time.

Consumption and development since the 18th century

The age of the steam engine

Since the invention of the steam engine in the 18th century, a consumption material productivity, there has been tremendous development and wide use of production consumption such as in sailing, mining, transportation, smelting, tool manufacturing, spinning and weaving, and so on. The productivity of consumption society has developed dramatically, giving rise to the industrial revolution and the age of the steam engine.

The age of electrification

Since the 19th century, electrical power has been widely used and has forcefully promoted the generation and development of a series of new industries such as electrodynamics, electrometallurgy, electro-machining, and telecommunication. The age of electrification came with the development of technological social productivity such as the invention of the internal combustion engine and diesel engine, and science and technology like organic-synthesis chemical technology.

The electron, the computer, and information production develop towards intellectualized consumption

Since the 1940s, the modern scientific revolution of atomic energy technology, electronic computer technology, and space technology has developed rapidly. The productivity of the consumption society has developed its greatest historical stage. There has been unprecedented progress as computers, and international and web-based information are used for intellectual purposes.

Science and technology

The wave of technological revolution is promoting the course of human development with unprecedented impact. Technological competition between countries is at the core of economic and military competition and even national strength, proving the assertion that 'science and technology are the primary productive forces'.

Productivity is the capacity of human beings to reform and conquer nature and acquire productive materials from production consumption to scientific research (the awareness and creation process of consciousness, perception, wisdom, and inspiration) consumption:

> Productivity = [(consumption + laborer + means of labor + subject of labor) + science and technology] + organizing process of production management

As will be readily seen, science and technology are the most important elements of productivity. The level of productivity depends on the content and degree of application science and technology. In all ages, the application of each scientific achievement has developed social productivity, wherein the application of high and new technology achievement has developed productivity with great progress. Furthermore, it has changed the old production mode and living mode and created new production modes and living modes, created new civilization and new culture, promoted political, economic, military, and social activities in society to move towards a new pattern – a higher and higher form.

The development of the entire society and even every social field is scientific revolution caused by new knowledge and science and technology created by consumption consciousness, wisdom, scientific technology, and consumption itself. The assertion 'science and technology are the primary productive forces' is wise. Productivity cannot make progress without new inventions in technology. Though the human is the most active factor in productivity, the production condition will be restricted and development speed will be limited without science and technology.

However, science and technology are not directly equivalent to productivity; they must be transformed through certain conditions:

1. Scientific achievements must satisfy consumption demands. Moreover, the larger the consumption demand is, the larger the ability of transforming to productivity is and the larger the transforming value will be. But the lower the consumption demand of consumers, the lower the ability of transforming to productivity is and the smaller the transforming value will be.
2. Mature new technology and high and new technology (new technology and high and new technology that can be put into scale production) are available. Achievement in the laboratory without a successful pilot test cannot be transformed into productivity. It is an important link in the transformation of achievement in the laboratory to be successful in the pilot test.
3. In the development of new technical achievement, the conditions for development and production should be satisfied, including the funds (minimum fund), equipment, and tools required in the technology development and all the supplementary conditions. If a minimum fund as well as corresponding equipment and tools and supplementary conditions are not available, even the best scientific achievements cannot be transformed into productivity.
4. People with talent are needed to develop and produce technology. Talent is the most active, revolutionary, vital, and crucial factor in the transformation from science and technology to productivity.
5. Only when market sales service talent is available can the new technical achievement be acknowledged and accepted by consumers and be transformed rapidly into practical productivity.

6. Advanced organizational process of production management is also necessary for science and technology to be transformed to productivity and to produce the proper effect. We can easily find out in the formula of productivity that the organizational process of production management has multiple relations with productivity. If the whole organizational process of production management is scientific, the power of the transformation from science and technology to productivity will increase several times over; otherwise productivity energy will be reduced exponentially.

To sum up, since the beginning, mankind has out of instinct used consumables and constantly created new needs for consumption and desires, perceptions, and wisdoms. During its long history mankind has been engaged in living consumption, creating new consumption of production tools – new productivity of consumption society. This has created living consumables and social consumables in the process of social civilization. The survival and development of mankind is not possible without consumption, to say nothing of the process of human civilization. The three industrial revolutions show that consumption is the source of the process of power of social civilization.

Section 6 Consumption creates scientific research and science and technology and drives the progress of social civilization

War is consumption. It is a form of social consumption. Futurologist Toffler (1970) suggested that wars in the future, either in planning or imagination, will consume the tax we are paying today. War is undoubtedly a pure consumption action, which consumes human, material, and financial resources. Its final 'product' is not a material product whose value has been realized but national security (including national wealth and power for some countries). Military expenditure (including army expenditure and war expenditure) is deducted from state finance and directly enters the military consumption process (living, equipment, and maintenance), most of which is used in the consumption of special products for the military and does not enter the reproduction process as productive investment. Marx (1867) said that in a direct economic sense, a country's producing war industrial products was like investing part of their capital in water. It can be seen that war is not only a kind of direct consumption, but also consumption with a huge cost.

Since a class society and alliances among nations developed in human society, there have been two kinds of war. One is the war of domestic class struggle – the revolutionary war between the classes who govern, exploit, and suppress laborers represented by the corrupt superstructure and the classes who are oppressed and exploited to fight against the governing class for the living consumption demand of survival. The other is the war between nations and between the just and the unjust – aggressive war. Its purpose is to plunder and use the consumption resources and consumption wealth of other countries. The purpose of the just war is to protect the consumption resources and consumption wealth of the aggressor country.

No matter what kind of war it is, it consumes social wealth; therefore, war is consumption. On the one hand, war consumes social wealth and destroys social stability, causing huge damage and loss to human life and property, so this is the evil side. On the other hand, war ends corrupt and reactionary governing regimes and founds a new regime. The new regime is a superstructure, which can represent the social economic base, gross productivity of the consumption society, and the gross production relations in society. It can liberate the productivity of consumption society and promote the development of the three major consumptions.

Consumption and war between clan tribes

Early in the period of primitive, clan, or tribal society, war often occurred between clan tribes, with the purpose of destroying natural resources required to survive and the consumption wealth of others, and protecting the tribe's own resources and wealth. War played an important role in the history of the Chinese nation.

Consumption and war in a slave society

The Xia Dynasty was the first slave-society dynasty in China. Jie was the last of the Xia kings. Jie lost the people's living consumption. Shang Tang won the people's heart for living consumption. Army of Shang Tang made such an inexorable march of progress that they beat Jie of Xia in Mingtiao (Fengqiu, Hennan nowadays). The governing of Xia Dynasty was finished. Xia Dynasty lasted for about 500 years from the 21st century B.C. to the 16th century B.C.

The Shang Dynasty was destroyed by the tyranny of King Zhou, who exercised his despotic power after becoming the king, causing the regime's decline. In addition, the subordinate ministers had other plans. King Wen of Zhou stood up to fight against and won people's support for a society of living consumption, and succeeded in defeating the army of King Zhou, with the help of his son, King Wu of Zhou. Thus, overthrew Shang Dynasty and founded Zhou Dynasty. The civilization progress of the three major consumptions in society was promoted during a certain historical stage.

Consumption and war in feudal dynasties

In the later period of the Zhou Dynasty there were difficult wars between lords. Several powers searched for supremacy in the Spring and Autumn Period and the Warring States Period. After the First Emperor of Qin unified China, the slave system ended in China, and the country began to enter its first feudal dynasty. During this period, there was serious war consumption and war promoted the progress of civilization. There came Sun Wu and *The Art of War*, Confucius' traveling around the states, Lao Tzu and *Tao Te Ching*, Guan Zhong, Shang Yang, the Mohist doctrine established by Mo-tse, and so on. All these cultural and political advances have influenced Chinese culture development to the present day.

It was a historic contribution of the First Emperor to unify China. However, the second emperor of the Qin Dynasty was fatuous and power was grasped by Zhao Gao, who killed loyal ministers. The politics was so decadent and rife with corruption that there were severe shortages of consumables. Chen Sheng rose to fight against the Qin Dynasty in Daze Town in July and was beaten and killed in December. The revolt lasted for only half a year, but it aroused all the country to fight against the Qin Dynasty. Many warlords rose, making the decadent Qin Dynasty gradually extinct. Later peasants revolted, because of their inadequate living standards. Xiang Yu, King of Chu, and Liu Bang, King of Han, who were both leaders of peasant revolts, fought for supremacy. Liu Bang won and killed Xiang Yu in the end, then founded the Han Dynasty.

Liu Che, Emperor Wu of Han, decided the general situation through wars

Emperor Wu of Han was an outstanding monarch in Chinese history; he accepted the great Confucian Dong Zhongshu's suggestion of rejecting various schools while honoring Confucianism only, and took culture as the spiritual strength to govern the people. Based on governing through ideology, centralized government came into being.

In order to protect the security of the northern border, to prevent the destruction of the consumption wealth of the Hun lords, and to promote economic development in the frontier areas, Emperor Wu of Han took many significant measures, turning a defensive strategy into large scale anti-aggression wars against Hun. While defeating Hun, Emperor Wu of Han enriched frontier defense through vast immigration. In 138 B.C., he sent Zhang Qian, a famous explorer, to fulfill a diplomatic mission to the Western Regions and ally with Dayuezhi (an ancient tribe) to defend against and attack Hun. Emperor Wu of Han also expanded territory in the south and the west, making the Yue people and a few clans in the southwest mix together better. Emperor Wu of Han migrated the three conquered tribes of Yue to the Yangtze River basin, the Huai River Basin, and the South Sea, making them live together with Han people. They were well gradually assimilated. The situation of general unification which had begun with the First Emperor of Qin was completed. During the process of exploiting the southwest region, Han people popularized and transmitted iron production tools and advanced Han culture to those areas, promoting local economic and cultural development and improving the development of their three major consumptions.

War consumption culture in the Three Kingdoms

War consumption culture in the Three Kingdoms period still has great impact on Chinese history. In the period of the East Han Dynasty, there was corruption and internal, intrigue in officialdom. While being corrupt themselves, officials also tried to fight against each other for power and did not care for the people at all. In 174 A. D., the 20-year-old Cao Cao was appointed as the north official of Luoyang to be responsible for public security in the capital. He formulated regulations, which could not be violated by anybody. The uncle of Qian Shuo, a eunuch who was favored by Emperor Ling of Han, went out at midnight, which violated the command of curfew. He was sent under guard to Cao Cao, who immediately told the guards to beat him to death with sticks according to the command. Order in the capital was greatly improved from then on.

In the later period of the East Han Dynasty, a struggle took place among Cao Cao, Sun Quan, and Liu Bei, resulting in the tripartite confrontation of three kingdoms in the end. It was a period in Chinese history when war culture had huge influence.

The period of the demise of the Sui Dynasty and the flourishing of the Tang Dynasty

Emperor Yang of Sui was very corrupt. Living consumption of the people could not be guaranteed and peasants were struggling hard to survive. Peasant revolts occurred all over the country as peasants asked for living consumption to survive. They would die if they did not rebel. Li Yuan and his sons determined to change sides and fight against the Sui Dynasty. They did their best to destroy the Sui Dynasty thoroughly and then founded the Tang Dynasty.

When Emperor Gao of Tang came to the throne, he designated Li Jiancheng as the crown prince, Li Shimin as King Qin, and Li Yuanji as King Qi. Knowing that he was inferior to Li Shimin in talent, Jiancheng, the crown prince, was so jealous that he conspired with his younger brother Yuanji, King Qi, to kill Li Shimin. Li Shimin started a mutiny in Xuanwumen, seizing the position of crown prince and later inherited the throne. Li Shimin had talent in literature and military affairs. He was good at listening to suggestions from others and using talents properly. He ruled the country wisely, loved his people well, and punished the criminal relatives equally as other criminals who gained the heart of people longing for living consumption. Thus, he created great achievement in his Zhenguan period, the age of the Tang Dynasty.

War consumption by Genghis Khan, the great hero

Genghis Khan, Emperor Tai of Yuan, was named Temujin. After 1201, he conquered several tribes including Tataer, Naiman, Mieercang, and other small tribes for three years in succession; then he beat Zhamuhe and unified the whole Mongolia. In 1206, all the slaveholder lords held a general meeting on the banks of the Enen River. They unanimously supported the 44-year-old Temujin, as the khan of the whole of Mongolia, honored as 'Genghis Khan'. It also symbolized the official establishment of the first unified regime in the history of Mongolia.

After the establishment of the unified Mongolian empire, Genghis Khan began the plan of marching southward and unifying the whole country. In 1218, he sent his army to attack West Liao and then West Xia, defeating the troops of West Xia. In 1211, the Mongolian army attacked Jin and occupied Zhongdu. In 1219, Genghis Khan led his army to invade Hualazimo (the Central Asian part of the Soviet Union, Afghanistan and Iran, nowadays), which had 400,000 soliders, and the wars of invasion and expansion began. The Mongolian troops did not stop until they reached what is Georgia, the Caucasus, and Russia today.

Genghis Khan changed the situation of the long-term struggle and battle among the Mongolian tribes, strengthened economic construction, and played a progressive role in the development of Mongolian society.

War consumption during the Kangxi and Qianlong reigns in the Qing Dynasty

In the later years of Ming Dynasty, politics was getting more and more corrupt and the frontier defense was getting looser and looser. Jianzhou Jurchen, a branch of the Jurchens in northeast China, took the opportunity and expanded their force. Under the leadership of Aisin Gioro Nurhaci, they gradually became strong. In 1616, believing that the time was ripe, Nurhaci came to the throne and honored himself as the khan with the support of the Eight Banners lords. The state title was decided as Great Jin, which was called the Later Jin.

Huangtaiji, the son of Nurhaci, inherited the sovereignity and unified China. The Qing Dynasty came to its heyday during the age of Kangxi, the grandson of Huangtaiji. When Kangxi took over the reign, he eradicated Oboi and began to decide state affairs. He pacified the 'Revolt of the Three Feudatories' and quieted the divisive behavior of Zheng Jing, the son of Zheng Cheng-gong. Then Taiwan and the Pescadores returned to the domination of the Qing Dynasty. Kangxi headed the crusades against Geerdan three times from 1680 to 1697, the captain of Junggar in Sinkiang who always invaded inward. The chaos caused by war was gradually calmed and aggression among northern minorities was prevented. From then on, the Qing Dynasty commanded the whole country and passed to the frontier. Kangxi completed the great undertaking of the unification of the motherland, which had been a great dream of all the people since the Ming Dynasty.

Emperor Qianlong was shrewd in literature and military affairs. He paid much attention to the development and expansion of agriculture and advocated land reclamation, guaranteeing that the consumption demand of the population for grain would be increased year by year. For this, he formulated various policies and measures to develop agriculture and develop the economy. Qianlong emphasized the integrity and unity of the country. He started several wars in frontier regions and suppressed the tribal revolt of Junggar, Hui, and Big and Small Jinchuan. In order to better safeguard the territory, he ordered that the name of Western Regions should be changed to Sinkiang (new territory in meaning), and assigned generals and counselors to Yili to administer the military and governmental affairs in the north and south Tian Mountains; thus the frontier defense in the northwest was permanently solidified.

After the prosperity and growth during the reign of Kangxi and Qianlong, the economic development and overall national strength of China had lagged behind the world because of their prejudice against science and technology. The consumption resource and wealth of China have long been destroyed and divided by conquering imperialist countries.

China was first invaded by the imperialist countries such as the Russian Empire early in the reign of Kangxi. The war for the border area began when the Russians attempted to invade the vast Chinese territory. According to the Treaty of Nerchinsk, signed in 1689, the border between China and the Russia Empire was defined as the Eerzuona River and the Geerbiqi River, and eastward along the Stanovoy Range to the sea. China had the territory east of the rivers and south of the range while Russia had the land west of the rivers and the north of the range. Russia promised to destroy the Albazin fortress and withdraw troops from Chinese territory. There were no border issues for 150 years after that, and the frontier was peaceful.

In the later years of the Qing Dynasty, various imperialist powers began to invade and divide China abetted by the corruption of the Qing Dynasty and the misery of the people. The first Opium War broke out, followed by the indemnity. After the first Opium War ended, western powers signed the Sino–French Treaty of Huangpu, the Sino–British Treaty of Tianjin, the Sino–Russian Treaty of Tianjin, the Boxer Protocol, and the Treaty of Shimonoseki with China. After more than 100 years, the consumption resources of China had been divided up by the world powers, and vast Chinese consumption wealth had been plundered.

During their whole history, feudal dynasties oppressed and exploited the vast laborer class and made it difficult for them to survive. The repeated revolts of the laboring masses, such as the peasant uprising led by Li Zicheng and the huge peasant uprisings of the Taiping Heavenly Kingdom, demonstrated how the laborer class rebelled for the purpose of guaranteeing its own survival and living consumption.

The rise of the Chinese bourgeois democratic revolution finally changed the above-mentioned violent system of dynastic replacement. Under the leadership of Sun Yat-sen, the temporary government of the Republic of China was founded in Nanjing on New Year's Day 1912. Sun Yat-sen augustly took the oath of office with the people's approval. Feudal imperialism, which had lasted for more than 2,000 years, had collapsed at last. The ancient land of China became a bourgeois republic. It was a great milestone in history.

Consumption and war in capitalist society

In 1927, Chiang Kai-shek betrayed Sun Yat-sen's three guiding principles of allying with Russia, allying with the Communist Party, and supporting workers and peasants and began to slaughter communists and progressive workers and peasants. Owing to their survival consumption demand, the Chinese Communist Party led workers and peasant masses to carry out nationwide revolts such as Armed Uprising in Nanchang, the Autumn Harvest Uprising and the Guangzhou Uprising, and they began the long-term life-and-death war against people-suppressing reactionaries with Chiang Kai-shek as the leader. During this process of struggle, the War of Resistance against Japan was added then. On October 1, 1949, the proletariat, vast laboring masses and patriots, who had been led by the Chinese Communist Party, gained the victory of the Liberation War and founded the People's Republic of China.

Lenin led the Russian proletariat to overthrow the government of the Russian Empire and founded the first socialist country of Soviet Russia.

The French proletariat carried out the revolutionary struggle of the Paris Commune to fight against the barbarous exploitation through the capitalism, but were eventually suppressed by capitalists.

In the primary capitalist society with pure private ownership, the cruel exploitation of capitalists and resistance through the strikes of proletariat never stopped.

The aggressive war of Japan's occupation and its war consumption

In 1873, the Meiji government issued the Recruiting Order, thoroughly breaking the feudal samurai's privilege to control military affairs and beginning to implement a general compulsory military service system. At the end of the 19th century, as Japan expanded more quickly, the status of the army increased and its political influence gradually exceeded that of the cabinet, and a militarism system was established in Japan.

In 1874, Japan invaded Taiwan and compelled the Qing Dynasty to sign the Treaty of Beijing, an unequal treaty. In 1879, Japan officially absorbed Ryukyu. In 1876, the Japanese government compelled the Korean government to sign the Japanese–Korean Treaty of Reconciliation – the Treaty of Ganghwa – letting Japanese power enter Korea and preparing the way for their invasion of Korea and China later. After the Sino–Japanese War in 1895, the defeated Qing Dynasty was compelled to sign the Treaty of Shimonoseki with Japan, with an indemnity of 30 million tael of silver.

Through the Treaty of Shimonoseki, Japan occupied Taiwan, the Pescadores, and Korea for a long time, deepening their exploitation there, and taking them as a springboard to further invade China. World War I broke out in August 1914. On August 23, Japan declared war against Germany. Fishing in troubled waters, they not only sent troops to seize German power in Shandong, China, but also occupied the Marwill Islands, the Mariana Islands, and the Caroline Islands in the South Pacific under Germany's leadership. From the 9.18 Incident in 1931 to 1932, Japan operated as a puppet government of 'Manchukuo', putting northeast China under Japanese colonial rule.

In 1937, Japan's Hirohito government started an aggressive war against China, beginning with the July 7 Incident and the September 13 Incident. Thereafter, with the increase of Japanese power and fascist's power over the army, Japan set up a fascist alliance with Germany and Italy, and in the end started World War II.

Just as Mao Zedong predicted, Japanese aggression inspired the spirit of the Chinese people to fight. China conducted a difficult anti-aggression war for eight years, breaking the Japanese dream of invading China and dominating East Asia. Many invaded Asian countries were anti-Japan, and there was an anti-fascist movement throughout the world. After the Pearl Harbor Incident, the United States joined the world anti-fascist camp. With the effect of these factors, the process of the death of Japanese imperialism was quickened.

The Russian Empire

During the 100-year history of the Russia Empire from the early 19th century to the early 20th century, invasion never stopped, fuelled by war. Russia endlessly destroyed consumption resources and consumption wealth through war consumption, while wealth was consumed in endless wars.

In April 1828, the Russian Czar Nicolas I started the war against Turkey with 150,000 armed soldiers. In 1830, the Russian Czar sent an army of 5,000 soldiers to suppress the Polish national revolt against Russia. In 1853, in order to obtain greater power along the Black Sea, Russia sent troops into Turkey. The isolated Russia was defeated in the end and compelled to sign a treaty in March 1854. In 1877~1878, the Russian–Turkish War broke out again. Meanwhile, the Russian Empire was intensifying its aggression against its neighboring country in the east – China. Within several decades, Russia seized about 1.5 million square kilometers in the northeast and the west of China and obtained many privileges, which damaged the interests of China. At the end of the 19th century, the national territory of Russia was finally determined. After 350 years of violent annexation and colonized expansion, the territory of Russia had sharply increased from 2.8 million square kilometers to 22.8 million kilometers, making it a huge empire across Asia and Europe. However, Russia's essential weakness was disclosed by the loss of the Japanese–Russian War in 1904.

The revolutionary war and war expansion of the United States

During the 126 years from 1607 to 1733, Britain built 13 colonies along the Atlantic from New Hampshire in the north to Georgia in the south, which later became the 13 original states of the United States. From 1752 to 1755, the population in the colonies sharply increased to 1.06 million.

In October 1765, the delegates from nine colonies held a meeting in New York and passed a law whereby British colonial peoples and local British people would enjoy the same natural rights and freedom, asking the North Americans to resist British trade. Between September 5th and October 26, 1774, the delegates from 12 colonies (no delegate was sent from Georgia) met in Philadelphia to hold the First Continental Congress. General unity was realized. On October 14, the Declaration of Rights was passed, stating that colonies would cease economic relations with Britain, and instead would support the movement to resist trade with Britain. On May 10, 1775, the Second Continental Congress was held in Philadelphia. It was suggested in the Congress that each colony should establish a new government to replace the colonial office. A military decision was passed by the Congress on June 15, 1775, which was to organize and equip an official army (the Continental Army). On July 6 1775, the Declaration on the Reason and Necessity of Force was passed through, alleging that those in the army would 'prefer to die as a free man, rather than live as a slave'.

The American War of Independence had three phases: the war in defensive stage from April 1775 to October 1777; from October 1777 to March 1781, the phase of strategic stalemate started with the symbol of the victory at Saratoga when the main battlefield moved to the southern region; and the strategic counterattack stage from April 1781 to September 1783. On September 3, 1783, Britain and America signed the Treaty of Paris. Britain officially acknowledged the independence of the United States.

The United States expanded its territory westward by way of war, destroying consumption resources. The American frontier rapidly moved west between 1800 and 1860. In the later 18th century and early 19th century, pioneers from western New York State came to the west through Kentucky and Tennessee and to Georgia in the south. Twenty years later, the frontier had moved to Ohio, Indiana, and Illinois and later to Michigan, Wisconsin, and Minnesota in the north, to Louisiana, Alabama, and Mississippi in the south. Later, the United States expanded its territory in two directions. In the southwest, it added Texas in 1845, and gained California, Nevada, New Mexico, and most of Arizona after a war against Mexico during 1847 and 1848 while half of the Mexican territory was destroyed. In the northwest, the United States threatened with diplomatic force and occupied Oregon in 1846. In the end, the two expansion lines met in California, completing its occupation in the west.

The United States gained independence by war consumption, and then expanded the consumption resource of American territory by war consumption.

The Spanish Empire

Spain is in the Iberian Peninsula, the southwest of Europe. The national religion is Catholicism. During the fights against Arabian rule, Spanish Christians formed several small countries, then gradually unified and formed several bigger Catholic countries.

Spain fought against the rule of Arabian kings to liberate Iberia from 1076 to 1492. Spanish troops entered Granada, where the last kingdom of Arabs in Spain resided, and ended the Muslim rule in Western Europe, completing the five-century-long movement of regaining its lost land.

After years of war, Spain gained a great victory and vast territory consumption resources and wealth. However, the huge consumption for wars depleted its state treasury. Queen Isabella even sold her jewels to cover the expense. In 1492, Columbus led three ships Saint-Maria, Pinta, and Nina, and 120 sailors to sail west. They discovered Cuba, Haiti, some other islands and tobacco, and occupied the northern seacoast of Haiti and established the first colony 'La Navidad'. Columbus made three more voyages. He died in Bali in 1506.

Spain conquered the West Indies through war. The islands discovered by Columbus in his first voyage were called the West Indies, to distinguish them from the real India. Half a year after Columbus returned to Spain, he started his second voyage, which was a real colonial journey. Columbus' crew had a fight with local people on arriving in Haiti. The battle was a decisive one in the history of Spanish colonization in America, and a typical event with universal implication in the American Indian genocide history. In 1496, Bartolome Columbus, the younger brother of Columbus, founded Santo Domingo City in Haiti, which was the first permanent Spanish colony in America. In 1502, Obando, a big lord, established the seat of government officially in Haiti. Based in Haiti, the Spanish extended their colonization in all directions. They occupied Puerto Rico in 1508, taking San Juan as the main colonial settlement. They entered Jamaica in 1509. They began the blood conquest in Cuba in 1511 so cruelly that the Spanish Bartolome Falasikasas who went with them was infuriated and thought they should desist. He began a holy war to save the local natives. He was the famous 'Disciple of Indians'. The establishment of San Diego in 1514 marked the completion of the Cuban conquest.

Spain conquered Mexico by war consumption. After establishing themselves in the West Indies, the Spanish began their expansion on American continent. In 1518, Kanlaskesis, Governor of Cuba, decided to send Cortez to conquer Mexico. At the end of 1520, Cortez surrounded the Aztecs with more than 800 Spanish soldiers, 2500 Indian soldiers and 60,000 Indian allied troops who had arrived successively at Cortez's order. The city was occupied on August 13, 1521. At the cost of 240,000 people's death from battle, starvation, and disease in the city, Cortez win the victory over the consumption resources of the invaded territory. After burning the city, the Spanish forced the Aztecs to change the city's name to Mexico City.

The miracle of Spanish Pizarro's conquest of Peru

The Spanish invaded Peru to conquer the Incan Empire. Spanish troops were courageous and good at fighting. The invading troops consisted of only 180 persons and 27 horses. From January 1521 to 1532 they killed the Emperor Atahualpa and founded a colonial government. By 1535, they had occupied all the territory of the Incan Empire and destroyed huge consumption wealth.

Spain conquered the Philippines, realizing the dream of being a global empire in Europe, America, and Asia. After conquering America and Africa by war, the Spanish dreamed of conquering the Philippines and China, founding an Asian colony, realizing a global empire. In April 1571, Legaspi led 230 men on a voyage to Manila in 23 fast ships. In May, he declared that they had occupied Manila, beginning Spanish colonial rule. Afterwards the Spanish gradually occupied other places of Luzon. Philip II realized his dream of occupying Asia and a 'sun-never-set empire'.

Wealth plundering by Spain

Spanish colonists thought that directly destroying Indian wealth was a simple but temporary method. The Spanish planted sugar canes and produced sugar in the colonies, and then they sold the sugar in Europe, creating an industry with high profits. In 1493, the Spanish took livestock to America for the first time, beginning stockbreeding in America. Spain also cultivated mining resources in their colonies.

The history of Spanish colonial development was one of aggression and bloody national war and an evil history of destroying foreign consumption resources, destroying foreign consumption wealth and conquering foreign nations. The perishing of many Spanish colonies was the consequence of a progressive revolutionary history of resisting destroying consumption resources and fighting for survival by the colonial people.

Consumption and war of Britain

The reasons for Britain becoming the 'empire the sun never set on' can be summed up in two ways. First, the Glorious Revolution broken out on July 30, 1688, in England. The revolution set the foundation for the British constitutional monarchy system, and provided advantages for developing capitalism rapidly in Britain. Second, British industry developed rapidly. Especially after Watt invented the steam engine in 1787, the Industrial Revolution started and developed, rapidly making Britain an industrialized and powerful nation. Because of the industrialized production consumption of capital commodity and commodity exchange, Britain became a militarized and powerful nation, and the productivity of its consumption society multiplied. As a result, Britain resisted the invasion of French army led by Napoleon, facilitated the forming of the Anti-France Alliance five times, and finally defeated Napoleon.

From the 17th century to the end of the war between Britain and France in 1763, Britain had already established a huge first empire centered on its North America colonies. The establishment of the First Empire symbolized that Great Britain had become the most powerful colonial empire in the world and provided a broad exterior market for Britain to become a 'world workshop' later.

The first colonial war contending for British hegemony was the Augsburg Alliance War from 1689 to 1697, which was also called 'the King William'. During the period from 1702 to 1711, Britain and France fought over the Spanish succession again. Britain became the biggest winner in this war. Britain expanded its empire, strengthened its sea power, and developed its foreign trade to gain greatest benefits. From 1759, the British army defeated the French Mediterranean Sea Fleet and Atlantic Fleet successively and basically eliminated the French marine military force. When the war ended in 1763, Britain signed the Treaty of Paris of 1763 with France. This treaty laid the foundation of the British Empire; Britain set up the global hegemony over its colonies and commerce; and Britain unceasingly turned India, the West Indies, South Africa, and Australia into its colonies. The British colonial empire provided the consumer market and the material resources market for the merchandise created in Britain industrialized productive consumption. In the 18th century, the commercial trading circle, which radiated from Britain to all its colonies, had been formed.

Before industrialization, Britain had already developed an external market. Both the exchange of consumer goods and the demand for foreign consumer goods stimulated production and promoted the birth of the Industrial Revolution, which was a breakthrough of the traditional production mode.

The success of Britain's Industrial Revolution and the war extended territory and consumable resources. There were several reasons why the Industrial Revolution first occurred in Britain:

- The application of technology transformed production; in 1787 Watt invented the steam engine, which promoted the Industrial Revolution.
- The technological revolution made industrial production move into a large-scale industrial production pattern. Thus it changed the economic market and promoted the development of industry over agriculture, making the national economic structure transform from agriculture to industry.
- The development of the economy and productivity of the consumption society symbolized that the capitalist social factors had bred, grown up and matured in the feudal society. Then the bourgeois revolution and transformation could succeed and be consolidated and developed unceasingly.

After the Glorious Revolution in Britain there was a constitutional monarchy and a bourgeois democratic revolution. It guaranteed and promoted the development of a liberal capitalist economy in Britain.

Britain completed the Industrial Revolution in the 1840s, allowing Britain to assume the position of world industry overlord. In 1850, British products constituted half the output of the world's metal consumption product, cotton fabrics, and iron, and two-thirds of the coal output. Other

British industries like the shipbuilding industry and railroad construction held first status in the world. In 1960, Britain produced 40–50% of the world's industrial consumables and 55–60% of the European industrial consumables. In 1850, British foreign trade accounted for 20% of the total world trade and increased to 40% ten years later. The pound became an international currency. The rapid development of the British industrialized economy strengthened its comprehensive national power enormously, and the national defense consumption became more powerful and the warships, cannons, fast guns, and lightweight weapons developed rapidly. These all increased war's aggressive force and further expanded the cost of aggression and the destruction of consumption wealth in the colony.

British colonial war consumption created the empire the sun never set on. Britain became the first industrialized country as a result of the Industrial Revolution. The history of Britain as the ruler of its colonial empire lasted for 350 years and Britain reached its developmental peak the 19th century; in 1800, the British empire included 1.5 million square miles of territory and 20 million people; in 1900, the British empire owned 11 million square miles of territory and ruled 390 million people, which accounted for one-quarter of the globe and one-quarter of the global population at that time. However, Britain's native territory consisted only of 240,000 square miles. Nearly half of British territory consumption resources were obtained after 1874. The scale and commercial value of the newly obtained territory resources would go far beyond those of France and other big powers. The formidable British navy was the most important factor for Britain to carry on successful colonial expansion. The vast empire offered Britain favorable strategic advantages.

The British invasion and rule of the colonial territories and the national wars against the British colonial rule began to have a serious effect on national policy. The Anglo-Boer war was a watershed in British imperial history. Before this war the empire grew unceasingly, but afterwards, the empire was in decline. The British government proposed to establish a common customs regime in 1903 to guarantee that the empire would last forever. Each colony took a negative attitude. These two big tentative plans of imperial federation and imperial customs system were realized in the end, which indicated that the empire was quietly declining. The Colonial Conferences were held in 1902 and 1907 and changed their name to the Empire Conferences later. The Empire Conferences provided huge manpower and physical resources for Britain in World War I and made great contributions to Britain's success. But at the same time, the Empire Conferences offered every colonial government an equal status with the

British home government day after day and provided a bigger power for the centrifugal trend of the colonies. When World War I ended, especially after the anti-colonial ruling revolution of martial consumption and struggle for independence in India succeeded, the Great British began to collapse globally.

The French Empire

The period from the end of 10th century to the middle of the 15th century could be regarded the French Middle Ages. Before 1302, France had been under the feudal monarchy system, in which the king's authority gained the acknowledgment of feudal dukes, and the king was the sovereign of the highest authority.

After Philip IV ascended to the French throne in 1285, he combined national territory. The Anglo–French dispute over territory from the early 14th century to the middle 15th century became the reason for French unification process at that time, in particular. As the final victor of the Hundred Years War, French King Charles VII regained the British royal territory consumption resources in France. But part of Calais was still occupied by the English; some aristocrats still maintained relative independence in the country, and the reunification was still not completed. During the rule of Louis XI (from 1461 to 1483), some feudal aristocrats headed by the Duke of Burgundy (bold Charles) formed the Public Welfare Alliance. In 1477, Charles died in battle at the Nancy campaign, and Louis XI seized the opportunity to take back the kingdom of Burgundy and Pierre Cardi. Therefore another big barrier to French unification was eliminated. Around that period, Louis XI took back the aristocratic territories of the Duke of Ajanta, the Duke of Armonk, and the Duke of Provence, one after another. He created his own kingdom with brand-new spirit and became the starting point of French prominence and power.

France moved toward consumption for an aggressive expansion to plunder resources from consumption for the justice war. For geographical resources, France had been in the middle of war with powerful countries for a long time. France was also in a war in which it invaded other countries to extend territory and take their consumption resources and wealth for a very long time.

From 1337 to 1453, the Hundred Year War between Britain and France lasted about 116 years, on and off. During the war, France was split into several parts, which separated into separate kingdoms; henceforth, three Frances came about.

In the later period of the Hundred Years War, the French people's national consciousness continued to develop and patriotic defense of the emperor became the theme at that time under inspiration of St Joan of Arc. Therefore, the extension of royal power was provided with a stronger social basis. It was in this situation that French King Charles VII (1422–1461) gained the victory that his ancestors had long dreamed of. The most important victory was the acquisition of taxing power and a spared standing army. During the rule of Louis XI (1461–1483), no effort was to strengthen royal power. By the end of the 15th century, the French economy had recovered from the war's destruction. After the 16th century, a capitalist handicraft industry developed very rapidly. Together with the prosperity of industry and commerce, French agriculture accelerated the process of disintegrating the feudal lord system and the building feudal landlord system. And the Price Revolution started in the end of the 15th century directly caused the rise of 'noblesse de robe' and the decline of the 'sword aristocrat'.

Until the time of Louis XIII (1610–1643), the centralism of the feudal monarchy and the state's power was strengthened. And the earliest newspaper in French history, *Quest France*, was launched in 1630, which was used as the vehicle for his centralized politics. Another important action was the establishment of the French Research Institute, which was an official cultural organization attempting to standardize activities in the cultural domain throughout France. In March 1661 Louis XIV succeeded to the crown and further strengthened royal power. He began to change just French wars to foreign aggression, plundered the martial consumption of consumption resources and wealth in other countries, and fought over European hegemony. During the 54 years when Louis XIV reigned, France was unexpectedly in a state of war for 31 years. Until July 1686, the Holy Roman Empire, Spain, Holland, and Sweden formed the Augsburg Alliance against France. In 1688, Britain joined the alliance, and the alliance started the war against France. After this war had gone on for ten years, Louis XIV stopped the war to sue for peace. They signed the Ryswick Treaty in 1697, and France withdrew from all the territories it had occupied after Nimewigan Treaty. Louis XIV moved toward empiric decline and the aggressive expansion war of consumption resources ended.

The rise of the European Enlightenment preceded the revolution. People probably started to know nature scientifically during the 16th century. In 1564, Copernicus published *On the Revolutions of Heavenly Spheres* in which he proposed there was a the heliocentric universe. Galileo (1564–1642) and J. Kepler (1571–1630) proved and developed this theory further, not only realizing the astronomy revolution but also arousing a revolution in the view of nature, scientific epistemology, and methodology. Thus the general and fuzzy understanding of nature developed into thorough and careful research. Bacon (1561–1624) in Britain was the first man to research the scientific method systematically and he treated it as the principle of investigating knowledge. He named his work about scientific methodology *New Instrumentalism* to show he was the founder of scientific methodology. Descartes (1596–1650), the founder of analytic geometry, elaborated the mechanical materialism in 'the physics' in his book *Principle Philosophiae* and regarded nature as a unified material world. The essence of nature had malleability. God's first push made material particles in chaotic state form a swirling motion and organized them through exclusion and attraction.

April 28, 1684, was the greatest day in human history because on this day Newton proposed his *Philosophiae Naturalis Principia Mathematica* to the Royal Society of London. Kant (1724–1804) was both a philosopher and a natural scientist. In the field of philosophy, he was the founder of German classical philosophy while in the field of natural sciences he was famous for proposing the hypothesis of the nebula originated in the solar system. Hegel (1770–1831) said that the essential factor of truth was the concept, and the real form of truth was a scientific system. Based only on concept, the life of science could become an organic system. Only by being taken as a science or a system could knowledge be realized and expressed. French philosopher and mathematician Baska invented the first mechanical drive computer in 1787. Watt invented the steam engine in 1787. Adam Smith (1723–1790), in *An Inquiry into the Nature and Causes of the Wealth of Nations*, revealed the relations between the bourgeoisie and the working class, the contradiction of the relations of exploitation, commodity production, and exchange of currency and capital, and the facts that consumption commodity exchange created the merchant class and wealth.

In Europe at this time culture was very progressive and the development of newspapers, the publication industry, and printing promoted the cultural propaganda and educational movement. The so-called Enlightenment was a public opinion campaign before it was a revolution. This movement encouraged oppressed and exploited slaves in extreme misery to struggle for their benefits and consumption survival, and agitated that true revolutionary action must be the conducted on the basis of a good plan, organization, and leaders to realize their goal.

The armed uprising in Paris on July 14, 1789, was a great revolution of the bourgeoisie fighting against the feudal dynasty of Louis XVI. Capitalist social factors were already mature in the French industrial developmental process and in the French feudal social matrix.

The great French martial consumption of revolution in 1789 had significance for human progression. It is clear when studying the historical background and reasons for the French Revolution that such a revolution could erupt in France only at the historical stage of that time. And at the same time, martial consumption made martial talents such as Napoleon heroes. But it was martial consumption that destroyed itself finally.

Napoleon plundered consumption resources and wealth

The French Revolution in 1789, after the success of the bourgeois revolution, stilled Jacques Song's right-wing dictatorship and established the Thermidorian Party to supervise the government; and it led the revolution to a national war of patriotism. In October 1797, France and Austria signed the Canburgh Fumieul Treaty, which stipulated that Austria should acknowledge France's seizing of Belgium, the Rhine's west bank, and the Republic established in northern Italy. This was an acknowledgment that France occupied the 'natural border' that it had dreamed of for several centuries, which consisted of the Rhine River, the Pyrenees, and the Alps. After the defeat of the anti-French alliance, France began to rise as a hegemonic state.

After Brumaire's coup d'état in 1799, Napoleon had no choice but to defeat the foreign enemy to maintain his powerful national status. After the victory in the Marengo Campaign over Austria in 1800, Napoleon used confliction inside the Anti-French Alliance to isolate Britain, which was forced to accept negotiations. In 1802, England and France signed the Armin Treaty, which marked the end of the Anti-France Alliance and the establishment of French superior status in Europe.

Napoleon proclaimed himself emperor and unofficial martial consumption of hegemony and counter-hegemony competed with each other. Since the French Revolution, Napoleon had embarked the supreme ruling position in France with a slogan of national revolution, and obtained the French people's reverence and respect, becoming a national hero. But he announced himself Emperor of France in May 1805 to equate his position with that of a feudal emperor. It led to the opposition of powerful countries in Europe because he attempted to dominate Europe like the Roman Empire had done.

The countries of the Anti-French Alliance battled with France on sea and on land separately. The British Navy gained a total victory in the Trafalgar Naval Battle in October 1805. The Spanish army, French army, and French navy, superior to the British navy in numbers, were annihilated completely. Napoleon's attempt to land on the British Isles was completely defeated. But in the land campaign, the French army won a total victory. Next Napoleon defeated the fourth Anti-France Alliance. With a need for allies to cope with Britain jointly, Napoleon was extremely magnanimous to Russia after defeating it. In July 1807, both countries signed the Treaty of Tilsit, and carved up some of the land of Russia's former ally, Prussia. Under Napoleon's economic blockade, Britain also fell into isolation in politics. During 1807 and 1808, British trade was facing many difficulties and exports dropped dramatically. Especially in 1808, custom tax value and declared value were dropping a little more drastically than before; the loss of the European market was also a heavy loss to Britain's economy. However, blockade and anti-blockade was a double-edged sword. It caused huge financial problems to Napoleon and became the reason why Napoleon was defeated.

Napoleon's empire was made to pay for his actions because of the cost of his aggressive wars. After the anti-France revolution erupted in Spanish capitals in May 1808, the revolt spread rapidly to every region of Spain. Meanwhile, the Portuguese fought against French invasion. In August 1808, Britain sent the young Wellesley (later Lord Wellington) to command troops and land in Portugal. The Peninsular War started. With the support of the Portuguese army, the British army ambushed the French army from Portugal. Being defeated repeatedly, Napoleon exhausted the consumption wealth of his empire, which began to decline.

The Napoleonic Empire then defeated the fifth anti-France alliance. After defeating Austria and signing the Vienna Peace Treaty, Napoleon's Empire continued to grow. From 1810 to 1811, France had successively annexed the Netherlands, Warri in Switzerland, and various states in Germany to the north of Lippe and Traver River. Meanwhile, Napoleon had also increased the intensity of the blockade against Britain. Blockade and annexation combined became the two big props of the Napoleonic Empire. Napoleon's expansion and the economic blockade seriously harmed and further threatened the assets of Britain and Russia. Dissatisfaction toward Napoleon caused the rebellious behavior of the Russia czars. In June 1812, Napoleon commanded large-scale armies of 700,000 soldiers to invade Russia. In December of that year, when the French army finally withdrew from Russia, of Napoleon's 700,000 soldiers only 50,000 or so were left. Napoleon's invasion of Russia failed, and accelerated the collapse of the Napoleonic Empire.

At this time, Britain – Napoleon's main enemy – organized the sixth anti-France alliance. In October 1813, the two parties fought in Leipzig. Napoleon's army was badly defeated and the Napoleonic Empire disintegrated rapidly. On April 6, 1814, Napoleon was compelled to abdicate. The Napoleonic Empire was thoroughly destroyed. On May 30, 1814, France signed the First Paris Peace Treaty with the anti-France alliance. The Napoleonic Empire was dead.

Napoleon III

On May 30, 1814, France signed the First Paris Peace Treaty with the Anti-France Alliance and announced the demise of the Napoleonic Empire. Louis XVIII succeeded to the throne of France. In June 1814, Louis XVIII signed the new constitution called the 1814 Charter. In its 74 articles, it displayed concessions to the achievements of the Revolution and reflected orthodox ideology and the tendency to restore the legitimacy of the ancient regime. After the death of Louis XVIII, his younger brother Charles X succeed to the throne; the Bourbon dynasty further intensified to restore 'the throne and the sacrificial altar' as 'theocracy politics' in the social construction, and launched a vengeful counterattack. Parisians became angry and launched a revolt on July 27, 1830. On July 29, the Louvre and Tuileries Palace were seized by the rebels, so the rule of Bourbon dynasty ended.

In February 1848, a mammoth people's revolution to overthrow the old feudal dynasty finally erupted. The following general election had the new political power come into being. As a result, Louis Bonaparte was elected as the Republic's president; he had no direct relation to the February Revolution. Louis Bonaparte took on the restoration of the empire his uncle, Napoleon Bonaparte, had started; he eliminated all barriers and made a coup in December, 1851. In 1852 he put on the crown of Napoleon III, started the second empire following the same old disastrous road of warfare. The foreign policies of Napoleon III were to implement an amicable consultation policy with Britain and a practical policy with Germany. In 1870, it was ended by the surrender of the army and its commander Napoleon III in the Franco–Prussian war, which initiated the revolution of the Paris commune. This revolution had significant worldwide historic importance. Afterward in 1871 Germany defeated France and annexed France's Alsace region and part of Lorraine, which realized the unification of Germany.

The Great Revolution of the Paris Commune

The Paris commune was a proletariat political power, established by Paris workers after the revolution on March 18, 1871. It was the first attempt to implement a proletariat dictatorship.

On September 2, 1870, Napoleon III was defeated and surrendered in the Franco–Prussian war. Parisians began the revolution on September 4, and overthrew the second empire, but the fruits of victory fell into the hands of right wing bourgeoisie republicans and the monarchic Orleans party members who established the national defense government. On February 17, 1871, L.A. Thiers took the post as the head of French government. On

February 28, the French–German peace treaty was signed. France ceded Alsace and big piece of the territory of Lorraine to Germany, and paid 5,000 million francs in reparations. The Thiers government humiliated the nation and forfeited its sovereignty, which aroused enormous indignation in the people. The Paris populace requested to establish a commune to supervise the government. On March 15, representatives from 251 camps in the national self-defense corps selected a Central Committee. In the early morning of March 18, the Thiers government sent the army out to attack Montmartre and the Ceaumen high land, attempted to capture the 417 cannons from national self-defense corps, and arrested the Central Committee members, thus triggering an armed uprising. In the evening, the national self-defense corps controlled the entire government and the bridge over the Seine in Paris. Thiers, the government members and their army, police, and government officials fled from Versailles in a panic. On March 26, Paris carried on the election, and on March 28 the Paris commune was established officially.

There were various reasons for the failure of the commune. At that time, France was not mature enough to let a socialist system substitute for a capitalist system. The class power balance between international and domestic affairs was disadvantageous to the proletariat. At the time of being defeated in the Franco–Prussian war, the French bourgeoisie was extremely weak, thus the revolt achieved success. Once Germany and France signed the peace treaty, the Bismarck government would support the Thiers government to suppress the commune; the power balance would radically change. The commune's revolution did not obtain powerful coordination from the revolutionary movement of others, nor support from farmers; it fought a lonely battle, which would inevitably invite defeat became of the great disparity in strength. Because of the historical limitations of the French proletariat, certain serious errors were made. For instance, it did not grasp the opportunity promptly when the enemy was unprepared to march into Versailles; it did not confiscate the French Bank, which had assets of three billion French francs, and gave the bank the opportunity to provide funds to the Versailles government, and so on. In this critical period of warfare, the insiders of the commune committee had a serious difference of opinion about the gravity of the situation and the emergency measures it should adopt. The majority and minority parties emerged regarding the establishment of the nation saving committee, its authority and composition, and in the middle of May it was once on the verge of splitting. This indicated that without a mature proletariat party to lead the revolution, without a explicit guiding principle, it was impossible to unite the revolutionary ranks, or to adopt the correct tactics to sustain the revolution.

The success and failure of the Paris commune brought huge enlightenment and instruction to the world proletariat and the general toiling masses:

- The proletariat and working people should not abandon themselves to despair or accept brutal oppression and exploitation willingly; they should revolt and seize power when the opportunity is mature.
- They had to learn the strategy of revolution, establish their own core of leadership, learn how to organize a revolution, and acquire the methods and experience to lead a revolution.
- Once the revolution succeeds, there must be correct policy and strategy to develop the revolution's achievement and advance the development and construction of the new government.

Consumption and unification and expansion during the German War

National united war of German anti-aggression

The German people suffered a lot during the war. Germanic peoples had endured for a long time the bitterness and suffering as the results of invasion and anti-invasion war, domestic struggles among religious forces, and the struggle between the religious and crown forces.

Prussia developed from a small, wild, and impoverished eastern area. Prussia's King Arne Friedrich William I (1713–1740) built a powerful military over a long period of time. He carried out tyranny, broke down the Junker dictatorship, and weakened the aristocratic class of the direct intervention in government affairs. He had great success in internal affairs. When he died in 1740, he handed over the reins to his second son 'the soldier king'. Subsequently, King Friedrich developed martial consumption supported by the concept of a 'supremacy of national interests'. Military expenditure is the greatest consumption of the country.

During the seven year European war from 1756 to 1763, the country and army of King Friedrich went through severe tests, resisted the united offensive of Austria, Russia and France, and preserved the resources of affluent Silesia. After 1763, King Friedrich started the reconstruction of the country. He undertook a series of reform measures to recover and increase national strength. However, all these served to build the military. In 1780, Prussia became a military camp during peacetime.

The 1820s was the beginning of modern industry in Germany. The handicraft industry underwent extensive development and transitioned to machine manufacturing. During the 1850s and 1860s, Germany had transitioned from an agricultural country to an industrial country and was involved wholly in world trade. Germany's economy remained prosperous except for short-term depressions. German industrial strength already had been close to that of France. In the 1870s, machine manufacturing in Germany had surpassed England and ranked first in Europe. The development of industry made the whole economic structure and class forces of German society increase rapidly, especially in Prussia. Most Germans began to become capitalists, and Prussia had turned from a feudal monarchy into the bourgeoisie monarchy, which was necessary to unify Germany. After the 1850s and 1860s, Germany's industrial revolution and economic development had been a coercive power promoting unification.

In September 1862, Bismarck took the post of prime minister. He made the 'iron blood speech' on September 30, 1862, and claimed that the contemporary major problem then could not be dealt with through speech and resolution, but through iron and blood. Prussia was moving in the direction he indicated. Germany launched three dynastic wars and began to achieve national unification.

In autumn 1862, when Bismarck discovered that recurring problems in Schleswig-Holstein had intensified once again, and it was closely linked with the German national movement and the endeavor of liberalism, he intervened in the national movement immediately. After thorough planning, Austria and Prussia attacked Schleswig by alliance in July 1864 and defeated Denmark army quickly. Bismarck launched war against Austria in the second unification war and reshuffled the Austria Empire into a binary monarchy – Austria-Hungary in February 1867.

During the days after July 13, 1868, Bismarck provoked the wrath of Napoleon III by a modified telegraph published in a newspaper. On July 19, France declared war on Prussia. Germany soon smashed the French army and achieved unification, safeguarding resources and national wealth, and Germany economic development increased rapidly. The destruction of Napoleon III triggered the revolution of Brumaire 18th in Paris.

Consumption during World War I

The reigning period of Kaiser Wilhelm II (1890–1918) was called the Wilhelm period. In 1914, the two hostile European empire groups were getting ready to fight and slaughter. Germany started the war. The Attentat von Sarajevo occurred on June 28, 1914, and became the fuse for World War I. The conflict had turned into a war spreading into the whole of

Europe and all over the world within a month because of the German government's behavior of adding fuel to fire. The Berlin uprising began on the morning of November 9, 1918. Emperor Wilhelm II fled to Holland. Hohenzollern in German history ended like this.

On November 8, 1918, German delegates were forced to sign the cease-fire agreement to end World War I. The Germany Empire was destroyed in the World War I it triggered. World policy for Wilhelm II failed. Not only was the country in disaster, but also the king himself abdicated and was exiled. His sorrowful result shows that pursuing power politics blindly eventually leads to failure.

Consumption during World War II

Germany ceded land consumption resource and consumption of war reparations after the failure of World War I. The result provoked the resistance of German citizens who thought that the signer of the Versailles Peace Treaty was a national traitor and should be boycotted. By means of national resentment against the terms of the Versailles Peace Treaty, Hitler came to power and developed the Nazi system, which was called 'national republic body' theory. He claimed that war was 'the fight of lineage to lineage and race to race' and the purpose was to accomplish the mission of defending the ethnic group and race and establishing the country of a 'national republic state system', a national elite-led country. The principle of leadership by 'a national elite' was put forward. The leader is the representative of the interest and will of the nation and has absolute ruling power over the populace. Hitler declared that he was the only person who could consciously realize the three factors called 'ethnic value', 'individual value', and 'self-protection potency' in order to strengthen national forces and resist 'national defense', 'democracy', and 'pacifism', which weakened nationalism. And he was the only one who should possess absolute leadership.

Hitler's national ideology was that Germanic peoples were the most superior in the world and should lead the world. Hitler's inflammatory speech was not only full of superficial and vulgar sadness for the German romantic tradition, but also took advantage of the sentimentality of the middle class in Weimar Germany and aroused Germans' national feeling. Hitler won the favor, connivance, and support of the upper class including right wing conservatives, army military headquarters, civil officials, and some landlords and industrialists, and became the prime minister of Germany as a result of a political coalition. Thereafter, Germany went into dark age of 'the Third Reich'.

Nazi Germany's aggressive nature was immediately displayed after Hitler came into power. He uncompromisingly withdrew from the World Disarmament Conference and the League of Nations in order to shake off the shackles of the Versailles Treaty, and he publicized and legalized the work of rearmament. He subsequently continued to carry out military adventurism to sound out the response of the international community. On the early morning of September 1, 1939, German troops crossed the border of Poland and launched a blitzkrieg strategy for war without a declaration of war. On September 3, 1939, Britain and France declared war on Germany, signifying the official start of World War II. People from various countries fought against Hitler. By March 24, 1945, the Red Army pushing forward from the East and American and British allied forces from the Normandy landings in the west liberated Europe. On May 7, 1945, Germany surrendered. On August 15, 1945, Japan surrendered.

Conclusion

Seen from the consumption developmental process of primitive human beings, we have solicited and created consumption materials ever since human life began. In the process of consumption, humans created family, clan, tribal society, and county prototypes of primitive community social systems. Mankind's living consumption level has risen gradually because of the invention and creative development of productivity. In the development process of human living consumption, social consumption, and research and production consumption, part of human living consumption remained. A typical example was war captives. If they were not killed, they would be left as slaves. Thereby the slavery system came into being. Slaves created surplus consumption products, and the development process of three major consumptions also led to a slave society.

Furthermore, fine division of labor came into being in the process of production consumption because of the development of the productivity of a consumption society and the handicraft industry, especially the division of labor between agriculture and industry. Class, class oppression and exploitation, anti-oppression and anti-exploitation, and war expenditure developed. After the steam engine was invented, centralized proletariat ranks (working class) and class emerged after an intensive machine production developed. Humans created social elements of the feudal society in the consumption process because of the development of the productivity of the consumption society in the slave society. As the elements of feudal society gradually became mature in the development process of the slave society and new social system, the feudal society was established through reform and revolution. This process is a continual affirmation process of the development and progression of feudal society elements. It is also a continual negation process of the outdated slave society, and the process of gradual and partial quantitative changes toward the ultimate qualitative change. The birth of the feudal society was an affirmation while the demise of the slave society was a negation.

As the rule developed quantitatively, capitalist social elements were constantly brought about because of the development of productivity of a consumption society in feudal society. As the factors of capitalist society developed and became mature, gradually in the process of feudal society's progress and development, as well as through social change or bourgeois revolutionary war consumption, feudal society was eliminated; a capitalist social system and socialist revolution were created, and a socialist system was established. The emergence and development of society were created by the three major consumptions, and family and nation were also created by consumption.

Civilization and the progress of human society are represented in the consumption for new technology and technology progress, which creates consumption for new and advanced tools and creates the progress of social civilization, which marks the scientific and technological level of productivity of a consumption society.

War consumption is the root of all evils even though it has a positive side. It was war consumption that created countries. The new countries' superstructures act on the three major consumptions and thus the social economic foundation is more solid and the productivity of a consumption society is liberated, which makes social production relations better adapt to the development of productivity of consumption society so that new countries promote the civilization of society.

Mankind has entered the 21st century and created productivity of a consumption society with new technology and constantly pushes human civilization into new stages in the course of the development of the three major consumptions. Three major consumptions of mankind affect capital commodity production and free commodity exchange, which will benefit all countries. In recent times, global commodities of capital production and exchange have permeated into various countries and regions, although conflicts of interest and power exist in these countries and regions. However, as many countries' economic interests are melded together, a military power launching a worldwide war would do harm to the interests of consumption countries if it neglected other countries' consumption interests in such a world pattern. Besides, other countries would inevitably unite for their benefit and defeat the aggressive war consumption for plundering consumption resources and consumption wealth. The instigator of war is bound to fail finally. This pattern will stop or delay the occurrence of world war. There was an interval of only 20 years between World War I and World War II. Although World War II ended more than 60 years ago, there has been no world war since then, as people recognize that what affects one country affects others, as all countries intermingle through economic globalization and mutual interests.

The people in the world should fight against all unjust wars, build harmonious worldwide communities, and develop the productivity of a consumption society, thus pushing forward human beings to develop from one civilized and progressive stage to a higher level. World peace and human harmony are the eternal themes of constant demands and aspirations of humans.

11

Thinking methods and consumption practice

It is often felt in doing certain kinds of specific work that it is hard to keep up with the requirements of the new era and tasks, difficult to perform the work well and to keep the solutions of problems flexible, which result in the fear of hardship. And all of this is not due to work attitudes like reluctance to do the job and laziness. Instead, we do it harder and wholeheartedly want to do the job well. It is just that we feel our ability falls short of our wishes; work results are not satisfactory and we get the opposite of what we want.

The root of these problems lies in the way of thinking. It is an omnipotent golden key, capable of guiding various specific and complicated tasks, providing clues or solving different problems rising in work. Now let's talk about seven basic thinking ways that can guide realistic work.

Section 1 Concept and importance of thinking method

First, it is necessary to identify the conception of the thinking way and the difference between thinking and the thinking way.

Thinking

What is thinking? Briefly, thinking is the whole process of thinking, understanding, and concluding or summarizing and reflecting the human brain's cognition process of the objective matters in the real world, which take the forms of concept, judgment, reasoning (inductive reasoning or deductive reasoning), hypothesis, theories, and so on. Thinking, as a kind of human creativity, not only reflects the objective world, but also actively reacts on the objective world through practice. Marx (1867) said:

> Many architects are put to shame by the skill of bees in building hives. But the aspect that makes the lamest architect wiser than the most skillful bee at the very beginning is that he has finished the hive in his mind before he starts it with beeswax. The results of his work at the end of work have already existed in the imagination, namely existing in concept. He not only changes the forms of natural objects, but also achieves his own goal in the objects. He knows this goal which serves as a law to determine his activities and ways.

This famous statement of Marx compliments man's ability to think. Thinking plays a significant role in social life: people understand the laws of nature and society, people figure out purposes and plans with the help of thinking, and transform the world by following these purposes. What is more, the truth of thinking is also tested in practice.

What is the thinking way? It is ways and activities that guide people to think. People try to understand, transform, and utilize the natural world instinctively and naturally with diversified levels of quality and experience. And the thinking way is the cognition way that directs people to understand, transform, and utilize the natural world in accordance with the general or special laws of things. Thinking helps one work out complex problems within a given context, thereby improving one's level, capability, and speed of reforming and utilizing the natural world.

When doing something, we should first clearly know the purpose or the expected aim, and then work out corresponding plans according to this purpose to take the relevant measures and identify proper strategies. The mentioned links constitute the process of thinking. On the other hand, the thinking way involves such aspects as adhering to principles, using ways or means, and taking corresponding measures. The thinking way runs through the whole process of cognition and is included in thinking. The more flexible and consistent with objective laws of thinking the thinking way is, the more objective people's cognition is, the stronger the people's capability to transform nature. And meanwhile, they change from being passive to being active, stepping from a limited realm of inevitably into the realm of freedom. Therefore, it is appropriate to say that thinking is to understand the natural world, whereas the thinking way is the way and activities to understand, transform, and utilize the natural world.

There is a popular Chinese saying: 'Knit the brows and you will hit upon a stratagem', and this is the forming process of thinking ways. Whether thinking ways are right or wrong comes from the correct judgment and induction (or deduction) of objects, namely the correct thinking ways. Thinking is the way and method of understanding nature and guiding people to understand, transform, and use nature. Transforming and using, instead of understanding, is the objective. To transform nature, we need to understand it. In any specific issue, there are many objective conditions. That is our understanding of events and the thinking results. Can we resolve these problems? We need to refer to thinking ways.

Thinking and thinking method are both subjective. It is necessary to check whether the thinking way is right or not though practice. No matter what we do, we should first figure out plans, and then we act, and whether we can succeed or not lies in examining carefully, summarizing cautiously, and verifying faulty and inconsistent aspects. And that is why it is crucial to address the dovetailing of subjectivity and objectivity. The cognition of a problem and the method of solving the problem are subjective, and whether the subjectivity can dovetail with the objectivity of reality should be tested in practice. It is not a theoretical issue but a practical problem whether people's thinking is an objective truth. People should prove the truth of their thinking in practice, namely the reality and the power, also this sideness of the thinking. As for whether thinking divorced from practice is still realistic is purely a scholastic question. Chairman Mao Zedong also said: 'There is but one truth, and the question of whether or not one has arrived at it depends not on subjective boasting but on objective practice. The only yardstick of truth is the revolutionary practice of millions of people.'

People's understanding is always behind the objective reality (people's understanding of nature) rather than ahead of it. This is the basic viewpoint of materialism. But rational thinking, by concepts and reasoning and the like, can overstep the objective and this overstepping, whether it is correct or not, has to be proved through practice. Practice is the origin, a material substance is the origin, so we must go back to the origin to verify the truth, which leads us to the point of making the subjective conform to the objective. People's ideas, principles, policies, plans, and measures are subjective. During their implementation in practice, if the subjective are correct but fail to be implemented, no good results can be reached. Implement and good results can be reached. In the implementation process, if we meet events of objective complexity and variability that stop the original plan from implementation, what will we do? We should adjust our subjective way of thinking at any time. According to the new situation, we should make the subjective conform to the objective. Only by doing this can we do the job well. Or there may be no problem in planning but problems emerge in implementing the plan since the situation of yesterday is not the same with that of today. So, the subjective should always be subject to the test of the objective and be improved and perfected in practice to get the best benefits and the best performance. This is to analyze and solve a problem from the overall situation.

It is also like this in a specific situation. For example, in my practice, regional general managers are appointed at branches that are subordinate to marketing departments. They were believed to use the same working methods and assigned the same tasks. But with their different conditions and circumstances, the scales of policy to use are different. If all things are done using the same scale and standard, they cannot be done well. The qualities of leaders are widely different, yet they have control over policies, what he says is what should be done. Since he is the one who has the final say on policies, the depth and extent of his understanding is influential. The job cannot be done once the policy is violated and this needs adjustment. Besides, economic conditions are different in the southwestern and northwestern regions; the latter is way behind the southeast coastal areas in economic development. Formulating specific working methods according to this and imposing uniformity in all cases is not acceptable.

This viewpoint and method must be extended to specific work to solve the problems of rigid thinking. There are many policies now, but we lack the one to combine the local conditions and to improve it. We have to admit it as a fact; it reflects the deviation between thinking and thinking methods. We must solve this problem and adjust the way of thinking to meet the objective world and objective facts so as to do the job well.

Section 2 Seven basic thinking methods

Integrative system thinking

The integrative system thinking way is when the system as a whole (overall system structure) is composed of structural systems of various parts, and these parts are a unity of motion based on mechanical interrelations, interdependence, and interactions under certain conditions. The system factors of the different parts compose their own integrative systems, which is a unity of motion of mechanics and conditional interrelations, interdependence, and interactions.

The integrative system thinking way is to guide mankind to develop subjective and motivated cognition towards nature and things, and it is the thinking method used when doing any work, resolving any problem, or facing any event. Work should be guided from the perspective of unity, and in the flow system of the integrative organizational structure, system factors in different systems should be connected closely to ensure that it is a mechanical motion unity with organic and conditional interrelations, interdependence, and interactions.

If we want to solve a problem successfully, the integrative system thinking way and investigating thinking way should be used together to find out whether there is something wrong with the integrative system or with the structure of a single part or all the independent parts, or with the system connection of a certain part, or with a condition in the structural system. By analyzing using integrative system thinking way and investigating thinking way to check the failures, it is possible to solve the problem clearly and quickly in an orderly way.

When people get ready to do work, the integrative system thinking method also means that their cerebra start to study it from the point of unity, and then to work out a solution. The course of study is thinking. Where should we initiate the integrative study? The answer is to start with studying individual things, trying to divide the general law of the overall concept into specific laws, conduct detailed testing and thinking, and then extract the general law from the individual laws with the help of induction, try to obtain a comprehensive cognition through vertical, lateral, internal and external studies. But it is difficult to judge whether this cognition is right or not, so it is necessary to perform deductive analysis as a whole. In western philosophy, induction and deduction are considered as two opposing concepts with the former referring to parts-to-whole and the latter whole-to-parts. Engels stressed that induction is the premise of deduction and deduction is the argument of induction and the two are inseparable:

> The induction process cannot be figured out even if we exhaust all inductive methods of the world. Only by analyzing the process can we do it. Induction and deduction, just like analysis and synthesis, are certainly related to each other. We shouldn't sacrifice one and exalt the other to the skies, but instead, we should put each in the right place. And to do this, we have to pay attention to their inner connection and mutual complementation.

The overall systems thinking method covers a wider area, and is favorable toward the aggregated analysis and will not affect the overall result of the work even in case of ill-conception, or one would catch one and lose another and lead to the ill-coordination of different parts. We must resort to this thinking method in our large-scale work.

Here what is discussed is the thinking ways of integral thinking, not holistic thinking. The larger the scale of an enterprise and a company are, the higher the requirements on its ways of holistic thinking are. For those groups or enterprises with many industry products and a wide geographical span, if they don't have the overall situation in mind, it could lead to two mistakes. First, all departments and units might emphasize only the importance of their own department and ignore the existence of other departments; second, because some departments have large organizations and it makes no difference even if they lose one or two of them, then they might relax the requirements on themselves.

Both ideas are wrong. Each department is an integral part of the whole and is indispensable. Each department must have the overall situation in mind, make concerted efforts and so that overall work could be done better. For example, the decision of sale at a discount is made after analyzing the overall situation of national policies and enterprise competition at the decision-making level. When the decision is transmitted to subordinate agencies, if they can carry out the job from the overall perspective with holistic thinking, the work will be pushed forward smoothly. In contrast, if they only consider from their own local interest, there may be many difficulties, and the progress of the overall plan would be affected. Facts have proved that all those who have the overall situation in mind can give full play to their subjective initiative, overcome various difficulties and promote the whole work. Thus, holistic thinking plays an important role in specific work.

Logical thinking

Logical thinking is the rational cognitive process of reflecting objective reality actively with the help of concepts, judgments, reasoning and other forms of thinking. Through abstraction and analysis and thinking about the sensual materials, and the thinking process of discarding the dross and selecting the essential, eliminating the false and retaining the true, getting from one to the other, getting from the outside to the inside, logical thinking requires us to put the specific image and individual properties of things aside, reveal the properties and nature of things, form concepts and use them to judge and reason to reflect the objective reality generally and indirectly. Revealing the nature of things through abstractive gives it the features of consciousness, process, and necessity. The basic forms of logical thinking include concepts, judgments and reasoning. Logical thinking ways mainly include induction and deduction, analysis and synthesis, as well as from the abstract to the concrete and so on.

There are differences between the two concepts of logical thinking and the logical way of thinking.

The feature of logical thinking is that it is first based on the 'should-be' point; from this perspective it begins to establish a viewpoint, then propose illustrations, and then on the basis of illustrations begins to argue that the viewpoint is correct or to extract the viewpoint from tremendous arguments, and finally draws the logical and normative conclusion with induction and deduction. It is a thinking way in which the brain, with respect to the targeted objects, conducts induction, summary, abstract, and reasoning – an ordered thinking method of inductive reasoning. This thinking way presents the advantage of normativity and easy understanding.

The logical thinking way can be divided into *argumentum fortiori* and *argumentum contrario*, the former starts with induction, namely, from the individual to the general; the latter begins with deduction – from the general to the individual. Arrange the work in an orderly way; design it as a whole, and then the plans, measures, methods, tricks, strategies, details, and control, which are the positive thinking method of brain reasoning. Or it can be started from the bottom; making sure how to get higher and at last get to the top to form a tower. These are two kinds of reasoning: *argumentum fortiori* and *argumentum contrario*. The normativity and rationalization of this method is very helpful to keep one's presence of mind in guiding the overall work.

We should analyze the work with *argumentum fortiori* first, namely starting with induction; first study the phenomena and at last decide the final solution to the problem. For example, to identify a company's annual work, seeing it from the positive side, analyze first how the annual work of the whole company has been planned and implemented; analyze from the whole how the inspection has been arranged and how subordinates do it, what kind of problems emerge, what the reason for the problem are and why there is problem like this. When problems are particular, few and accidental, solve them from the whole to the bottom and it is a hierarchical solution system. Analyze a problem from the top to the bottom, but when everything is ok and basically reasonable at the top and problems still emerge, solve them from the bottom. If there are problems from the top to the bottom, then reasons for this general phenomenon should be analyzed from the top, from the whole rather than from the bottom.

This is *argumentum fortiori*. In the analysis, the reasons for the problems are basically at the top. So in summarizing the whole work of a year, we say the major policy is wrong, yet some local specific decisions are correct, but they failed to be implemented. People at the lower levels are responsible for the failure in implementation; yet the root lies in the poor correction and management at higher levels. If the lower levels don't carry out the work but get away with it, they will go on like this. Therefore, problems should be solved from the top; the relevant principle leaders should take the blame. The lower levels, at the same time, try to understand the problem and solve it level by level. This is *argumentum fortiori*. Don't blame the lower levels for not doing what they are told to do. Then who should be blamed for this? Tell him to do it but he doesn't. Then why not deal with him? Are leaders like these qualified leaders? Why not dismiss or replace him with a more qualified one? If you did this, the orders would surely be followed. With the logical way of thinking, find solutions from the top to the bottom. Problems emerge at the bottom, but the top is to blame. Inspect the work with this way of thinking.

Second, if few problems arise at the lower levels, and the whole are in good shape, only a few departments, people, and leaders are responsible, and then these people should take the blame without implicating the top levels. We cannot always believe that the top levels are to blame for all errors and all problems. This way of thinking is not scientific. It is the leader who should be responsible for shielding and not punishing a person who has made mistakes, while if the leader punishes him severely, it is not the leader but the subordinate who should be blamed. We cannot ensure every leader would do everything correctly and match the subjective to the objective. This is *argumentum fortiori*. On the other hand, seeing some specific work from the bottom up, which is correct and which has reflected the correct decision-making? Which have failed to show the decision-making level's guiding theory? Which of them are wrong? To find whether the whole objective, plan, and control are right or not, if the decision is correct on the whole, then the lower levels should take the responsibility for not implementing what has been decided.

The above-mentioned is to inspect work with logical thinking. Some people have such thinking: credits are mine; errors yours. They take the credit for themselves and put the blame on others, which is wrong. The work of leaders should first be inspected if the branches don't perform well. Leaders should first be charged with responsibility if their subordinates refuse to follow orders since it is the leader's incompetence that leads to the disobeying. If the leaders are competent, subordinates would certainly obey them. Thus, there is no reason to blame subordinates for everything. We should find out the reasons for the problems from the part of leaders: have they done everything properly? If one is a leader with this kind of thinking, can he do well at leading? If each level would follow, leading by levels, then the responsibilities of levels would be clear.

Sun Wu's maids of honor

From the story of Sun Wu training maids of honor we can see there is great power in logical thinking. Maids of honor enjoyed the special favor of the emperor and wouldn't follow anyone else's orders. They ranked only next to the emperor and would not listen to anyone else, which was the objective situation. The emperor required Sun Wu to train those maids to become soldiers capable of fighting, which was his objective. First, Sun Wu lined up the maids into two groups with the emperor's two favorite concubines serving as group leaders. This is the thinking way of Sun Wu. Before drilling, he announced a discipline. Hearing it, instead of following his requests, the concubines all began to laugh. When told to turn left or right, they all refused to obey him. Sun Wu accounted the discipline for the second time and told them to follow his order, or he would have them killed. But those maids all thought: I am the favorite concubine of the emperor and not afraid of you at all. You are nothing. They still refused to listen to him. Sun Wu then announced the military order for the third time: anyone who refused to follow orders would be punished according to the military law. In drilling, the maids still disobeyed him, so Sun Wu ordered to have the emperor's two most beloved concubines killed. After that, he chose two maids as group leaders and lined up the groups. When he ordered them to turn left, right, and face about, the maids obediently followed his orders.

This is a logical way of thinking, finding problems from the top to the bottom. When policies of the top are correct, but the bottom refuses to follow, you need to punish them and the problem will be solved. If Sun Wu had chosen not to punish them, and the drilling could not go on, then he, instead of maids, should be responsible. A work unit, objectively speaking, has a certain number of employees, who should be easier to manage than maids. Then it should be leaders rather than employees who should be responsible for bad organization and management, and it is also leaders who are to blame for the situation when orders are disobeyed orders and prohibitions are defied. Only in this way, can the overall and partial thinking and thinking ways be integrated and perfected. If the correct viewpoints are negated by wrong ones, the results would still be wrong, and finally, nothing would be done, and it would fall into a mess. Napoleon once said that a flock of sheep led by a lion can beat a group of lions led by a sheep. A smart leader can train his employees from sheep to little lions and make them dare to charge and struggle without fear of death. If the working methods and thinking ways of leaders are correct, such a group could be created. It could make cadres with low levels and qualities have those of high-level cadies; train those undisciplined and uncontrolled cadres into a united and capable group, which requires logical thinking to solve the problem.

Dialectical materialist thinking

The dialectical materialist thinking way, the opposite of the metaphysical thinking way, is to observe things from the point of their interconnectedness as well as their motion, change, and development – to solve problems with dialectical methods. Unlike the logical thinking way to conduct reasoning step by step, the dialectical thinking way, under the principle of the dichotomous approach, adheres to the principle that the principal contradiction determines the nature of things, the unity of opposites, and mutual transformation of contradictions. The principal contradiction can be transformed into a secondary contradiction, and a secondary contradiction, under certain conditions, can be transformed into the principal contradiction and only in this way can it be possible to speculate correctly. This thinking way is to analyze in a dynamic cause and effect of things in their unity of opposites, or it would be a wild argument with both parties claiming to be in the right. Bad things are said to be good ones and good things may be said to be bad ones.

Good things become bad

For example, a person or a team has made great achievements, which is a good thing, the mainstream, the principal contradiction, and the thing used to determine the nature. But if, with these achievements, one gets arrogant and complacent, it will probably lead to backwardness. The principal side of a contradiction would transform towards another side. The aim of the dialectical way of thinking is to provide a thinking way to stop the change from advancement to backwardness, to keep the principal aspect of a contradiction from changing to the secondary aspect of a contradiction. Understanding the dialectical way of thinking, you will be modest and prudent, both confirming your achievements correctly and at the same time knowing your deficiencies. Check yourself, correct the deficiencies and at the same time set the next task to gain better achievements, and moving forward to the new tasks one could avoid being arrogant. Thus, guided by this thinking way, one would be less blind and arrogant. There are also people who are more capable. Compared with others, we still have a long way to go. We can control our blindness and arrogance with this way of thinking.

Bad things become good

With the dialectical way of thinking we can change bad things into good ones. For example, a Panasonic TV user in Tai'an City expressed his complaints in the press after the explosion of his TV. This was bad for Panasonic since this meant the quality of its products was poor and this would bring negative attention to the company. But facing the unfavorable situation, Matsushita didn't act blindly or rashly. Instead, it sent staff to the user's home to make him understand that the explosion was because of misuse rather than TV quality. When the article appeared in the newspaper, consumers thought that the quality of Panasonic TVs was really good, and a bad thing turned to be good. This is the dialectical way of thinking. In short, the final purpose of using dialectical thinking to resolve a wide range of conflicts is to elicit good results, elicit good things from the bad, turn the good to the better and prevent it from changing to the bad.

Study the weapons of mastering dialectical way of thinking: one is to understand, transform and harness the nature and benefit mankind; the second is to understand and solve various contradictions in our three complicated consumption practices and attain our desired goals; the third, arming ourselves with dialectical way of thinking would make us smart, make less or no mistakes, and remain invincible forever.

Reverse thinking

The reverse thinking way, which is opposite to the logical thinking way and other general thinking ways, is a way to achieve the purpose of solving problems correctly.

For example, the story of horse racing by Tianji is a typical example of reverse thinking. It is a way of acting in a diametrically opposite way. According to the general, logical way of thinking, people would have their best horse compete with others' best and let the inferior horse compete with the same kind. But Sun Bin acted in a diametrically opposite way. He made his worst horse compete with the best of his opponent, the best of his with the second best of his opponent and the second best with the worst and at last he won. In the military, it is the normal logical way of thinking that if you attack me, I would defend. But Mao Zedong chose to lure the enemy in deep and make a backward thrust, attacking the enemies by surprise.

This is reverse thinking. Another method is to keep the enemy in check with a small force. There is an army, but not all of the army would be sent to fight with the enemy, but a small force is used to divert the enemy's main force and at the same time separate the enemy armies from each other. It is also reverse thinking to shift your battle situation by concentrating a superior force to destroy the small and weak part of your enemy. In our work, there is also situation like this. For example, when what needs to be dealt with is too much. You cannot dwell on this since there is too much work to be done. You cannot put your major attention to the details. Just put a little effort on these trivial tasks. The main focus of a manager should be on the general situation, the principle task. Wasting time on trivial matters would affect the overall work. In many cases, the reverse thinking way should be used to deal with such problems.

Reverse thinking is a very important way of working. For instance, the reverse thinking way is bound to be used in arguing for a scientific research project, in working out work plans and measures as well as in illustrating a point of view from a positive perspective. If it cannot be turned down, it is basically correct; if the program cannot be reversed, it is problematic, or incomplete, hereby we must improve or make a new program. When discussing in a meeting, we must pay attention to negative comments, which sometimes are proved to be true and thus are valuable. However, many times, negative comments are wrong. Leaders should centralize correct views through democratic centralism.

For a particular problem, consideration must be given to choosing a right way to solve it. Holistic thinking, logical thinking, dialectical materialist thinking or transposition thinking? Should it be done by a mixture of these kinds of thinking? We should seek the correct ways to finish tasks within our respective areas.

Transposition thinking

The transposition thinking method is the way that the thinker uses to consider a problem from the position of the people who is supposed to be the third party. We should think both from the perspective of leader and from those who are led, and the one who is led should think about how to do things and solve problems from the perspective of the leaders. And further transposition should be made by the leader or the one led for the sake of the third party to analyze and review the correctness of the thing. The transposition thinking way is that the brain studies the targeted thing by using the study methods of summarizing, induction, and the abstraction of tri-transposition. In this way, we can grasp the essence of things and conduct a rational and proper solution.

Confucius once said: 'Do not do to others what you do not wish others to do to you.' That is to say do not impose on others what you yourself do not desire. As a leader, if you consider something to be incorrect, then do not make your subordinate do it. This is transposition thinking: Understanding problems from the other's perspective, then things would be done well.

Another transformation, from the perspective of the third party, is to see whether the policies made are correct or not. As a saying goes: lookers-on see most of the game, which tells us the importance of transposition. Nobody is allowed to stick to his old way of doing things and doing things subjectively just because he is beyond the reach of the leaders. In this way, you cannot get the desired effect. Looking at yourself, you can never see clearly. With transposition thinking to observe problems, you will become more objective. Always from the perspective of leaders, you cannot analyze the problems comprehensively; while always standing at the position of the led, you may always blame leaders. If you were the leader, what would you do? In the past, there was a saying: if you are not in charge of the household, you would never know how expensive the daily necessities are, which means if you are not in that position, you would never know the complication and interrelations of everything. China needs to support 1.3 billion people. Can you solve the problem? Can you make them lead a life like Americans overnight? Definitely you cannot since conditions are not the same at all! Not standing in the position, you have a lot of disputes, while standing there, how will you deal with it? Only by experiencing this personally can you understand the true face and difficulty of the problem.

In an enterprise, leaders, when doing everything, must take into account the reality of their subordinates, must place themselves in the position of the led, consider what they would do if they were the led and then make plans for courses of action, especially in the aspects of the distribution policy, ideological work, and management regulations and policies. As the led, one should think if I were the leader, what is the correct thing to be done? Only in this way, can we see clearly the right and wrong, the correct and incorrect and highly unify our thinking and hold together to form an ever-victorious and invincible team.

Creative thinking

In order to carry out work in a creative way, it is necessary to master the creative thinking method. Try to develop one's savvy, inspiration and understanding; try to be a purposeful, careful and attentive man; follow the principle of being practical and realistic and then one would have creative thinking ways, savvy and inspiration. Creative thinking way is not confined to original knowledge, but is ready to think independently and is good at doubting and proposing questions. It is critical to be skillful at asking questions and commanding the thinking approach to work creatively. Many ideas are made in work. But many people would doubt whether these ideas will work and whether they conform to the local reality. With independent thinking, if we find former concepts are not correct, we need to bring up our new ones. This thinking way is characterized by positively seeking difference, that is, to be inclined to think out approaches different from others; keen observation, great novelty, and initiative. The creative thinking must be active to doubt about the routine management practices, put forward new ideas and opinions as well as suggestions for improving impractical methods; in this way, a person can be of great initiative. In addition, this thinking way has the advantage of putting forward new ideas and hypotheses.

Through vast experience you gain in practice, through observations of various complex factors in dynamic changes, and based on rich scientific knowledge and association, the rational thinking you get is creative thinking. The first characteristic of this thinking is strong doubt. If you doubt one way, then you should try to solve the problem in another way. Your leader may tell you what to do, but if you doubt it will work, you should consider replacing it by another way. Creative thinking comes from doubt, and after that imagination begins.

For instance, seeing a cup, we might notice one of its disadvantages: failure to preserve heat. Then, imagination begins to function. Seeing a thermos bottle with good heat preservation, we think whether its liner could be reduced and put into a cup. This is creative thinking, so the vacuum thermos cup is produced. Imagination is the manifestation of the creative thinking way. In the process of imagination, one may be hit by inspiration, when we integrate all complex things and a new thing appears in one's mind; this is the function of inspiration and thinking recognition. Aircraft have evolved from flying birds and gradually became more mature. Inspiration and thinking recognition are another manifestation of creative thinking. Creative thinking, as rational thinking, whose correctness must be determined by deductive thinking. For example, imagine the production of the aircraft. Whether the imagined craft could work or not needs to be crystallized by deductive thinking and at last tested in practice to show whether the design is right or not.

In researching and using creative thinking ways, we should dare to innovate in research to break the old-established concepts, have the courage to imagine and conduct scientific experiments, and then we can invent and create something. In our work, we mustn't simply copy 'books' and follow regulations. Instead, we must carry out investigation and study, combine 'books', documents, and regulations with the reality of the local time and place, and explore working methods that fit the reality. We should carry out the work with creative methods, and only in this way can we have prominent achievements. Sanzhu Company is a national company with wide regional differences. It has no choice but to rely on good thinking ways to perform excellently. All achievements of new experience and inventions are those of creative thinking and of the recognition of savvy and inspiration thinking.

'From prominence to balance, from balance to prominence'

The thinking way of 'from prominence to balance, from balance to prominence' is a general law in the process of things' motion and development, and is used to guide work on the basis of thinking cognition. For example, the growth of an independent tree is prominence and development; stretching out twigs and leaves in the process of making prominence is the so called balance; continuous growing is prominence and the branches and leaves in growth is balance; this process repeats and when the tree stops growing, the final balance is to guarantee its safety. At that time, except for special situations, the tree generally begins to decline and gradually dies.

Trees growing in dense forests keep their balance by interdependence, so they are short and thick and don't have as many branches as a single tree. Because of the density of the forest, trees in a forest compete for sunshine, air, and growing room, thus those which stand out quickly and grow faster, yet at the same time, they balance each other to ensure their stable and secure growth. In the process of standing out and competing for growing, trees that fail to achieve that would be washed out.

In business management and development, management is balance and development is prominence. Just like a half bucket of water, if you manage it well and do not let it leak a drop, it is still just half-full and would be reduced by evaporation. Only by adding water to it, would there be more water, and adding water is standing out. If the bucket is filled with water, then the peak of balance is reached. At this time, you need to transform the bucket to increase its capacity and then develop a new balance.

In the development of group work, many people would work at the same time on the same job. Because of the differences in their understanding of the work, the skill mastery, savvy, and inspirations, the achievement of work would be different. Among these people, some would stand out with prominent achievements and create work experience, which is called prominence. The group leaders guiding this job would organize all the staff to learn from the man with great achievements and experience, which is called balance. This is the thinking way of prominence and balance used by leaders to guide work.

When the whole group begins to learn the advanced experience and achieve the advanced level of an advanced person, another new advanced experience of the advanced characters will appear, which can be regarded as new prominence. Leaders then regulate for new balance, to organize the mass to learn the new experience and try to catch up with or even exceed the model; the process repeats but with advancement and development.

Nowadays, a lot of work lacks flexibility of methods, which need to be stimulated by creative thinking. The working method of the past is cramming; the management is high centralization; accounting, marketing orders, and plans are also centralized. But now we've shifted and changed. The top only distributes the guiding ideology, based on which the lower levels should work creatively rather than do what they are told to do. The central idea only covers two efficiencies, and then it is up to one's capability to find out how to improve these two efficiencies. It is just like the eight immortals crossing the sea; each one shows his or her special prowess.

All in all, we should use these seven ways of thinking comprehensively and in a mixed way, using different methods under different situations. If one can free oneself and not work with a simple, rigid, imperative, fully copied, and completely obedient method, one would become a fairly flexible and constructive leader. Facing these problems, one would weigh various conditions, use comprehensively all kinds of thinking ways and create a lively and vibrant working scene. These seven thinking ways are a golden key with which one can unlock numerous doors. Use your brains, pick up this golden key of thought, and make yourself smarter through application, training, testing, repetition, progress, and sublimation to push forward the flourishing of your career and achieve better two efficiencies. It is also the realistic significance of these seven thinking ways.

Section 3 Apply materialistic dialectics to discuss consumption law

Philosophy is knowledge about world views. Marxist philosophy is the product of the scientific development of the past, the results of human theoretical thinking, which is a solid scientific system summed up in consumption practice and then proved by it. Therefore, in our exploring the law of consumption, we should learn more philosophy. Marxist philosophy is a unity of materialism and dialectics, and materialist dialectics is a kind of science about universal connection and development. The motion process of all things exists and develops in a dialectical way. Therefore, only by adhering to materialist dialectics can it be possible to recognize the true features of three important consumptions.

Analysis of 'change' and 'unchange'

Materialist dialectics holds that all things are changing and developing, and change is absolute, while the unchanged is relative, and there is no absolutely unchanging thing.

Of course, all changes, no matter what kind, happen under certain conditions. The internal cause is the basis while the external cause is the condition of change. The growth of knowledge depends on constant learning. If we only count on knowledge we've learned before and don't keep studying, then our relative knowledge becomes diminished. People change under certain situations. For example, the dignified war hero Liu Qingshan went to Tianjin after liberation. With the change of environment, he changed from a hero to a sinner. Some people may not have had much merit before, yet with their study and hard work in a new environment, they became people with great achievements in our socialist construction, like Wang Jinxi, the man who made great contributions in the oilfield.

Therefore, we must discipline ourselves in work, manage based on regulations instead of trust. Before you trust a person, don't appoint him; after you appoint him, don't suspect him. This is our human resources policy, which, however, can be used to replace the management system. Thus, we must improve the management system and strengthen institutional management. Some comrades still fail to see why we should do so. Actually, strengthening the management system is a requirement of the sound development of enterprises, and everybody is supposed to understand its significance, removing the ideas that an auditor's inspection means there is no confidence in you. It is a misunderstanding to consider the audits of auditors to be a kind of distrust. Hence it is imperative to know that all things are changing and developing.

Relations between principal and secondary contradictions

There are usually many contradictions in one thing, among which one is primary, and others are secondary. The primary and secondary contradictions in the position of dominance determine the nature of the thing. Therefore, I repeatedly contend that leaders must concentrate on the principal contradiction; otherwise it is hard to make any achievement. For example, as a branch manager, what will you focus on since there is so much routine work even in small organizations with all their elements? Obviously it is sales that must be concentrated on, for it is the principal contradiction. As long as the sales volume is increased, other work can be led to good performance. If we try to grasp everything and deliver our energy, nothing will be done well. Thus, it is suggested to learn to grasp the principal contradiction skillfully.

Of course, the principal contradiction and secondary contradiction can be transformed into the other under certain conditions. For example, as a branch, sales are the principal contradiction, and others such as the staff's life and welfare are secondary. However, if the staff often work overtime to open up the market and finally the sales volume increases at the cost of the staff breaking down owing to fatigue, caring for staff's life becomes the principal contradiction. Under such circumstances, the manager should put the sales issue aside to care about sick staff and let them feel the warmth of the collective. In this way, when sick employees recover, they will work harder, leading to better performance in sales. This is a virtuous circle. On the contrary, if the manager ignores the transformation of the secondary contradiction and just stresses sales with no care for the staff's life, the staff's enthusiasm will be undermined, which in return affects the sales performance.

Another example, in a company, sales are also very important. But since last April, our client began to stop buying from us. Although with some effort we won at last and kept on selling our products, a potential crisis emerged, and whether we have competitive products and can continue to grow steadily, such a fundamental strategic problem has become the principal contradiction. Therefore, in these circumstances, I decided to establish a research institute immediately and develop our own products, in which I put most of the manpower and resources and generally left sales in the lurch. In this way, although our income was reduced by three to four million in 1993, we managed to solve our principle contradiction. When a manufacturer of some product cut off their supply, the new generation of viable preparation Sanzhu Oral Liquid initiated in China and developed in-house was produced. It has ensured our steady development. Thus, in grasping the principle contradiction, we shouldn't neglect the mutual transformation of the principle and the secondary contradictions.

Universality and specialty of contradiction

There are contradictions everywhere and anytime and contradictions of different things have particular features of their own. For example, everybody wants to survive as healthily and long as possible, and every time when they get sick, they want to be cured. This is a universal problem. However, there is an exception – some people want to commit suicide. In special circumstances, they refuse to live; this is a special problem.

Another example is that the living standard in China now is low, and awareness of health protection of the Chinese is relatively poor. They focus their attention on curing the illness rather than on health protection and illness prevention. The illness–treatment phenomenon is a universal problem. As a result, when selling Sanzhu Oral Liquid, we publicized it with a fixed position of treatment. However, it is a different case in some cities such as Shanghai, Dalian, Beijing, and other economically developed cities, with relatively high levels of culture and strong health awareness. Thus, in these areas, it is advisable to place more stress on the function of health protection of Sanzhu Oral Liquid in advertising. Understanding this truth, it will be easier to work effectively. This is the contradiction between the universality and particularity of problems. Understanding this truth would be quite helpful to make your work easier. The 'ten principles of marketing' we have formulated just sets down a norm in the company, hence it is the universality of contradictions rather than specific programs; it is definitely unacceptable to apply it mechanically.

Everything, including nature, is complicated and changeable; all exist objectively and regularly and can be understood and yet are hard to understand. There is a gradual process to understand all this. During our understanding, transforming, and utilizing of nature, these three important consumptions are both finite and infinite understanding. So only by mastering the laws of contradiction, dialectical materialism, and these seven ways of thinking (or 'golden keys') can we better understand and transform nature, solve all contradictions that emerge in our work and affairs during the three important consumption practice, and then achieve our periodical objectives.

In short, we should probe the law of three important consumptions with materialist dialectics. In this way, we can work actively and achieve success.

12

The law of thought and leadership management

Section 1 The importance of following the law of thought and improving soft management

All thinking activities of human beings arise from three important consumption processes while no thinking activities are separate from them. It is the task of ideological and political work to guide people to unify the extremely complex thinking incurred during the three important consumption process to the correct thinking (sometimes wrong thinking), meanwhile help people to solve specific issues incurred for multiple reasons. The thinking issues are complex; we cannot deal with them with simple moralizing. We should observe thinking laws to solve new situations and issues incurred in the three important consumptions.

Ideological and political work is the legacy of our party and army. Every victory of our work is closely connected with strong and forceful ideological and political work. Resorting to Marxism-Leninism and Mao Zedong thought, the older generation of proletarian revolutionaries enlightened the progressive proletariat and intellectuals, established the Communist Party, further increased the Party organization by deeply and extensively promoting Marxism-Leninism and relying on ideological and political work, led grandiose workers' and farmers' movements, set up the people's army, and enhanced the army's morale with an effective ideological and political work. Under suffering and difficult conditions, the Party fought with a strong will to seize the victory in the anti-Japan war and defeated Kuomingtang reactionaries. Mao Zedong (1987) said:

> During the past fifteen years, our Party observed and will observe revolutionary and Bolshevistic tradition, which is orthodox in our Party, including everything good politically, organizationally and in working style, which is undeniable. Without this great tradition, our party won't be sustained, united, and cemented and we won't obliterate intra-Party mistakes, win revolutionary victory by fighting with the enemy and establish the Communist Party as the big one winning the trust of the people and different social classes... On the basis of People's War and upon such principles as unity of army and people, commanders and soldiers and disintegration of enemy, People's Liberation Army establishes its own strong and forceful revolutionary political work, which is an important factor for us to defeat the enemy.

Since the founding of New China, besides the correct route and policy, ideological and political work continues to play a very import role in gaining victory of the war to resist America and aid Korea and the socialist transformation. The unit of politics and economy, and politics and technology is undoubted and will remain so. This is loyal and professional. The word politics will still exist in the future. However, the meaning has changed. If we are always engaged in businesses and overlook ideological and political work, we will emerge as directionless economists and technicians, which is very dangerous. Ideological and political work serves economic fundamentals and ensures the completion of economic and technological work. However, ideology and politics are commander and soul. If we relax a little on ideological and political work, the economic and technological work will be led astray. Without the strong and forceful ideological and political work, the implementation and execution of correct routes and various policies will encounter enormous difficulty and resistance.

The ten-year turmoil of the Cultural Revolution misled people's thought, with cases involving unjust, fake, and false charges piled up. The third plenary session of the 11th Chinese Central Committee began to rectify wrongful cases, systematically correct mistakes in various fields and adjust several policies, ideological, and political work to conform to the building of four modernizations in China. Because of the remaining 'leftist' influence, people don't understand well the newly formulated policies catering to the development of new scenarios. Under such circumstances, it is very important to do good ideological and political work. Deng Xiaoping (2002) said:

> We should put ideological and political work in a very important position, seriously do it well without relaxation. This work involves

> Party committees, management at various levels and each party member. We should be target-focused and careful in this work. In order to make this work popular with the masses, the most important factor is that each Party member, especially those serving in a leader's position should start doing first themselves when this work involves the mobilization of masses. Therefore, in order to do good ideological and political work, we need to improve the Party's leadership and the leadership system.

If we fail in ideological and political work, the correct policy of the Party's central committee won't be smoothly executed; the adjustment of the national economy and four modernizations won't be smoothly realized. Therefore, ideological and political work is the lifeline for the development of the national economy and the realization of the four modernizations.

Existence determines ideology. Since thought, ideology, and politics emerge from certain economic fundamentals, ideological and political work, with the development of different economic rules, interests, and interrelations, different thought, ideology, and political views will unavoidably form their their own rules. Ideological politics emerging from socialist economic fundamentals and superstructure represents the fundamental interests of the broad masses. In the fight against capitalist ideological politics, proletarian ideological politics looms and forms its own rules. It has become a science to study and master its rules. In order to do good ideological and political work, we have to study the rule of ideological activity for the emergence of thought. When we apply this rule to the soft management of enterprise, we might get twice the result with half the effort.

Section 2 The law of ideological tendency of thinking activities

Materiality of thinking

Each thinking activity of man is a reflection in the brain of a certain form of the motion of matter. Since human beings are advanced animals, we are capable of initiative thinking, able to summarize, induct, and abstract to a certain extent. The concept is formed by analyzing, or integrating unfamiliar substances or the combination of both. What distinguishes the human from the animal is thinking capacity. Thinking is the most advanced mental activity with new form of quality. Human thought is the reflection of a certain social material culture in the brain's thinking activity.

Since thinking and thought are a reflection of a certain form of matter, in class societies, people live at a certain rank of class and all ideas and thoughts are marked with the trait of that class. Ideas immune from the impact of class do not exist. Neither does the thinking above the support of materials.

Effects of thinking and thought on matter

Since thinking and thought exist in a certain motion of matter, a correct thought will strongly boost material development while an outdated, decayed, or wrong thought in a leading position can severely impact and hinder development. When the principle of steam was discovered, Watt, the famous scientist, inducted and carried out repeated experiments, and finally the steam engine was invented and its application boosted the rapid development of the material civilization of the whole society. Based on the discovery of the nature of lightening, Franklin inducted and carried out experiments many times to invent the lightening rod while the extensive application of electricity brought human beings into the electric era. There was the same enduring process for the discovery of the molecule, atom, and ion. Marxism-Leninism and Mao Zedong's thought represented the advanced proletariat thought of human beings, which guided the proletariat class to transform the world and gain a significant victory. The victory of the October Revolution, China's New Democratic Revolution and socialist revolution, is forceful proof of this.

Under general conditions, when a person is in a progressive mood, he will work efficiently; when a person bears a wrong thought or has a depressed or unhappy mood, his work efficiency will be relatively low. Therefore, thinking and thought are a reflection of a certain form of matter, and they can be used to affect matter at the same time – 'matter transforms into spirit and spirit into matter' to promote things to move forward continuously.

Thinking and thought of tended regularity

Thinking and thought are a reflection of a certain form of matter. The motion of a certain matter has its own regularity and tendency, which constitutes the characteristics of variety of matter and the difference between each. Since the motion of various matter has its own regularity and tendency, upon its reflection in human thinking and thought, the thinking and thought with regular tendencies comes into being. For example, when politics and economy are unstable or in a transformation stage, most people will tend to be waiting, expecting, and hesitating. In such a context, if people are not educated with correct thoughts and policies, the speed and anticipated effect of the overall revolution will be compromised. Therefore, the work of scenario education matters, which will be the first priority of leaders, tolerating no negligence.

When education on ideological politics tends to be neglected, the corrupted capitalist ideology and its culture and art will surely be flooded, poisoning Party members, cadres, and the innocent young generation. In such contexts, human thought was plagued, which damaged the Party. Faced with such a reality, we need to promote the correct advanced thought, forcefully propagandize righteous people and good deeds, carry out integrated education with typical good deeds, and inflict severe penalties on those who behave badly.

When the immediate interest of most people is involved, people's minds tend to fluctuate. For example, in 1976 and 1979, the national government was determined to adjust salaries of 40–60% employees. However, 90% of people tended to raise their salary to a higher level. Before the official start of salary adjustment, smart leaders should take advantage of such a mindset, and send out a new call for 'four modernizations' in a timely manner. Most employees imposed stricter requirements on themselves and competed to complete various production tasks. To a certain extent, the analysis of such a mindset will always disclose the simplest fact: people need first to consider food, beverages, clothes, shelter, and transportation whatever the social consciousness is.

When the salary adjustment was officially started, the thinking and thought of people turned from the tendency of raising their salary to whether it could be realized. In such an environment, people tended to compare their advantages to others' disadvantages, displaying unstable emotions. The main method of ideological and political work at this moment was to guide people to understand the meaning of the salary adjustment, treat themselves and others correctly, and understand the correct attitude they should have when their salaries couldn't be raised. What was more important, the exemplary force of management at various levels was a force for ideological and political work. Each Party member should always keep in mind that the pioneering and exemplary functions of the Communist Party members are very important.

When the salary adjustment work basically ended, the thought of most people soon returned to a stable phase under the atmosphere of a solid thought foundation when the salary due to employees was adjusted.

However, we should be clear that even a few irrational phenomena would cause dissatisfaction in some people.

Leaders should follow the necessary rules of the development of such an ideological activity. We need to face mistakes that occur at work bravely and patiently educate some people without correct thinking and offer aids to people in need. After some time, the thoughts of these people would gradually return to normal.

When activities of human thinking form a kind of mindset, another form of mindset is covered. Therefore, inexorable laws of the activity of thinking are applied to do ideological and political work so as to prevent thinking and thought from developing in an extreme direction. Materialistic dialectics is employed to solve problems. For example, at the stage of growing up, a person should encounter qualitative leaps physically and psychologically. Reason will be compromised by sensation. Relations of love and study could extend to the extreme and improper tackling of a love affair, which would severely impact study and work. Therefore, we need to guide young people to handle relations of love, marriage, study, and work correctly.

At a certain stage, the over focus on production efficiency of all employees would lead to production safety and normal operation of equipment being overlooked; when incidents of human injury and equipment damage were caused investigation of responsible persons was started; the mindsets of the employees would turn from focusing on production to the treatment of incidents, and employees would tend to be over-cautious and depressed and thus affect production efficiency. A correct handling of such a tendency required leaders to focus especially on production safety during a production boom, operate strictly by the rules, and educate employees to eliminate potential safety risks at the burgeoning state. In case of serious incidents, materialistic dialectics should be employed, clearly analyzing the cause and liabilities for the incident and immediately adopting remedying measures.

Section 3 Educate people with advanced culture and thought

Due to the unbalanced development status among different industries in various regions, Chinese people have different economic statuses. The advanced cultural ideology is fighting fiercely with all outdated thought every minute. If the thinking and thought of the public are left unrefined, people could lack a common language and will. During the periods of reform and opening up, and the emancipation of minds, economic restructuring is an arduous and complex task. We have seen many existing problems and will encounter many unanticipated problems. In order to complete this task and ensure the uniting of thought and actions, we have to strengthen and improve the ideological work effectively. Or else, the ideological turmoil is unfavorable for political stability. Once the advanced correct thought on behalf of people is mastered by the masses, it will become a material force to transform society and the world. Therefore, we should work hard on the following:

1. Strengthen the study of advanced theory. It is difficult for most people to study and extensively read basic theories. Therefore, most people should grasp the fundamental things of policy. We need to understand China's existing policies, actual working experiences, and problems deeply through repeated discussions and guide people to discuss them intensively. Only in this way can we handle them well and use them to guide actual work.
2. In accordance with existing policies, study materialistic dialectics, which may deepen our understanding of the theoretical basis of existing policies, and at the same time help us gradually overcome and correct various erroneous ideas and thoughts.
3. Based on various wrong thoughts incurred in living consumption, scientific production consumption and social consumption, use materialistic dialectics to guide people to discussion to gradually overcome and rectify various wrongful thoughts.
4. Attach importance to theoretical study and elect a qualified theoretical supervisor to guide people to grasp essential points and explain them in simple way.
5. The leadership management should lead in study and promote the learning experiences of masses.
6. Improve various institutions for study (including part-time and amateur) and the learning system.

Section 4 Three important consumptions and ideological work

Living consumption, social consumption, and scientific research and production consumption are the most essential activities of human beings. Living consumption is essential for people to survive. Production consumption is an outcome of living consumption. During the whole process of living consumption, production consumption, and social consumption, different kinds of thoughts came into being. Even in communist society where social classes have been eradicated, there are still correct and wrong thoughts.

Without living consumption, social consumption, and scientific research and production consumption, there won't be any thinking and thoughts. Therefore, thought arises from living consumption, social consumption, and scientific research and production consumption and, at the same times, affects those three important consumptions. Ideological and political work will be carried out combined with the three important consumptions, and we need to correct wrong mindsets in time. Delayed correction will adversely impact the completion of the production task and product quality. For example, an employee who held an irresponsible attitude towards work because he was unsatisfied with his bonus produced a defective product. The relevant leader discovered it and held an incident analysis meeting that same night. The leader timely found out about that employee's mindset and operational mistake and formulated correct measures. This correct method helped to raise the product eligibility rate from 50% to 85% and the task was completed beyond the quota.

Section 5 The general law of thinking by young people

As a general rule, young people think less and are apt to accept new things and be courageous, but at the same time they are immature and have less social experience. During the transformation from being a teenager to being a young person, a person will gradually grow mature physiologically. Their thinking about study, work, love, marriage, and so on at a certain stage will fill their whole mindsets.

Keeping company with good and talented people explains the huge influence of the environment on human beings and it is important in exerting deeper influence on the young.

In our country, we cultivate and educate the young generation with right advanced thinking. However, we need to clearly realize that the remaining feudal thought and corrupted thought of materialism poisoned the pure soul of young people like the plague. When serious facts are reflected in the brain of the young, the ideas and thoughts they form can be divided into four common tendencies:

1. *Being diligent and hard working*. We need more work in finding more efficient ways for the younger generation to master techniques to make great contributions to national development. During study and work, when love and marriage are touched upon, young people should think carefully and regard their career as the first priority. Some would take advantage of sincere love to promote study and work.

2. *Being not so ambitious in study.* Young people should seek to be self-sufficient and lead a stable and comfortable life by finding the right person to marry who has some skills.
3. *Being arrogant and superficial.* There are some people who are arrogant and superficial, particular about jobs, and rely on parental influence and superficial economic conditions.
4. *Being corrupt.* There are a few people who indulge in a corrupt capitalist life, empty-minded, seeking economic benefits by any means to satisfy themselves and their counterparts.

In study, work, love and marriage, young people tend to have ten kinds of thinking and thought:

1. Superficial, vain young people are impressed with appearance, beauty, wealth, and reputation, which is a biased aesthetic view.
2. A sober-minded young person will generally attach importance to inner beauty, industriousness, ambition, and love appearance and beauty but not pursue them too severely. They enjoy a harmonious family, work hard, and are active in work with little ideological fluctuation.
3. Some feel self-abased due to misfortune or suffering or severely impressed by the misfortune and suffering of others. These groups of people generally attach great importance to inner beauty and find a kind husband or wife with an active working attitude. Generally speaking, they don't pay much attention to study and work, tend to stay silent and self-contained.
4. Some are innocent and immature. Boys or girls easily fall in love, generally in adolescence, and thus should be correctly guided so that they can hold the right attitude towards the world outlook and the relationships between life and work.
5. Pretty, sober-minded, and far-sighted girls are generally aggressive, smart in work, and simple in lifestyle, and very patient; they focus on finding talented, enterprising, industrious men with inner beauty to love; they like external beauty but don't pursue it too strongly, while talented, sober-minded, practical, far-sighted, strong-willed men tend to find a pretty, sober-minded female to love.
6. Instant love is usually the beginning of first love. Although unfamiliar with each other, the two admire and respect each other (including personality and style). They have a good impression of each other, which is usually the starting point of recognition and friendship.
7. Isolated young people are always stubborn in their own personal opinions, usually silent, become very talkative when meeting someone

conforming to their opinions, like to choose sincere, honest, and enterprising partners to love.

8. Persons rich in love usually have multi-level aesthetical values, and are radical. Their family is usually interested in economics and politics. They are talkative and outdo others in their intelligence and appearance. When the love affair is touched upon, they may think many others conform to their tastes. The second possibility is that they may soon select their favorite love, showing love and care. Outside, they usually show affection or love for other men or women. Third, rich love may make a person dislike the old while pursuing the new.
9. Young people who regard love as a sacrifice for selfish desire are not capable themselves. With regard to marriage, they would like to find a counterpart with influential family background, which may bring them political development or economic satisfaction.
10. People who are arrogant and unfortunate in love usually outdo others in intelligence and appearance, and enjoy skills and reputation. They don't have a clear understanding of themselves, faltering in love and work. They place higher demands on love, forgetting the principle that everyone is not perfect. Therefore, they fail to find their Mr. or Ms Right. With the passage of time, they have to shoulder the consequences of love.

To sum up, adolescents usually have ten mindsets. Arrogance is the big enemy of love. Industriousness and loyalty makes the bridge of love, while fatuity is the mire of love. We should strengthen education about equality, dignity, and self-respect for the young, and severely criticize any behavior hurting others' dignity while the serious violators should be punished and educated.

When we are engaged in the education of young people we should:

- forcefully promote the advanced model of young people in various fields, actively guide them, and make them develop on the right healthy track
- arrange the study of politics, business, and entertainment activities of young people to avoid ideological emptiness
- pay more attention to both ends, and influence the middle
- use the good as a roadmap helping the backward to catch up with the advanced and promoting the middle.

In this way, we can promote the enthusiastic, move those who are neutral forward, and let those who are resistant to change catch up.

Because of the prevailing pessimism and depression, and contempt for older people by backward young people, and the neutral mindset of others, we should be very patient when dealing with ideological and political work of neutral and resistant people. During the process of motivation and influence, we should be good at finding their achievements and advantages, detect very tiny progress they have made, and avoid attaching bias and sarcasm to them.

We should be good at dealing with the mindset of the individual according to four categories of tendency and ten thinking and thought rules. We should insist on opening one lock with one key. Let experience cultivate and educate the young with personal experiences. It has been proven that the aforesaid method is very effective.

Section 6 The law of thought under special conditions

When we encounter special circumstances during work and study, new thinking and thought activities are generated. Studying and grasping laws of thought under special circumstances, we can actively prevent the generation of negative factors and convert negative factors into active factors. It is necessary to study what kind of problems one encounters, at what age and what time, and what kind of thought is produced.

When people are sick, lying in bed, they hope that their relatives or friends will come to see them, and carefully watch others' attitudes towards them to detect levels of concern about their illness. If the sick person is unmarried, they worry a lot about their future love, marriage, and so on. In these circumstances, their leaders and friends should visit them, help them solve problems, which will help the person who is ill to calm down and recover quickly, and make a contribution when returning to work. After returning to work, sick people easily accept criticism when making mistakes as they regard criticism as a kind of sincere care. If nobody cares about them when they are sick, they will then complain and hold negative attitudes towards work. It will be very insignificant to do ideological and political work then.

When people are praised, rewarded, and have succeeded in reform, joining the Party and Group or have been promoted, it is easy for them to become proud and conceited, which leads to them lagging behind. In such circumstances we should avoid such negative thinking at an earlier stage and carry out education with the dialectic method. When people are criticized, encounter setbacks, retaliate, fail in reform and innovation, join the Party or group, are not satisfied with promotion, mistreated in retirement, unsatisfied with work transfer, irritated by unreasonable job assignment, they will become annoyed, depressed, and complaining and abusing at work. It is said that difficulty and setback are the fate of humans. We should establish a real outlook on growth and maturity and regard setback and difficulty as the dynamics for moving forward.

When people are in trouble, have family difficulties, re unhappy with their children's marriage, or if newly married, cannot afford an apartment, they easily become worried. In these cases leaders should make a family visit in person and help to solve the actual problems as best as they can.

People who like to do what they are good at, but are misused, will complain or get angry. Under such circumstances, the relevant leader should reflect the actual condition to the superior to shift the misused person to the right post. We need to guide and educate these kinds of people to correctly understand the complexities of things. It needs a process to solve problems. They should hold a positive attitude and adapt themselves to the new situation, help to facilitate their life and work so that they may change to like what they are engaged in, meanwhile, making contributions to national development and the well-being of human beings.

Section 7 Adhere to the guideline of coaching

One is apt to lose one's reason when in radical activities of thought. One cannot think causal factors comprehensively since being stubborn about one's opinion gets in the way, thus causing tension among family members, relatives, neighbors, classmates, colleagues, superiors, and subordinates. We should be serious in handling these contradictions.

During year-end festivals, couples quarrel since they are not rich enough to give cash to parents in economic difficulties in rural areas. Improper handling of such situations will cause severe consequences; for example, neighbors will quarrel or fight because of contradictions related to housing, land, water, electricity, or rumors. We should detect such contradictions in time and do ideological work early, stick to the reasoning method to persuade people; we should avoid contradictions escalating, adopt necessary administrative measures, be strict in criticism and education, and loose in seeking punishment.

Contradictions among colleagues are usually caused by rumor, mutual benefits, reputation, or work disagreements. We should educate employees to win awards and honors with legitimate effort, be immune to rumors, communicate and consult more regarding work disagreements, stick to problems of principle while they make concessions in tiny issues, and seek common ground while preserving tiny differences. Multiple reasons cause contradictions between superior and subordinate, cadre and masses; some result from the bad lifestyle of leaders while some result from the lack of abilities of leaders, who cannot meet the requirements of subordinates and masses.

These contradictions are universal and last for a long time. To solve these contradictions, leaders have to know people profoundly, rectify party style, and practice what they preach to people. Leaders should educate subordinates and masses to treat relations between immediate interests and long-term interests correctly. Leaders should bring good deeds to the masses in person; clarify reasons when something cannot be done in person, and take responsibility for organizing people to solve problems that can be settled with some effort.

Section 8 Care about people's living consumption

Personal interests are reflected most evidently, intensively, and sensitively in one's activities of thought, and are the most basic problems. Leaders are responsible for being representatives of the personal livelihood interests of people. Otherwise, various tasks and calls will not be accepted easily. During the revolutionary and warring age, the Communist Party educated and organized farmers to carry out the revolution. After the revolution, farmers were allocated housing and land. Wherever it is, our army will bring good deeds to people so that our army is popular with the public. The broad masses are ready to join the army to safeguard the fruits of revolution. During the revolution fight, they know the principle of making lifelong devotion to communism, and may stand the test of any hardships.

Mao Zedong once criticized those personnel who only focus on fighting while they neglect the livelihood of people, and pointed out that if we only mobilize people to fight without doing anything else, can we achieve the target of defeating the enemy? Of course not. We have to do lots of work in order to win. Lead the land struggle of farmers and allocate land to the farmer; enhance the labor enthusiasm of labor and increase farmers' production; safeguard workers' interests; establish cooperatives; develop foreign trade; and solve problems of clothes, food, shelter, daily necessity, disease, hygiene, and marriage issues related to farmers. All actual living issues related to the masses should be our concern. If we have noticed these issues, have them solved to meet needs of farmers, we can become true organizers of the farmers with them around us to support us. Comrades, till then, will we be capable enough to participate in the revolution? We will be fully capable till then.

It is because the revolution army led by the Communist Party truly cared about the living consumption of the masses that the masses really stand at the side of the People's Liberation Army and finally won the victories of the New Democratic Revolution, Liberation War, and Socialist Construction.

If a leader doesn't care to educate subordinates and broad masses, he cannot win their support and be a leader people will follow. For example, storing vegetables for winter in the northern part of China is the great concern of many people. If leaders manage to organize the purchase and transportation of vegetables to meet people's needs of living consumption, people can keep their mind on work and production. People, of course, react positively to such kind of leaders.

Section 9 Moral education

Morals are a code of collective living and conduct, which stipulate the obligations of people, relations between people, and relations between people and society. No morals can exist without society. The moral is not an abstract concept. With the change in social formation and economic foundation, morals change as well. When the economic fundamentals of socialist public ownership are established, broad masses become masters of the country and then socialist morals of citizens are generated. To love our socialist country is the profound expression of the new psychology, so are integrity, loving labor, innovation spirit, strong will, generosity, national equality, equality among men and women, respect for the old with love for the young, and so on. Morals are a reflection of a certain economic fundamentals, which must serve the politics and economy of this society. Morals are ideological power to solidify the social system and make it develop more powerfully. The greatness of Lei Feng comes from his consistent pursuit of morals in his very short life; he had made common but great contributions to social affairs, setting for us a good example of pursuing the right social morals. Lei Feng is praised by the generations that followed him. Once his spirit was mastered by the broad masses, it turned into a material force to transform society. The force of social consciousness sometimes outnumbers the power of law and directives.

Right morals have significant effects on constructing socialist material and spiritual civilization. Ideological and political works have to pay adequate attention to moral education, beginning with the concept of honor, 'five attentions and four beauties', combined with learning deeds from Lei Feng and other social figures. A citizen should love our socialist country, the Chinese nation, be ready to serve broad masses and bring good deeds to the general public. Leaders and politicians should preach in person, setting personal examples. To educate others must start with the educator himself or herself. For example, don't speak four-letter words; let the old, weak, and disabled take seats when taking the bus. If you do like this, the young will imitate you and the public will follow what you have preached; launch the campaign of the month for civilization and politeness, have comprehensive propaganda; moral leaders organize major activities and strive for marked achievements, set good examples, mobilize the public to learn, summarize and reward good deeds, forcefully promote good deeds and fine people, and gradually cultivate a socialist moral style.

Section 10 Style construction

Style as a reflection of the activities of thought

Chen Yun pointed out that the social style of the ruling party is related to the rising and falling of the controlling party. Meanwhile, the style of a unit or factory is directly related to the style of major leaders. As the saying goes that soldiers will follow the general while the grass will follow the direction of the wind. We will get a principle from this old saying that work styles of leaders have great influence on subordinates.

The power of a style

A style is a kind of silent order and power. The style of a team is determined by the style of the leader. The good style of a unit or factory is favorable for implementing the principles and policy of the Party, which will be confident of fulfilling its task and being brave to face the risk and difficulty, feel shameful for failing to complete the task. Or else, if they feel cowardly facing difficulty and risk, the order will lose power and function. For example, if a unit stops production because of loss of power for one hour, workers are willing to complete the task by voluntarily extending work hours for half an hour to finish their task. Because of mechanical problems, another unit stops production for 45 minutes. Workers left the production site, disobeying the order of leaders. Different styles have different effects.

The cultivation of a style

These are ways to cultivate a style:

1. Leaders teach by personal example as well as verbal instruction, and be strict with themselves and then other people.
2. Leaders promote good styles on every occasion, and criticize and correct wrong styles.
3. Leaders exercise good styles in practice, and are strict with rules. For example, we should highlight the attitude and discipline of completing tasks in case the implementation plan is not strictly abided to. We should have precise organization, strict requirements and discipline, and serious attitudes to implement organizational discipline.
4. The superior inspects the work of inferiors and their units, and especially the work style of leaders. The main method of solving problems starts with finding the causes from leaders. If we do this, we may possibly rectify an adverse style.

Section 11 Ideological education and strict requirements

We are all aware of the relationships between ideological education and strict requirements. However, two inclinations may emerge during actual work: when we attach importance to ideological work, we tend to think that ideological work is omnipotent. If we patiently work, anybody can be transformed. It is a bias; another scenario is that we tend to manage the economy through economic means while overlooking the function of ideological work. It is proven by practice that both tendencies are wrong. In order to make broad masses produce study and live in an order way, we need to require government, production leaders, and authority leaders to issue compulsory decrees. Without these administrative decrees, the social order cannot be maintained. This is commonsense to us all, which is complementary with solving internal contradictions among people with persuasion. Therefore, people in charge will hold on to advanced ideological and political work with the combination of strict requirements and law enforcement. Superiors criticize as severely as possible and punish as little as possible.

Section 12 Establish an ideological work net

Leaders at different levels are the backbones at work among the masses. They are hard cores of production, as well as the hard cores that ideological and political work depends on. If we can detect the mindset of people, we may achieve better effects in ideological work. Only when leaders and backbones conduct ideological work together, can ideological situations be grasped at any moment and problems solved in time. We build an ideological and political work net to solve contradictions by mutual respect, love, and help.

Section 13 The essence of ideological work

It is important to make clear that the essence of ideological work is to solve various ideological conflict. Materialistic dialectics holds that contradiction exists in everything. Therefore, in the ideological sphere, there is inevitably a series of contradictions, from living consumption, social consumption, scientific experiment consumption, and production consumption; there are contradictions. Without contradictions, social production and scientific experiment won't exist and living consumption won't be so colorful. The existence and development of contradictions promote the advance of social production and scientific consumption, and enhance the living standards of the masses. The influence of ideological work is to understand contradictions in a positive way, and to spur the productivity of consumption society to develop by leaps and bounds.

There are internal and external factors causing the transference and development of contradictions. The internal cause is the basis while the external cause is the condition of change. The external cause exerts its functions through the internal cause while the ideological work is the external cause. Therefore, in order to solve contradictions reasonably, we should grasp the internal factors of the contradiction. In this way, ideological work can be target-focused to deal with contradictions in a positive way.

The contradiction is universal as well as special. Therefore, we should differentiate when dealing with ideological work.

Section 14 Become skilled in the holistic method

For contradictions of universality, the work method of 'open all locks with one key' will be employed. Contradictions of universality are contradictions that have something in common. If this method is employed in dealing with these kinds of contradiction, these contradictions can be solved efficiently. For example, life and work are the most basic contradictions. If people are happy they can work efficiently; conversely, they will work at low efficiency in poverty and apathy if they are unhappy. Therefore, life has a direct influence on work. Meanwhile, work also has direct influence on living consumption. If we work well, enjoy a rich material life, the spiritual life will be fulfilling, and the material and spiritual life will correspondingly be enhanced. Therefore, as an ideological worker, we should make the care of people's life as our first priority, mobilize the initiative of all employees, and promote the smooth progress of work. The smooth development of work will enhance the living standards of the masses, generating a virtuous circle. On the other hand, where there are work difficulties, we should inspire people to fight for happiness, ascend the career ladder, and work hard, getting rid of worrying and negative thoughts. If not, ideological work will become empty preaching, losing calling force.

Under the condition of a socialist market economy, contradictions between collective interests and personal interests are universal. No group can get rid of this kind of contradiction. Not properly solved, it will adversely influence work. In order to solve this contradiction, we mainly use materialistic, spiritual, cultural, and information forces to mobilize the work initiative of people. Meanwhile, we should help people to hold a noble world outlook to broaden horizons so that personal and regional interests should give way to collective and overall interests. Finally, the collective interests will defeat personal interests, and we will work hard to make contributions to the development of our country, which is a strategic view.

As a member of a group, we should also build the noble collective outlook. Or else, we will be restricted in a little personal space to achieve nothing. With regard to Sanzhu Corporation, the unconventional fission-like rapid development in the economic tide is closely attached to the noble outlook of each employee. Since the establishment of the company, we constantly base ourselves on dedication; hold four banners of compatriotism, devotion, hard work, and frugality; regard the promotion of high-tech products and transferring them into social productivity as personal responsibilities and missions; and attach equal importance to social interests and economic interests. As a result, the meaning of an enterprise is enhanced and the senses of responsibility and mission of employees are strengthened. We, therefore, automatically get rid of some narrow ideological concepts and effectively reinforce the professionalism of the staff. The unity of national interests, collective interests, and personal interests has become the mainstream of the enterprise's thought. During the process of three important consumption processes, 157,000 working staff made solid friendships, which deserves lifelong remembering.

The method of 'open all locks with one key' also manifests itself in how to grasp principal contradictions, by virtue of the fact that principal contradictions determine the development of things, and that once principal contradictions are settled, other contradictions can consequently be solved. Therefore, we need to grasp principal contradictions in dealing with ideological work. Generally speaking, when the immediate interests of most people are involved, they will become the principal contradictions there and then. Ideological and political work should start from the principal contradictions. For example, when the decision of the salary adjustment of some employees is made, it will soon become a principal contradiction. The ideological personnel should actively carry out work by following this principal contradiction.

The contradiction will vary in different stages of salary adjustment: prior to salary adjustment, most employees look forward to salary rise; therefore, they set stricter requirements of themselves and are active in work. At that moment, the focus of ideological work is correctly guiding people to know deeply the meaning of the salary adjustment, correctly treating oneself and others, displaying the exemplary force of management, educating the public with action and stabilizing emotions of the masses to ensure the normal progress of production and work.

When the salary adjustment is finished, the focus of ideological work is to do well channeling and loosening 'deadlock'. We need to realize deeply and recognize bravely the mistakes in work and rectify them. We need to patiently and fully educate and offer help to those employees who cannot correctly realize the meaning of salary adjustment for their actual difficulties so that their burden may be alleviated, their spirit lifted, and they will work to realize the meaning of the salary adjustment without any negative side effects. In summary, with the development and change of contradiction, we need to note that mental labor and physical labor cannot be effectively combined and their initiatives won't be displayed with only simple institutions and discipline.

Section 15 Become skilled in the work method of 'one key to open one lock'

Principles of ideological work include listening, channeling, and leading. We need to put ourselves in others' shoes and adopt reverse thinking to lead employees to look forward and unite various thought towards a common goal. We need to respect personality and the rights of humans, attach importance to equality and democracy, and avoid being bullish.

The contradiction is universal as well as unique. We need to adopt the method of opening all locks with one key to solve contradictions of universality. Contradictions of individuality are contradictions that have their own individuality at different development stages for different groups. An ancient saying goes 'each family has its own difficulty', which refers to the specialty of contradiction. We need to adopt different measures to solve different contradictions. Sanzhu Corporation's development also brings us many contradictions. Ideological chaos and work passivity will be caused without strong and forceful ideological work to influence the development of the company. Our rapid development lies in the fact that we do ideological and political work from various aspects. For example, when the company is initially established, some management rapidly grows in practice; meanwhile, such vicious mindsets as conceitedness and pride came out. We issue an article on the relationship between talents and the stage.

We assert the importance of talents on starting business and explain in theory and practice that talents need a stage to display them. Without a stage, talents will fulfill nothing. Meanwhile, we call employees to study this article and circulate it in various meetings. Therefore, we correct arrogant thought to ensure the healthy growth of our team. In order to assert micro interests, I focused on explaining the dialectic relations of micro interests and macro interests, emphasized the importance of macro interests on the development of capital, and thus corrected the wrong idea of splitting and sharing all the profit among employees.

Section 16 Emphasize ideological work for intellectuals

Intellectuals are a special group with a unique life and value concept, especially since they have been used to a lifelong income without crisis since they originally worked in institutions and state-owned units. Facing a performance-based distribution mode and work method in Sanzhu, a private company, they needed time to get used to it. Therefore, we needed to adopt a special method to deal with the ideological work of intellectuals. Sanzhu Corporation is a centralized place for intellectuals. Here, 90% of managers boast of an academic degree above college level, and they are the business backbone and hope for the enterprise to explore new markets. If the ideological work cannot catch up, it is a waste of talent as well as internal consumption of the enterprise. Some state-owned enterprises cannot function well, not because of a talent deficiency but because they don't attach much importance to the ideological work of the intellectual. Therefore, since the establishment of our company, we regard talents as the priority of priorities and attach great importance to the ideological work of intellectuals.

The key to ideological and political work of intellectuals does not lie in preaching, but in action. First of all, we must respect them for their personality. The spirit of not succumbing to a bowl of rice among ancient intellectuals still prevails in the intellectuals of today. Therefore, we need to respect their personality and adequately confirm their life values and labor to make them realize their life value during labor. At present, the whole society considers talents are our treasure. However, such kinds of treasure are not rewarded in social status. But here in our company, we really treat talents as treasure.

Second, we care for intellectuals especially when it comes to living consumption, and know what miseries intellectuals go through and try to solve them. Generally speaking, most intellectuals lack social communication skills since they are more engaged in their profession. Therefore, they tend to encounter more living difficulties. Under such circumstances, it becomes very important to be concerned and care for them. Instead of coming from ritual, this care comes from being treated like our relatives, a sincere love. In this way, they will really think that they are one of us instead of just being an employee, and will display initiative as masters of the company. Therefore, I have done a lot in caring for the lives of employees, in particular experts, ranging from finding jobs for their family members, family telephone installations, and balcony allocations.

All these are my concern. I also provide cash aid to facilitate their work and reduce their worries about living expenses. In this way, they will display their full talents during work, and honor the enterprise. Besides, the principle of distribution according to work should be strictly observed. We should not be afraid of income gaps with people devoting more work getting more payment, less work, less payment. Sometimes the income difference can be three times or five times. In this way, people devoting more time to work will become much happier and people devoting less time to work won't complain either.

The impact on intellectuals by ideological and political workers is tremendous. In Sanzhu Corporation, I regard it as fundamental that the company takes resources from society and must make contributions to society in return. All behaviors of the company start from devotion, such as delivering relief products to old soldiers and advocating the establishment of a caring fund. We educate all employees to carry out work in accordance with the law and regard 'dedication to society' as our motto, which encourages the intellectuals a lot and creates the best stage for them to realize their own values. In such circumstances, if we do ideological work in detail and with care, all problems can be solved.

In summary, ideological work, which is universal as well as special, is very necessary. If the ideological works can be faithful to fact, the purpose of ideological work can be realized.

Generally speaking, all thoughts of ideological activities are reflections of matter, the product of internal and external activities of matter, the three important consumption processes, which are contradictory as well as interconnected, and have different stages and activities. Besides, they have their own rules. These units of opposites and struggles among different matters and in different stages are internally connected and follow some necessary rules. These units of opposites and struggles will be reflected in the thoughts formed in our mindsets and follow some regularity. We study these rules in order to master and use them.

When we mastered different rules of thinking in different spaces, time, and conditions, various thoughts will necessarily arise. Then we can be deal with ideological work. During the process of study, we should pay attention to universality and individuality, which requires us to master the inner psychological activities. It is an important ideological and working method for us, which prevents us from making various mental and metaphysical mistakes and helps us eliminate subjectivism and bureaucracy. This is one of the reasons why we explore ideological activities and the generation of ideological rules.

13

Leadership management art and method

The work of management at all levels is complex. How do we enhance leadership performance and management efficiency in a balanced way? It needs the application of scientific leadership management art and method. As society progresses, leadership management art and method innovate. To improve incessantly and renovate leadership method and art in leadership management work is a basic requirement to enhance leadership capabilities.

Section 1 Study consumption law and improve leadership management art

Art is the perfection and enhancement of methods. It is a way of being creative, a higher-level method, and is the perfection and enhancement of methods. In addition, art is also included in the scope of strategy.

Leadership management art is generally displayed in the following ways.

The art of democratic working methods

If we want to make good use of democratic working methods, we have to be adept in transforming personal opinions into everyone's opinions; adept in discovering advanced experience from the masses, refining typical advanced examples and then using them to educate everyone; and adept in utilizing the art of mutual education.

The art of enlightenment

Enlightenment intrigues people by providing convincing explanations and examples to find associations among things and gain insight from the process. It is mainly manifested by:

- exalting comrades with creative working experience and shed light on their work
- cultivating and create new typical examples to enlighten people to associate, observe, and think in this way
- enlightening the working methods of subordinates
- solving various kinds of contradictions in work and life in an artistic way.

We should first learn to put ourselves in another's shoes.

The art of grafting one twig on another

This can be done by:

- sponsoring activities beneficial to government and society; in the process of donation, promote appropriate images and products that are most suitable for Sanzhu
- supporting social groups, and conducting charity activities to graft images to product promotion
- associating with social groups and government divisions to celebrate a certain holiday.

By conducting these activities together, we promote our image onto holiday celebrations.

The art of concern for people's life

Examples are:

- caring for trifles in the life of subordinates, solving problems for employees, showing love to them and helping them.
- keeping an eye on employees who catch cold or are in hospital
- congratulating employees who get married or have a birthday.

The art of advertising promotion

Examples are:

- using the news; reporting a piece of news is not art, but creating a new piece of news out of an existing piece of news is art
- promoting literature
- serving the Lord by the power of Lord.

The art of solidarity of leaders and subordinates

Examples are:

- talking to those who suffer from contradictions so as to let them communicate their emotions and feelings
- praising and encouraging their virtues
- talking to and treating others with utmost sincerity
- caring for them
- when subordinates get nervous, talking to them about casual things to make them less nervous
- leaders commanding employees through rationality, strategy, and policy to ensure consistency.

The art of being humorous

Leaders need to have a funny conversation style and be good with vivid metaphors. Being humorous and good at coming up with inspiring strategies should be consistent. The way to grasp this art is first to learn language skills and then to pay adequate attention to training and practice. Artistic language full of humor, and vivid metaphors help us express our intentions and feelings so as we get what we want.

The art of provocation

The best way to persuade a general is provocation, which can be used to activate employees' working enthusiasm, faith in winning, and spirit of fighting to the death and bravely killing enemies. The technique of this method lies in hiding the real goals of leaders, and making use of a kind of art to trigger feelings. The highest point of the human spirit can be triggered and leads people to working goals.

The art of persuasion

Persuasion and provocation are consistent with the art of strategy. Their goals and methods of instruction are in accord. But the way of exerting them on different people is not the same, especially for those who are experienced and sophisticated. When it comes to those people, no provocation will be applied, but persuasion. The virtue of the art is that its concrete application varies with individuals.

The art of leadership 'prominence – balance'

'Prominence – balance and balance – prominence' is a law by which everything develops. We will apply this law to economic work on our own initiative, stressing management benefits and development benefits, and in daily work by stressing cultivation and selection of good examples from which others should learn, forming waves of development.

The art of grafting one twig on another

Based on the circular spiral law of philosophical cognition, all matter and thinking derived from matter can be repeatedly grafted. After grafting, there are changes in the new substance, and one can see different results. In practice, we apply the 36 stratagems and military strategies and tactics of Mao Zedong to commercial battles.

The art of sensory expression

This can be done through:

- *Touch*. A good design of products entails a good sense of touch. When people talk to each other, and if you impress them with senses of touch, understanding and trust, your communication with others will go well.

- *Sight.* Sight is expressed as what we do and the products we make are reassuring and can be accepted or approved by others.
- *Feelings.* Through friendly communication, building friendship, and increasing emotional intercourse.
- *Colors.* Colors can be used to trigger man's emotions, initiative, and desire.

The art of language techniques

The art of language means strengthening solidarity and coordinating it with the implementation of working methods. When talking to someone one should try to aim at the right point at which one can start a conversation with others. In public, first of all, we should be aware of the characteristics of those we are faced with and find common ground where we can converse with them, and consequently have empathy with people. In addition, we should learn a conversation style of being both blunt and implicit. Compliments and praises are a language of beauty people like to hear. If compliments and praise are applied in a good way, they can help arouse people's enthusiasm. We often say that we should guard against arrogance and rudeness and be modest and discreet. But being modest has certain limits. If you are way too modest, you will become a hypocrite. Euphemistic language of criticism can be misunderstood.

The art of voicing opinions to leaders

Be courageous enough to express opinions to leaders, but when it comes to expressing them, we should use euphemistic expressions: choose the way that suits the occasion best.

The art of assembling leaders

There are three stages:

- Optimize assembly. Use one's own wisdom to graft and assemble wisdom of others to create new approaches and art.
- Entrust assembly to others.
- Hold brain-storming meetings to obtain new ways of thinking and to align our way of thinking with that of others.

The art of conversing sincerely with peers and colleagues

First of all, see the big picture, and take the big picture into consideration, which will be the starting point when we consider and deal with problems. Respect your colleagues, raise and discuss questions with them, instead of being arrogant. Try to be good at putting forward some different opinions and being faithful to the truth. Consider things as they stand, rather than deny everything. Adhere to principles and flexibility.

The art of being good at rejecting

We must learn to be good at rejecting. Neither do we tell others what to do, nor do we hurt them.

The art of being a detective

There are four stages:

- Throw a stone to clear the road. When we are not so sure of something and do not have any clue, why don't we take our problems to other people for advice. We can judge what is right and what is wrong from their reaction.
- Detect by setting points and by sampling. If we want to know the big picture, we'd better set some typical points (good or bad) to detect, explore, or investigate.
- Induce others to get what you would like to know.
- Detect under cover. Send other people to lurk.

Section 2 Learn to apply 38 methods

Based on leadership management experiences and my long practical leadership management experiences, I have concluded that the following 38 kinds of working methods are effective:

1. *Set overall objectives in the correct way and implement them in stages.* First of all, set the goals you are striving for and then summarize them to formulate a scheme of implementation. Classify objectives as long

term, middle term and short term. Measures have to go beyond objectives in order to achieve the objectives.

2. *Hold on to facts and be consistent between the subjective and the objective.* First, conduct research and investigation. The right decisions only come from research and investigation. Second, find principal contradictions and principal aspects of contradictions within a certain range of time, and focus on them to give impetus to ordinary contradictions to be resolved. Third, learn to research and investigate: know exactly what the goals of investigation are; be clear about the outline of the investigation; choose typical cases to analyze – the so-called 'dissect a sparrow'; become fully aware of adverse effects exerted by initiative on the objective.
3. *Formulate correct and feasible stratagems, strategies and policies.* Do this by: creating the right macro stratagems and macro strategies, based on the conditions of the subjective and objective goals and tasks of groups, determining macro stratagems and macro stratagems, formulating tactical macro approaches; determining correct macro stratagems and micro strategies; macro strategies need to be ensured by macro strategies, and need still more micro strategies – concrete tactics to be realized; formulating feasible macro strategies and micro strategies and policies or codes of behavior drawn up under a certain historical period; they are concrete while strategies are guidelines and means of fighting, and are abstract; policies and strategies underlie macro stratagems. Policies serve stratagems, and a certain stratagem is certain to be associated with a certain policy.
4. *Show leadership and control.* First, categories of control: single line control – program control; double line control – two lines of execution and inspection; superior and inferior supervision control; double way supervision control — control of the execution system and control of the guarantee system restrict each other. Second, control of minds: a positive guide is used to uphold healthy tendencies. Third, control of public opinions. Fourth, lay stress on typical examples, enhance publicity, and stimulate overall development.
5. *Be democratic.* Democracy is a way and means, not an end. Democracy consists of three conditions: that leaders will be good at transferring their own correct ideas to others in a democratic way; that leaders will adopt democracy to solve problems whenever they do not know what to do; that leaders will try to make their mind rich and profound, and become involved with the masses. When finding correct thoughts, methods, typical examples, and conclusions, leaders can promote them.

6. *Use the mass line.* The mass line is a working method by which correct thought and typical examples are extracted from the masses and then applied to the masses. The best examples and experience are sorted out and subsequently promoted among the masses. The power of example is used to educate people.
7. *Combine material and spiritual stimulation.* In the primary stage of socialism, most people tried to make ends meet; therefore, the stimulation of materials had to be used as a means to motivate their enthusiasm. Meanwhile spiritual stimulation was also needed.
8. *Organize study classes.* Study classes can help solve problems and can be organized to study useful theories. They are centralized. They can help encourage wide discussion and encourage people to exchange opinions, which complement each other, and solutions are enhanced. Study classes can set up barrier teaching and case teaching, which can help improve the working ability of managers so as to achieve a high degree of unity of thought.
9. *Conduct ideological work according to laws of thinking.* General and special laws of thinking can be used to conduct ideological work. The so-called 'one key to all locks' is the thought of grasping typical examples. Problems of cognition can be solved by one approach. But individual problems should be solved using the appropriate method, the so-called 'one key to one lock'.
10. *Protect the overall situation at the expense of the partial situation.* To be a leader one needs an understanding of the overall situation, so a leader has to let go of some partial interests for the sake of overall interests. When balancing pros and cons, choose big interests at the expense of small drawbacks; when balancing major losses and minor losses, choose minor ones over major ones.
11. *'Play the piano'.* This is a working method of grasping work in a comprehensive way. One issue stands out at a certain time, but extra attention must be paid to other aspects to coordinate work. It is a process of motion characteristic of being vivid and dramatic as well as a combination of being slow and fast.
12. *Praise and reward.* One method is to praise someone at a small meeting; a second is to praise and reward someone at a large meeting. Another way to praise and reward someone in a live conference, which entails promoting advanced experience and giving impetus to overall work.
13. *Use a vertical level inspection.* In the level inspection leaders are required to inspect after they assign work. Superiors check up on inferiors who then inspect people inferior to them. This kind of

inspection is carried out until the lowest level is inspected. Another method is called for, the anti-perspective method of inspection. That is to conduct anti-perspective inspection down to the lowest level of work, which can help prevent us from being bureaucrats.

14. *Rely on backbone employees to create a snowball effect.* Rely on your backbone employees, and then expand them to create a snowball effect. The work has to be performed steadily and firmly, otherwise, a situation of 'half-cooked rice' will emerge, which means a job has not thoroughly been done.
15. *Show trust and emotions to subordinates to stimulate their self-confidence.* As a leader, one must have confidence in subordinates. In the meantime cultivate emotional relationships with employees, for emotions are able to help increase mutual trust and loyalty. Since self-confidence takes half the credit for successful businesses, the self-confidence of employees has to be stimulated and built.
16. *Eliminate chaos.* First evaluate people on their current performance rather than that of the past. Then implement strict discipline starting with all levels of leadership; meanwhile, leaders have to be strict with themselves and undertake ideological and political work primarily through praise. Leaders should organize rapidly to rectify groups and teams, and try to solve and balance various kinds of contradictions under the new leadership.
17. *Deal correctly with the relationship between credibility and institutionalized management.* It is important to handle the relationship between credibility and regulation well.
18. *Manage employment properly.* The management of employees is central to management in general. For good employment it is necessary to select talent appropriately. Put each employee in the right position.
19. *Show authority and legal management.* Developing a center and authority is necessary for ideological management combined with institutional management. The management of the whole network is incorporated in the range of the management of institutionalization, normalization, standardization, and elaboration.
20. *Use contradictory management and cooperative management.* Execution and supervision restrict each other, and decentralization and centralization are also contradictions, which should be reasonable and appropriate. Consolidate the unity of thought and organizations to confine non-organizational activities, putting aside minor differences so as to seek common ground. Manage in a centralized and unified way and require subordinates to obey leaders.

21. *Use internal and external fields.* Step out of the internal range and perform work on the external field under unfavorable conditions.
22. *Know that 'the weak hampers the strong' and 'the strong defeats the weak'.* Employ superior forces to destroy enemies. A small team of troops fights a war of prevention, blinds and hampers the enemy's superior forces.
23. *Make use of contradictions and diverting contradictions.* When crises happen internally, divert the perspective of internal contradictions and conflict to lighten or resolve them.
24. *Decentralize for the sake of contradiction handling.* The effects of decentralization are that they motivate members of the leadership group to act on their own initiative, and they specify the rights and duties for each level and person so as to make sure every piece of work is attended to under the control of a responsible employee.
25. *Re-educate.* Enhance the whole quality level of leadership through in-service education, which entails professional training in employees' spare time, and combining off-the-job training with amateur training and in-service training.
26. *Use flexible publicity.* Public relations involve internal and external parts. Internal public relations aim to motivate staff to move forward toward the same goal. External public relations win more support from society and leaders.
27. *Set an example.* A leader has to set a good example by uniting his subordinates, and caring for them; helping the group to pull together and work hard; and setting an example on all occasions.
28. *Grasp the connotations of institutional management and behavioral management.* First, improve and perfect an institutionalized, standardized, and detailed routine control and management system, which is the most important code of connotation. Second, detailed management procedures make it easier for quality management, which guarantees the quality of products. Third, attach great importance to the influence of spirit and human behavior.
29. *Manage according to the 'Charter of Anshan Iron and Steel Company' and 'Daqing Spirit'.* This is essential for being a leader. Implement 'two participations, one reform, and three combinations', 'three honest', 'four strict', 'four identical' reforms, and you will succeed. *Two participations*: the cadre should go to the grassroots to conduct deep research and participate in work in a designated place at the proper time; technical workers and workers' representatives should participate in management – the decision-making, the formulation of regulations and work plans, etc. *One reform*: reform the company regulations,

technology, and processes, etc. *Three combinations*: the leadership management committee integrates the administrative cadre, technical cadre, and workers. *Three types of being honest*: be an honest person; speak honest words; do honest things. *Four types of being strict*: strict organization, strict discipline, strict requirements and strict attitude. *Four types of being identical*: it should be identical whether the leader is present or absent; it should be identical with or without being checked by personnel; it should be identical in good or bad weather; it should be identical in daytime and at night.

30. *Make good use of new technical tools to perform management.* Modern tools can help people conduct management most directly and effectively. They are a means of great importance to improve the level of management and working efficiency.
31. *Focus on the most important issue as well as other minor ones.* What we should do to apply this way of work is muster enthusiasm at each level, so that work will be carried out in order.
32. *Put ourselves into others' shoes.* We think about problems from the opposite perspective, which helps improve our thinking and the correctness of work and enhances the level and authority of leadership.
33. *Understand network construction.* The network construction will be improved and perfected as quickly as possible, and then deepened and refined. It is essential to establish the network well and check up on it regularly.
34. *Punish and reward managers.* The faster a manager is rewarded, the better. When punishing managers, one should criticize them harshly and slowly to prevent them from being emotional. But under some special circumstances, the punishment of a manager is supposed to be dealt with promptly but righteously.
35. *Hold regular meetings.* Hold meetings regularly with managers of a certain rank to report, research, and discuss work, and solve problems. Afterwards hold office meetings to deal with problems in a way which makes leaders have enough time to do much more important things.
36. *Lure the tiger out of the mountains and steal beams and pillars to replace them with rotten timbers.* The tactic of luring the tiger out of the mountains means luring your enemies away from their base so as to seize each opportunity. The tactic of 'steal beams and pillars and replace them with rotten timbers' has the connotation of altering the content and nature of things by way of deception. In marketing sales, especially in a very competitive market, these two tactics will be taken into consideration.

37. *Drop the bait, cast your net wider, and get driven to do something*. These tactics are commonly used in the military and in market competition. These tactics have to be employed flexibly in commercial battles.
38. *Play to score, and win the majority*. Leaders must know exactly where they stand and what kind of people they are faced with when speaking, behaving, and making decisions. The first thing for a leader to do is to define himself and his work, and survey the approaches by which people's enthusiasm will be stimulated to a maximum degree. A leader employs appropriate language to narrow the distance by all means from the people he deals with. Pay attention to speaking method and art, for good methods can ease contradictions rapidly to help relieve embarrassment and clear up barriers in work in a smart way.

We all know these working methods, but what counts is understanding how to apply them.

Section 3 Talents, career and platform

Talents, enterprise, and platform are basic elements of productivity development in consumption society.

Enterprise needs and trains talents

Talent, enterprise, and stage are three important conditions for mankind to push the development of the productivity of consumption society and to make contribution to society. The three are interrelated and interact, and all are indispensable.

Talents are required for building up enterprise. In order to work out a great enterprise, we need talents with different abilities, levels, qualities, and characters. Talents with ability and good character can provide reliable guarantees for the enterprise. The enterprise needs talents, which can only be identified and reflected during the process of building up the enterprise.

A platform for establishing the enterprise

A platform (or condition) is required for talents to establish the enterprise. Talents cannot exert their intelligence without platform or condition. There are two kinds of platforms: one mainly has objective conditions, the other will be set up by the creator after creating the condition. In reality, one usually creates the condition for enterprise for individuals rather than at beginning when the condition is available. The condition individuals create is the stage when a platform is set up.

Step onto a big stage to achieve great enterprise

The enterprise and stage are complementary to each other. Enterprise determines the size of the stage, while the stage plays a part in the proceedings of enterprise, accelerating or suspending enterprise. A small stage can only achieve a small enterprise. In order to make more contribution to society, you must be engaged in great enterprises on a big stage.

Section 4 Matters needing attention for marketing management

Clear mind and define tasks

What is our strategy adjustment? It keeps giving priority to the medium and small sized cities to establish chains and shops. As only the network can provide benefits, we must accomplish network size to obtain a stable sales volume.

What is a strategy adjustment? Just select the right learning model to follow and combine it with innovation.

What are tactical adjustments? It means making improvement and innovation on the basis of the existing tactics. Combine the experience in marketing and promotion with service marketing, which is a basic tactical adjustment.

Deeply penetrate the front line and market

We should realistically take the initiative to complete tasks in a better way: 60–70% of the factory leaders' time should be used to stay in the workshop, where they can identify problems as field management is the uppermost working method in a factory. And as for the market managers, especially top-level officials, 60% to 70% of their time should be used to investigate the front-line market and consumers so as to ask for their advice, learn from their experiences, and identify problems for a timely solution. The experience should be discovered early and be promoted in a timely manner, and the problems should be identified quickly to find an early solution. We must learn to use information for communication so as to promote our work efficiency. And the work should be carried out in a realistic and creative way.

Transform three motives into productivity

The future work is to further sum up the experience on how to transform three motives into productivity. We should carefully pay attention to the formulation and implementation of three-motive policy. When carrying out this policy, we must focus on the detail and understand and implement the principle that the detail is the key to success and failure. The inspection work should check that details are well done, where the problems are, and who is responsible. All of these should be taken seriously and cannot be considered trivial.

Improve the quality of management level

After the adjustment of the strategies and tactics, the key issues lie in the quality, discipline, and execution of our management team. We must emphasize learning, including learning from books and learning in practice, to accomplish the achievement, and then put the knowledge and experience we learned into practice. There is a no-boundaries philosophy inside the enterprise philosophy of Sanzhu, which mainly emphasizes the idea of learning without boundaries, at home and abroad, or learning for our own use.

Whether the above-mentioned content can be implemented, the key lies in whether our top-level officials at all levels can use these points for self-discipline. If not, the leaders are deceivers. As time goes by, the authority and appeal of leadership will decline. Therefore, top-level officials at all levels should take the lead everywhere. The market front-line staff must be much younger; this is the important principle of the organizational work of cadres.

14

National macro leadership management

All human activities are in the process of consuming and creating consumption. Human beings get consumption materials from nature and create consumption materials ceaselessly in order to meet their consumption demands, which have been increasing continuously and developing and improving. In the activity process, new productivity of the consumption society, new production relations, and the combinations among them are created continuously. Production comes into being in the combination of productivity and production relations. And then production creates products demanded in consumption, consumption pattern, and a new consumption level.

The process of capital commodity production and exchange explores and improves the exploitation of consumption commodity channels and socialized commodity exchange. In the modern period, the process of capital commodity production and exchange of the whole of human society yields narrow production relations, production relations of corporation behavior, generalized production relations of the whole society, relationships of the economic base and the superstructure, and the relationship of human consumption and nature. These relationships in activities create basic contradictions and dissipation structures of society. Multiple complex enterprises are the cells of the social economic base, and the non-productive organizations, such as social organizations, parties, religions and so on, combine in the three important consumptions process of the whole society. However, there is no individual, family, social organization, party, religion, or nation without activities of the three important consumptions, and there is no politics without consumption.

The process of three important consumptions gives birth to contradictions between the productivity of the consumption society and production relations, contradictions between the economic base and superstructure, and contradictions between the three important consumptions and nature.

This creates social contradictions of a country, nation, and external nation (the contradiction between country and country). The core of all of these contradictions in one country is the creation and distribution mode of social consumption wealth, and the legal mode, in which individuals and organizations get the social consumption wealth and that the amount of social consumption wealth is gained. Can all of these be identified by people's value system and be relatively equitable or seriously unequal? (Absolute equity does not exist forever.) The amount of people's survival consumption and enjoyment consumption in the social consumption wealth determines purchasing power, consumption consciousness, consumption mode and behavior, and mode and behavior of social activities.

From this we conclude that all human activities are not separated from the three important consumptions. In the three important consumptions activities, the management of humans' own consumption process, production consumption process, and demanding and creating process activities for materials of consumption for the three important consumptions demand that people create the best and most useful living consumption materials, social consumption materials, and spiritual and cultural consumption, with minimal research funding and production consumption, to achieve a more equitable distribution of total social consumption wealth.

It is a complicated and important mission to resolve the national internal contradiction and create a better solution to internal contradictions among the people and establish a happy, prosperous, and harmonious society, which is the responsibility of the national superstructure, of enterprises as the basic social economic gem, and of all the families as the most fundamental gems of a society. Individuals and non-producing organizations, parties, and religion need a scientific management method to exert positive effects to construct a harmonious society. However, all these activities are involved in the process of the three important consumptions, so scientific organization management should be adopted, and the management can be classified into two types: consumption and macro management, and consumption and micro management.

The macro management of consumption is an integrated management for the three important consumptions of national superstructure. Micro management of consumption is a corporation's production consumption, sales service management, and the household living consumption management of the family. The goal of the macro management of consumption is to keep the national order of the three important consumptions, normal activities, and normal research to satisfy people's ever increasing material and spiritual consumption needs, and to guarantee national security and stability and the harmony of society, and to make contributions to the harmony of the human world and the rapid and healthy development of the three important consumptions and national profits.

The goal of the micro management of consumption is to ensure an enterprise produces more and better valuable commodities with the lowest production cost, to get more business and social profits through satisfying consumers' needs with high quality sales service, to maximize the productivity of the consumption society, and to take on social responsibility. Besides, it ensures that an enterprise properly resolves the contradiction between productivity and production relations, between the national interest and corporate interest, between the corporation and society, and between corporations' production consumption and nature.

The management of household living consumption is the basic consumption target and management for human life. The goal of management is to increase the limited consumption fund and to properly arrange living consumption to improve its quality. Because the resources of the consumption fund and people's ever increasing material and spiritual cultural consumption needs are complicated and inconstant, they influence general social economic activities and have some significance to the micro management of consumption.

It is important to clarify the elements of national conceptions, national management, and comprehensive national strength when discussing macro consumption and management.

Section 1 National factors

Territorial elements

A country is a certain terrain including domains, territorial seas, national airspace, and a boundary, which belong to all people who reside in this terrain. Territory is a consumption resource that all people rely on. Countries usually use boundaries that are established according to history or treaty with its neighboring countries.

People elements

All people are masters of the national territory; one or more nations that live on this land are the people of this land. People are possessors and dominators of this country territory. The benefit of a country is the people's benefit. The power of a country is endowed by the people.

Legitimate national power system elements

Government is a power institution that represents the interests of the country and the people. Government keeps national security, ensures people's benefits and rights, exerts power equitably, guarantees the stability of society, and constructs a harmonious society. It ensures people's normal life, production, and social activities, and deals with people's internal contradiction. It takes the responsibility of maintaining friendly interactions and equitably resolving contradictions between countries. It develops the productivity of the consumption society, the national economy, and international trade with other countries to satisfy people's ever-increasing material and spiritual cultural consumption needs.

System elements of superstructure

The superstructure is a social ideology established on a certain economic basis and the summation of a political and legal system, organization, and facilities. The superstructure includes the political and ideological superstructure.

The political superstructure is the political and legal system established on a certain economic basis, and national machinery and political organizations such as the army, police, courtrooms, prisons, government departments, parties, and the organizations of social politics.

Ideological superstructure is social ideology with an economic basis including political ideology, law, moral, philosophy, and religion. Superstructure is a unification of ideology and political relationship in essence between people.

Legal system elements

The western capitalist society is a democratic political system, and the Chinese socialistic society is the people's democratic political system. Both of them use laws to regulate civilians' behavior in living consumption, social consumption, scientific research, and production consumption. The national constitution and the law system that takes the constitution as its parent law are established by the people's congress in China and by the national congress in western countries. The national constitution and laws represent people's benefits, and people's rights are protected and restricted by them.

Section 2 National systematic and integral management functional factors

In national management law the nature and the scale of the national management determines the national management mode.

Consisting of management elements, national management is an overall management system, a comprehensive leading method of managing objects, purposes, methods, means and strategies, tactics, policy, law, and so on, and a systematic thinking method, so as to control the practical processes of the three important consumptions through:

- national political organizations, the country is organized and managed in and manage orderly, integral and organic way
- sovereignty of territory, territorial waters, and national airspace
- defense of people's normal living, production, democratic power and morality, safety, stability of all social activities and the social harmony.
- tools, mechanism, facilities
- national superstructures
- development of the national economy to macro control the law of market economy (natural economy law of consumption)
- constitution, law, rules – the yardstick for people's behavior and they regulate people's behavior
- resource allocation
- social wealth allocation
- civil education and high scientific research education
- consumption of social security
- protection and construction of the human living environment
- national strategy, tactics, policy, and decision-making
- constituting and implementing national policies
- constructing harmonious society based on laws and social morality
- supervising and monitoring
- national diplomatic activities
- developing international trade.

Section 3 The comprehensive national power factor

Comprehensive national strength is spiritual power as well as the information system, and it is the evaluation standard between countries on an international level.

The general elements of comprehensive national strength include:

- national resources
- economic power
- cohesion of the people's will
- level of productivity of consumption society
- military power
- level of social development and progress
- diplomatic power
- the integrated organic combination of the organization and the government's ability to control.

Among these eight elements, the integrated organic combination of organization and control of the government system's ability to control is the core, and no power can be brought into play without organization.

Section 4 Macro consumption, and social consumption and wealth distribution management

To ensure a relatively equitable allocation of the general national wealth there are seven requirements:

- to develop and create wealth to ensure the deserved consumption wealth of the nation
- to ensure the capital investment in national security and social stability consumption
- to ensure capital investment for development of social consumption wealth and revenue generation
- to ensure capital investment for the consumption of newly emerging forces that don't create consumption wealth
- to ensure the consumption of those who have lost the ability to create consumption wealth because of old age, illness, or injury
- to ensure the minimum consumption level of the unemployed
- to ensure the minimum living consumption level because of laziness and the transformation of criminal groups.

The distribution and redistribution policy of national consumption wealth is made by the nation on behalf of the fundamental interests of all citizens, and, accordingly, national finance establishes revenue and expenditure budget plans and implements it. It is important:

- to manage national security consumption and judicial, social, and public security consumption
- to manage distribution principle and policy
- to manage whether the payment amount use decided by the fundamental policy is well funded
- to manage whether the beneficiary group receives the living consumption materials (or capital) it deserves
- to discuss the improvement, correction, and coordination of policy according to information feedback, and to establish and perfect a complete program
- to supervise and monitor systems.

Section 5 Living consumption-centered macro-market regulation and control under a state-led economy

The relationship between scientific research and production consumption of people's living consumption and the scientific research and production consumption of social consumption

The scientific research and production consumption of people's living consumption is fundamental. Food, clothing, shelter, and transportation are the most basic consumptions for people. During the development of people's needs consumption for living, its own contradictions come into being – the natural contradiction of shortage of supply and over supply. Meanwhile, the contradiction between the development of social consumption (including people's public living consumption and the consumption of the social superstructure itself) and the development of living consumption comes into being, because the development of people's living consumption level cannot be separated from the development of the productivity of consumption society, and the development of the productivity of the consumption society should put the production consumption of the second industry in the primary position, which is the basis for the development of the productivity of the consumption society.

Only in this way can we make rapid development in the production consumption as the basis of people's living consumption and social consumption, and meet the ever increasing needs of people's living consumption and social consumption. The nation should implement macro control over market finance and the law of economy, in which the dominant economy takes living consumption as the center so as to exert the advantages of market finance and the natural law of economy and to avoid disadvantages at the same time.

Establish an information collection and research center at a nationwide, macro level for the three consumptions markets, to provide valuable and correct information to the national decision makers for reference

The information content (comprehensive information at home and abroad) should include:

- the proportional relationship between the categorized information and the information of scientific research and production investment and the consumption of living consumption
- the proportional relationship between high-grade living consumption for enjoyment and scientific research and production consumption as well as development forecast
- the current situation of R&D of new technologies and potential information
- combined information between basic scientific research and production
- technology property in the technical protection phase, expiration times, and market situation information
- the ratios between investment in scientific research and production consumption of the social basic industries, investment in scientific research and production consumption for social consumption, and investment in scientific research and production consumption for living consumption
- the current situation of the overall proportional relationship between direct living consumption and residential income; and the proportion between the investment in basic social construction and the investment in people's living consumption and social consumption
- the proportion between the investment in basic social construction and the investment in basic raw materials of scientific research and production, and the effective rate to driven living consumption
- the proportion of import and export trade in the investment and production of three domestic important consumptions
- the categorized competition situation in the international market: demand situation on developed countries' market; demand situation in developing countries; potential market hopes; strategies to enter the international market
- the configurable competition situation in the consumption resource market
- the development situation and future potential of high level of technology

- the market forecast of the supply–demand relations on the proportion between living consumption and scientific research and production consumption
- the market forecast of the supply–demand relations on the proportion between social consumption and scientific research and production consumption
- the balanced forecast on the improvement of people's living consumption level and the consumption power of scientific research and production
- the forecast on the influences of the improvement of people's living consumption level to social consumption
- the forecast on the living consumption influences of the excessive increase of national investment in scientific research and production consumption on the social consumption, and basic construction and production consumption to social consumption.

Guiding, controlling, and adjusting investment in production consumption from the macro perspective

Macro control and management instruments include:

- control by tax policy
- control of investment in production consumption by financial instruments
- control of investment in production consumption by administrative instruments
- control by resource distribution instruments
- market management and control
- legal management and control, for example, anti-monopoly laws.

Section 6 Macro consumption and financial management

During the time when monetary finance dominated commodity production, exchange, and consumption processes, the nation dominates and controls financial firms and market management, which is the bounden duty of the sovereign nations responsible for people's living consumption rights and interests. During the process of joining together the three important consumptions of the world through the macro consumption chain, it is of great importance for countries in the world to combine together to manage the laws of world market finance and economy, which can guard against the serious harm of financial and economic crisis and promote the sound and rapid sustainable development of the world economy.

The national central bank and management of financial enterprises

The national central bank must strengthen the management of financial enterprises to play their roles, control financial enterprises, and implement absolute control over and absolute leadership of financial enterprises according to the following principles:

1. The state has the right to implement an absolute control of the leading national bank.
2. The state has the right to hold controlling shares in large security companies.
3. The state implements strict monitoring and regulation to operating enterprises in mutual fund, security, and warrant markets according to law.
4. The state monitors the operating conditions of all banks throughout the country and sets loan loss provisions standards for bank risks. When operating errors reach a certain poor standard, the right to operate will be rescinded and a designated bank which operates well will merge with it. The state will protect the depositors' interests from harm and implement macro management of the three important consumptions by controlling the operating rights of financial enterprises by:

    - managing economic operation through the supply amount of the monetary market
    - adjusting the deposit amount of the depositors through interest rates
    - stimulating market consumption through loans
    - adjusting the investment direction of various trades and industries through loans
    - implementing service to guide the investment direction of funds owned through a bank
    - strengthening the management of financial instruments because the circulation of financial instruments instead of paper currency is directly related to the amount of money issued.

Financial enterprises

Banks carry out operations by special means and they are enterprises operating and managing through loans. The internal rule of the financial enterprise's operation is the black box or black-box operation, which is a process of changing small and scattered golden eggs into big ones with deposits as the core and the safety of credit loans as the core of the benefits.

These are the levels of management in banks:

- The head office is the impersonal entity, the general operating and managing unit.
- The provincial sub branch is responsible for the leadership management of the bank's lending and borrowing business.
- Municipal and regional subsidiary banks take responsibility for the detailed operation of the loan business.
- Branches in counties and districts (working offices) take charge of examining and approving specific operations of the loan business and the leadership and management of the deposit business.
- The savings agency is the specific unit for deposits and payments and is not in a position to release loans.
- Except for the function of managing the national economy, the operating purpose of the bank enterprise itself is to take profit from operating currency.
- The risk of operating lies in the possibility that loans once released may not be paid back, and thus be bad loans, and become the losses and deficits of the bank.
- The purpose of bank management is to ensure the need for the economic managerial function of the state, ensuring operating profit, avoiding operating losses from undesirable loans, avoiding waste and illegal violation in operations, and improving the bank's working efficiency and operating efficiency of banks.

Black box operation

If A represents registered capital, B represents deposit taking, C represents loan releasing, D represents balance or surplus between debit and credit, E represents the negative:

$A + B - C = D$ taking a deposit with a low interest, releasing loans with a high interest and taking profit from it.

A + B – C = E is called balance credit, which is a loan business in the form of payment promise or currency claim. Banks lend credit balance (amount of money above their own stock) and take the interest profit with no-cost payment interest.

To enhance the management purposes of the financial industry, in addition to the above-mentioned seven national macro-control effects, but also because of the non-transparency of bank operations with deep black-box management, countries need to strengthen controls to prevent crisis, avoid jeopardizing the interests of depositors, and endangering social harmony and stability.

Consumption and stock market management

The stock market has a great impact on financial markets, and stock market management is responsible to shareholders:

1. Enterprise listings change the fixed capital and intangible capital of the assets not for circulation into capital commodities and push them out for exchange in the market. That changes the fixed and intangible assets of the enterprise into small stake commodities, and pushes them into a particular market and transaction as commodities.
2. Normally, when business efficiency and profit margins are announced in the market, the higher the profit margin the higher the profit amount, and the value of stocks will rise accordingly. It is the manifestation of the market value revaluation of the enterprise's stock if stocks expand in a certain time, and the stock market value of the enterprise will decline or plunge when there is a loss or low profit in operational efficiency.
3. Enterprise equities are commodities of quantified enterprise capital (including fixed, liquid, and intangible capital) and the price in the transaction process is also affected by supply–demand relations.
4. The stock price is also affected by supply–demand relations in the international trade industry, as well as the impact of important events related to listed enterprises.
5. Enterprise capital changes into a tradable commodity through being listed on the stock market and then transacts on the stock market freely. There are business companies and individuals involved in the stock market trading business, trading freely. During the operating process, there are general shareholders who purchase shares to make investment based on the promising results of a business for the purpose of taking the enterprise's profit revenues.

To sum up, you can draw the following conclusions:

1. The stock market is a special financial market.
2. The stock market is the operating market for buying and selling capital. The core of the ups and downs of stock prices is the enterprise's operational efficiency, and normally the stock prices of the stock market fluctuate with the operational efficiencies of the enterprises as the core gauge, which can reflect economic development.
3. Now that the stock market is the commodity market and is directly affected by business–benefit ratio and profit amount, the stocks of the capital commodity are influenced by the supply–demand relations.
4. The ups and downs of the market price of the capital stock are affected by supply–demand relations and by the hype influences of securities companies operating stocks, so the country should manage stock and commodity transactions of capital strictly.
5. The capital stock of private enterprise coming on the market is a manifestation of progress.
6. It is also progress for the state-owned capital enterprises listed on the capital stock market.
7. The nation should implement scientific regulation of the stock market, the special trading market.

The need to strengthen financial management

Financial management must be strengthened:

- to prevent and reduce the impact of international financial crisis on domestic economic development ensuring that the living consumption of domestic consumers is relatively stable
- to ensure the country's money is stable, thereby enhancing the financial credibility of currency in the process of international trade
- regulate supply–demand relations between domestic consumers and consumption commodity and regulate the export trade according to the domestic needs of consumption to ensure that the demand of domestic consumers is relatively balanced, which is helpful to the stability of prices
- to balance international payments and increase foreign exchange reserves (including gold and silver) to promote economic development in China.

It can be strengthened through foreign exchange controls and foreign exchange flows systematically, which can increase the country's foreign exchange earnings and reserves. The country must have sufficient foreign exchange earnings, and procurement capacity in international trade thus increases.

Relatively adaptable financial control protects the capital investment security of the nation and prevents losses from major fluctuations of the stock and securities value. Use foreign exchange controls, encourage exports and limit imports, and adjust employment opportunities.

Section 7 Social security consumption and management

The government manages state affairs according to law. Legal boundaries are clearly defined for all behaviors of the nation, and going beyond the boundaries will be illegal or criminal. There is a strict limit between breaking the law and committing a crime. Breaking the law is not equal to committing a crime, but criminals break the law.

Management functions at all levels of public security systems: the courts, the military and other government institutions belong to the state machinery and superstructure, and all laws and regulations of the superstructure belong to the category of the social constitution. All of their spending belongs to social consumption costs. How to achieve the best result for the security of society with minimum consumption is the purpose of management. Comprehensive security management should be strengthened through professional law enforcement agencies, grassroots organizations of state power, and people combining to implement 'network security'; by adding legal education courses from primary school to university; and by implementing a thorough social security system review to reduce the cost of social security.

Section 8 State security consumption and management

The purpose of a nation's security consumption is to protect the territorial integrity of the country and prevent a split, protect the consumption resources of national territory from another country's invasion and occupation, and protect national consumption wealth from another country's plundering, which is in the supreme interest of all citizens: the national interest comes first. Therefore, it is not only the country's affairs, but also the citizens' responsibility to strengthen the construction of modern national defense and strengthen national military education and training.

The overall consumption of national defense construction and national security is national security consumption. The construction of modern national defense must be supported by advanced technology and strong economic power. If the nation's productivity of consumption society falls behind because it has an underdeveloped economy, then a strong national defense force would not be established, and the nation would be bullied.

The management of a country's security consumption investment is to use limited national defense spending on national security to improve the military's fighting capacity to the largest extent; this is the purpose of a nation's security consumption, which is extremely important:

- to ensure the scientific nature of the investment in national security consumption so as match war needs
- to advance the investment process
- to ensure the effectiveness of combat strength in the investment process.

The country must advance the kind and quality of weapons through reducing waste and frugal consumption because the excellent quality of a weapon is a soldier's life.

The country should annually examine national security consumption and effectively enhance national defense power; improve the fighting force and the quality of its weapons; and avoid unnecessary consumption. Corruption and military expenditure waste are serious crimes committed against the nation and people's life.

Section 9 State consumption and management

Reform national bureaucracy to cut consumption to reduce the country's financial support for the population to reduce the nation's own consumption.

It is very difficult to simplify and restructure a government. The success of such reforms lies in the top leadership's determination and methods, and strategies and policies to carry out the reform. The broad public servants are the key to support understanding, policy, strategy, and method art.

Staff increases in national government and increases in consumable costs do not equal an overall increase in the productivity of the consumption society. The bureaucracy and corruption resulting from consumption costs do not have a positive impact on the development of the productivity of consumption society, but hinder it. Therefore it is necessary to decline financial payment for the nation's own consumption.

It is necessary to carry out a hypothetical model analysis of a nation's consumption management.

Section 10 Consumption and employment

It is important for society to solve the re-employment problem as the result of labor saving following advanced productivity of a consumption society. The following methods can be adopted:

- Develop tertiary industry and develop labor intensive industries with fine processing of commodities (with policy support).
- Develop small and medium enterprises on tight profit margins.
- Develop urbanization of small cities and towns, agricultural products and commodity processing and modernization, service industry and modernization, to absorb the surplus agricultural labor force.
- Develop production consumption in the fruit processing industry, in livestock breeding and aquaculture.
- Encourage individual entrepreneurship.
- Support the production consumption in labor intensive industries with fine export processing.
- Develop production consumption in exporting productions and develop general living consumption and high-tech industrial consumption, and so on.
- Support and develop the quality training for the surplus labor force. The key is to adjust the development of enterprises and individual entrepreneurships based on finance, taxes, administrative policies, and services so as to increase the employment rate.

Section 11 Education, scientific research consumption, and management

National education and scientific research are the driving forces to enhance comprehensive national quality and improve comprehensive national productivity of consumption society. This can be done by strengthening the management of education and research funding, curriculum design, and guiding ideology at all levels of education.

The guiding ideology of education is to cultivate patriotic workers with knowledge and self-esteem. National public servants should incessantly improve their practical experience and ability. We must select talents, train them, and make them become mature. We cannot simply select public servants from students without practical experience.

These are the ways and means of education:

- Strengthen patriotic education and social morality education from primary school. Strengthen physical training and geographic and fundamental knowledge.
- Strengthen philosophy and natural science education from junior high school, but the guiding ideology should be carried out from beginning to end during education and scientific research. Patriotic education and social morality education should be carried out from primary education to higher education.
- If higher education is not combined with scientific research, it is a kind deception and crime committed against the nation and people. Scientific research must be closely combined with university education. Strictly forbid investing in image projects, while the already-funded project should be converted into a science lab.
- higher education and scientific research; the professor should lead students to practice in firms. If professors of technology are not engaged in scientific research and lead students to conduct scientific research in the lab, their title of professor should be removed.

Reform the entrance examination method gradually, and we may refer to the educational mode of western developed countries, especially the credit system for graduation adopted by universities.

For education and scientific research consumption and management, a systematic and integrated scientific management should be implemented:

- Save funds to prevent wasteful expenditure.
- Ensure there is education and scientific research spending to achieve program objectives.
- Ensure the quality of teachers improves and clearly define and classify areas and disciplines for financial expenditure.
- Ensure the university is governed by a headmaster with relevant professional knowledge, to release control on one hand, and to

strengthen evaluation on the other, to ensure that advanced talents and scientific research results boost the rapid development and progress of materialistic productivity.

Section 12 Consumption import and export trade management

International trade is the concentrated expression of economy and politics, and a concentrated expression of economic and political relations between a country and another nation or multi-nations. The commodity exchange in international trade is consumption. If there is no consumption demand, there is no trade. It is consumption that affects the commodity exchange and development of commodity channels. There are three differences between international trade and domestic trade:

1. *Expanding trade opportunities.* These are the main benefits of international trade. If we do not open up international trade, some countries and regions cannot have balanced development in living consumption, and materials and mental culture consumption because of differences in climate and resources, technology differences in scientific research and production consumption, and differences in culture and civilization.
2. *The existence of sovereign states.* Cross-border trade involves the citizens and manufacturers of different countries. Each country is a sovereign entity and carries out management control of the cross-border population, commodities, and capital flows, which is different from domestic trade.
3. *Exchange rate.* Every country has its own currency, and in trade transactions both parties need to establish a common international currency as the ruler of commodity exchange value – the exchange rate.

International trade

These are some factors relating to international trade:

1. *Diversity of natural resources.* Differences in consumption resources of various countries and differences in production conditions make it possible to trade among countries, which means the three important consumptions between countries need to complement each other.

2. *Lifestyle preferences and consumption differences.* Even if all the country's consumption resources and production conditions are the same, if the commodity consumption habits and preferences differ among countries, then there is a need to trade in commodities among countries.
3. *Cost differences.*
4. *'Comparative advantage theory' held by Ricardo.* In 1810, British economist David Ricardo revealed 'the principle of comparative advantage' – that the international division of labor was favorable to one nation. Ricardo proved that if both parties involved in any trade specialize in the production of commodities with comparative advantage, both would benefit from it. Under the condition of free trade, each nation shifts its production to the field with comparative advantage. Meanwhile, underdeveloped countries enhance their economic development through learning advanced technology from developed countries. The problem of overproduction is solved for developed countries that have discovered a new consumption market. To gain more comparative benefits, developed countries invest in the underdeveloped ones to make use of the power of cheap labor in the latter.
5. *Comparative advantage.* A surprising conclusion may be drawn that small countries benefit more from world trade. They can trade at a world market price much different from their domestic prices, because of their small influence on the world market price. This is why small nations benefit a lot from world trade, while big powers cannot benefit as much as they expected.
6. *Equilibrium price ratio.* Once trade is initiated, the world market must form a price system according to the needs of consumption and the supply in the market. The price ratio cannot be determined without further information. However, the intervals of the location of the prices can be settled. The prices are certain to be between those of the two countries. The specific ratio depends on the needs of consumption, in that consumption determines everything.
7. *Multi-commodities.* When two nations or regions produce a wide range of commodity at a constant cost, these commodities can be put in order according to the comparative advantage or cost.
8. *Triangle and multilateral trades.* It is beneficial to participate in triangle or multilateral trades where many countries are involved, because bilateral trades are generally unbalanced

9. *Trade protectionism.* Ever since Adam Smith, economists have held different views on trade protection. They argue that trades can facilitate the international labor division which is favorable to every country. Free and open trade can make it possible for each nation to increase its production and consumption, so living standards all over the world can be advanced. Nevertheless, trade protectionism gets in the way of comparative advantages.

Analysis of demand–supply relations of the trade and tariff

A tariff can raise commodity prices, reduce consumption and imports, and enhance domestic production. The impact of a quota is the same as that of a tariff in nature. A prohibitive quota (prohibiting all imports) is equivalent to a prohibitive tariff.

Though there is no fundamental distinction between tariff and quota, subtle differences exist. Tariffs can raise public revenues or make it possible to reduce some other taxes, which can make up for the losses that consumers of importing countries suffer. However, profits made through price variance resulting from the quota go to importers or exporters who are lucky enough to get the import permit.

Tariffs result in economic inefficiency. The economic losses of consumers surpass the total of the public revenues and the extra profits the manufacturers make in the process of imposing tariffs.

Tariff collection can:

- encourage domestic production of low efficiency
- raise prices so consumers' purchasing taxed commodities is not efficient
- increase public revenues.

The first two add to economic costs because they are inefficient.

Under the guidance of Ricardo's comparative advantage theory, free trade benefits consumers of the trading countries. Then why does every country want to set up international trade barriers? Economic theorists put forward these reasons for economic protection:

- the non-economic view – to sacrifice some economic welfare to support other aims of the country
- misunderstanding economic logic
- Analyses based on market power (the consumption attracting power of consumers) or the faultiness of the macro economy.

Be aware of the 'millennium round' of Seattle

The Seattle meeting may just be regarded as a respite on the long way to market access, but the Seattle meeting could become a turning point in ten years or so. It symbolized the termination of open policy market strategy in most countries. Some nations will set up new trade barriers, especially in the fields (such as financial services and e-business) where international laws are not established.

Develop market free trade and management

There are many elements affecting free world trade. In the process of consumer commodity exchange in the import and export trades between different countries and regions all over the world, it is inevitable to carry out trade management protection in the form of tariff policy.

Establish and follow the management of the legal system that is relatively fair in international trade. Each nation should fully understand the trade law of comparative advantage.

Section 13 Social security consumption and management

The establishment and development of the consumption security system in the world

Nowadays, only a few nations have established a social security system. Before October 1, 1949, there was no social security system at all in China. After the founding of the People's Republic of China on October 1, 1949, national social security systems such as a retirement pension for workers, free medical care, immunoprophylaxis, and so on were gradually set up.

Consumption status quo of Chinese social security

The relationship between the development of the population and the beneficiaries of social security

Table 14.1 shows the life expectancy of some countries in 1997 and in China from 1940 to 2005.

Table 14.1 Life expectancy in some countries in 1997 and in China in 1940–2005

Country	Year	Life expectancy (years)
Australia	1997	78 and above
Canada	1997	78
France	1997	78 and above
Greece	1997	78
Israel	1997	78
Italy	1997	78
Japan	1997	66–79
Singapore	1997	78
Spain	1997	78
United States	1997	72
China	1940	35
China	1950	49
China	1980	70
China	2005	72

Population development and periodic law of social security in China

Most of the current beneficiaries of Chinese social security were born around 1940, and their baby boom was around 1963. Their children will retire in around 2023, which is the second peak of Chinese social security. The baby boom for those born in 1963 was around 1989. The third peak of Chinese social security is around 2050 for those born in 1989. The third retirement peak is around 2075.

The status quo of social security after 2000 in China

All those born around 1940 required social security period from around 2000, the first peak of social security in China since the establishment of the People's Republic of China. There is no doubt that the large population of the old and aged constitutes a heavy burden to families and society. Social pressure increases daily because for some time, although there was a retirement system, a social security fund was not deposited into special accounts in advance to increase in value to ensure the fund's use in the future. More often than not the social guarantee fund is collected from current production consumption and working expenses to be a guaranteed pension for current retirees, which increases current financial pressure.

There is much public debate over the most effective way to prevent a funding crisis. Two main solutions have been put forward: reform the current system or establish a new total accumulation system based on private personal accounts. Both ways have substantial support, but no decisions have yet been made.

Source of the social security fund and the management of consumer payments

Sources and direction of the national guarantee fund

Health care expenditure in the United States reached US$1.4 trillion in 2001, taking up 14.1% of the GDP. National health care expenditure is spent mainly on in-patient care (33%), doctor service (23%), prescription medications (10%) and home nursing (7%). The rest of the fund is spent on other personal health care services.

Since 1965 when Medicare for the old was initiated, the government has played a more and more important role in health-care financing, from 25% up to nearly 41% in 1990 and still soaring. In 2001, the government provided 45% of health-care expenses in the United States.

Sources of the social security fund and management of the consumer payment

In the days of China's planned economy, the retirement fund for national public servants and workers and staff in corporations, medical care, and immunity funds all came from state revenues (including the housing fund). After the establishment of the market economy under the guidance of macro control, tax (retirement tax, health care tax, housing fund tax and so on) accounts, grant-in-aid, and insurance are all used in medical care. Part of personal social security is covered by social insurance. Fiscal revenue covers all the personal social security of well-to-do villagers in the countryside. Part of the third kind of funds (retirement, health care, and housing) is covered by the local group, part by personal funds, and part by children and other revenues. Public subsidies cover part of it. Cooperative medical service is fully implemented in the countryside in China. A certain amount of money is granted to each peasant as a medical guarantee from the central government.

Consumption and management of social security

In countries with backward education, children begin to participate in whatever labor they are capable of around 13 years old and create consumption wealth. In most countries, especially in developed countries and some developing countries, children at the ages of 10 to 18 are in the consuming period of receiving an education. In those countries, those at the ages of around 18 to 24 also belong to the consumer group by taking advanced education. In those underdeveloped countries and regions, there are still small parts of people in the same age group receiving advanced education. For the manual workers who receive little education, the best working time is from the age of 13 when they participate in whatever labor they are capable of to the prime working age of 52, which is also the best working period to create social consumption wealth. On the other hand, the best working time for those who mainly do mental work with supplementary manual labor increases by five years (to receive higher education) to the age of 57, and generally can extend to the ages of 62–65. Generally speaking, after the age of 52, it is unsuitable for manual workers to do any heavy physical labor. Light physical labor can still be undertaken by those aged 57–62. It is stipulated in Chinese labor law that one should retire at the age of 60; the retirement age in the United States is 65.

The life cycle of consumption

The round rule figure of life cycle consumption and consumption creation by humans is shown in Figure 14.1.

Since we have known that the time for pure consumption wealth constitutes 40% of a human's life time, while the time for creating consumption wealth (consumption at the same time) takes up 60%, we should act as shown in Figure 14.1.

1. The nation adopts economic levers such as tax collection to accumulate funds so as to ensure the consumption of those who are either too young or too old to create consumption wealth.

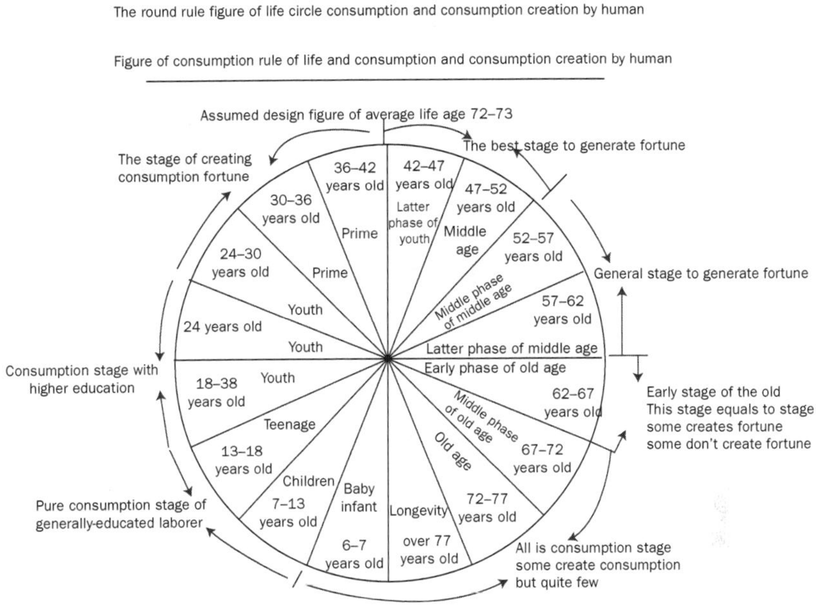

Figure 14.1 The life cycle of consumption and consumption creation for humans

2. Those who are capable of creating wealth with a relatively high income should accumulate funds for their later years and the education of children. The country and individuals should share the responsibility for social security.

Consumption of the social consumption wealth for the disabled

This can be done in the following ways:

1. Work hard to achieve prepotency. Prenatal examination must be undertaken to prevent the birth of a disabled fetus.
2. Increase social security and free care for infants and children, as far as an epidemic prevention system is concerned. Whatever hardship the economy may go through, the cost should be met to prevent disabilities.
3. Reinforce the management of the physically and mentally impaired, so as to reduce the number of people with non-disease disabilites.

Section 14 Consumption and resource allocation management

Protect, manage, and exploit natural resources

A nation's natural resources are non-renewable, so the following actions are required:

- Prohibit short-run exploitation of natural underground minerals.
- Reduce wasting of resources and make comprehensive use of the resources as much as possible.
- Protect and foster resources.
- Use and management should be carried out for the development of seaports, and the protection and utility of running waters, out of consideration for the comprehensive overall configuration to avoid waste.
- The principle of saving and giving full play to the productivity of consumption society should be followed in the exploitation of all the other natural resources.
- Research, develop, and create new resources for consuming.

There should be mutual beneficial configuration and development of the management of domestic and overseas consuming resources. All human beings and nationalities of every country live in a certain place defined by legal boundaries, with the three important developing consumptions. All nations should develop the resources reasonably and mutually on the basis of mutual benefits.

Configuration and management of intellectual resources

Intellectual resources are mainly the protection, configuration, and management of intellects and scientific knowledge and technology (including intangible assets such as patents, brands, and so on). The advanced productivity of intellects and advanced science and technology, which is the motive power for the development of human civilization, is the most important element in creating consumer social wealth. The golden key to develop the three important consumptions is to develop education and scientific research, introduce intellect and technology to each other with proper care given to the talented persons, and protect, manage, and rationally allocate intellectual and technological resources.

Configuration and management of capital consuming resources

The government should carry out the configuration and management of capital consuming resources from the standpoint of the regulation of macro consumption. Under the guidance of national overall systematic management, let companies, trades and professions develop independently with all their strength instead of exploiting and developing companies in every field of work.

Section 15 Consumption and population management

The development of the three important consumptions is always closely interrelated with population growth, the needs of living consumption, and people's increasing material, spiritual, and cultural needs. Without the needs of consumption, there would be no motive for the three important consumptions. Excessive growth of the population sets back the development of the three important consumptions.

Historical development of the human population

The population has been slow to develop in history. There have been humans for several thousand years. Until 1950 the world population was 2.486 billion, and the total output of grain was 689 million tons. It resulted from the extreme backwardness of the productivity of the consumption society and the exploitative private-ownership system.

Ever since the middle of the 20th century, especially after World War II, the three important consumptions and the world population have developed rapidly. The world population increased from 2.486 billion in 1950 to 5.8 billion in 1997. In about 50 years population growth surpassed the total of the population of several thousand years of human history. The grain output increased to 2.096 billion tons with a net increase of 1.407 billion tons compared with the output of 1950.

Consumption and population management in China

Table 14.2 shows how gross national income, population, and annual grain and meat outputs have risen between 1946 and 1997.

Table 14.2 Rise in gross national income, population, and annual grain and meat outputs in China, 1946–1997

Year	Gross national income (Yuan)	Dollars per capita	Annual grain output (million tons)	Annual meat output (million tons)	Annual sugar output (million tons)
1946	23.39 billion				
1949	35.8 billion	27 (or about 50 dollars in another algorithm)			
1956	627.8 million		182, with 290 kg per capita	6.9843	
1984	1.04357 billion		407, with 397 kg per capita	15.25	3.801
1997	1.23626 billion		493, with 402 kg per capita	52.688	7.0258

The rapid population growth in China results from the superiority of the social system and the liberation and development of the productivity of a consumption society.

Population growth of the developed countries and developing countries

This is a summary of the population growth of some developed and developing countries:

1. *Population in Britain.* The preliminary data collected by the British statistics department show that the population was 60.21 million in Britain at the end of June 2005 following the wave of Eastern European immigrants. It was the first time that the population had surpassed 60 million in official estimates. The growth rate of the British population was at its highest level since the 1960s.
2. *Population in Germany.* The Wiesbaden Federal Statistical Office in Germany showed that the population of eastern Germany will go on decreasing: it is expected there will be 12 million there in 2020, while in 2001 the population was 13.7 million. The statistics department states that this reduction in population is due to emigration and a higher death rate than birth rate. It is expected that until 2020, the younger population of eastern Germany will decrease by 28%, twice that of western Germany.

3. *The population in Europe* has declined sharply, which is a time bomb threatening economic development. The European Commission is concerned about the decreasing population in European countries. The decline of abor forces and the aging population problem can hinder the economic development of European countries.
4. *An aging population creates a burden on economic development.* With the decreasing of the birth rate and the continuous extension of people's lifespan thanks to medical development, the aging population undoubtedly brings about a certain pressure on the social economic development. Nowadays, the ratio of the active labor force to the pensioners is 100:35. However, if this tendency goes unchecked, the ratio will reach 100:75 around 2050. The pensions in Germany, France and Italy all come from taxes. As a result, national taxation will increase as the population of pension holders soars. Though the problem hasn't caused conflicts in society, it will turn from bad to worse as time goes by.
5. *Constant negative growth of Japanese population.* In 2005, the Japanese population saw negative growth for the first time. The declining birth rate and the increasing rate of aging have induced a series of social problems. Many people expressed concern that labor force reduction could lead to revenue deficiency and society couldn't bear the burden of the increasing aging population. Some analysis points out that the decline of the Japanese population is directly related to the decreasing birth rate. Problems such as late marriage, high housing and education costs are the main causes of the Japanese women not wanting to bear children. What Japan should really do now is to pay close attention to the wellbeing of the people, establish good-neighborly relationships, promote economic prosperity, and achieve peaceful development.

Growth and management of the world population

The United States

The US population grows at a high rate that is extraordinary in developed countries and holds the third place in world population after China and India.

American population growth owes much to the country's immigrants. In recent years, the American population is increasing mainly because of the increase of immigrant population and their offspring.

The United States allows well-educated and highly qualified immigrants to enter the country, so college students in other countries, especially developing countries, can become qualified US immigrants with no cost to the USA. This increases the international competitiveness of the United States.

Spain

Among western European countries, Spain is one of the countries in which childbirth is encouraged. If a married couple gives birth to a child, the government grants a subsidy of €300 (about 3,000 Yuan). The more children a couple has, the more subsidies they get.

Japan

Japan is one of the few eastern countries that encourage childbirth. Since 2006, the Japanese population has decreased, one year earlier than was expected. This is because the costs of raising and educating a child are very high. Support payments include the human-capital investment in the child and losses the mother experiences in raising a child at the expense of sacrificing her job. The Japanese government made an ineffectual effort to promote childbirth.

Russia

Couples of child-bearing age are taxed for not giving birth in Russia. For historical and economic reasons, the Russian population grows slowly, with even negative growth occurring in recent years. For many years, the Russian government has taken various measures to promote childbirth. Recently, some people in Russia have suggested that couples of childbearing age who deliberately have no children should be fined or pay taxes.

India

Influenced by religion and traditional customs, the phenomena of early marriage, multiple births, and even child marriage are very popular in India. Family planning is thus difficult to implement, especially in remote areas and countries. In recent years, more and more people from all walks of life have realized that the unlimited increase of the population has seriously hindered India's economic development and social advancement. The call for the government to take effective measures to restrict population growth is increasing.

China

According to its own national conditions, China has adopted family planning as a national policy. It turns out that the implementation of the policy is correct. Research reports show that the large number of people that China does not need to support from 1971 to 1998 as a result of the country's family planning policy has saved 6.4 trillion Yuan as the potential upbringing cost for families, and 1 trillion Yuan for the country.

Thus the pace of population growth is directly related to the development of the productivity of consumption society, the three important consumptions, the wealth distribution policy of the social system, and fertility awareness. Its relation with nature is a unity of opposites. It is an inexorable law that humans and nature should be coordinated with each other and develop in a harmonious way, or humans will be punished by nature.

15

Enterprise leadership management

In its development process management science has developed with the creation of human consumption and the process of consumption creation. Before scientific management was put forward by Frederick Winslow Taylor, an American writer, the management of enterprise production and operation fell into experimental management. After the steam engine was invented, enterprise production became an intensive, large-scale production. Taylor summarized practices in his scientific management theory, *The Principles of Scientific Management*, published in 1911. Then in 1916, Henri Fayol, a Frenchman, summarized his practical experience in *General and Industrial Management* on the basis of Taylor's scientific management. By then, enterprise management had developed from management of production processes into management of operation processes.

Max Weber, a German who established the theoretical administrative organization system, is called the father of organization theory. In the 1920s, scientific management developed into management science, which was represented by George Elton Mayo, Abraham Maslow, and Douglas McGregor in America.

The development of contemporary management mainly involves the social system school, the decision-making theory school, and the contingency theory school. The social system school is represented by the American scholar Chester Barnard; the decision-making theory school is represented by American scholars Herbert Simon and James March; the system management school is represented by Fremont Kast and James Rosenzweig; the empirical school is represented by Drucker and Dale; the contingency management theory was established by F. E. Fiedler, an American who put forward the contingency leadership theory in the 1970s. Management science is sure to keep on developing with the development process of the three important consumptions practices.

Consumption and enterprise management matter a lot to enterprise. In order to straighten out their relations and function, we need first to be clear about the concepts of enterprise and management.

Section 1 The concept of enterprise

Enterprise is a cell of a social economy and an organizing form by which mankind asks nature for consumption materials and creates the movement process of consumption materials. Enterprise runs with dissipative structure. The process by which enterprises produce products is a consumption process. An enterprise's production activity is a process during which it has a relation with nature, and it is a reflection of the relationship between people or between people and society, which must adapt to the complicated natural and social living environment. Consumption is the traction force for the production, marketing, and operation of the enterprise.

There is a boundary between the entrepreneur and capitalist. The operational philosophy and behavioral features of an entrepreneur are to bear the responsibility of the enterprise operation, and to produce maximum enterprise benefit with minimum consumption expenditure. The interests of an enterprise are divided into two: profit interests and social interests, including producing and selling useful and popular products, to generate tax, settle social employment, take care and make contributions to public welfare, and make contributions to extended reproduction for the enterprise's development.

The operational philosophy and behavior of a capitalist

The only purpose of operating an enterprise is for profit. Any means can be applied to earn interest and profit, including harming the interest of many consumers and the public. An entrepreneur and a capitalist have the same purpose of achieving profit through careful operations, but a capitalist does not have a sense of social responsibility.

An entrepreneur's purpose to pursue profit is not for the sake of profit. An entrepreneur regards the operation of an enterprise as a social business. The enterprise must make profit since it is the life-blood unit for social economy. Without profit, an enterprise would go bankrupt, not to mention its social responsibility and interests. The social responsibility assumed by entrepreneurs should be based on the enterprise's profit, or else entrepreneurs couldn't realize their social responsibility.

Although capitalists hold mercenary operation ideas, objectively, they still assume a certain social responsibility. The maximization of profit itself is equaled to the realization of social responsibility. Without social interests, an enterprise cannot realize profit interests, which is the contradictory unity of the opposites. The operation concept of an enterprise determines its behavior. The overlooking of social responsibility in the pursuit of profit hurts consumers and other social interests. Enterprise is bound to belong to society, so is the money. Nobody could bring in fortune at their birth or bring it out at death. Fortune comes from society, to society it will finally return. Therefore, the enterprise operation ideas of a capitalist should be the same as those of entrepreneurs. We need to learn from Japanese Panasonic and other entrepreneurs and strive to be excellent entrepreneurs.

Section 2 The concept of enterprise leadership management

Modern enterprise management is a people-oriented scientific management process, during which the research, development, production, marketing, and service of an enterprise are systematically integrated by functional elements with technical tools, working methods, enterprise culture, and management modes. Lower consumption costs are applied to produce more high-quality consumption products, so as to achieve better double-purposes.

The functional elements of enterprise leadership management include organization, decision-making, the consumption objective, planning profit targets, resources allocation, enterprise rules, discipline, allocation decision-making, strategy, tactics, stratagems, monitoring, safety assessment, and so on.

We should discuss the future direction of the modern enterprise from two perspectives: the correct relations of the enterprise and the individual, and the future evolution of the enterprise's organizational form.

The enterprise and the individual are equal. The enterprise should meet the needs of the individual; meanwhile it influences the individual through its resources, responsibility, and effectiveness, as shown in Figure 15.1.

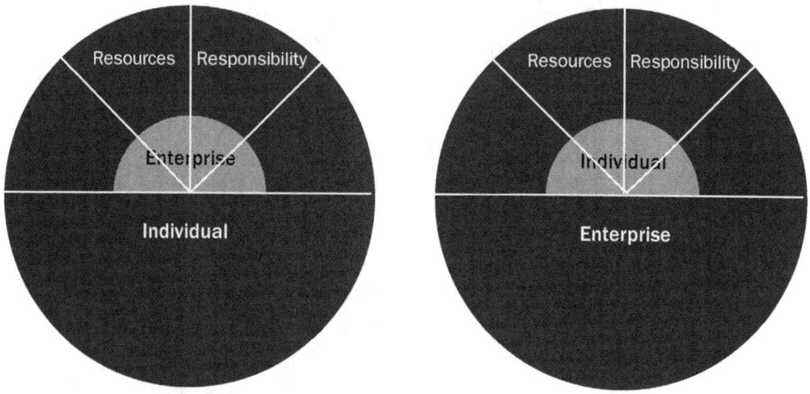

Figure 15.1 An individual's demand of an enterprise

The relationship between the individual and the enterprise

The relationship between the individual and the enterprise is:

1. *Demand-oriented.* The individual asks the enterprise for pay, wages or salaries, status, opportunity.
2. *Resource-oriented.* The individual can provide the enterprise with intelligence, imagination, creativity.
3. *Responsibility-oriented.* The individual is responsible to the enterprise for active force, influence, power of organization.
4. *Effect-oriented.* The individual desires from the enterprise promotion opportunity, leadership capacity, a sense of achievement.

The enterprise's influence on the individual

Similarly, the enterprise's influence on the individual is:

1. *Demand-oriented.* The enterprise asks the individuals for proper profit for the company, practical contribution to the company, the elimination of anyone not beneficial for the company.
2. *Resource-oriented.* The enterprise can provide the individual with a working environment to satisfy the individual's social demand, pay to the individual from enterprise profit, assistance for individual growth.
3. *Responsibility-oriented.* The enterprise desires that individuals can display leadership capacity to drive working, effectively utilize enterprise

resources, bear all responsibilities within the range of rights to balance rights and responsibilities.

4. *Effect-oriented.* The enterprise hopes that, in a team, individuals can enable the company to grow constantly, gain more profit for the company, grow together with the company.

When we compare these orientations one by one, we may clearly define the correct relations of the enterprise and the individual. The future enterprise has five orientations:

1. *Hugeness.* Enterprises must focus their efforts on establishing management status in the fiercely competitive international market, while the diversified organization can easily lose. Only the centralized huge enterprise can make profit. That is why mergers and acquisitions at present are so popular.
2. *Specialization.* The future operation of the enterprise will be oriented to experts and professionals. Outsiders cannot deal with professional business any more. The rich hire experts to operate enterprises for them. The expert is responsible for making a proper profit. Only to separate investors from actual operators can rights and responsibilities be measured separately, and supervision must be strengthened to avoid deviation from proper enterprise orientation.
3. *Cross-border operation.* The shortcoming of a single country is that the survival of enterprise can be threatened when there is turmoil in the domestic market. Therefore, a modern enterprise should explore overseas markets to balance risks.
4. *Capital popularization.*
5. *Free competition.*

The future development of modern enterprises should depend on the five above-mentioned orientations. The success of an enterprise will depend on whether the five orientations can be met.

In the above analysis, the enterprise knows the demand of employees, and employees know the demands of an enterprise; this is very important to the leadership and strategic decision making of the enterprise.

Section 3 The philosophy of enterprise leadership management

These are some of the characteristics of the philosophy of enterprise leadership management:

1. *Values.* Enterprise effectiveness and consumers prevail. Everything will center on consumers' demand and will serve consumption, with consumer satisfaction as the supreme goal.
2. *Boundless concept.*
3. *Market-orientation.* To pursue consumers' demands, enterprises should create new needs of consumption, serve consumers, and satisfy them.
4. *Social responsibility.* The enterprise comes from society, serves society, contributes to society, and returns to society.
5. *Enterprise development and management philosophy.* Enterprise development is emphasized while management is applied for balance; this is the rule emphasis–balance, balance–emphasis.

Enterprise renovation and renaissance requires:

- cutting off non-profitable units
- revitalizing derelict assets
- reforming the institution and carry out restructuring
- developing new sales modes by developing new high-tech products to win the favor of direct consumers in the road to rebirth for enterprises.

Enterprises should be human-oriented, respect human rights and dignity, and manage people according to national law and enterprise regulation. People are masters, managing things, material, and property to realize community integration of society, enterprise, and individuals.

In enterprise development consumers will prevail. Everything will center on consumption and serve the consumer. The demand and trust of consumers is life for an enterprise's existence.

Highlight enterprise development: without innovation, the enterprise will fail. Balance is management regulation, improvement, and reform to conform to enterprise development. Enterprise development and management are a dynamic process and a unity of opposites.

Information screening is essential as consumption determines everything in the modern enterprise. It is very important to investigate and collect extensive and complex consumer information and screen scientific intelligence to provide accurate, refined, and detailed information to leaders so that decision-making mistakes can be avoided.

Enterprise leaders combine strategies and tactics according to the information of targeted consumers, formulate a series of decisions, organize trials to gain experience, and then launch large-scale development.

Gradually modify mistakes to conform to market development rules: carry out executive monitoring on the enterprise's plan; modify the plan by inspecting it to correct mistakes to ensure there is balance–emphasis and emphasis–balance in development.

Use various convenient and fast communication networks for information screening: establish basic information databases and the latest information database. The most valuable information is the most recent information.

Create an information screening database through comparative, historical, and forward analysis and by building value information.

Information without value is a disaster to the decision maker. Information authenticity is the guarantee for successive decision making, otherwise decision-making mistakes will be made, causing catastrophe and failure of the enterprise.

Section 4 Consumption, control, and management of enterprise operation planning budget benefits

The whole process of the enterprise's operation activities is the process of consumption and consumption generation. The enterprise is a social economic cell. Enterprise operation is a process of creating benefit, which is influenced by environment and competition.

The enterprise's double benefits are the social benefits and the enterprise's profit benefit. Double benefits are generated during the process of production consumption and the final product consumption by consumers. Social benefits include products with use value (including consumption during the production process) directly consumed by consumers, taxes, employment, and so on. The transformation of scientific results into the productivity of the consumption society create civilized progress, generating new technological products with use value during the production consumption process. Consumption by consumers indicates social civilization and progress.

The enterprise's benefit is profit, which is why it is called profit benefit. During the creation of social benefits, the enterprise creates surplus labor value or surplus product wealth, which is in a relation of the unity of opposites. Without social benefits, there won't be enterprise profit benefit. Without enterprise profit benefit, the enterprise will go bankrupt, failing to create social benefits. Besides, investors enjoy a little portion of enterprise profit benefits; the rest is transformed into consumption funds for reproduction, generating social interests. During production, the enterprise creates a commodity with use value that is consumed by consumers. The generated surplus labor value – surplus product wealth, which is called the rule of profit benefits and social benefits – functions in any society.

By scientific budgeting, the enterprise will define operation results, financial status, and achievements in the future operation in the form of a monetary amount and quantity, so as to monitor and control operational activities of the enterprise and various business divisions, and accomplish comprehensive management of the entire enterprise. In utilizing this tool, we should conduct an integrated analysis of the social environment, natural conditions, and internal environment of the enterprise for the production consumption, operation planning, and budget and profit management. The overall process of enterprise planning and profit estimating should focus on benefits, which are the internal driving force for enterprise development. Enterprise development and marketing are external factors for competition and development, which is an indication of the fundamental rules of enterprise.

Operation planning and budget management has a strong causal relationship with enterprise operation effectiveness. As a saying in China goes: 'Eating cannot impoverish us, wearing clothes cannot impoverish us, without planning, we will always be poor.' It just illustrates the importance of plan management and summarizes income, operation, and saving.

We can summarize the purpose of operation management in the following way. During the operation process, we use minimum expenditure to create maximum income benefits. However, enterprise consumption and operation management are not simple theoretical topics, most importantly, they are practical topics. Theory comes from and is superior to practice, guiding practice. Theory is not the repetition of practice, which should be tested by practice and improved and developed in practice. Practice always prevails. Most entrepreneurs who achieve large or small success are not theoreticians at the beginning. During practice, their successful experience conforms to economic rules. Sticking to these rules, they gradually achieve success. The rule belongs to theory. However, most successful entrepreneurs fail to summarize and sublimate their practice to draw theoretical conclusions. Experience is very practical, guiding you to create higher income benefits with minimum input consumption in the operation process.

My explanation of the relationship between consumption and the budget control, operation planning and effectiveness management of the enterprise, based on theory and practice, has a practical implication. It should not be static or unchangeable management theory, and should develop in practice since the management model is confirmed by operation purpose, advanced production tools, process, and mode.

The management mode of sales service is confirmed by the budget mode of the purpose of sales service. Due to constant development of high-tech productivity, the constant change of the production modes, the operation management mode also constantly changes. Change is absolute, which better conforms to the development of the productivity of the consumption society. Invariance is relative, the need for stage balance, which safeguards the need for the development of productivity of consumption society.

Formulating a plan

An enterprise's consumption, budget control, and operation planning management will be formulated in accordance with the long-term, medium-term, and short-term strategies and tactics of the enterprise. The long-term plan usually covers more than five years, the medium-term plan covers two to five years while the short-term plan usually covers one year. The short-term plan is subdivided into monthly plans. It is the general method and rule for plan formulation. Middle and short-term plans are implementation plans; in particular, the yearly plan is the specific implementation plan. Sometimes, some part of the long-term and medium-term plan will be juxtaposed with the short-term plan. Although the operation plan budget and control benefit management are formulated based on objective reality, they still belong to the subjective scope while the objective practice is in motion every minute. The plan should be tested by reality. Therefore, during the implementation of the plan, leaders should monitor and control the implementation process, summarize experiences, and correct problems. They should carry out a plan check every half-year to rectify the plan to ensure the completion of the short-term plan. At the end of each year they should summarize the experiences and lessons in the implementation of the short-term plan and then formulate a short-term plan for the following year. At the same time, they should modify and improve the medium-term and long-term plan.

Analysis of system management for plan budget benefits

Enterprise makes investment with the purpose of achieving a targeted benefit (enterprise benefit and social benefit) by means of its management model. The management model of the enterprise determines the target benefit first, and then the budget of sales, cost, and expenditure is formulated while it is controlled by means of budget management, so the planning of enterprise investment and the scientific nature of the enterprise's managements are greatly improved.

Further analysis on enterprise benefit budget management

The study of the relationship between the enterprise's sales revenue and the benefit from the perspective of management is called cost–volume–profit analysis. While determining the operation objective of an enterprise, the balance point between the enterprise revenue and consumption cost, the breakeven point, will be found first, which is the prime basis for the formulation of the enterprise's objective. By designing a model, we can carry out monitoring and a decision-making analysis on the determinant variant among three varying factors. See Figure 15.2.

Profit = sales income-variable cost-fixed cost
Profit = sales volume × unit price-variable cost-fixed cost

There are five stages:

1. Confirm the rectangular coordinate system, with the horizontal axis representing sales volume and vertical axis representing cost.
2. Find the value of fixed cost a from the vertical axis and use horizontal axis o and point from vertical axis A as the starting point to portray a line of fixed cost F parallel with horizontal axis.
3. Use horizontal axis o and point from vertical axis A as the starting point and unit variable cost as ramp to portray overall cost line V.

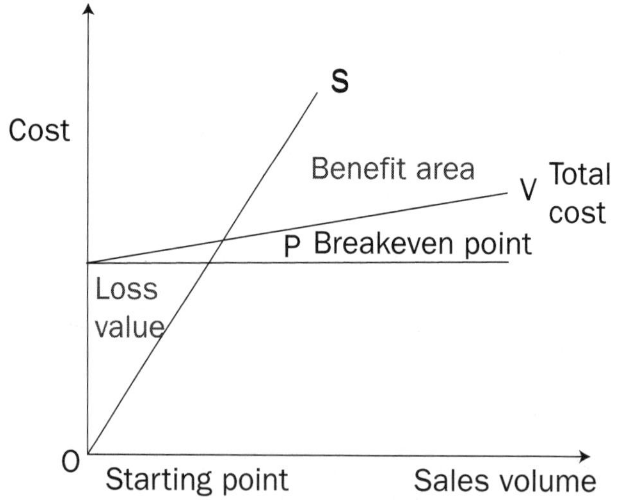

Figure 15.2 Cost–volume benefit loss and profit function and breakeven point

4. Use the origin of the coordinate as the starting point and unit as the ramp to portray sales revenue line S.
5. The crossing point of the sales income line and the overall cost line is the breakeven point P, indicated as P in Figure 15.2; the upper right side of the breakeven point is the profit area while the lower left side is the loss area.

In this figure we find the balance point of enterprise income and overall cost. Profit is made when the sales income is above the balance; under the balance, loss is caused, which is the primary basis for formulating the enterprise goal. Certainly, there are many variable factors for enterprise profit, which are fundamental.

The management of enterprise benefit budgeting from the perspective of a profit and loss equation

Under the condition of ordinary relative market and regular enterprise operation, the enterprise's profit and benefit are unknown. Then the existing resources of the enterprise will be utilized to reasonably arrange and develop the sales volume and revenue of consumption commodities, to control their cost, and to achieve profit benefit. When the objective is determined, scientific and systematic budget planning and profit management will be carried out.

The formula of sales volume required for achieving target profit is:

$$\text{sales volume} = \frac{\text{fixed cost + target profit}}{\text{unit price = unit variable cost}}$$

The formula of unit variable cost required for achieving target profit with established sales volume is:

$$\text{variable cost of unit price} = \frac{\text{unit price} \times \text{sales volume} - (\text{fixed cost} + \text{profit})}{\text{sales volume}}$$

The fixed formula required for achieving target profit under the condition of established sales volume is:

$$\text{fixed cost} = \text{sales volume} \times (\text{unit price} - \text{unit variable cost}) - \text{target profit}$$

According to this profit and loss equation, the profit budget model can be displayed by cost–volume benefit diagram as shown in Figure 15.3.

There are six stages:

1. Confirm the rectangular coordinate system, with the horizontal axis representing sales volume and vertical axis representing cost, sales income, and profit amount.
2. Find the value of fixed cost a from the vertical axis and use horizontal axis o and point from vertical axis a as starting point to portray a line of fixed cost F parallel with the horizontal axis.
3. Use horizontal axis o and point from vertical axis a as starting point and unit variable cost as a ramp to portray overall cost line V.
4. Use the origin of the coordinate as the starting point and unit as the ramp to portray sales revenue line S.
5. The fixed cost line uses target profit interest b as distance to portray target profit interest line T parallel with the fixed cost line.
6. Use target profit interest line as the basis and portray V line including target profit and overall cost parallel with V line. The crossing point X of VO line and sales income line S is the balance point to realize target profit benefit, called budget breakeven point.

According to the cost–volume profit interest diagram under profit budget management, we may see that under fixed cost, if the unit price rises, the slope of sales income will increase and the crossing point with VO line based on target profit will go down. Thus, the target profit will be realized in advance. The target profit can be realized with a relatively small amount of sales income. This is shown in Figure 15.4.

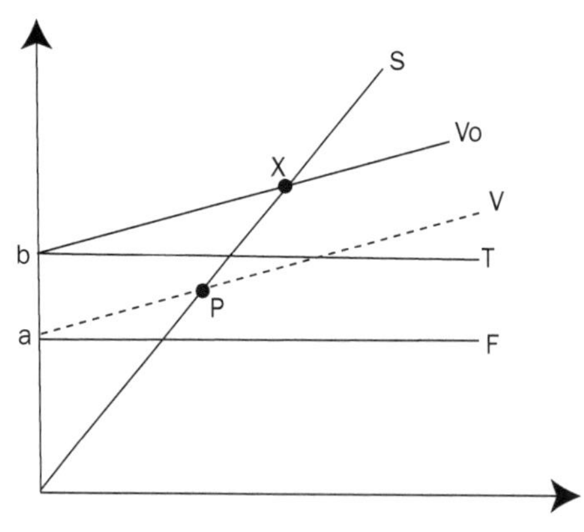

Figure 15.3 Cost–volume benefits under budget management (1)

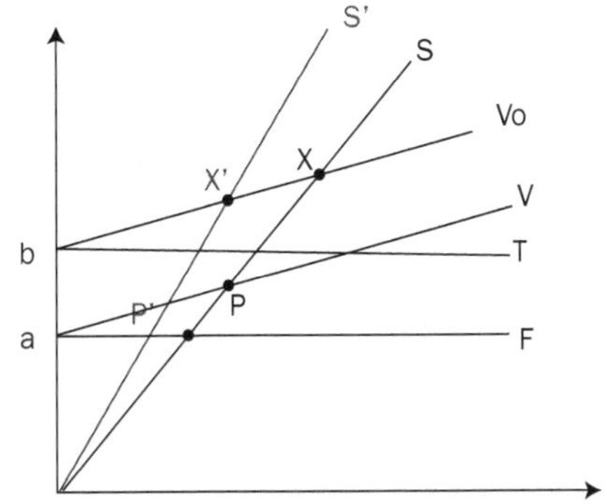

Figure 15.4 Cost–volume benefits under budget management (2)

Under a fixed unit price, if the unit variable cost rises, the ramp of VO line based on the target profit interest will correspondingly drop and the crossing point with sales income, the breakeven point, will reduce too. Thus, the target profit interest will be realized in advance, as shown in Figure 15.5.

Under a fixed unit price and a unit variable cost, if the fixed cost reduces, the VO line based on target profit interest will move downwards parallel to it, as will the crossing point with sales income, and then the target profit of the enterprise will be realized under relatively low sales volume. If the sales volume continues to grow, the over-target profit will be acquired, as shown in Figure 15.6.

This analysis illustrates that the fundamental principle of the management mode of profit benefit budgeting is that sales volume and cost are worked out by demand budgeting to achieve target profit on the premise that the target profit is established, and the enterprise can obtain over-target profit

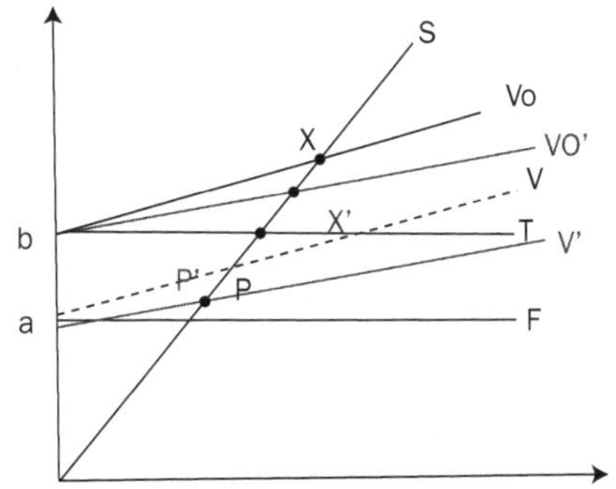

Figure 15.5 Cost–volume benefits under budget management (3)

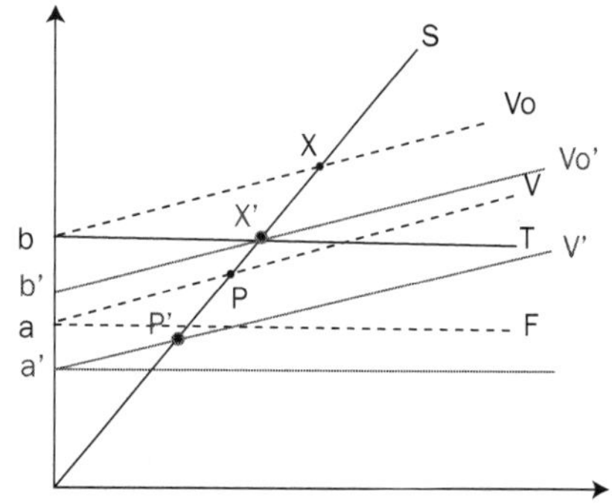

Figure 15.6 Cost–volume benefits under budget management (4)

by expanding the sales volume and reducing cost on the basis of determined sales volume and cost. If sales and cost budget, cash budget, research and development expenditure budget, and so on are considered from the perspective of long-term decision making, these budgets are connected to form enterprise benefit budget management.

Analysis of the budget balancing point of budget management with a focus on profit benefit

The crossing point of sales revenue and total cost under the budget management mode with a focus on profit benefit is called the budget balancing point. At X point shown in Figure 15.3, the budget balance point is the direct basis for investigating whether the target profit can be realized by profit benefit budget management.

The significance of the budget balance point is that the realization process of the target profit can be visualized, and the financial meaning of the balance point over budget can be explicitly portrayed. The triangle area under the budget balance point indicates the realization process of target profit. The VO line contains the target profit benefit and total cost. The crossing process of this line with the line of sales income S is also the process of the realization of the profit target. The crossing area of VO, S, and J vividly depicts this process. The upper right area of the budget balance point, the right area with the crossing of S and VO, indicates the over-budget profit benefit area or over-target profit benefit area.

The crossing point of sales revenue and total cost under the budget management mode with a focus on profit benefit is called the budget balancing point. This point is of great significance in budget profit benefit management. In additional to normal situations, it also manages estimated market sales volume and total cost and profit benefit. It is important to strive for technical reform or increase sales revenue or take measures to reduce cost to guarantee and develop the target of profit benefit. It is the basis for the system of enterprise leadership management.

Figure 15.7 shows the management system of enterprise profit benefit budgeting.

In the budget system of enterprise profit benefit, all budgets compose a complete and supporting budget system, which is the carrier of profit benefit budgeting. In the system of profit benefit budgeting, sub-budgets have close connection and a certain order. The close connection indicates every budget supports and depends on all the others. Target profit benefit is supported by every sub-subject, and every sub-budget attaches itself to the target profit benefit.

The target profit is subdivided into sub-budgets, the completion of which is a forceful guarantee for the realization of the target profit. Meanwhile, during the compilation of the budget, each competent department should communicate under the guidance of the budget compilation principle, which should be the reference of the budget formulation in each department to avoid the irrational phenomenon that a budget may be favorable to a specific department but not to the enterprise. Sub-budgets are interconnected and the order is irreversible.

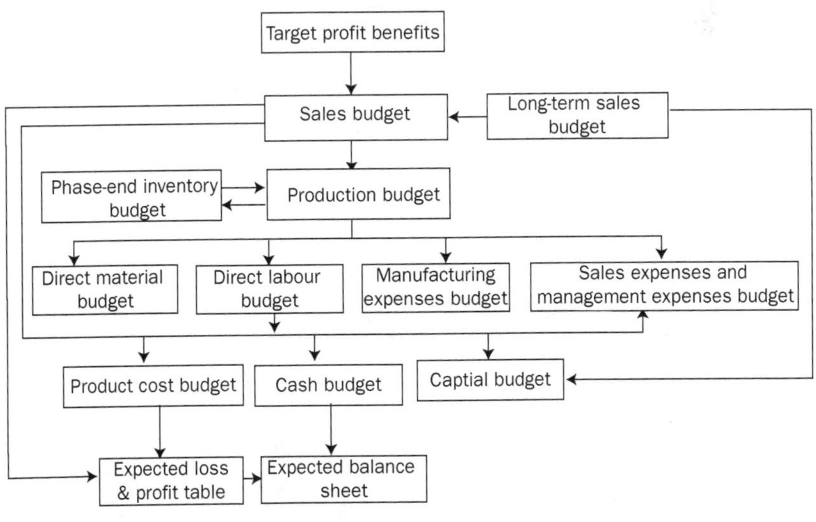

Figure 15.7 Enterprise's profit benefits budget management system

Under a vertical organizational structure, the enterprise budget plan is subdivided into the budget responsibility of various cost centers. The person responsible for each cost center is responsible for the costs in the area. Having analyzed operation activities, the basic cost center regularly sends cost information to the superior cost center. Having summarized the subordinate cost information, the superior cost center will report to its superior, and this continues up to the investment center at the maximum level, or the cost control center, which regularly reports the plan to the budget plan management committee.

Under a horizontal organizational structure, the enterprise's budget plan is also subdivided into budget responsibility of various centers. The basic cost center regularly submits the analysis report of actual cost to the superior cost center. Having summarized relevant information, the cost center at this level will submit it to the superior profit center. Having summarized the responsibility cost and income, the profit center will report it to the superior investment center, or the cost control center. Having summarized the budget completion situation, various centers will report the corresponding information to the corporation headquarters. The person responsible in each cost center is responsible for responsibility cost in its area.

Having analyzed operation activities, the basic cost center regularly sends cost information to the superior cost center, which summarizes the subordinate cost information and reports to its superior till the investment center at the maximum level, or the so-called cost control center, which regularly reports the plan to the budget plan management committee. Having submitted the budgeting management of operation profit benefits to special organs for disposal, the corporation reports to the budget plan management committee.

The organizational system is the basic environment for the fine operation of enterprise profit effectiveness and budget management mechanism. The realization of the target profit benefit should be established on the perfect organizational system, which mainly includes the budget management committee, special budget department, and budget responsibility network.

The budget management committee consists of the board chairman or general manager, and responsible persons of relevant departments. During the management process, they are in core leadership positions, whose main responsibility consists of organizing relevant personnel to decide target profit benefits, review, study, coordinate, and balance various budgeting items. It is the supreme management organ of profit benefit management. The special budget department is directly affiliated with the budget management committee, in charge of the management of the budget plan.

The budget responsibility network is the main body responsible for the budget, consisting of the investment center, profit center, and cost center. Different responsibility centers have different status in the profit budget management system with the investment center on top, the cost center on the bottom, and the profit benefit center in between. The investment center, profit benefit center, and cost center build the responsibility chain network, which is an all-round network including the responsibility of each department and employee. Depending on the organizational form of the enterprise, the organizational structure of the budget responsibility network is usually vertical and horizontal in form, as decided by enterprise leaders according to the conditions based on principles of convenience and strictness.

Budget variance analysis is the analysis of historical data, which does not guide production and operation (production consumption is viewed as operation) unless it is carried out sensibly and frequently (preferably once a week). The cause of budget variance mainly involves the internal working efficiency of the enterprise and the change of external elements. For the analysis and treatment of budget variance, different treatment measures are taken in accordance with the specific cause of the variance.

Ownership of responsibility for budget variance incurred by internal work efficiency should be clarified according to the controlling principle. Performance should be correctly evaluated. Combine actual performance of each budget executive body with its immediate interests through the reward and punishment system, confirm the resulting improvement measures according to reasons, and actively find new benefits growth point. If the change in factor variance incurred by external factors is a long-term trend, the operation strategy of the enterprise will be affected, which should be an investigation factor for the next phase of the budget compilation. We should properly adjust the budget goal of the next phase. On the contrary, the confirmation of the next phase of budget goal will not be influenced. Meanwhile, determining the responsibility for budget variance incurred by external factors, the principle of equal risk benefit should be followed, and risks caused by variance should be shared by various responsible organs, enterprise operators, and subscribers.

In the management model of profit benefit budgeting, budget variance analysis will begin with profit benefit variance analysis. Profit benefit variance will be gradually decreased and put into other elements related to target profit benefit, and these related elements will be analyzed one by one, so as systematically and fully to represent the cause of the actual profit benefit in budget period being above or below the target profit benefit. Figure 15.7 roughly shows the relations of various elements forming profit benefits variance. The main factors influencing the realization of the target profit benefit include sales income, sales and various variance costs, fixed costs, and management costs. During the disposal of the budget variance analysis, apply different treatment principles to different responsibility centers. Generally speaking, if a cost center can turn out products of the same quality at a cost lower than budgeted, it signifies better performance of the center.

Although management expenses belong to fixed cost, regarding the profit benefit budget, the reduction of management expenses will directly increase the profit benefits of an enterprise. Therefore, during variance analysis on management expenses, the enterprise should make reasonable judgments about work quality and service level with regard to other management systems (such as evaluation system of talents' performance), cement this phase level, and actively seek an improvement principle to treat budget variance fairly and objectively. The profit benefit variance of the profit benefit center should be supplemented with non-currency measuring methods, including productivity, market positioning, product quality, employees' attitude, social responsibility, balance of short-term and long-term goals, and so on.

Tables 14.1 to 14.7 illustrate the information required in budget plans.

In case there are fluctuations in enterprise budget, profit, and effectiveness control and price positioning, the budget and profit plan should be adjusted.

$$\text{Formula: retail price} = \frac{\text{factory product price+anticipated market cost+profit}}{\text{total anticipated sales volume}}$$

These are some explanatory points:

1. The retail price of a full-competition product is the upward and downward price confirmed by market demand and supply relations. The enterprise fully realizes profit benefit with reduced cost.
2. The retail price of a semi-competitive product should be determined by the sales model, with reference to the retail price of a non-competitive product.
3. Price confirmation of a non-competitive product (including patent products and new-tech products) and a non-fully competitive product should consider risk expenses.
4. Self-marketing is the same as agent marketing. Both should ensure that there are sufficient expenses and operating profit in the operation process.

Table 15.1 Information required in a firm's budget benefits management plan

Items		Quantity	Amount	Per capita benefits	Profit rate	Total expenses rate	Labor benefits rate	Project expenses rate
All employees								
Total revenue								
Total cost								
Cost of various items	Direct manufacture cost							
	Indirect manufacture cost							
	Sales cost (expenses)							
	Transportation cost							
	Tax							
	Scientific cost							
	Environmental cost							
	Management cost							
	Other costs (including rewards)							
Quality management	Rate of finished product of preceding year							
	Planned rate of finished product of this year							
	Enhance benefit rate of finished product							

Table 15.2 Information required in an annual sales plan budget (Yuan)

Items	Price	Remaining sales loss & benefit	First season		Second season		Third season		Fourth season		Total yearly amount	
			Quantity	Amount	Quantity	Amount	Quantity	Amount	Quantity	Amount	Quantity	Amount
Product A												
Product B												
Product C												
Product D												
Product E												
Product F												
Product G												
Total												
Of which												
Sales in cash												
Sales in credit												
Collect remaining Payment of preceding year												

Table 15.3 Information required in an operation profit benefits budget of service production enterprise plan (Yuan)

Items		**Quantity**	**Amount**	**Per capita quantity**	**Cost expenses rate**	**Note**
All employees						
Total revenue						
Total cost						
Classification of items of total cost	Direct cost					
	Indirect cost					
	Taxation cost					
	Environmental cost					
	Management cost					
	Others					

Table 15.4 Information required in a budget for an inventory finished product (Yuan)

Unit production cost (Yuan)	Unit	Quantity	Amount
Direct material			
Direct manpower			
Manufacture cost			
Others			
Unit product cost			
Phase end inventory product cost			
Phase end product inventory (pieces)			
Half of shelf life passing (loss and profit in risk phase)			
Inventory loss and profit			

Table 15.5 Information required in a sales expenses budget (related to performance) (Yuan)

Cost items	Actual number of report year		Budget number of plan year		Comparison	
	Amount	Taking up percentage of total	Amount	Taking up percentage of total	Amount	Taking up percentage of total
Salary and bonus of sales personnel						
Transportation cost						
Packing cost						
Advertising cost						
Insurance cost						
Traveling cost						
Other cost						
Office cost						
After-sales service cost						
Renting cost						
Environmental cost						

5. Product pricing is crucial. If the price is too high, the sales and operation results will be influenced. If the price is too low and can be raised in a timely manner, because of insufficient profit and expenses, the product cannot be developed and market of the product cannot be exploited, losing the enterprise's double benefits.

There are many such examples. There are successful pricing experiences in Sansui Corporation, successful pricing of many products, including Sansui Oral Exposed Liquid; there is also failed product pricing (very good

Table 15.6 Information required in a departmental management expenses budget (Yuan)

Expenses items of department	Administrative department (division)	Technology department (division)	Labor and capital department (division)	Education department (division)	Financial department (division)	Logistics department (division)	Office	Total
Salary								
Calculated benefits								
Traveling expenses								
Office costs								
Depreciation costs								
Repairing costs								
Training costs								
Water and electricity costs								
Others								
Total								
Non-cash outflow								
Anticipated cash outflow								

Table 15.7 Information required in a cash budgeting management plan (Yuan)

	Jan		**Feb**		**Mar**		**Apr**		**May**		**Jun**		**Jul**		**Aug**		**Sep**		**Oct**		**Nov**		**Dec**	
	Income	**Expenses**	**Income**	**Expenses**	**Income**	**Expenses**	**Income**	**Expenses**	**Income**	**Expenses**	**Income**	**Expenses**	**Income**	**Expenses**	**Income**	**Expenses**	**Income**	**Expenses**	**Income**	**Expenses**	**Income**	**Expenses**	**Income**	**Expenses**
Loan																								
Debt																								
Revitalization																								
Others																								

Note: cash flow management is the blood flow management of enterprise.

products, patent products, and so on), with experience and lessons very dear to the enterprise.

The enterprise takes as it focus profit benefit management, adopting budget profit benefit plan management, which is an integral systematic project. The table is a tool of the management process, but the tool can be improved or replaced. However, the profit benefit of the enterprise is not calculated, except through decision-making, balancing, and mobilizing all employees to participate in its management by giving full play to their creativity and wisdom in the operation management and enterprise development to create management benefit and development benefit in the process of plan management.

The budgeted profit and effectiveness is the goal of enterprise operation planning, which is a kind of power and motivation. The active distribution policy is the direct source of employee dynamics. To implement enterprise planning, budgeting and profit management, the employee rewarding mechanism should be implemented in the whole area of responsibilities, rights, and benefits, and should be made specific to individuals to mobilize the enthusiasm of all the employees. Meanwhile, we should pay adequate attention to quality training of all employees to let them participate in quality management, with work quality ensuring product quality to achieve impeccable quality goals. If the leader focuses attention on just accounting management while overlooking development, only the management is emphasized and the risk is intolerable, which will consequently adversely impact the development of enterprise. The management has a bottom line, but development is infinite.

The way out for an enterprise is the market. The enterprise should keep a close eye on direct consumers, and the commodity exchange channel is the bridge used to reach the target, direct consumers. The way out for the enterprise is satisfaction and favoring the product's direct consumers and the shared goal of the manufacturer and the distributor is the direct consumer.

Various manufacturers and distributors direct consumers together, resulting in complications, and severe risks in market competition. The market changes so quickly some things cannot be planned. Therefore, managers will use planning and budgeting to strengthen accounting management and will study the competition in the market and the new demands from consumers, and improve their own policy and mode of sales service to satisfy the continual new demands of consumers. Then they can grasp the initiative in market competition; if they are passive, the targeted benefit of the operation plan cannot be realized.

The dynamic model of target operating profit

The control and management of planning and budgeting of target profit benefit of an enterprise begins with compressing costs.

Reducing the enterprise's cost consumption is the internal work of enterprise management; talents are the source of enterprise wealth. Talents need a stage or opportunity to show the capabilities, while the stage needs talents for existence. Reducing enterprise costs begins with cutting personnel with low labor efficiency. When the number of employees of the enterprise decreases and labor efficiency rises, costs are reduced and enterprise profits are increased. Personnel costs can be reduced by:

- enhancing the comprehensive management capacity of managers and increasing labor efficiency through education and training
- applying more advanced management tools to increase management work efficiency and reducing the number of managers to the maximum extent, to improve labor efficiency and save management expenditure
- strengthening workers' business technology knowledge and practice; in this way the enterprise improves workers' proficiency levels on business technology, increases labor productivity and product qualification rates, and enhances the level of material management and use of raw materials and auxiliary materials; the number of backward employees will be reduced every year to increase labor productivity
- carrying out a piecework labor system for employees in the production line to calculate their salary by the piece; for operating posts to which the system cannot be applied, labor time should be checked to utilize the time relatively effectively and an overall rationing system and check by quality standard rationing, personnel rationing and salary rationing, and so on should be implemented, so as to eliminate employees with low labor productivity.

In this way the number of enterprise employees is reduced, labor efficiency is enhanced, costs are lowered, and the enterprise's profit is increased.

Table 15.8 shows an example of the annual target operating profit benefit of Enterprise A.

When the total revenue of Enterprise A stays the same, the enterprise improves the level of business proficiency through strengthening personnel training and enhances the level of workers' labor skills and improves the level of piecework labor; while the original management tool stays unchanged, the application of management by objectives and responsibilities improves the use of eight work hours to non-piecework posts (any unit or post to which piecework cannot be applied will be managed by post rationing), workload rationing, personnel rationing and work quality requirement rationing, salary rationing, bonus rationing, and target responsibility management rationing (excluding internal management of the enterprise). Therefore, the finished product rate is increased by 3% to 99%; 10% of cost – 270 million Yuan is saved; the increased benefit of 270 million Yuan caused by management is divided by the original basic benefit of 300 million Yuan to get 90%, or 270/300 = 0.9, and the management benefit rate is increased by 90%, and the labor benefit rate is increased to 19%. It can be seen that while sales revenue is not increased, only by strengthening the internal work of enterprise management is the annual profit of Enterprise A increased to 570 million Yuan from 300 million Yuan; the profit amount is increased by 90%, and the profit rate is increased to 19% from 10%.

Let us continue with Enterprise A, on the basis of 10% reduced cost consumption, management expenditure is reduced by 10% in the second year, travel expenses are reduced by 10%, environment expenses are reduced by 10%, and other consumptions are reduced by 10% and 5.832 million Yuan is saved. In the second year, the gross profit of Enterprise A is increased to 628.32 million Yuan from 570 million Yuan in the first year. Therefore, through two years' internal management of the enterprise, while the annual sales revenue stays the same, 3 billion Yuan, the annual enterprise benefit is increased to 628.32 million Yuan from the original 300 million Yuan.

Let us continue with Enterprise A; in the third year, the annual cost of the company is reduced by 10% through managing and reducing raw and auxiliary materials – 37.2 million Yuan. Hence the direct cost consumption is reduced to 874.8 million Yuan from 0.972 billion Yuan, and the enterprise benefit is increased to 725.52 million Yuan in the third year.

It can be seen from the above analysis that under the condition of fierce competition in the market, especially full competition of products, when it is difficult to increase the total sales revenue of the enterprise, it is advisable, practical, and feasible to increase the operating benefit of the enterprise by practicing internal management and strengthening comprehensive enterprise management while the original sales revenue stays the same. Furthermore, the benefit can be doubled. However, the method has limitations, for product cost consumption is limited rather than limitless, and cannot be reduced any more when a certain level is

Table 15.8 Sample annual operating target plan

Item	Number of personnel	Per capita labor revenue	Amount	Per capita labor efficiency	Per capita cost	Finished product rate (%)	Percentage of total cost in revenue	Percentage of single cost in total cost
Number of personnel	15,000	0.002						
Total revenue			30					
Total cost consumption			27		0.0018		90%	100%
– direct cost consumption			10.8					40%
– indirect cost consumption			5.4					20%
– environment cost consumption			1.35					5%
– consumption of scientific research and technical development			1.35					5%
– consumption of travel expense			1.35					5%
– transportation cost consumption			1.35					5%
– consumption of year-end reward			1.35					5%
– supervising cost consumption			0.27					1%
– consumption of management cost			2.7					10%
– other consumptions			10.8					4%
Finished product rate						96%		
Total profit			3				10%	

Note: per capita annual sales revenue generated: 200,000 Yuan, and benefit created for the enterprise: 20,000 Yuan.

reached. That is exactly the limitation of management benefit. An enterprise must develop, or it cannot have scale or enhance the double benefits – enterprise development benefit and management benefit (discussed otherwise) – to the largest extent. Now let us return to the market consumption competition of the enterprise.

Assume the product of Enterprise A is in a full-competition market during the process of sales market competition. The equilibrium profit rate in the market is 10%, and the original profit rate of Enterprise A is 10%, which is equal to the average profit value of comprehensive market competition.

During the process of fierce competition in the selling market, the average profit rate decreases to 5%, and some poorly operated enterprises with an original profit rate of only 4% are sure to be closed. When the enterprise profit rate is 5% or a little higher, the profit rate of Enterprise A is still 19.184, and the profit is 150 million Yuan, hence 725.52 million Yuan − 150 million Yuan = 575.5 million Yuan.

Assume in the fifth year (calculated from the first year in which Enterprise A is assumed), the average profit rate in the market decreases to 3%, and a large number of enterprises are closed. The profit of Enterprise A is reduced to 508 million Yuan from 575.5 million Yuan. In the fourth year, with the absolute advantage in fierce market competition, Enterprise A takes over a closed factory, and carries out production technology reform (because Enterprise A has huge capital) and improves advanced technical equipment. In addition, technicians and managers are assigned to operate Enterprise B, achieving sales revenue of Enterprise B of 2 billion Yuan. Enterprise A itself expands its factory and production, increasing the sales volume of 1 billion Yuan, increasing to 4 billion Yuan from the original 3 billion Yuan. Hence the sales volume is doubled during the process of fierce competition. Although the average profit rate in the market is only 3%, the profit of Enterprise is increased to above 1 billion Yuan because of its doubled sales volume and the merit of increased scale. Furthermore, in the sixth year, because of the fierce competition in the selling market, the selling price returned to 7% from the reduced price owing to supply exceeding demand, and the original level of supply–demand relations is restored in the sixth year. Suppose the retail price level under the supply–demand relations in the first year creates an average profit level of 10%.

Now Enterprise A has an annual sales revenue of 6 billion Yuan and a sales amount of 6 billion Yuan × 24.8% (profit rate) = 1.45104 billion Yuan (profit). We can see that its sales are doubled, and that its annual profit is 1.451 billion Yuan/300 million Yuan. Because of the development of the enterprise, the profit benefit is multiplied by 4.8 times.

According to the above-mentioned six years' development process, Enterprise A stands firmly in the market competition by strengthening internal enterprise management and reducing cost consumption. Other enterprises are closed or operate with little profit. Owing to its management advantage, high product quality, high finished product rate, and low cost consumption, Enterprise A gains a profit rate higher than that of other enterprises in the industry and achieves further development and nearly 4.8 times of annual benefit. There are two lessons from this. First, we should practice the internal work of enterprise management, enhance product quality, and reduce the consumption cost of the enterprise to the largest extent. Second, we will develop the scale of the enterprise, winning by scale. The scientific development of an enterprise is a huge (but not limitless) prospect, which is the task of an entrepreneur. Enterprise A will be the most successful enterprise in the world. The entrepreneur is Jack Welch, who is a successful and great entrepreneur.

Section 5 Reinforce enterprise goals, and develop and initiate non-comprehensive market competition products to improve two enterprise efficiencies

The products of non-full market competition involve products with proprietary technology and new characteristics that are popular with direct consumers. The product for value innovation used in Blue Ocean Strategy, the traditional American wine industry, consists of seven elements:

- the price of each bottle of wine
- the elegant and high-taste logo attached on the packaging and the label on each bottle with the prize-winning declaration; the mystic winery is used to emphasize the artistic and scientific nature of the winery
- highly invested marketing; raise the popularity of the product in the fiercely competitive market and win the favor of distributors and retailers on a kind of wine
- the reputation and historical background of the winery (list names of manor and castles and historical era when the wine factory is established)
- the brewery quality of wine

- the complexity and elegance of wine
- seven wines of different kinds ranging from chardonnay to merlot, made according to different brewery to satisfy the tastes of customers.

Some wines have been among the most competitive products worldwide. However, the US winery invented seven value elements of the commodity to make wine in this factory very popular with consumers. The wine has been successful in the full-competition sales market and US wine has the third leadership position in the global market. Competition in this industry, valued in US$20 billion, is very fierce. Wines from California dominate the domestic market, with two-thirds the sales volume of US wineries.

Casella Wines in Australia uses a four-step action framework for innovation (Figure 15.8), and has launched Yellow Tail Wine with great success.

In order to break the relationship of the tradeoff between differentiation and low cost and to create a new value curve, there are four problems of great significance for challenging existing strategic logic and business models:

1. The new value curve promotes the pursuit for differentiation and low cost in the enterprise, so as to break the relationship of the tradeoff between value and cost.
2. It can remind the enterprise that the enterprise should not increase its cost structure and over-design products and service only for growth and creation. Many enterprises are caught in such situations.
3. It is easy and can be understood by managers at various levels, so that it can be fully participated in and supported by the whole enterprise during strategy implementation.

Deletion	**Adding**
Brewery terms and prizes of honor Brewery quality Highly invested marketing	Higher than affordable wine price Participation level of retail store
Reduction	**Creation**
Complex taste of wine Wine category Reputation of grapery	Quantity drink and selection Interests and risk

Figure 15.8 Innovation characteristics of Yellow Tail Wine

4. It drives the enterprise to strictly consider every competition element in the industry, so as to find out the assumptions implied in the industry, which are usually unconsciously taken for granted by competing enterprises.

Figure 15.9 shows the strategic layout of Yellow Tail Wine.

With regard to high-level or affordable wines, we attach importance to other competitive elements, such as complex taste and the brewery quality of the process and oak fermenting. Wine insiders say that the sweetness of Yellow Tail Wine reduces the quality of the wine, which goes against the traditional taste, art, and wine-making process of superb wines. This may be unreasonable as some customers prefer Yellow Tail Wines.

This company breaks the traditional manufacturing mode and promotion means of wines, creates a new, unique manufacturing and promotion mode, and wins marketing success based on consumer preference.

Figure 15.10 shows the four step movement framework. The first step is to delete long-term competing elements in your industry. These elements are usually taken for granted, although they are valueless or their value is reduced. Sometimes, the value emphasized by the buyer experiences fundamental change, but the competing enterprises don't take corresponding

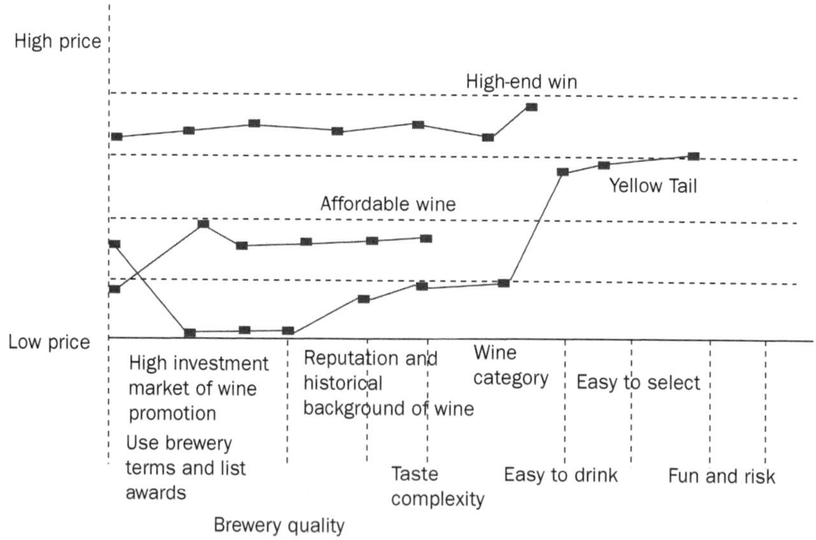

Figure 15.9 Strategic layout of Yellow Tail Wine

action to counter these changes, or even don't detect such a change. This is a 'habitual blind spot', which cannot be detected.

The second step is to make a decision on whether current products or service are over-designed, just to match and beat competitors. Under such circumstances, offerings by the enterprises exceed the need of customers, or the cost of the enterprise suddenly increases, both of which yield no good results.

The third step is to explore and eliminate the reluctant compromises made by consumers.

The fourth step is to find new sources of buyers' value and create new demand so that the strategic pricing standard can be changed.

Working through the first two steps (removal and reduction) can help you to understand how to reduce cost below your competitors. Research shows that enterprise managers seldom systematically remove and reduce investment in competing elements, resulting in increasing cost and a more complex business model. In contrast, the latter two issues teach us how to enhance the value of the buyer and create new demand. These two issues let us systematically explore how to provide new experience and reduce the cost of enterprises. What is most important is deletion and creation, which enable the enterprise to go beyond the level of competition to pursue the goal of maximizing values. They force enterprises to change competing elements and make current rules of competion insignificant.

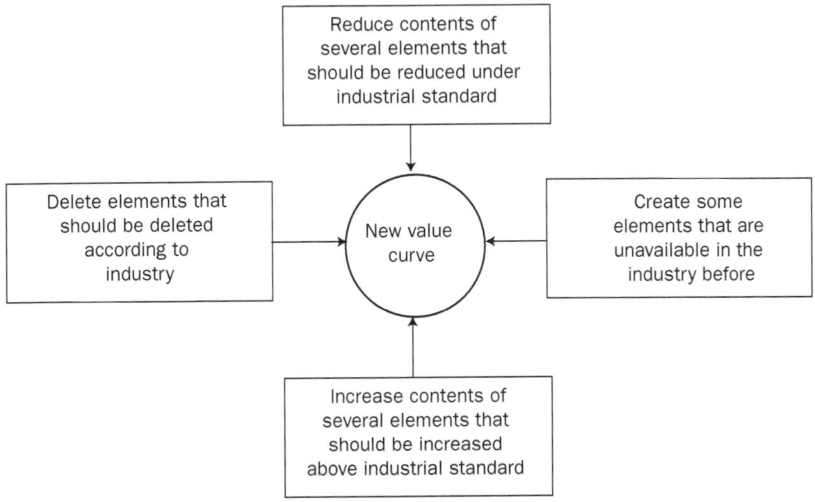

Figure 15.10 Four step movement framework

The analysis of the innovation thinking in the wine industry by Yellow Tail Wine demonstrates that we should be good at detecting old and habitual thinking, and recreate the innovation in a product to inspire consumer desire for it, thus creating a new differentiated product with characteristics. The product is a non-full competition product with low relative cost. The retail price should be relatively high. In response to products needing promotion, transportation, advertisement, and marketing costs should be considered. The profit margin of distributors should be relatively high. Only in this way can distributors prefer to operate. Consumers are ready to purchase because of the differentiation and freshness of the product, bringing profit to the product manufacturer as well as the distributors, which is also the rule for creating new differentiated consumption products.

Improve the management of profit benefit budget and develop a patented product without competition

If the patented product can meet a market demand, it will be a consumer-preferred product. Since it is the consumption product solely produced by the enterprise, the product enjoys patent protection in the sales market, without competition from other products of the same type and quality (the competition from replaceable products is possible), therefore, we define a patented product as a product with relatively little competition. Patents, trademarks, copyrights, and other intangible protection-rights assets belong to the scope of enterprise management, which will be monopolized products at a certain time, space, and locations with certain technology since its price is far away from its value. With the expiration of a warranty period this technology will be pushed onto the market for the general public. Other enterprises can produce this product losing the protection of the patent. Sales of the product at the same quality will be popular, with prices rapidly declining to a relatively low level. The product enters the full-competition market.

The invented Sanzhu Oral Exposed Liquid I chaired is the first high-tech product of our company with a patent (patent number: ZL93115272.0, initiated in China and leading the world trend). When the product is launched on the market, it was popular with the broad masses. In 1994, sales revenue in the first year after launching was RMB 0.125 billion; the second year it was RMB 2.35 billion, the third year RMB 8.04 billion, the fourth year RMB 7.75 billion, with total taxes, RMB more than 2 billion.

Both assets accumulation and social benefits are good. Another patented invention chaired by me is Fuxinkang Oral Exposed Liquid (patent number: ZL95112116.2). In the first year of its launching in 1995, sales revenue was RMB 0.5 billion, achieving many economic and social benefits. We are applying for international patent for this product and the invented ecological cosmetics I Chaired-Economic Beauty (patent number: ZL97112152.4). It earned sales revenue of RMB 0.5 billion in the first year after its launch in 1995.

At the beginning, the patent product of Sanzhu Corporation was relatively non-competitive. With the development of its competition in the market and rapid expansion of new-tech products and similar replaceable products, the price of the patent product gradually reduced to approach the optimal market rate, finally leading to full market competition.

Bill Gates from Microsoft invented the patented technology of computer chips, taking the monopoly position in the international sales market, with a product price far deviating from value rules. The enterprise made a good profit and developed fast to be listed in the global top 500.

Therefore, the prime task for the development of an enterprise is to build up new technical and differentiated products in the market and to create a new demand from consumers. Through enterprise activities of marketing and promotion (sales and management are discussed otherwise), consumers can know, accept, buy, and even prefer new technical products, realizing the social benefit value of new technical products and the operating value of the enterprise, which are necessary to realize the enterprise's development benefit.

Taking an overview of the progress of global civilization, we may discover that its various historical stages were initiated and created by a new tech product for consumption. Therefore, new creations made by the enterprise should be the source of dynamics for its development.

Section 6 Consumption and enterprise decision management

During the whole development process of the enterprise, decision-making will always exist. Decision-making management includes industrial investment decision-making: who should buy the product produced by the enterprise; how should the information on the consumption market be investigated; how should raw and supplementary material and production tools be selected; and how should decisions on resource allocation, and short-term, medium-term, and long-term targets be made.

Since production process and tools decide the production mode, and the production mode decides the management mode, decision making regarding the management mode, management contents, enterprise culture, regulations, and discipline should be made according to the production mode, which should then be modified in the implementation process. We may say that the management and development process of double benefits is a process of decision making and modification on decision making, in particular, decision making on the development investment of enterprise, which is an important issue of the enterprise. As long as the decision-making is not wrong, issues caused during the development of an enterprise are easily solved. If the decision making of the enterprise is wrong, it will cause irrecoverable loss, which will be the maximum loss of the double benefits of the enterprise. We should transfer the arbitrary decision making of the enterprise leader to the assessment and decision making of the management group to avoid decision-making error.

The decision-making committee

An enterprise decision-making committee centering on the president and general manager, which is the supreme authority of the decision-making level of the enterprise, should be established. The committees should include the vice president for the market or the general manager, the financial director, and the person in charge of the market information department of the enterprise, and external consultants hired to take part in decision-making; Decision-making does not mean that the minority is subordinate to the majority, instead, it means scientifically evaluating the credibility of data, the feasibility of investment capital's return cycle, and the potential and medium-term or long-term possibility of selling in the market. A positive decision can be made when the success rate is 70% and the risk is 30% while a negative decision should be made when the evaluated success rate is 60% while the risk is 40%. Why can a big decision allow 30% risk? The development of a sales market involves a dynamic social change process, with multiple variables and unanticipated factors. Any scientific evaluation report cannot contain all unanticipated factors. Therefore, even the best decision making contains risks, which just brings more development and investment impetus. That is the reason for the existence of venture capital. The decision-making process and the final decision-making plan display knowledge, wisdom, experience, education, and a cognitive level of understanding and inspiration.

The duty of a decision-making committee

The decision-making committee will not be in charge of the management of the double operating benefits of the enterprise but make significant decisions of the enterprise. Its duty is to evaluate and make decisions about the significant problems of the enterprise throughout the management process of double operating benefits. Once a decision is made, it will be carried into practice by the president and the organization's business administration organization.

Monitor the process of implementation and management decision making

The implementation process will be monitored and evaluated regularly once or twice a year, and will be adjusted to reduce the loss caused by wrong decisions as much as possible. Therefore, enterprises must try to ensure that correct and scientific decisions are made, or serious and uncorrectable loss will occur.

Correct decisions of Sanzhu Corporation bring huge success while important decision-making mistakes cause big losses (due to incorrect information). Therefore, enterprises should seriously summarize experience and lessons, which are important for the enterprise leaders and the enterprise.

Section 7 Consumption and organization management

Organization management is a very important element of enterprise management. Management functions of enterprises are realized by the work of the organization. The organization is power. When the enterprise has a scientific target plan and wants to realize this target plan, the first priority is to organize all resources allocation and implement them according to functional elements to realize the final target plan of the enterprise. However, the organizational development process is a test of the organization itself. It is a guarantee of the organization if the structure is strict, discipline clear, requirement severe, and attitude serious. Organizational work can enhance and develop consumption productivity of society at the maximum level, reduce cost consumption of the enterprise at the maximum level to raise double-benefits goal of enterprises.

Organizational management is the first priority of enterprise management, and does not only apply to enterprise management. Any kind of group activities needs organization. Without organization, anything will be in a mess, with no power. No targeted task can be realized (whether big or small) without organization. Individual heroism sometimes exerts great power; without organization, it is very insignificant. The hero has to be combined with the broad masses to strive to realize the plan's target. Only then, can a hero become a true hero.

Enterprise form of organizing

The configuration of the enterprise management mode is the behavior model of the organization's structure set in accordance with the enterprise's production purpose, production mode, subject of labor, and the need of all the enterprise's resources allocation. It should be established according to the size of the enterprise itself, such as flat mode, matrix mode, layer mode, and so on.

Organization structure should be simple and scientific

Organization structure should be simple and scientific. In order to set the organization structure scientifically, tight links and cross-linkage functions should be provided in it, which is guaranteed by strict discipline. The requirement for the execution of discipline should be severe; the treatment of problems should be serious, or else the organization's power and characteristics will be lost. Management leaders at various levels should discover whether management is proper. For example, if the organization establishes a center, department and divisions, with one leader managing three or four units, or even as many as six units, bureaucratic mistakes will emerge if there are too many employees under one leader, which will affect their work. For example, the organization of the army usually adopts the system of three above three, or four above four. It will no longer be scientific with five above five system.

Bureaucratic organization will be strictly controlled

Bureaucracy is when leaders command and make decisions without considering the actual situation for a period of time. Bureaucracy is behavior that doesn't conform to actual conditions, which is a frequent mistake made by leaders. Therefore, bureaucratic organization is a formidable enemy for management, the source of every fault during the management process and the source of wasteful consumption. Bureaucracy brings the enterprise's management organization into failure.

To overcome bureaucracy, organization overlapping should be strictly avoided.

Reduce the number of assistants. Too many assistants are the root cause of bureaucracy. Due to too many assistants, the first leader will work by depending on assistants, who won't go further and listen to reports. The first leader will just make decisions and command relying on reported information. Personnel will not truly report pros and cons of an issue since all this is connected to their responsibility, power, obligation, and interests so as to cause major leaders to make bureaucratic mistakes.

Overstaffing in an organization is the root cause of bureaucracy. It keeps major leaders away from practice, causing bureaucracy, which cannot be controlled by people's will. Overstaffing in an organization is sure to cause excess employees, low work efficiency and productivity, and serious wasteful consumption.

Organizational power is generated when humans exploit and create consumption materials from nature; this encourages the fight between humans and nature, among human groups, and even among nations. Therefore, enterprise management should regard organizational management as the first priority of leaders.

Section 8 Consumption and consumption object management

The target consumer group of products will be managed

Before investing in production, the object of consumption for a product must be positioned. At the same time, the positioned object of consumption will be studied, with or without competitors, full competitors or non-full competitors, and then a study should be carried out to exploit or gain some direct consumers who are ready to consume the product. Meanwhile, you should study competition on the same type of products from other enterprises or replaceable consumption products. During the fierce competition process in the sales market, use consumer management to increase the loyalty of consumers for your products to enhance the sales volume and double the benefits of the enterprise's consumption products.

Object of consumption during production process

All consumptions of the enterprise in creating new consumption commodities are included in the production process of the object of consumption. Only when all consumptions in the production process are transferred to a certain product, which is becoming a new commodity consumed by the direct consumer, can the value of production purpose be realized.

Consumptions during the production process include the consumption of subject of labor, the consumption of tool depreciation, the consumption of management expense, the consumption of labor expense, and the consumption of social environment expense. The selection of the object of consumption is important to determine consumption cost and product quality.

The selection of targeted consumers determines the consumption cost and quality of products. Disqualified raw materials, poor production instruments, and unskilled laborers would result in high consumption costs, poor products, and even poor operation, loss, or closedown of the enterprise.

Section 9 Enterprise object management

An objective has the power of appealing, attracting, and generating cohesion. It can mobilize every group related to the targeted interest. Therefore, any scientifically feasible target can generate the power of appealing, attracting, and generating cohesion (three forces). However, it will be guaranteed by strong and powerful organization.

Based on its operation targets, the enterprise decides its objectives in the near, medium, and long term, which are divided into high, middle, and low level objects. In this way, fulfillment of the objectives can be guaranteed and arrogance can be avoided. The meaning of designing the objectives of three stages: the first objective should be based on the current foundation, a higher objective that the team is confident to realize through hard work. Based on the first objective, the second objective task ascends to a higher level, which is possible to realize with hard work while the third objective task has an expectation value, with hope to realize.

In the process of ensuring the realization of the first objective, all employees are fully confident to realize the objective with hard effort. Without the power of appealing, attraction and cohesion, arrogance will appear and negative factors will be induced, which is unfavorable to enterprise development and interests and the development of employees. Besides, this arrogance is an intrinsic ideological activity. When the objective at this stage is completed, leaders can smoothly shift the fighting force and collective enthusiasm to the second objective. In this juncture, the spiritual power of the team will smoothly transfer into huge material power to possibly realize the second goal if it is within the target period and there is time for forward development. Then leaders can channel team power to the third objective to strive for the realization of the third objective.

At the end of the season and year, we need to organize to summarize seasonal or yearly experiences and lessons and carry out relevant rewards to encourage advanced groups and individuals. However, the rewarding should be fair and justified. For this, excellent models should be fairly selected. We then reward these models to make them display exemplary force for moving everyone towards the new objectives. We should be careful to prevent unfair and unjustified praise and reward. The standard for rewarding should be performance based and these rewards will encourage everyone to follow. Or else, the realization of new objectives will be severely influenced.

Section 10 Consumption and the management of resource allocation

The enterprise production and operation management process are also a consumption process of resource allocation. Resource is an important objective used in enterprise management, which is also an integral element of the productivity of the consumption society. It includes laborers, capital, land, raw and supplementary materials, tools, technical processes, machinery equipment, product sales, models, time, information, solar power, air, wind, living environment, and other important resources.

The level of consumption and resources allocation management is closely related to the double benefits of the enterprise's operational management, which is an integral indication of leadership capacity, leadership method, and the art of core leaders. While studying the development of the enterprise productivity in a consumption society, the enterprise leaders will first study enterprise resource, analyze its advantages and disadvantages, make the most of integrated advantages and overcome disadvantages, unleash the power of the organization, and organically create the best double benefits of the enterprise through systematic and integral management.

Section 11 Consumption and enterprise management mode

Consumption and management mode of productive enterprises

The management of a productive enterprise will be determined by the production mode, which is determined by the production purpose, production technology, and process and production tools. Since production purpose, production technology, and process constantly develop, and new production tools are constantly invented, the production mode should change constantly. Because of the constant change of the production mode, the management mode must change with the change of the production mode to adapt the development of productivity, or the development of productivity of the consumption society will be impacted and hindered. This is one of the important reasons why enterprise management is a topic of study.

For example, the management of the production mode of the family workshop is totally different from that of the intensive production mode of steam engine industrialization; the management mode of a labor-intensive production mode is different from that of a new high-tech intensive production mode; and the management mode of a general labor-intensive production mode is different from that of an intelligent and automatic production mode.

Therefore, the management mode should be determined based on the actual production mode to make the management mode adapt to the production mode so that the maximum productivity of the consumption society can be displayed.

Sales management mode (including operating and selling enterprises)

Sales of the consumption commodity produced by enterprises

The management model of enterprise product sales will be determined by the objects of consumption of their consumption commodities and the supply–demand relations in the market.

When supply falls short of demand, the spot cash sales management model of a manufacturer's via direct authorizations to the retail stores (supermarkets) or wholesalers is relatively simple, but the manufacturer will have close and friendly relationship with distributors since they replace the manufacturer to serve consumers directly. They serve and manage consumers – they complete sales on behalf of the manufacturer (under the pretext of guaranteeing their own interests).

The enterprise organizes sales itself. A large enterprise carries out the integration of research, development, production, and sales, and the internal operation of the enterprise during the selling process. Totally different from the first management mode, the management mode involves a group. Scientific research and the manufacturer adopt a workshop-style management. The overall management structure of the enterprise contains the front house (market) and back house (research and production) with the latter guaranteeing the supply–demand relations of the former. The sales market adopts a system of independent legal subsidiary. The group establishes head office for each sales market (sales department of group) to command enterprise planning and manage sales of various subsidiaries. Various provinces establish provincial offices to substitute for the corporation to be in charge of running the management of sales in each province and region, each subsidiary is in charge of management of regional and town offices. This is the leveled management system.

Sales management is the direct handing over of the product produced by the factory to the sales company for sale. Accounting disposal should be carried out first inside the group. The group company also adopts the accounting treatment for financial management of independent subsidiaries. Group enterprise should encourage internal trade among independent subsidiaries as a way to manage operations and sales. That is the marketing management mode of direct sales to consumers by subsidiaries and workshops.

The financial center of the group directly rules the financial management of subsidiaries all over China; product sales, collection and labor expenses should be managed by a central financial center. The deposit volume of various subsidiaries should be limited and the excess should all be remitted to the financial center of the group, adopting a centralized management mode. The finished product warehouse of the production factory establishes a second level warehouse management model, with the primary finished product warehouse established in the factory while the secondary product warehouses are kept in various provinces and regions. Direct management of the factory ensures the supply in the sales market. Sales cash from various offices and workstations should be deposited in the corporation's designated accounts (only deposits are allowed; withdrawal is prohibited).

The aforesaid management ensures that the cash flow of 2,200 offices and 13,500 workstations of Sanzhu Corporation around China can enter the subsidiaries' account at the right time, with cash turnaround as fast as 27 days. Meanwhile, the smooth development of the sales market and sales channel of the consumption commodity should be ensured. Rapid development of the promotion process greatly encourages productivity in the consumption society.

The management mode of product sales agents of productive enterprises

When the commodity production enterprise does not want to or is incapable of organizing its own sales team, it may entrust a regional or national agent for sales. The marketing management mode of such a factory is usually very simple. The main task is to select an agent with selling and enterprise planning capabilities and emphasize profit distribution during negotiations in accordance with the mutual benefits principle. The ideological mode of the agent is to reduce the agency price as much as possible while the manufacturer tries to preserve a certain profit margin. In particular, in response to the full-competition commodity, under the condition of supply exceeding demand, the enterprise should make the maximum concession on profit to agents. Only when acquiring the maximum profit margin from the manufacturer can the agent get the space to plan marketing operations and sales in the market.

Under this marketing mode, the large agent dominates the manufacturer and rules the sales market of consumers to make a relatively high profit.

The management model of business enterprise

The marketing mode of advertising promotion

In accordance with consumption demand characteristics of the sales market, a business operation seeks consumption demand and creates a new consumption idea to lead the desire for it. Create a new marketing model to promote consumption based on consumer satisfaction.

Advertising for product marketing is the marketing model of venture investment. If the enterprise planning fails, the enterprise will incur a heavy loss or even fail. If there is successful advertising, better profit benefit will be achieved. The advertisement-marketing mode has certain rules, which are important:

1. The tactical policy is to pay adequate attention to attracting large and appropriate groups, with differentiated characteristics when choosing consumption commodities.
2. Enterprise marketing planning will grant a cultural soul with a new selling point to the commodity.

3. The product will be sold in pilot sales in middle-sized and small cities, and then, based on that experience and lessons learned, the experience will be perfected for future development.

Tactical policy of investment in advertising

These are the tactics of investing in advertising:

1. During the process of advertising promotion in the pilot sales market, pay special attention to the popular advertising message in promotion planning. Any advertising that cannot be understood and accepted by the public should be avoided.
2. Once investment is made in advertising, promotion will not be stopped because the intended purpose is not reached, but the contents of the advertising message should be adjusted or else the overall scenario will fail.
3. Once investment is made in advertising, personnel will be organized to trace 24 hours a day whether investment is in place and whether the effect of advertising meets the expectation and the reason behind it, so as to adjust the contents of the advertising as soon as possible.
4. Experienced marketing should follow immediately. Explain the skills required to volunteers according to plan and summarize a typical experience to encourage promotion.

Conference marketing and its management mode

Conference marketing mode

Conference marketing is a systematic and integral marketing mode. Distribution agents have specific standards to select the consumption commodities of manufacturers, which will adapt to the needs of consumption of specific consumption groups.

The specific service group is a kind of marketing mode, under which a specific group is invited for promotion in a specified place and time. During the marketing process, a specific pre-sale service plan is formulated and includes the site service plan and after-sale plan. This must be organized to train special sales service personnel to adapt to the consumers' needs. Implement a rational interest allocation policy among the sales personnel and couple performance with special meeting locations to promote the task of the service group.

Conference marketing management

Figure 15.11 shows the organizational structure of conference marketing.

Control of the conference marketing network

Using its exclusive agency product, the marketing company plans and organizes an expert panel to deliver lectures on its marketing network. Every independent node in the network will be controlled by the control model of five elements: exclusive regional agency, sales in hard cash, business personnel training, large profit margin, and the policy of a special year-end reward. The corporation uses hard cash for settlement in its development outlets, free of risk. Under the control of five methods (product, regional agency, expert lecture, personnel training and price) of the corporation, various regional sales outlets can only sell the products purchased by cash with the reliance on the help of the corporation, to finally realize scale benefits of both sides.

Spreading method of typical experience

A pilot will be provided first, and then when successful experience is acquired, successful experience will be studied and spread; the experience will be popular during the promotion development process to increase sales volume. This is the management mode of sample guiding rolling development. The marketing mode of the sales market, whose basic rule is to center on the direct consuming group constantly innovates and develops. Against all creating ideas and creative marketing modes, the consumer-centric rule won't change to achieve the satisfaction of consumers.

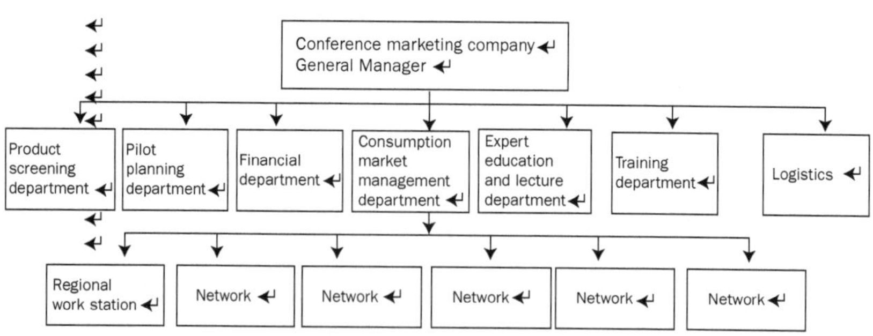

Figure 15.11 The organizational structure of conference marketing (flat management) – raw material inventory budgeting

Section 12 Consumption and enterprise regulation and discipline management

The firm by-laws regulate investors according to national requirements. Series of regulations in an enterprise are the guarantee to realize the internal operating objective plan of the enterprise and the guarantee for the systematic operation of the enterprise. These regulations have a legal nature in the enterprise, which will not conflict with national laws. They belong to rules within the scope of national law, such as the financial system, the cost management system, the cash management system, the logistics management system, the labor assets personnel management system, the knowledge and technology management system, the archive management system, the storage management system, the hygiene management system, and the production and quality management system. Included are such things as an employee training system, factory, plant management system, equipment management standards and systems, the production management system. Also included are the process discipline check management system, production technology experiment management system, raw and supplementary material, the packing material checking system, the technology analysis system, the process flow and post operation management system, substandard product management system, production record management system, production water and quality checking system, the quality archive management system, the quality incidents management system, periodical family visiting system, product sampling observation system, the product quality analysis system, the product quality auto checking system, the quality inspection department sampling system, the quality standard formulation and management system, and the production site checking system.

An enterprise's discipline is the guarantee for all the management behaviors of the enterprise. The discipline itself has definite requirements and standards. It is the enterprise law to guide the behavior of all the employees of the enterprise, which should not be violated, or severe punishment will be applied. We should have a serious attitude and strict requirements in the implementation of discipline. If the discipline cannot be seriously implemented, the enterprise will not go far. Inside the enterprise, all employees are equal against legal regulations and discipline, with nobody above enterprise discipline and regulations.

In summary, enterprise management should be incorporated through the by-laws into discipline management, with everything in the enterprise operating in accordance with the law and regulations, which is the hard management of the enterprise. Sanzhu Corporation boasts seven chapters of production enterprise and production task management, seven chapters of workshop management, four chapters of quality standard management, volumes of financial management by law, and eight chapters of routine management, with each chapter having detailed rules.

Section 13 Enterprise distribution policy and management

In the process of internal enterprise management, the distribution policy is the core of all dynamics, consisting of equity benefit distribution, benefits distributions of senior leaders, general leaders, and management personnel, senior technicians and general technicians; distributions of workers' interests; and the distribution mode of salary and bonus.

The distribution policy is closely related to the immediate interests of each member. The distribution policy decides how the enterprise members acquire social wealth, their purchase power, consumption capacity and level, which are the survival and development needs of all people and important requirements for building a harmonious society on enterprise.

The enterprise's distribution policy also belongs to the superstructure. Therefore, the distribution policy of the enterprise is within the general scope of the national distribution policy. The enterprise has the sovereignty to formulate its own policy, which is subject to national regulations, taxation laws, and other economic means.

The prime task of enterprise management is to study and formulate the distribution policy of the enterprise. The standard required for formulating the enterprise's distribution policy will be fairness and justice. The policy must be able to inspire and mobilize the enthusiasm and activity of personnel, make them do what they should do, and inspire them to work creatively.

Section 14 Enterprise strategy, tactics, plan and management

Strategy

Enterprise is the economic cell of society. All operation activities of the enterprise are elements of the social dissipation movement. Enterprise development is a spiral development led by three important consumptions; it is developed in mutual competition. The survival, decay, or elimination of an enterprise is a natural phenomenon, which is an inevitable consequence of economic development led by consumption.

In order to ensure competitiveness and development, the enterprise must discover a strategy to succeed in competition. The strategic decision of the enterprise is of great significance for the direction of the enterprise, such as low-cost strategy, talent strategy, development strategy, new technology development strategy, novelty strategy (including blue ocean strategy), product quality strategy, market competition strategy, brand, and so on. The process of studying, formulating, and implementing strategy is the development process of enterprise management – the process of routine enterprise management and the development process management. It is also a development management process with emphasis and balance. Among specific projects and various systems, the process is not a balanced and parallel development but a coordinative development with focus and emphasis. During the marketing process there are 'six firsts':, quality first, technical content first, service first, network first, environment first, and management first.

During the competition by products, we should give the first priority to product quality. To meet the maximum need of consumers with high-quality products is fundamental and the key to market competition. Technological content should be first. Only those products with high-tech content and huge market potential can have fundamental competition. During market exploration, we should focus on service first. The development facts of countless enterprises at home and abroad indicate that consumers are ready to buy products from those enterprises that really regard consumers' satisfaction as the standard of service value and provide an efficient service for consumers with improved service.

During service marketing, we should insist on 'network first'. The network is scale; without scale, there won't be scale benefits. Either in cementing the current market of products or developing new product markets, we should attach importance to network scale and improve operation efficiency and the benefits of network. In addition, during marketing we should attach importance to the internal and external environments of the enterprise: 'environment first'. Without a favorable environment, nothing can be fulfilled. Environment is the condition for enterprise survival. Therefore, internally, we should attach importance to ideal education and cement the building of enterprise's cohesive and centripetal force, enhance the cooperation and unity of the employees; externally, we should build a good enterprise image, product image, and brand image to seek support from all walks of life and create favorable external and internal environments for the overall development of the enterprise. During the operation of the whole enterprise, we should follow 'management first'. Flexible and efficient management mechanisms and precise and accurate management systems are crucial for the effective operation of enterprise.

The six firsts are not parallel, but a consideration of the overall operation of the enterprise at different perspectives. Therefore, we should always insist on these 'six firsts' and treat them with a view to strategy.

The marketing plan of the enterprise is the crystallization of wisdom and creativity, the soul of product marketing. Marketing strategy, tactics, policy, and stratagem are the life of marketing enterprise.

Tactics

Tactics serve a strategic objective. A strategic objective is the 'target', while tactics are 'arrows' or 'swords'. The two make up the unity of oppositeness. Once the strategic objective is determined, the tactics, policy, and strategy will be formulated to realize the strategic objective, and tactics implementation will be guaranteed to achieve the purpose of a strategic target.

Manoeuver

Manoeuvering is the method to achieve the strategy, indicated by certain rules, which determine the development life of the enterprise together with the policy of the enterprise. Policy is open standard behavior, while a manoeuver does not disclose the objective directly but involves lateral or other regular behaviors that serve the realization of the objective plan. With dual nature, manoeuvering has functionality as a management rule and strategy as a method. The service objective of manoeuvering is strategy while the functionality objective of the working method is specific persons. However, the implementation of all strategies and manoeuvers are conducted and executed by persons.

For example, in the competition for direct consumers, the enterprise with relative weak strength should avoid big cities with fierce competition and develop in medium and small cities with relatively weak competition. Having won trial successes and acquired experience and learning, and a certain competing force, the enterprise should improve itself, develop, and expand to large cities. It is a manoeuver of strategy. The overall strategy aims at the sales market. It is the method of manoeuvering to take sales markets in medium and small cities, which serves the realization of strategic objectives.

To learn and study application strategies is the art and capability of leadership and the commanding level of the overall system. Therefore, in order to ensure the enterprise will gain better benefits with far-sightedness and advantage, major leaders of the enterprise should use strategy, policy, and manoeuvers to organically combine management benefits and development benefits.

Section 15 Enterprise consumption and assessment management

Formulating assessment standards

Complete assessment standards will be formulated to serve as the basis for the performance assessment of specific units or individuals in the enterprise, instead of assessment by subjective judgment of leaders. The content and standard of the assessment will guide personnel to move forward. If the enterprise aims at profit benefits, the assessment standard is the systematic assessment standard focusing on benefits; thus all employees will take profit benefits as their goal. If the assessment standard centered on sales, the employees would focus on sales instead of profit benefits. The assessment would result in higher sales volume. Although employees get their due interests according to the assessment standard, the profit benefit of the enterprise would be relatively low or even at a loss. Therefore, the management of the operation activities should be focused on benefit to assess sales volume and develop scale benefits.

Setting and organizing the assessment unit and personnel

Based on assessment standards, the enterprise assesses all its operational activities, which is the conventional work of the enterprise and major enterprise leaders. With this working method, enterprise leaders can work with assurance, speak words based on facts and figures, command with calmness, and manage with order, which is an indication of better enterprise benefits. These activities should be carried out:

1. During the process of enterprise consumption, all work should be provided with an assessment standard, and leaders can assess, evaluate, commend, or reward anyone at any time.

2. Regular monthly, quarterly, and annual summaries, assessments, evaluations, commendations, and rewards should be made.
3. An assessment system centering on the professional assessment unit and responsible persons should be established.

Only in this way, can the leader have a timely basis for assessment, commending and rewarding, and making fair, justified, systematic, and integral assessment results so that all employees will follow the commending and rewarding. Justified criticism can be easily accepted and all the public will be satisfied to correct its mistakes. The enterprise team can displace cohesive and fighting power. When major leaders of the enterprises shift the fighting force to the objectives, huge materialistic force can be displayed.

Section 16 Supervision

The need for supervision provided in enterprise

Consumption and management in the enterprise's operational activities should be carried out in accordance with articles and clauses, regulation and discipline. Enterprise regulations are the code of conduct to standardize the operation activities of enterprise employees. Supervision exerts no functions on discipline-observing employees. Supervision is directed to non-compliant behavior during the process of enterprise operation. What is more important, these non-compliant persons severely disrupt the display of the team's force and operational tasks cannot be completed in time. These behaviors will harm the enterprise's operation and marketing. Every non-compliant person will be supervised, identified, and punished, and then the normal operation and marketing of the enterprise can be ensured.

Establishing regular supervision and auditing departments

The enterprise will provide a full-time regular supervision and auditing organization to supervise and inspect the enterprise's operation and marketing process on behalf of the board of directors and the highest manager of the enterprise, and the large enterprise will establish supervisors' meetings, a supervision department, and auditing department while the small enterprise will establish a supervisor and full-time auditors to carry out regular work, which is very important.

Section 17 Safety management

Modern enterprise management pays most attention to people, and security is the most important management element. Security awareness and security precautions will be carried out in all activities during the full course of development from factory building to production and operation. Security is an important indicator of qualified enterprise management, and is a very important element of the value of the double operating benefits of the enterprise.

Section 18 Development of enterprise operation consumption management and team building

Every operating activity of an enterprise is a collectively organized team behavior rather than an individual behavior. The team cannot have fighting strength without the guarantee of organization and discipline. Once the plan objective of the enterprise is determined, the building of organization and the team strength will be reinforced, or the objective task may not be completed.

Section 19 Consumption and product quality management

Product quality as an element of productivity of the consumption society

The evaluation of product quality is based on product quality standards. Product quality has broad social property. The factors influencing product quality are numerous, complicated, and take a long time to be formed. In the production process of the same type of product in different periods and stages, different enterprises have different quality standards and requirements. Some products apply to national standards while other products apply to enterprise standards, with varied requirements on product costs, since productivity value in producing the product varies a lot. For example, the difference and value difference of 90% eligibility rate, 99% eligibility rate and 100% illegibility rate (the product is rejected due to the substandard) will directly influence the enterprise's economic interests, intelligible brand assets, property rights, and the value benefits of product.

The quality of the product is productivity, the realization of whose function is restricted by the internal management conditions and management levels of the enterprise, laborers' skills, the technical level of production means, and the quality level of the subject of labor, and so on. All these factors influence quality standards and develop in constant change. If an enterprise can turn out eligible quality products popular with consumers with less input and lower cost, products produced by this enterprise will become popular with consumers and the enterprise will develop very quickly. When the product produced by an enterprise is no longer popular with consumers, the enterprise will go bankrupt. Therefore, quality is the lifeline of an enterprise. The enterprise should ensure and constantly enhance product quality. The enterprise should implement a comprehensive whole-process standardized and responsible overall system management of product quality. Comprehensive quality management is the core of enterprise management, which is the most important thing. The finished product level of product quality marks the level of the enterprise's comprehensive management.

Policy, discipline, and organization of enterprise quality management

Product quality is the life of an enterprise. The enterprise must establish regulations, policy, and discipline to manage product quality. The policies, regulations, and disciplines should be made to ensure employees full participation in quality management, to guarantee product quality with their work quality, and to combine part-time and full-time personnel in the quality management division. For example, with regard to the quality insurance system, Jinan Sanzhu Pharmaceutical Co., Ltd. has established the Quality Management Committee led by the general manager.

Section 20 Enterprise management

An enterprise manages people by regulations and manages tasks, materials, and properties by people. During enterprise management, the institution may standardize people's behavior, but be incapable of managing human thoughts and consciousness. During the modern era when mental and physical labor are combined, mental labor has become the main labor of society. Compared with the era when productivity was underdeveloped, physical labor, hard physical labor in particular, declined greatly. Compared with the management of pure physical labor, difficult soft management methods for mental labor and labor integrating physical and mental elements have witnessed fundamental changes. Therefore, hard management

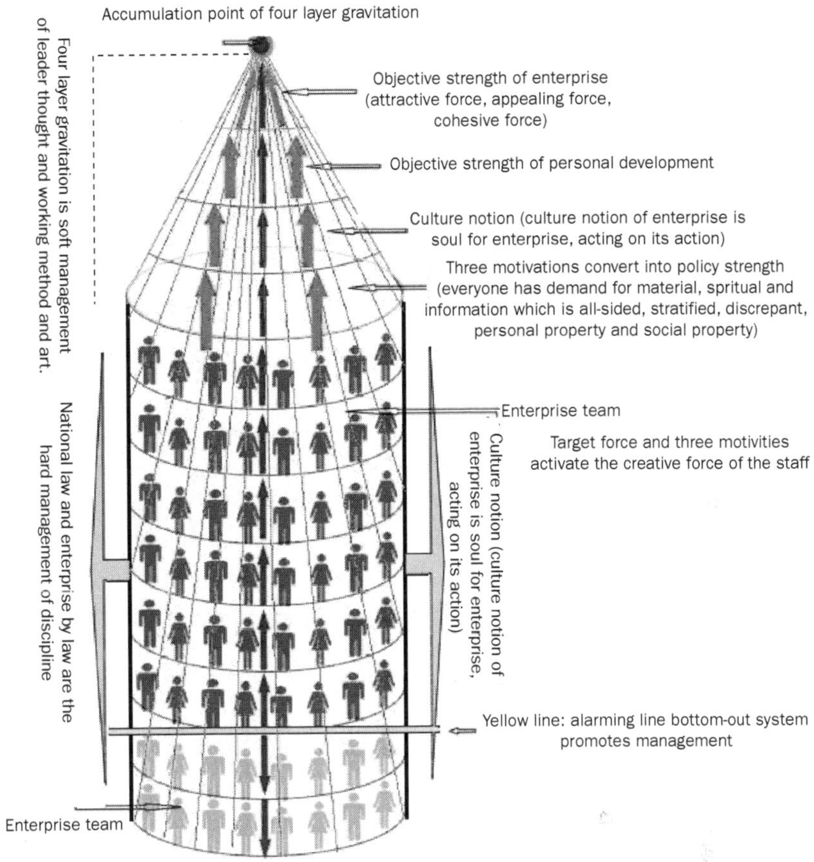

Figure 15.12 Different functions within enterprise management

and soft management are both proposed: merciful management and merciless management (everyone is equal in discipline, adhering to 'four strict' rules). Figure 15.12 illustrates the different functions within enterprise management.

Notes

1. The people in the column represent groups in the enterprise.
2. The two straight black lines on each side of the column represent national law and the regulations and discipline of the enterprise, used to standardize the unified action of all members.

3. The yellow line under the column is a warning line that represents the last-one-out system, a propelling force for all members.
4. The vertex of the cone in the upper part of the diagram is the accumulation point of four-layer gravitation, including leaders' integrative competence, leadership thinking methods, working methods, and artistic soft management.
5. There are four types of gravitation: of the enterprise goal, of individual development goals, the enterprise culture and concept, and policy transformed by the three motives, which is the direct gravitation of all employees. (These are explained below.)
6. There are four levels of gravitation from top to bottom. The upward blue line represents life force and the infinite vitality of personnel. All employees on the first level accept material, spiritual, and informational gravitation. Everyone has material, spiritual, and informational demands, which are direct, comprehensive, stratified, and differentiated, with personal nature and social nature. The second layer is thought governing the gravitation of cultural ideas and soul. The third layer is the gravitation of the individual development goal. The fourth layer is the gravitation of the integration of the overall development goal of the enterprise and individual development goals.

This type of management will convey the integrated management results of the leader's capacity, thinking method, working method, and art.

During the management process, we need to implement six working methods:

1. Formulate the objective and task.
2. Formulate the standard requirement of the objective and task.
3. Define the person responsible for completing the task.
4. Set the time requirement for the objective and task.
5. Specify the discipline of rewarding and punishing for the task.
6. Seriously summarize experience and lessons; move forward by promoting achievements and correcting shortcomings.

The implementation of this six-step working method is a matter of principle, judging whether a leader is qualified or not. Some managers are too merciful and not strict, and do not achieve a win-win situation; others are too strict and not merciful, which results in low efficiency and poor results. The above two working methods and attitudes must be resolutely corrected.

There are three formulas to judge leaders' work:

Assignment of definite task – check = zero result

Assignment of definite task + check = poor result

Assignment of definite task + check (with awards and punishment) = superior result

16

Marketing leadership management

Section 1 Concept and development of marketing

Productivity is one of the links of consumption in the consumption society. Products are consumed by consumers through the sales process, thus realizing their use value. The long history of mankind is the process of three important consumptions in which living consumption and social consumption drive the development of scientific research and production consumption. During the process, new needs of consumption are created, and then the needs act upon consumption. The ever-increasing material, spiritual, and cultural needs of consumption of human beings drive the economy to move forward in a spiral way. Therefore, the marketing of the three kinds of consumers' demands is referred to as 'marketing of consumers' target demands large market system service'. The marketing of the large market service system is the soul of enterprises.

With the competitive development of capital commodity production and exchange, the overall supply–demand relations of society turn from a seller's market into a buyer's market. While competing to meet various consumers' demands, the manufacturers and dealers create various kinds of marketing modes and marketing means.

The common purpose of production and exchange is to win the preferences of various types of consumers and achieve the value of products. However, the conception of marketing is interpreted differently in different historical periods. In the developing history of marketing, some new concepts emerge every ten years, which encourage research, guide the practice of consumption, and arouse controversy. No matter how controversial, they must provide light and heat; they must be solid; they must not be a flash in the pan; they must improve our abilities to understand, predict, and control reality. People are often disturbed by the shortage of scientific concepts rather than the excess of scientific concepts.

As early as 1937, those sociologists who founded the American Marketing Association began to study marketing. So far, they have been constantly developing their theory, seeking to give a more scientific definition to guide marketing. Early studies show that marketing is a discipline and should have a core concept. For example, the core concept of economics is shortage; the core concept of political science is power; the core concept of anthropology is culture; the core concept of sociology is group. The core concept of marketing is exchange.

A set of common-sense concepts is derived from the concept of exchange. Then there emerge the concepts of demand, desire, product, value, satisfaction, and market, which fill in the blanks in marketing. These concepts contain insights on exchange.

During the historical development process, academic marketing began to transfer to schools of business from departments of economics in the 1950s. The development of marketing helps entrepreneurs build and protect the thinking system of the market.

Around 1950, in an address to the American Marketing Association, Neil Borden began to use the concept of 'marketing mix' and identified 12 elements within it. Borden said that he was enlightened by James Clinton's words in 1948 that the enterprise manager functions as a decision maker, an artist as well as the combination of various elements. Borden pointed out that marketing experts were concerned with whether marketing and advertising personnel (who consider the creation of demands as the primary function of advertising) could go further.

In 1950 Joel Dean, in his discussion of an effective pricing policy, used the conception of 'product life cycle'. Dean described the market development period, market expansion period, maturity period, and so on. Subsequently, Theodore Levitt (1965) spoke highly of the concept. Since then, the concept of the product life cycle has undergone numerous modifications. However, so far it is still a controversial issue that interests many people.

Wendell Smith (1956) introduced the concept of rich connotation in market segmentation. There are differences in the history of different markets. They have different needs and interests. Smith required companies to conduct detailed market segmentation studies instead of just product differentiation. He considered market segmentation as a strategy. Today we are more inclined to see it as the division of the market into a number of competitive parts. Then the company decides to choose the part and tactics to meet the needs of this part.

Jerome McCarthy (1960) put forward the well-known 4P combination, the marketing mix of product, price, place, and promotion.

Theodore Levitt (1960) published the famous concept of marketing myopia. It is characterized by an emphasis on product rather than customer demand.

In 1963, William Glazer (1969) put forward the lifestyle conception (achieving sales by observing behaviors of social consumers and studying products demanded by consumers).

In 1967 John Howard and Jeddish Sheth (1969) put forward the buyer behavior theory and pointed it out that a marketing organization should base production on sales, and observe the behavior of consumers, study the needs of consumption, and organize marketing.

Philip Kotler and Sidney Levy (1969) proposed the idea of expanded marketing, in which marketing can be applied to all behaviors (including those of organizations, people, places, and ideologies).

Gerald Zaltman and Philip Kotler (1971) proposed the conception of social marketing, which is marketing expanded to include social goals.

In 1985, the American Marketing Association provided a new definition of marketing, whereby marketing conduct extends to the systematic combination of social and public relations, political skills, social welfare activities. Thus marketing is not only reflected in the activities of enterprises, but can also be extended to non-profit organizations and public bodies.

To sum up, the conception of marketing is constantly changing. However, no matter how it changes, it must meet the three important consumptions needs, which are the core of marketing. I call it 'marketing of consumers' target demands large market system service' and the details will be discussed later.

The key of this concept is that it will be meaningless if the consumer parts with consumption. The demands of consumers diversify society, so marketing should be carried out according to the detailed classification of consumers' demands. The consuming process has various relations with society, which also has the scope of a 'great market'. The consumer's consuming process is a complex social marketing process. At the moment, it is a buyer's market of capital commodities production and exchange. The competing aim of marketing is the direct consumer and the homogenization of marketing methods. The key point is that whoever can win the preference and satisfaction of the direct consumer is the winner. So, in the process of winning the consumer's preference and satisfaction, the quality of marketing and service determines success or failure.

The marketing conception can reveal the essence of modern marketing and guide marketing practice. However, the conception of marketing keeps developing along developing consumers' demands.

Section 2 Large market system service marketing directed at consumer target needs

The sellers' market

In a sellers' market, overall commodities in society are in short supply – there is a shortage of commodities. As the Chinese saying goes, mud on the radish is not washed when it sells well. This means that consumers do not find fault with the quality of a commodity if it is difficult for them to buy the commodity they need. As long as they can purchase the commodity from the suppliers, they are easily satisfied. The marketing process is characterized by a trading exchange process. As a result, it is common that marketers do not show enough respect for the human rights of consumers in a sellers' market.

The buyers' market

In a buyers' market, overall commodities in society are in oversupply: there is an excess of commodities but a shortage of consumers who want those commodities. When consumers buy the commodity, they are critical about product quality. Sellers should provide a fine service and show respect for the rights of consumers. Consumers' interests are protected by society and the law. In a buyers' market, manufacturers and dealers have to change their ways of thinking and acting in the marketing of products to meet consumers' demands and preferences in order to achieve their marketing purposes. This whole process involves government intervention and the participation of all aspects of society. Marketing has become a broad, socialized issue for social and public relations.

Relationships between a buyers' market, consumers, manufacturers, and dealers

Because of the relative shortage of consumers' demands, manufacturers and marketers compete to meet these demands. In this competitive process manufacturers and marketers provide a variety of services and behaviors, so as to gain consumers' preference for their products, enable consumers to buy their products, and upgrade consumers' status and rights. It is difficult to satisfy consumers who are critical about products. The protection of consumers' rights and interests improves. Manufacturers and marketers are forced to improve their product quality and service quality. The national government strengthens the monitoring and management of product quality and makes laws to protect consumers' rights and interests.

Consumers are 'supporters' of manufacturers and marketers (also known as 'God')

Since consumers dominate the manufacturers and marketers, production is based on sales. If products produced by manufacturers are not recognized and purchased by consumers, factories will close down; workers will lose their jobs; investors will lose money. As long as products produced by manufacturers are recognized and purchased by consumers, the factory will be able to develop; investors and dealers will make a profit; all staff, production workers, and marketing personnel will earn wages, laborers' protection tax, and welfare. With money, basic human needs can be met. The money, which comes from consumers, is the wealth created by consumers. Consumers support manufacturers and marketers. Manufacturers and distributors are also consumers (it is not an absolute opposition, but a different division of labor in a certain time). The production process of manufacturing enterprises is also the consumption process of products from other enterprises, showing the process of the productivity of the consumption society.

Respecting consumers' rights and interests

All members of society are consumers, with their own independent thinking and behavior rights. As long as they do not break the law and other regulations, they should be respected by other members of society.

Consumers, including consumers in the production process, have the right to choose satisfying products, offer criticism and rational proposals for manufacturers and marketers, and have their rights and interests protected. Any forced purchases and sales are illegal acts that violate consumers' rights and deserve the criticism of consumers and the community as well as legal sanctions.

Staff of the marketers should not only show respect for the rights and interests of consumers, but also act as consumers' consultants, providing knowledge on health. treatment of diseases, how to recover from diseases, and changes of lifestyle that lead to poor health. They should recommend relevant health and disease rehabilitation products, learning materials, and products of daily use to consumers, and establish friendships of mutual trust so as to enhance consumers' health and longevity.

Marketing personnel need to provide consumers who are capable of enjoying consumption power with spiritual commodities and services to build friendships and develop long-term commodity sales relationships. This will promote sales and harmonious relationships in the community and make consumers loyal to the enterprise and its products.

Section 3 Analysis of the concept of large market system service marketing directed at consumer target needs

The relationship between consumers and marketers

As previously stated, all members of a society are consumers. In a certain period of time, space and job position, you are a consumer and I am a marketer or a producer. Outside the workplace everyone is a consumer. Everyone is in the consumption process and is closely linked to society. Particularly after detailed division in the production of commodity, members of society all create consumption products and consume social commodities.

The products we consume are shipped from one place to another or from one country to another, so the products are gained through marketers' transactions or the process of international import and export. In this process, the products are subject to management by the country, laws, decrees, and policy, as well as transportation and storage. The products should be traded at a specific trading place or site in order to meet customers' needs. This comprises a large social marketing concept, not just limited to a simple relationship between marketers and consumers.

Relationships between consumers, target demands, and system service

Manufacturers and marketers have a common goal to meet consumers' demands. When products in the same industry are of almost the same quality, all enterprises are in the direct pursuit of customer satisfaction with different degrees of expectation, which is constantly improved. For each manufacturer and marketer, the key to success lies in meeting consumers' demands. Therefore, manufacturers and marketers must decide on commodity pricing, transportation, sales outlets, pre-sales service, marketing service, and after-sales service; seek advice; improve services; and establish long-term relationships with consumers and so on. All the above elements are part of the system service, with each element functioning as an independent small system. Each system is a complete whole, constituting the service structure of the whole system.

Analysis of relationship between consumers' target demands and system service marketing

As we have stated, all members of society are consumers; production is consumption, and producers are consumers. However, a commodity cannot satisfy all members. For example, foods are consumer goods that everyone needs, but everyone has their own preferred food; again, everyone needs clothing, but everyone has their own preference for clothing. Consumers' demands are affected by work, lifestyle, and purchasing power. Different age preferences and different purchasing power lead to different consumption target demands of consumers.

Marketers fix consumers' target groups for their products according to different consumers' target groups. If marketers cannot correctly target consumption groups of their products and blindly improve system service marketing, it is 'pointless' service marketing, which results in serious waste or the total failure of marketing, business losses, and even corporate failures. However, if an enterprise selects target consumer groups accurately and gains their preferences with service planning, the enterprise will be able to achieve its marketing purposes.

Classification of consumption of food consumers' target demands

First, consider the classification of popular food consumption groups, and meet their different demands and preferences; second, consider the needs of groups with different purchasing power; third, consider the needs of groups of different ages.

Target needs of consumption for medical and health products

First, consider the demands for popular medical and health products; second, consider the needs of groups with different purchasing power;

third, consider the needs of groups of different ages. Since health care consumers have an urgent need to enjoy this type of consumption, marketers must meet their needs and spread knowledge of health at the same time.

Clothing needs of target consumption groups

First, consider the consumption needs of most people; second, consider the consumption needs of groups with different purchasing power, of different ages, and with different preferences. Consumers who enjoy consumption are the target group of all marketers in different sectors.

Consumption needs resulting from ethnic and regional lifestyles

Over a long period of time, people in different regions have formed habitual ways of living consumption. It is necessary to respect people's lifestyle and meet their consumption needs; meanwhile consider improving backward consumption ways, thereby improving their quality of living consumption.

Creating new needs for consumption

People's living consumption and material and spiritual culture are growing continuously and will never stop. Therefore, scientific research should be undertaken and products should be manufactured to meet the growing consumption needs. When the new products are produced and not recognized by consumers, they are products without competitiveness in the market. After new products are made, manufacturers and marketers locate target consumers, popularize the products, and increase consumers' awareness of the advanced products.

Meanwhile, it is necessary to train volunteers who choose a free shopping experience. Increase consumption desires and awareness of target consumers through the volunteers' remarkable consumption experiences. Get the innovative products to meet consumers' demands during the marketing process through the assurance of service and public relations. It should be known that the cost of research and the production of products needed by consumers is high, and marketing expenses are high as well. Therefore, the retail prices of products sold in the market should be much higher than the fixed cost of the factory, raw and auxiliary materials, and the variable cost. The retail price should cover research costs, production costs, costs of product knowledge and consumer awareness, the enterprise's risk-taking charges, and the entrepreneurial profits. If the price is not set rationally, the marketing process is bound to fail, as incontrovertibly proven through harsh realities.

Summary

Therefore, during the marketing process enterprises should first decide what the target market group for their products is. Too, the planning of marketing programs and implementation of the system services ensure successful marketing; otherwise even a minor error is likely to lead to partial failure.

It is shown that if manufacturers and marketers cannot constitute a system of service and carry out systematic service management, the needs of consumers cannot be met. Enterprises should first decide on target consumers of their products and make plans for marketing the large market system service. Thus, with only the awareness of meeting consumers' satisfaction and without thinking about large-scale marketing, the purposes of marketing cannot be achieved; only with awareness of service marketing and the conception of a large market can consumers' needs be met. Without scientific positioning of target consumers, marketing of a large market system service does not exist. Thus, satisfaction of target consumers is the core of marketing.

Section 4 Consumption, marketing management and marketing mode

The marketing of consumers' large target market system service is a socialized marketing process and also a process of pursuing the consumption satisfaction of target consumers. Systematic service marketing influences the organization of various aspects in society, the participation of the people, the great market systematic service structure and the increase of marketing cost. The purpose of management is to control and manage the consumption during the social marketing process, carry out comprehensive budget-control management, achieve good enterprise marketing benefits – enterprise benefits and social benefits – with relative low consumption costs.

The marketing model is based on consumers' demand. In order to achieve the purpose of marketing, marketers must first use all their power to research products for target consumer groups, purchase convenience, and preferences. The means to satisfy their demands, the marketing model of alternative products and the marketing situation should be paid more attention. The marketing model is the prerequisite for successful marketing. If the marketing model cannot meet the objective satisfaction of consumers, other marketing measures cannot function. This is because sales management and marketing planning measures are developed according to the marketing model. Unless it adapts to the needs of the marketing model, the marketing measure cannot play its role.

Marketing model elements and categories

Supply and demand elements of marketing

Table 16.1 shows the supply and demand elements of marketing.

Different combinations of various elements constitute different marketing models. Different marketing models keep on changing, especially when there is a buyers' market. Business marketers continuously change marketing models in order to track the target population and to meet their preferences and satisfaction. Enterprise marketing management and planning varies with the marketing model.

Marketing models of a traditional social channel

In the marketing mode for products with full market competition, if the quality of products is the same, manufacturers, during the marketing process, win consumer preferences through product price, quality, channel, environment, and relationships, so that products are offered at low prices and purchased at convenient locations. These might be:

- large supermarkets
- small supermarkets in residential areas

Table 16.1 The supply and demand elements of marketing

Producers' marketing	Products price consumers outlet sale service environment relationship
Consumers	Demand value producers convenience consumption satisfaction environment relationship

- fixed fairs and scattering markets
- department stores and shops
- shopping malls, commercial buildings, supermarkets, and other retail models
- units for commercial purposes such as pharmacies, supermarkets, hospitals, specialist hospitals, clinics, nursing homes, kindergartens, and so on
- other places such as cinemas, gyms, bookstores of product marketing, schools, training courses, meetings, and commercial conferences.

Products with half market competition are manufactured by a few manufacturers to meet the needs of target consumers. Such companies' competition for market consumers is conditional. Not every manufacturer is able to produce technical products or new functional and multi-functional products, and only a few manufacturers can control the production of products. Marketing composed of a few manufacturers competes for consumers' preferences and satisfaction in order to achieve their marketing purposes. For example, China's beverage market, mainly Coca-Cola, Sprite, Cola, and Nongfushangquan, compete for consumer preferences to achieve their marketing purposes. Another example is the donkey-hide gelatin product. In the market the products of Pingyin donkey-hide gelatin plant, Pingyin Dong E donkey-hide gelatin factory, and several other plants compete for consumers. Different combinations of elements are adopted to meet consumer preferences to accomplish sales.

Some products are marketed without market competition. The products are any proprietary technology products and products with the new technology at a certain stage of monopoly, and differentiation products. The products that no manufacturers produce on the market are non-competitive. The marketing model for manufacturers is to take combined elements, and determine target consumers. The target consumer should recognize the quality of products. To be successful consumers must know about the product and the product must sell for the right price. If the price is too high and consumers have low purchasing power, it is impossible to attain sales. If the price is too low, sales cannot cover marketing costs and cannot be efficiency and effective. This will inevitably lead to marketing failure.

The building of the right environment and relations including social relations and consumer relations in the marketing process is very important, and the living condition of enterprises and the condition for the marketing process.

The model of marketing of consumers' large target market system service is that the services before, during, and after sales are provided for target consumers. Convenient channels of purchasing are provided to ensure efficiency and effectiveness. This kind of marketing model is employed by many corporations, such as Sanzhu oral liquid, Heart K, Melatonin, Wahaha, Wuliangye, and Maotai.

Service-oriented marketing

The conference-marketing model combines the system elements of the pre-sale, mid-sale, and after-sale services that meet the special needs of the consumer target groups by a single product or multiple products. The special needs combine the consumption demands for physical products and spiritual culture. Service marketing achieves sales purposes. It is system services marketing that centers on the elderly population with spending power.

Direct marketing is a model in which the producers sell directly to direct consumers. The direct marketing model around the world is not producers' directly selling to direct consumers, but a hierarchical mode that is established according to the operator's desire for rapid wealth obtained from consumers' consumption and investment means.

These are some new marketing modes with television and network as the media:

- *TV direct sales.* Manufacturers or dealers set up shopping centers or stores on TV, which they promote through advertising and display. According to the characteristics of television sales, service elements are combined to form a new model of service marketing system, thus achieving marketing objectives.
- *Internet online marketing.* Manufacturers or distributors make domestic and foreign online marketing settlements with direct consumers through the network, online malls, shops, or business relationships. Online contracts and procurement have greatly promoted the development of marketing, and will play a tremendous role in promoting the development of the three kinds of consumption.

These are the four operating modes of marketing:

1. *The internalized enterprise-marketing model.* This is when the business organizes marketing companies on their own and establishes subsidiary marketing companies in the provinces, cities, and counties for their

own products. The promotion organizations are built under the level of subsidiary companies. The company's products run through their own marketing structure of system services. Each independent subsidiary is also an independent corporation. Under the leadership of the parent company, each subsidiary has the right of its own independent accounting management. Most products are entrusted to pharmacies and supermarkets for sales while the company has promotions through meetings.

2. *Manufacturers entrusting products to marketing companies.* Marketing companies adopt independent marketing modes. They negotiate with producers and decide the retail price of the agent's products and the retail price in the market and a series of conditions to ensure the implementation of marketing. Then they regulate the marketing model, and manage the implementation of planning.
3. *Conference marketing.* This is designed to meet the special needs of specific consumers' demands for spiritual and material services.
4. *Direct marketing.* This depends on consumers' ways of investing and businessmen's desire for wealth. It consists of direct and multi-level marketing. In China the multi-level marketing model is illegal. It should be recognized as legal that their own products are sold by themselves, and should be advocated.

Section 5 Marketing management mode

The marketing mode decides the marketing management mode. A marketing mode must have a suitable management mode, which serves the marketing mode. The purpose of this marketing mode is to decide what the lowest management costs to achieve the best sales are so as to make the most marketing profits. These are the most important decisions in marketing, and they should be made every season.

Section 6 Consumption and marketing culture

Marketing culture

Marketing culture is the soul of 'marketing of consumers' large target market system service' and an important part of the corporate marketing culture. The orientation of the marketing culture varies with enterprises, such as 'customer is God', and so on. The marketing culture of Sanzhu Group is that consumers are the parents of enterprises, striving to be small advisers for consumers, and centering on consumer preferences and satisfaction as the highest standard.

Enterprise culture is the whole of enterprise

Culture is broad and narrow. In the broad sense, culture is made up of material culture and spiritual culture – the whole of the relations between human consumption and the progress of natural history. In ancient China, the connotation of narrow-sense culture is culture, education, and achievements in culture and education. The broad-sense culture is the sum of the material and spiritual productive capacity, the material wealth and spiritual wealth acquired in the process of human social practices. Each society has an appropriate material culture and spiritual culture, and with the progress of the social material production, the popularity of producers' cultural and technical level, education, literature, art, and science is an important criterion of cultural development in a certain historical period. The narrow-sense culture is mental production capacity and intellectual products, including all forms of social ideologies, the natural sciences, technical sciences, and social ideology. Sometimes the term refers specifically to knowledge and the facilities related to education, science, literature, art, health, and sports, which are distinguished from world outlook, political thinking, and morality.

A culture formed by a social concept is a socio-political and economic reflection, and at the same time it affects the politics and economy to some extent. Its development is a historical succession. A new culture always evolves by relying on the results of the old culture. With the appearance and development of the nation, national culture is also affected to some extent by the physical environment. The nearer it is to primitive times, the greater the influence the physical environment has. Religious culture and various ideologies are also great influences. In a class society, culture reflects the ruling class's thought and the concept of ethics that is dominant in the spiritual culture. In *Capital*, Marx said that the class dominating the material means of production also dominates the spiritual means of production. Therefore, the minds of those without the spiritual means of production are generally dominated by the ruling class (Marx, 1867).

Advanced socialist culture is created and developed on the basis of inheriting human outstanding cultural heritage in a critical way. It is the common spiritual wealth of all members of society and plays a role in the progress of social civilization. Sanzhu Group's corporate culture is a culture grafted on three kinds of culture: the advanced culture of socialism with Chinese characteristics; fostering the strengths and circumventing the weaknesses of traditional Chinese culture – Confucianism, Legalism, and Taoism; and the study of Western culture, learning its advanced science and technology, management experience, and corporate marketing experience.

The conception of corporate planning

People's wisdom and creative ideas on the objectives of the enterprise are called 'creative intelligence'. It is the arsenal of marketing measures and creates the soul and culture of products. Besides the new desires of consumption demand, the loyalty of consumers, a corporate brand, and new values are created. For example the marketing planning of Sanzhu Group is 'Sanzhu oral liquid, convincing oral liquid'; and that of Wahaha planning is 'Wahaha, an appetizer for you'.

Selecting products

Market size and brand strategy

The overall marketing plan of enterprise products develops on the estimated market share of consumer spending and is implemented in stages. The marketing strategy scale of Sanzhu Group takes five years to occupy the national consumers' market. And the short-term goal program in the first-year, the mid-term goal plan of two years and long-term goals program of three to five years are developed. In the actual market development, it just takes three years to accomplish the goal of the entire strategic plan.

Strategic objectives of new product development

New product development is an important means of market competition and an important business strategy for long-term sustainable development. Only by means of patented newly differentiated non-competitive and semi-competitive technology products can there be rapid development and enterprise efficiency and effectiveness, thereby achieving rapid and sustained growth of the enterprise. When focusing on new patented technology products or new products with technology differentiation, the marketing also reserves new technology and functional products of the next generation to be ready for the cyclical decline of the product; in the meantime, developing and updating a new generation of technology products is self-transcendence and leads to continuous development of new technology products.

Focus strategy

These are elements of the focus strategy:

1. *Centralized management of funds.* Highly centralized funds are managed by the financial center of the headquarters by means of a financial management company or revenue and expenditure management system. It is similar to bank management that transfers the funds to triple flow capital value.
2. *Centralized and unified corporate culture.* A unified group culture and philosophy, unified code of conduct, and unified corporate internal image make staff recognize the value of the enterprise and create strong solidarity and cohesion; externally the enterprise will be accepted by the public and a good social image will be established.
3. *Low-cost.* The reduction of the production consumption and enhancement of product quality yield are fundamental to corporate profits and competitiveness to meet the 'marketing of consumers' large target market system service'. The competitive process of products, especially the products in the overall market competition, is a process of competition in the high quality and low cost of consumer goods. Whoever has superior quality and lower costs than average is a winner.
4. *Innovation strategy (unconventional strategy).* Production, management, research, and marketing should embrace constant reforms and innovations to ensure long-term vigor and vitality of business. In particular, there should be sophisticated scientific research on consumer demand using high technology, which is the reserve force of the sustainable development of enterprises.

The strategy matrix of product service

The strategy matrix of product service is a marketing model of systems market services. It has the following strategic features:

1. *Building specifications.* To build a series of specifications on products before and after sale, and to refine the service structure and control management.
2. *The reform of management organization.* This is brought about when service causes all business activities of enterprises to be truly customer-centric. It is necessary for organizers of modern enterprises to make a big change. And independent organizations that are parallel with production and marketing and provide services for customers should be established within the enterprise. They will have a commitment to service throughout product sales. At the same time the content of services needs to be beyond the previous narrow service areas. The prevalence of a telephone service in the West and China is a typical example. The telephone hotline service is a major business of the service sector. Any customer who calls the dedicated hotline of the service department of an enterprise can obtain services related to the product. Such hotlines are free: costs are paid by the enterprises.
3. *The concept of service.* The concept of service perpetrates all the economic activities of enterprises. Since service has been regarded as a new factor of the marketing mix, the concept of customer service has run through the whole service process from product design to the after-sale service and has been employed in the strategy of the product life cycle. In all stages of the product life cycle, sales and service activities are combined. At different stages, the corresponding service is provided to extend the product life cycle, thus improving marketing effectiveness.
4. *Relationship service marketing.* Salesmen in the marketing process establish trust with consumers. Consumer information is recorded in the service card files of the salesmen, who maintain friendships with consumers by telephone. The consumption amount is recorded in the performance evaluation of the salesmen. When consumers' consumption reaches a certain volume of sales, the salesperson calls the consumer to receive a prize, and meanwhile makes a new round of promotions for repeated purchase. When there is a new marketing campaign, the salesperson informs the consumer to participate in the activities and that this activity offers preferential goods and a bonus for them and their friends. In this way, a chain promotion is formed.
5. *Hospitality service sales.* During service marketing, the products should be sold with hospitality. The warm service to consumer B from salesperson A will motivate the consumer's feelings. When consumer B purchases the same products, that person will specifically look for

salesperson A to buy from, so the sales volume of salesperson A will expand. Especially in conference marketing, the sales staff provide enthusiastic services for lonely elderly people, calling them grandpa or grandma when they make a home delivery. They also help the seniors in cooking and washing dishes, call them regularly, and tell them to take medicine on time. The seniors are moved and do not know how to respond. So they buy the salesperson's product as a reward to the salesperson. Because of the salesperson's enthusiasm toward consumers with special needs, the consumption is not just material; more importantly, it is the satisfaction of spiritual and cultural consumption. It is well known that there are no worthless services. The passionate spirit can meet the service whose value is embedded in the products. It is similar to the idea that the value of a cup of coffee in cafés and at airports is totally different from its value at home. It is the value of the serving place and service that adds to the retail value of coffee.

Co-marketing strategy cooperative marketing type

Three types of cooperation are required in a co-marketing strategy:

1. *Horizontal cooperation.* This is the parallel cooperation in specific marketing activities of enterprises. For instance, the two companies work together on developing a new product, or they cooperate on product advertising and sales promotion, or to provide the network of distribution channel for each other's products. Horizontal cooperation is most likely in the same industry, which is a foundation for the international division of labor.
2. *Vertical cooperation.* This is the cooperation in different marketing activities of enterprises. Enterprises undertake a marketing activity to form the advantage of cooperation. For example, Novo Company in Denmark is a small company producing insulin and enzymes with certain technology and production advantages, but its ability for sales is poor. So Novo cooperates with the US partner Bristol-Myers Squibb, which has marketing activities in North America, so Novo has overcome its own weaknesses by acquiring the strong points of Bristol-Myers Squibb Company, which has achieved very good results.
3. *Cross-cooperation.* This cooperation exists mainly between the enterprises in the same industry and companies in different industries. With the continual application of a corporate diversification strategy, this cross-enterprise cooperation has been increasingly accepted by

enterprises. It is also known as all-round cooperation, whose great importance is increasingly attached to international marketing. Consumer target groups demand large market system services; marketing and the consumption of productive forces are developing rapidly; the internal environment and external environment of enterprises are changing; and marketing models and measures develop with the new needs.

Objective gathering strategy

At a certain time, space, and location, enterprises gather humans, finance, and materials to develop different products with established targets. According to the different demands of consumers, corresponding consumption strategies and ways are adopted so as to make a breakthrough at the key point and achieve marketing success. For example, in the early days, the integrated force of Sanzhu Company was not strong. However, the gathering of internal and external relations and power in the scientific research ensured the scientific research project proceeded quickly (integrated cooperative research) and the ultimate success of the scientific experiment. Then in the marketing process, the gathering of human, financial, and material resources was successful in a market trial.

Tactics and strategy

Tactics and strategy determine the satisfaction of strategic objectives. Once the strategic objective is decided, the most important factors in the satisfaction of consumers' demand are the system services details, tactical skills and strategic approach, and marketing. An error in detail often leads to overall failure.

Organization guarantee and management

After making decisions about product selection and choosing marketing models, strategies, tactics, and policy, the top priority for marketing firms is the organization guarantee. The key for marketing success is the selection of the leaders and groups that fit with the purposes of the above-mentioned tasks. The marketing team is recruited and established to ensure the realization of objectives and tasks. Selecting, educating, and employing are the tasks of the personnel center (or personnel department) and the first task of the main leaders:

1. The criteria for recruitment should be promulgated.
2. Training should be organized. This includes simulation training and practical training. the Sanzhu Company's cadre school (17 volumes of training materials with several million words), teaching, and other activities.
3. Talent is evaluated and selected through performance; anyone unsuitable is not appointed.
4. The policies on wages and incentives should be jointly studied and formulated with the financial department so as to motivate the enthusiasm of all the staff. The 'three motives' (material motive force, spiritual motive force, and informational motive force) is the theoretical basis for policy development.
5. The assessment criteria of personnel in the marketing system should be managed to build an excellent team.

Six best practices

The marketing process should adhere to the 'six bests': best quality, best technical content, best service, best network, best environment, and best management.

Best quality should be sought throughout the product competition. High-quality products and satisfying consumer needs to the greatest extent are the basis of competition and the key to market competition. Best technical content means only products with high technology content and great market potential can be competitive. Best service should be adhered to in the process of market development. Foreign and domestic business development proves that when manufacturers give priority to consumers' needs and provide effective services, consumers will purchase their products. Good networks bring scale efficiency. Either in the market consolidation of existing products, or market development of new products, we must focus on network size and increase network efficiency and effectiveness.

Additionally, the marketing process has to pay attention to the best environment. There will be nothing without a good environment; that is the survival condition of enterprises. Therefore, we should focus internally on the education of corporate philosophy, strengthen cohesion and solidarity, and enhance collaboration and unity between internal staff; externally, we should foster a good corporate image, product image, and brand image to win support thereby creating good internal and external environments for the overall development of enterprises. In the course of the entire business operation, the best management needs to be achieved. A flexible and efficient management system and accurate management rules are the key to the effective operation of the enterprise.

These 'bests' are not parallel, but the considerations for the overall function of the enterprise from different points of view. Therefore, we must always adhere to the 'six bests' and deal with them with a strategic vision.

Section 7 Handle nine major relations in the marketing process

The relationship between marketing and enterprises

External relations and market sales are two factors that complement each other in marketing. First, pay special attention to external conditions and ensure a fine external environment so as to steadily move forward. Second, the relationship between marketing and the internal environment improves the internal environment by ensuring unity within the team, by ensuring good planning work, and by strengthening training and improving staff quality.

The relationship between Sanzhu Oral Liquid and other new products

Sanzhu Oral Liquid is Sanzhu Group's leading product and the basis for further development of the group. However, more high-tech products must be brought into the market, so the group can develop steadily. Therefore we must show concern for the development of new products in the market.

The relationship between regional headquarters and subsidiaries, subsidiaries, branch offices and business divisions

When several business divisions or subsidiaries (branch offices) are established simultaneously in a city they should have a brotherly relationship and internal relationship. An integrated work unit should be established in the region, which will be responsible for coordinating their relationship. Regional managers and subsidiary managers should share resources and support new products.

The relationship between executive managers and operation directors

Executive officers, operation managers, and propagandists are closely related, none of them should be a bureaucrat. If the executive officer does not perform well, the person can be removed from the position; if the operation manager performs well, then the person should be promoted.

The relationship between marketing personnel and non-marketing personnel

Marketing personnel are involved in direct marketing and non-marketing personnel are involved in indirect marketing. They are both marketing personnel and are indispensable. Job responsibility should be detailed from subsidiaries to working offices, workstations, and propagandists. Bonuses should be linked with sales. Adhere to the principles of preciseness, prudence, carefulness, confidentiality, and firmness.

The bonus distribution relationship between operation directors and propagandists in subsidies and working offices

Incentive policies should be linked with operation directors and propagandists. Bonuses should be divided into several parts, of which a part is distributed to operation directors and a part is reserved for overall balance and annual bonuses. Fill gaps with the remaining funds, adjust independently and stabilize the entire sales force.

The relationship betwen subsidiary management, working offices, and township workstations management

Subsidiary management, working offices, and township workstation management are closely related to each other.

The relationship between urban marketing and rural marketing

On the one hand, the rural market remains the main battlefield of overall marketing in the future; on the other hand, urban work is still a priority. Be two-pronged: continue to develop and consolidate the rural market, and also capture the urban market.

The relationship between overall publicity and separate publicity

In cities the main publicity is handing out leaflets or newspapers. In rural areas the main publicity is also leaflets and newspapers, and publicity by word of mouth is used as well.

Pharmacies, wholesale departments, and hospitals remain the main marketing channels. Other channels can be set up, but they should be under strict control.

Section 8 Three basic points of marketing and dynamic leadership management

Planning, standardization, detailing, systematic control, and management

This has the following elements:

1. *Planning*. Planning can be divided into two aspects: macro regulation and control of the country, and corporate planning. The macro control of the country is not supplemented by administrative orders but by economic and legal means. Corporate planning is more rigorous. It is based on the needs of consumers, and centers on users.
2. *Standardization*. Standardization provides clear criteria and operational procedures for work quality and product quality. There should be standardized systems, supervision and monitoring procedures, standards, and refinement. For example, the standard parts of a machine can be applied to all the machines of the same type, which makes those standardized parts viable. If a part can only be used in one machine, it is of limited usage. Therefore, standard parts should be adopted.

3. *Detailing.* This is the working standard of rigor and precision. Our work should be detailed. If there are no detailed standards, there will be no good products, results, or achievements. Only if we adhere to the principle of providing detail can we identify and solve problems promptly, accurately, and efficiently.
4. *Systematic control and management.* Planning, standardization, and detailing are parts of a whole and we should study how to put them together. Systematic control and management involves combination in management. Only through systematic control and management can we bring various components together and ensure that each component plays its role.

Dynamic competitive marketing management

Competition exists all the time and crises occur repeatedly. This is the inexorable law governing competition in the market economy. This law functions around consumers' needs, just as price fluctuates around the value of a product. We have to study the law of consumption all the time, anywhere, and constantly develop new products and increase our competitiveness. We must continue to study consumers' psychology and the consumption market so as to meet the different needs of various levels of consumers. Stick to the idea of 'prominence–balance, balance–prominence'. The higher level should set a good example for the lower level so that the lower level can learn from the higher level.

Diagnostic marketing

In diagnostic marketing, marketing strategies and tactics should be studied first. If you set the wrong direction, one false step will make a great difference. Each company must diagnose its own situation and then make the right judgments. If the situation is clearly interpreted and the main and secondary contradictions are understood accurately, correct decisions can be made.

Diagnosing decisions is a process in which the subject is consistent with the object. To do this well we must pay attention to tactics in the marketing process. After correct decisions are made, tactics must be studied in the implementation process. It is important to combine overall planning and individual implementation. If leaders do not know how to diagnose decisions and combine and coordinate strategic decisions and tactics rationally, they will become blind.

We should first be not afraid of security issues. Be ambitious, and use tactics and wisdom to gain the greatest victory. Have fine relations with all departments in the region where the company is located. Secrecy ensures security. Some of our actions, especially some of the actions of managers and senior managers in headquarters, must be kept strictly confidential. To improve security, internal unity also matters. Treat employees as our relatives. In this way, we can unite as one, and small problems will not turn into greater ones.

Section 9 Apply operation research to improve marketing management

These are some ways to improve marketing management through research:

1. *Strengthen study to understand systematic operational research.* It is necessary to apply a holistic way of thinking and systematic and operational research. We can learn from practice and application; then we can we control the overall situation.
2. *Learn from the experienced by means of grafting.* When learning from experienced people, we should combine specific conditions to uphold the unity of the subject and object by grafting.
3. *Be good at accepting new things and methods.* Tabularization is a part of layout, which everyone should learn to use. Using this method, management will rise to a new level.
4. *Combine 'ruthless management' with 'enthusiastic management'.* This is a necessary requirement for modern enterprise management and a demand of human instinct, and also an integral part of Sanzhu's corporate culture. A leader should plan first and arrange the work with an iron hand. All the things above belong to the range of a plan. 'An iron hand' should be used in the implementation. Implementation and orderliness must be intensified and strengthened.
5. *Study with an open-minded attitude.* We should have a correct attitude to study advanced experiences and be open-minded. The secret of success is to persist in intentional learning.

Section 10 Strategies, tactics, guidelines and principles of marketing

These are marketing strategies:

1. *Market size brand strategy*. The enterprise makes an overall plan for consumers' share in the market, and then plans for regional market development, which will be completed in phases.
2. *New product development strategy*. This is an important strategy for the enterprise's long-term sustainability. Only proprietary technology products and new variant products can develop rapidly and create enterprise efficiency.
3. *Focus strategy*:

    - centralized financial management
    - centralized corporate culture
    - low-cost; this is fundamental in creating corporate profits and improving competitiveness
    - innovation (create something new and original); this is the reserve force for the sustainable development of enterprises.

4. *Product and service strategy*:

    - establish orderly specifications for pre-sales, sales, and after-sales processes, and refine service structure, control and management
    - establish independent organizations for customer service parallel to production and marketing and maintain the service function during the whole marketing process
    - adopt the concept of service is adopted in all the economic activities of the enterprises
    - relations and service marketing by salepeople to build relations of mutual trust with consumers, which can promote chain marketing
    - make sales with warm-hearted service
    - co-market through horizontal cooperation – the parallel cooperation of enterprises in a particular marketing activity; vertical cooperation of enterprises in different marketing activities; and cross cooperation among enterprises of the same and different industries.

5 *Objective concentration strategy*. In a certain period of time, space, and location, enterprises make use of human, financial, and material power

to achieve their objectives. They develop different products, adopt suitable strategies and methods on the basis of consumers' needs, and spare no effort to ensure breakthroughs.

These are marketing tactics:

1. *Turn from cities to rural areas to establish bases in rural areas.* Get into rural areas by using the tactics of 'mopping up'. We can either seize rural areas in mobile warfare before establishing a base, or establish a base before moving forward. These are cross promoted because different situations in different areas need different methods.
2. *Concentrate superior forces to fight a war of annihilation.* Only by concentrating manpower, material, and financial resources and continuing to emphasize them to the end can we achieve the expected effect. The leader's power cannot be used equally. The leader must concentrate on the object of fighting in a certain period of time and should work independently while others coordinate.
3. *Select a point to break through.* In marketing work, we should select a successful point to break through for each task and to find a model. If we go about several tasks at a time, we can do nothing. We should select a point to break through and find a model so that the staffs are hopeful and encouraged.
4. *Manage by division and division in movement.* In major cities, you will have poor results if you don't divide to manage. That is something we have not fully digested in marketing, so the work of major cities is still backward. Therefore, we must manage staff by letting them go down to specific functional areas through more detailed divisions of labor, and by ensuring the implementation of the strategies and tactics at each managerial level.
5. *Establish bases in neighboring counties.* We must establish a solid base for 'the war of annihilation'. Only the establishment of bases can ensure we can fight a war of position, and only the war of position can improve basic management. Mobile warfare should be combined with guerrilla warfare.
6. *Grade separation for comprehensive operation.* Integral propaganda on TV widens the range but we may also make some people focus on the hospital to make an assault on the fortified position. In this way, many kinds of tactics integrate and coordinate with each other, and the mutual infiltration function is very good.

7. *Integrate various tactics.* The assault on a fortified position, guerrilla warfare, mopping up, and a war of position should form a complete and comprehensive system and coordinate with each other in mobile warfare. Unlike single tactics, these integrated tactics require certain command capabilities from the leader.
8. *Use news and entertainment for propaganda.* News has strong reliability and authority. Therefore, we should make full use of news to enhance soft propaganda. People love to see and hear entertainment, which allows us to use this method to publicize the enterprise and products.
9. *Intersect the inside and the outside.* This is the tactics of intersecting the actions of blocking and attacking. Our outward attack of marketing is continuing with overwhelming momentum. Meanwhile, the supervision and examination department and the ministry of law should ensure internal honesty. In public relations, we should strengthen external relations of each level and each aspect.
10. *Intensify the effect and advance gradually.* These tactics should be combined through TV, newspapers, free consultations, terminals, and other forms.

There is one guideline of marketing: depending on high technology, create new needs of consumption, promote the theory, technology, function, and consumption ideas of a product, create a new consumption environment, and meet consumers' demands with excellent service.

These are some principles of launching a market:

1. Depend mainly on general propaganda and take specific propaganda as subsidiaries. General propaganda aims at the whole targeted market, emphasizing coverage and accuracy. Specific propaganda focuses on targeted consumers.
2. Depend mainly on the concept, mechanism, and efficacy propaganda and take image propaganda as a subsidiary. Image propaganda is based on functional propaganda. Only in this way can propaganda of healthcare products have the desired results.
3. Depend mainly on science and life columns in newspapers or on television and take advertising columns as subsidiaries.
4. Depend mainly on case surveys and take the cultivation of practitioners as subsidiaries. At the beginning of the market launch, register as many consumers as possible and then visit them to learn their consumption situation and help them solve problems in consumption.

5. Combine broadcasting propaganda and expert lectures. Let experts speak to enhance credibility.
6. Combine the publicity of popular science and volunteer medical consultation, disease prevention, and treatment.
7. Train and improve. Sanzhu Group not only improves the pharmacies, but also trains a team of high-quality promoters.
8. Publicize by making use of all opportunities. Participate in the government's public welfare activities and sponsored events to carry out publicity.
9. Publicity should be credible, interesting, and accurate. Fine quality and genuine efficacy of products are prerequisites.
10. Depend mainly on treatment propaganda and take prevention and healthcare propaganda as subsidiaries.

17

Family consumption and wealth management

The family is the most basic and the smallest unit in the social structure with the division of single-parent families and large extended families. In China, the history and social system that can be studied are changeable in the history of five thousand years. However, it never changes that the general population mainly participates in social activities with the family as a unit, and families are formed by blood ties and the kinship system. A village is made up of a number of families; a town is formed by a number of villages; a county by a number of towns; a region or city or province by a number of counties (districts); and a country is the superstructure and systematic social structure of a number of provinces.

In the stage of underdeveloped society with commodity production and exchange of capital, the form of the production consumption and living consumption was mainly enough for households. In the slave society and feudal society, the economic production means was mainly the family workshop. Until the birth of capitalist society, family enterprises still existed, while the incomes of social living consumption funds were also reflected in personal and family income. The expenditure of human living consumption was mainly in the family (all members) living consumption. Consumption was divided into two parts: household living consumption, the major part, and living consumption of social or collective groups and organizations whose expenses are paid by the social group.

Living consumption comprises material consumption and spiritual cultural consumption. The household is the minimum and the most basic cell of the social structure as well as an economic cell of micro living consumption.

We are going to study the formation, use, and financing management of consumption funds, the structure of living consumption, and the pattern of living consumption from the perspective of the household, the economic cell of micro-living consumption. The relationship between living consumption fund revenue created by production consumption in the primary, secondary, and tertiary industry, and the living consumption fund revenue created by investment in the production consumption of the social infrastructure is the relationship of internal connection among the three important consumptions. It is a law that the three consumptions affect the market, finance, and economy created by social development, which has both positive and negative aspects, namely the natural (free) law of the market economy with state intervention. It is the natural law that state intervention acts on the market economy.

Consumption and management are studied from the perspective of micro-economic cells, and personal and family living consumption. It is not only an extremely complex and dynamic process but also very specific. It is the process in which micro movements affect the overall situation, which is more conducive to understanding how the economy develops in an orderly and systematic way and is conducive to controlling the development and management of macro human consumption.

Section 1 Family living consumption fund income and wealth management

Household income and living consumption include personal income consumption and living consumption of all family members. Here the individual income and consumption will not be listed for convenience. All the personal consumption before marriage is included in the household living consumption.

The household living consumption capacity is determined by family income, and the way of living consumption depends on people's consumption consciousness, which decides consumption behaviors. I have discussed 'consumption practices and consumption consciousness'. Since household living consumption power is decided by household income, we first study the source of household income in various historical stages and then study it as a type of living consumption.

Underdeveloped society with commodity production and exchange of capital

Slave and feudal societies are the stages of an underdeveloped society with commodity production and exchange of capital. The characteristics are as follows. First is barter exchange. Second is the exchange for goods with a certain substance that has an equal value of currency (cattle, copper, iron, gold, silver). Barter exchange and the exchange of gold or silver, including notes and drafts on behalf of gold and silver, and so on, are exchanges of surplus products based on self-sufficiency. At this time, there were family workshops with commodity production, which had entered the stage of commodity production and exchange of capital, which is mainly represented after the mid-term feudal society. But the overall economic form of society was still the self-sufficient form, so it is called underdeveloped society with commodity production and exchange of capital.

Until the start of capitalist society, the form of economic base and economic activities was mainly commodity production and exchange with capital currency. In a capitalist society, the living consumption, social consumption, and research and production consumption takes the form of capital money – currency rules the whole process of economic activities. There remain minor self-sufficient economic sectors in remote and rural areas. And even for self-sufficient families, it is impossible to avoid the fact that surplus products enter the goods exchange in the form of currency. Here we should note that in a capitalist society currency has ruled the entire process of economic activities on behalf of commodities. The currency can be exchanged for any goods. The amount of money represents the value of certain goods, but it has limitations. For example, money can buy food and meat for eating, but it cannot be eaten as food. Hungry people need to eat. Even if they have a lot of money, they could starve to death without buying food. Comparing money with edible food such as grain and meat, food is the most valuable asset.

During the long historical stages of the slave society and feudal society, because productivity was very backward, living consumption and food consumption were the primary needs for survival. Therefore, a family must first guarantee their own consumption with the consumption materials they themselves created. The economic form is the major social economic form. The sources of household consumption are discussed below:

1. All family members who can work labor to create consumption wealth as the source of living consumption. After spending what is necessary on food other money enters the market for barter exchange for other products and life supplies to meet the needs of household living consumption and reproduction.
2. The business in this period is the family workshop. The source of consumption funds is from the products they themselves produced. The

products were exchanged with other means of production and reproduced in the market. Meanwhile, they exchanged their own goods with family agricultural commodities to trade for their own living consumption goods to meet their consumption needs. Their efficient management of income and expenses made the workshop business expand. In this long history of human society, people at that time created the national spiritual culture that is now called the primitive spiritual culture, which met the consumption needs of material and spiritual cultures of various nations and countries.

3. In the slave and feudal societies, there was no social security. Although in very bad years the country sometimes provided relief food and other materials (only a very few countries granted relief funds), it could not solve the problem.
4. In slave and feudal societies slave holders and landlords relied on the living consumption fund, land, tools, pasture, and fishing boats that they occupied to exploit peasants, herders, and fishermen of their revenue for consumption. The state and various officials also acquired consumption fund revenue from many laborers, and the state also collected commercial duties from landlords, pasture owners, and fishing masters. The revenue from opening industrial plants and commercial enterprises also became their consumption revenue fund and social consumption revenue fund, so they could afford the living consumption of enjoying the physical materials and spiritual cultures.

In this long historical period, because of social systems, disease, and weather, and for other reasons, many slaves and farmers lost their living resources, such as land and labor tools. They were forced to work for landlords, be slaves to the nobility, or rent lands from landlords to till. Such servants or slaves would unconditionally surrender production to the landlord, and have to pay a poll tax. There was very little income, so these people led a life of starvation or semi-starvation. Traders got consumption funds from profits earned from business trading, but they also had to pay the state poll tax. Therefore, there were few profits left for them to feed family members, so struggled on the death line.

Thus, in slave and feudal societies, every cent of ordinary laborers was carefully calculated and budgeted by them. Family members who would work created income to feed the younger generation and the older generation who could not work, forming the law of revenue and expenditure from generation to generation. Thus people raise children to look after them in later life.

The source of household funds and wealth management under a social system with relatively developed commodity production and exchange of capital

These are the sources of household funds and wealth management:

1. *Families with general salary income.* Consumption funds of these families relied mainly on wages (including bonuses and benefits), supplemented by other incomes, such as revenue from trading stocks, bonds, funds, lottery, amateur part-time work income, dividend income, investment income real estate, retirement pension, and medical insurance payments and other investment incomes. This situation is prevalent in families with general wages.
2. *Families with fat salary.* The main source of such household consumption funds is from high wages. Such a situation is more common among national civil servants and business managers.
3. *Families with small-scale business.* A part of the profits from investment in a business is used for family living consumption; the other part is applied to the families with further expansion of investment. This situation is prevalent in the small-scale family business.
4. *Families with return on investment and salary revenue.* These families have large-scale enterprises. In addition to business profits, they pay wages to employees.
5. *Some families in rural areas.* In rural areas, some agricultural products are not fully commercialized, and there are still a small number of families that produce for their own consumption with the remaining products entering into the market. In economically backward areas, income and expenditure is still mainly self-sufficient. Remaining products entering into the market for commodity exchange comprise a small percentage. This situation is more common in rural households. They are not only consumers of products they themselves produce, but also sellers.

The above five kinds of families with different sources of household consumption funds and with different ways of living consumption also have different means to manage consumption funds.

The first kind of family maintains household living consumption by relying on wages. The revenue management of this kind of household is divided into two categories; the first involves higher income families. Some families divide their incomes into several parts for home financial management. They first pay for social security or purchase a personal insurance policy, and then they maintain the daily living consumption. They also keep certain reserves for schooling their children, set aside some money to pay for their parents' needs in case of severe illness, and some money to supplement their own living consumption and healthcare needs when they get old. Some families choose to keep ,money in their saving accounts to earn bank interest payments; some families choose to invest in small business, real estate, stocks, funds, lotteries, and so on, in order to obtain larger gains. The other situation involves lower income families. They can only arrange for necessary living consumption. In addition to labor insurance, individuals are incapable of taking the extra money to make other financial arrangements. After the necessary living consumption is arranged, in case of special financial difficulty, they have to ask relatives and friends, national subsidies, or social assistance for help.

Families with large salaries usually draw part of their money for financing, such as stock investment (or investment by equity participation) or investment in funds, or deposits, and investment in real estate. They acquire more living consumption funds in various ways. While increasing their living consumption level and living standard, they also subsidize their aged parents.

The third and fourth kinds of families mainly acquire income by opening and running enterprises, and have sufficient living consumption funds and high levels of living consumption. In addition to bonuses, they usually have salary and capital investment income, such as profit and interest payments from various funds, stocks, deposits in saving accounts, and so on. Their income is used for enjoying the living consumption and reproduction consumption to expand financial investments and to enhance enterprise operation.

As the system of rural retirement pension has not been fully established, the source of the fifth kind of household living consumption funds will be guaranteed by their own financing. Part of the consumption fund relies on state subsidies, such as the yearly poverty alleviation funds in China to help poor farmers, the universal nine-year free compulsory education, the medical subsidy and security from the state for each farmer, subsidies to poor households and students, relief funds, freedom from agricultural tax and subsidies on grains, and so on, which are sources of living consumption funds. Some families have good benefits from agricultural and sideline products (such as pigs, chickens, and agricultural product processing). They have sufficient living consumption funds and experience in the financial management of consumption funds, so can generate income to increase their consumption funds.

Tables 16.1 to 16.3 show hypothetical charts of sources of household consumption funds and financial management.

Table 17.1 Hypothetical financial management of household consumption funds (Yuan)

Household	Consumption fund income	Expenditure of living consumption	Saved funds	Earnings of financing management				Total added value of funds
				Deposits	Investment funds	Business investments	Others	
A	120,000	72,000	48,000	1,440				49,440
B	72,000	48,000	24,000	300	5,000			29,300
C	72,000	48,000	24,000		10,000			34,000
D	48,000	36,000	12,000		3,000	1,000		16,000
E	72,000	60,000	12,000	300				10,300
F	120,000	120,000	0					0

Table 17.2 Hypothetical fiscal management of household funds (Yuan)

Household	Income	Expenditure	Total surplus in five years	Total added incomes in five years				Total
				Deposits	Investment funds	Business investments	Others	
A	120,000	72,000	240,000	7,200				247,200
B	72,000	48,000	120,000	1,500	25,000			146,500
C	72,000	48,000	120,000		50,000			170,000
D	48,000	36,000	60,000		15,000	5,000		80,000
E	72,000	60,000	60,000	1,500				61,500
F	120,000	100,000	80,000				10,000	90,000

Table 17.3 Hypothetical use of household living consumption funds in financing management five years later (Yuan)

Family	Consumption fund income	Expenditure of consumption funds	Total consumption funds	Using of consumption funds				Surplus
				Facilities and transport	Purchase of houses	Tourism	Pension reserves	
A	120,000	72,000	247,200	40,000	200,000			7,200
B	72,000	48,000	146,500		140,000			6,500
D	48,000	36,000	80,000				10,000	70,000
C	72,000	48,000	170,000	100,000		10,000	50,000	10,000
E	72,000	60,000	61,500	30,000		10,000		21,500
F	120,000	100,000	90,000	30,000		10,000	20,000	30,000

Analysis of household living consumption after five years

Now we analyse the household living consumption funds, income, and financing management of the six assumed families after five years.

A family with a higher living consumption income has more reasonable arrangements for living consumption. After subtracting 72,000 Yuan for living consumption from the annual income of 120,000 Yuan, 48,000 Yuan remains. The remaining is deposited in the bank with the interests of 7,200 Yuan earned after five years. The total consumption fund is 247,200 Yuan in five years. After five years, its surplus is 7,200 Yuan with the housing consumption of 200,000 Yuan, and domestic appliances of 40,000 Yuan. It is a prudent saving type of family good at careful planning and arranging expenditure based on income according to regular standards (never get involved in risky investment).

Family B with an annual income 72,000 Yuan, and living consumption expenditure of 48,000 Yuan per year has a balance of 24,000 Yuan per year, and is also good at arranging income and households expenditure. It is more adventurous family than Family A, but it leaves adequate room for security while making adventures. It deposits 10,000 Yuan per year for interest from the bank and takes 14,000 Yuan for risk investment with investment earnings of 25,000 Yuan. The total income of 146,500 Yuan with 140,000 Yuan used for housing investment consumption leaves a balance of 6,500 Yuan.

C family spends money but is good at investment. With the same annual income as family B, it has living consumption of 48,000 Yuan with a yearly balance of 24,000 Yuan that is involved in all-risk investments. It is lucky enough to get a better income of 50,000 Yuan. The cumulative revenue in five years is 170,000 Yuan. Five years later, it has a balance of 10,000Yuan with 100,000 Yuan paid for vehicles, 10,000 Yuan for tourism, and 50,000 Yuan for pension reserves. The family is careful to spend risk income with 50,000 Yuan remaining for the old age, which is very sensible.

Family D is the family with the least annual income and is also the most economical and conservative household.

Family E is the family with sound consumption. Though it has the same family income as families B and C, the income of the consumption funds varies greatly owing to the family's inability to manage their finances.

Family F has as much income as family A is a purely enjoying consumption household. There is no balance, with all the income of 120,000 Yuan in the first year paid out. From the second to the fifth year, its total is 90,000 Yuan with cumulative capital 80,000 Yuan and financing income of 10,000 Yuan. The family's consumption of facilities and transport is 30,000 Yuan, that of tourism is 10,000 Yuan, and that of pension investment is only 20,000 Yuan, which proves that the family has poor financing capacity.

These are six kinds of hypotheses representing possible families. From the household financing and consumption situations of these families, it can be seen that some families are good at spending their money wisely; others are not good at financial management and they arrange living consumption by relying on accumulated funds. Some are relatively good at financial management and arrangements of living consumption, and some enjoy consumption. Though they have high incomes, their consumption is also very high. According to the law of life cycle consumption and creation of consumption, it is necessary to make reasonable arrangements for family financial management and spending. In other words, in the cycle of creating consumption wealth, individuals need to accumulate certain pension reserves. When there are inadequate national pension funds, a family's reserves can make up for the inadequacy so as to ensure its consumption needs in later years are met.

Section 2 Family living consumption fund source and its relation with production consumption

After meeting the living consumption of material and spiritual culture for human survival, people begin to pursue enjoying living consumption, which is endless. This is also a process of continuous enhancement, which is accompanied by social progress. However, where are the living consumption funds and enjoyment consumption funds from to meet the needs? Since humans participate in social production with the family as a unit, the consumption needs of the material and spiritual culture are created; meanwhile, the desires of new consumption needs are also created, which also has an effect on consumption. The production consumption process that creates social consumption of material and spiritual culture must also create consumption funds for these products. The revenue and expenditure of consumption funds is determined by the social system and the law of social wealth distribution policy, and is also influenced by elements including production conditions, production capacity, and personal labor value, etc. Hence unfair and inequitable, and even very unfair and inequitable, distribution of consumption fund revenue appears.

During the same period and time, some people are struggling in the death line while some are leading an extremely enjoyable and luxurious life; some people are living in the oppressed and the ruled environment without freedom, whereas some are oppressing and ruling others. Here I mainly study the source and management of household living consumption funds rather than studying and resolving social contradictions. I have discussed the contradiction between living consumption and social class and the method of resolving contradiction elsewhere.

Section 3 Total production consumption creates consumption fund and consumption

Since the overall production consumption and social consumption are dynamic, it is hard to analyze them. Since the hypothetical model is static, it is easier to look into the dynamic internal law.

In the hypothetical model, C is the advanced capital; V is the labor wage; M is the profit tax; and D is total production. Subsidies of financial consumption funds are from profits. In the supply and demand market, it is assumed that the manufacturing investment in farming, forestry, animal husbandry, fishing, light industry, finance, commerce, and transportation is considered to be the total of production and social consumption goods. In fact, it is not all like that. This assumption is made to analyze the supply and demand in the market and study the inherent law of equilibrium in the market economy more clearly.

Assumption 1

Assumption 1 is the basic model. The total output value is one trillion Yuan, and the total capital of production investment in basic industry is 500 billion Yuan; that in farming, forestry, animal husbandry, fishery, and light industries is 400 billion Yuan; and that in finance, commerce, and transportation industries is 100 billion Yuan. It is supposed that labor wages (consumption funds) account for 30% of the total output value, and profits and taxes 20%. A certain amount is taken out of the profit and tax payment to subsidize the living consumption funds of poor people, to reduce investment in reproduction consumption to increase the total social consumption fund, in order to promote consumption to stimulate economic development. The market supply and demand is 500 billion / 395 billion Yuan, with a ratio of 1:1.67.

Assumption 2

The labor wage created by production increases by 45 billion Yuan, up to 345 billion Yuan, and the profits increase to 230 billion Yuan by 30 billion Yuan. 50 billion Yuan is extracted from the fiscal profits and taxes to be subsidies added to the labor wages of 345 billion Yuan, attaining consumption funds of 395 billion Yuan. The balance of market supply and demand is 500 billion / 395 billion Yuan and the ratio is 1:1.27. Here you can see the increase in investment in basic industries increased by 300 billion Yuan for the total social consumption funds (labor wage) while the financial subsidies living consumption funds of 50 billion Yuan make an increase in purchasing power of 80 billion Yuan. Since there is no increase in the total of social consumption, demand exceeds the supply.

Second, third, and fourth years

In the second year, the domestic investment is 250 billion Yuan, of which 180 billion Yuan is accumulated profits and tax over the previous year and other income funds. With the added foreign investment of 100 billion Yuan, the total investment is 350 billion Yuan. The investment in basic industries increases by 100 billion Yuan to 750 billion Yuan; the production investment in farming, forestry, animal husbandry, fishery, and light industries rises by 200 billion Yuan to 600 billion Yuan; that in the financial, commercial, and transportation sectors is up to 150 billion Yuan with an increase of 50 billion Yuan. There is an increase in labor wages (consumption funds) from 105 billion Yuan to 450 billion Yuan. With a 70 billion Yuan rise in profits and tax, profit increases to 300 billion Yuan. Thus, the market supply and demand is 750 billion / 450 billion Yuan and the ratio is 1:1.67 with a balance of market supply and demand.

In the first year, the consumption funds created by the investment in basic industries and fiscal subsidy to consumption funds raise the total purchasing power of society without an increase in total consumer goods, which leads to a shortage of supply in market. However, the investment ratio in the second year is adjusted with 180 billion Yuan in basic industries, 200 billion Yuan in the farming, forestry, animal husbandry, fishery, and light industries, and 50 billion Yuan in financial, commercial, and transportation sectors. In this way, the supply of living consumption increases with the market supply and demand toward balance.

In the third year, there is an increase in domestic investment by 240 billion Yuan and foreign investment by 100 billion Yuan, reaching 340 billion Yuan. 180 billion Yuan is invested in the basic industries, reaching 930 billion Yuan. With 500 billion Yuan invested in farming, forestry, animal husbandry, fishery, and light industry, profit is up to 650 billion Yuan; with 110 billion Yuan invested in financial, commercial and transportation sectors, it rises to 260 billion Yuan; and labor wages increase to 562 billion Yuan by 112 billion Yuan. The profits and taxes rise by 52 billion Yuan to 352 billion Yuan, and the fiscal subsidy consumption fund is worth 60 billion Yuan. Thus, the balance of supply and demand is 910 billion / 622 billion Yuan and the ratio is 1:1.81. There is a relative equilibrium of market supply and demand with mild inflation, which is good market supply and demand.

In the fourth year, there is an increase in domestic investment by 352 billion Yuan and foreign investment by 100 billion Yuan. 100 billion Yuan is invested in the basic industries, reaching 1,030 billion Yuan. With 252 billion Yuan invested in the farming, forestry, animal husbandry, fishery, and light industry, it is up to 902 billion Yuan; with 100 billion Yuan invested in financial, commercial and transportation sectors, it rises to 360 billion Yuan; and labor wages increase to 687.6 billion Yuan by 125.2 billion Yuan. The balance of supply and demand is 1,262 billion / 6,876 billion Yuan and the ratio is 1:1.81 with slight oversupply.

Summary

When there is an equilibrium of supply and demand and the supply exceeds the demand, it is required to increase infrastructure investment, boost investment in the development of basic industries, increase living consumption funds of individuals and households, and stimulate the development of living consumption; when the market is in short supply, it is decreased to reduce investment in the infrastructure and basic industries, increase investment development of consumer goods and industries in financial, commercial, and delivery services, and stimulate the development of living consumption so as to ensure market supply and demand. When demand exceeds supply, a simple tightening is unscientific. Instead, we should combine regulation of currency investment of production capital and the appropriate tightening policy, which is the correct approach of investment.

Seen from the above model, it is assumed there is no increase in the total population of the community, which is impossible but makes it easier to discern and analyze problems. The economic development is affected by social consumption. In the production consumption process, living consumption funds continue to increase with the continual increase in the purchasing power of people's living consumption and people's average living standards.

Section 4 Family living consumption is at the core of three important consumptions

The household living consumption is the core of the three important consumptions. Social and production consumption without individual and household living consumption is like a river without water, and nothing exists. The individual and household consumption needs for material and spiritual culture need increasing and such living consumption needs are moving forward without end. This requires the state to guarantee and protect them to ensure fairness and justice, which can create social consumption and individual and household living consumption to make continuous development of material and spiritual culture in both consumptions.

In the process of consuming social material and spiritual civilization, the consumption of productive forces and production relations and research and production consumption are created. In turn, research and production consumption creates individual and household living consumption in the material and spiritual culture; creates material and spiritual culture products for social consumption; and creates consumption patterns and consumption levels. It is now recognized that Engels' coefficient law measures household living consumption levels and standardized coefficient.

Household living consumption

The structure of personal and household living consumption changes with household revenue (consumption funds) and the development of social consumption productivity, and is influenced by customs and preferences. Consumption consciousness determines consumer behavior. Social consumption structure is also determined by the size of total social wealth used in social consumption and the development and change of the productivity level of the consumption society.

In the sequel of *On the Social Science Research* (1985), the renowned economist Yu Guangyuan states that a society produces a wide variety of consumer goods that are an important and basic factor in the provisions of social consumption, but this is only a prescription of social consumption. We know that under different social systems with different distributions of consumer goods among members of the community the result of distribution is the consumption of various social groups, namely what kind of goods and services people are consuming and the amount of consumption. Furthermore, social spending can be divided into the consumption of consumer goods disposed by the social public and the individual resident.

For the consumption of consumer goods dominated by the social public, consumers are still individuals. Consumer goods are first allocated to individuals with different consumption ways, which is also a specific provision of social consumption. In addition, according to consumer behaviors, social spending can also be divided into food, clothing, housing, transportation, social activities, and meetings. For consumption purposes, the analysis of the needs of survival and enjoyment or development makes social consumption have specific provisions. These various kinds of prescriptions combine the general rule of social consumption, which can be called social consumption structure. This is the consumption structure of consumer goods of a family's material and spiritual culture and those of social or public consumption. Social spending serves personal household consumption.

The law of Engels' coefficient formula

Engels' coefficient formula is the percentage of residents' food consumption and expenditure in total consumption expenditure, which decreases with the rise of revenue level. It is named after Ernst Engel who was a German executive officer and statistician in the 19th century. Engel noted that different income groups in Saxony spent a different proportion of income on goods and services, and with an increase in family income, the proportion of food expenditure became lower. This does not suggest that food had a lower status. It is not difficult to understand that with an increase in income and expenditure, though the proportion of food expenditure decreases, the currency for food consumption expenditure increases. The amount of food consumption at a lower level of economic development also increases, the quality of food consumption improves and people's nutrition levels are accordingly enhanced.

Engels' coefficient decreases with a rise in the level of revenue so within the growth of various consumptions, the growth of food consumption is relatively slow. The reason is that food consumption is consumption for survival, and when their survival needs are satisfied, people can spend surplus money on enjoying consumer goods. Motorcycles, cars, luxury cars, computers, mobile phones, luxurious housing and decoration, tourism, and home appliances are often high-end consumer products.

Engels' coefficient standard is that when expenditure on food consumption accounts for more than 60% of the country's total expenditure, the country or region is economically poor; if expenditure on food is between 60% and 50% the country or region is fairly wealthy; if it is 50–40% the country or region is relatively well off; if it is 40–30% it is well off; if it is 30–20% it is wealthy; and if it is below 20% it is especially wealthy. Engels' coefficient law is used to analyze personal household living consumption, the living consumption standards of vulnerable groups that are adjusted and alleviated by state, and the development of high-end consumer goods to meet the living consumption of wealthy individuals and households, thus promoting overall economic development.

Financial support, social security, and personal and household living consumption

The income of the group under the poverty line is increased through financial poverty alleviation and social security. It is assumed that in a region in which 40% of the total population is above the poverty line; 20% above the adequate food line; 20% better than well off; 10% wealthy and 10% especially wealthy. It is assumed that 50% of the population in this area has an adequate supply of food, with food consumption in meat and eggs accounting for 10% of food consumption expenditure. Soon there will be a shortage of food and an increase in the price of meat and eggs. Then the consumption investment in meat and eggs should be increased and the production of meat and eggs needs to be developed to ensure the market supply. Meat and egg industries need food as feed, which also affects product prices in the food industry and industries associated with the food industry. The shortage of food consumption can cause an increase in prices. If this happens, the state should regulate the investment ratio, increase investment in food production and consumption, and reduce the infrastructure investment so as to increase the supply of food consumption; meanwhile banks should raise interest rates to attract more residents to increase deposits and minimize the amount of currency in the market.

In this way, demand and supply will be balanced, and it is the same with prices. An improvement in residents' living standards drives overall economic development. However, the desire of well-off and very well-off residents to develop their personal and household living consumption cannot be driven by increasing the living consumption level of residents above the poverty guideline, and their consumption can only be driven by developing living consumption items for enjoyment – material and spiritual cultural consumption products.

Personal and household living consumption in wealthier households

Food consumption accounts for only 20–30% of the total revenue in wealthier households, and 70–80% of the total revenue is used to meet high-end products such as housing, clothing, cars, home appliances, televisions, mobile phones, computers, tools, and appliances. Spiritual cultural consumption includes enjoying concerts, theatre, dance halls, and nightclubs, high-grade hotels, tobacco, and alcohol, and tourism abroad with children.

Besides the 20–30% of people who are wealthy, enjoying consumption also includes ritual living consumption of national and social groups, and commercial living consumption.

Any product created by productivity of a consumer society, which is transformed from new technology, is considered a high-end enjoyment consumption good. The increase of the need to enjoy consumption drives the development of high technology's transformation into productivity of the consumption society. The development of the economy with high consumption, high technology research, high taxation, high accumulation, and high speed is driven; economic development in the circular spiral law is also advanced and continuous progress in social civilization and culture is propelled. As this happens the number of poor people gradually decreases or their income rises so they have adequate food and clothing, and the whole nation or region eliminates poverty and becomes prosperous.

However, this sort of development of the economy also reflects the problems and conflicts created by living consumption when there are income discrepancies. In a nation or region, those who spend their money on high-end consumer products waste social wealth, while other people have a poor level of living. Social contradiction is aggravated by such a serious unfair social phenomenon, which is also the fault of enjoyment consumption.

How to adjust and solve the contradictions? The state is responsible for controlling consumption and waste, the establishment of the social wealth distribution policy and tax laws, the redistribution of social wealth, and the improvement of living consumption funds for poor families so as to increase social security and comprehensively improve the lives of people. But there is no absolute justice. Through comprehensive analysis, the state should vigorously develop high and new technology to meet the increasing living consumption of material and spiritual culture. The fundamental purpose of human beings is to advance overall economic and social progress.

Enjoyment consumption and consumption consciousness of individual and household

When the need of consumption for survival is satisfied, people enter the time of well-off personal and household living consumption. Consumption consciousness decides what one consumes and how one consumes. While you may have the spending power, without consumption consciousness, you will not purchase. Although one has the spending power to enjoy high-level concerts, without that consumption consciousness, one is not going to enjoy the natural beauty brought by music. It is the same with the high-end nightclub. However, when you have the consumption consciousness of enjoying high-end cars, one begins to study the functions and advantages and disadvantages of various cars in order to buy one's favorite car. This is the feeling of spiritual enjoyment. When some people and families have strong consumption consciousness of clothing, they will study what kinds of clothes are the most fashionable, most beautiful or most handsome, and so on. There are those who like eating or playing and visit restaurants, hotels, nightclubs, and other entertainment every day; others are more interested in family housing and renovation, and tourism. Owing to the different preferences of consumption consciousness, individual families with the same income have different consumption structures for disposable income. The living consumption structure also has an influence on the development of production consumption structure. The different preferences of consumption consciousness decide one individual's consumption structure is behind the development of enjoying living consumption.

The interaction between personal household enjoyment consumption and others

It has been mentioned that consumption consciousness determines the enjoying consumption way and structure. The human is the smallest molecular in society, and the household is the minimum unit of society, and certain connections and interactions exist between individual and individual, individual and family, and family and family. It is assumed that in a unit with 30 employees, 20 families belong to wealthy households, in which ten households buy a house, five buy cars, and another five deposit money remaining from living consumption in the bank without buying houses or cars.

When the five families see 15 other families move into new houses, and drive their own cars to work, they begin to realize that they are happier than them. Because of that, why don't I buy a car or buy a house, since my income is no less than theirs? Thereby, consciousness to buy houses and cars is increased. Eventually, these five families buy houses and cars. Of course, when some people see others buy high-end clothing, they will buy high-end clothing too. It is the same with computer consumption.

Excessive living consumption of individuals and households

Those who spend money on household and personal consumer goods continue to economic development, and individuals and families' excessive consumption makes more contribution to the economy. The following are two excessive consumption plans for a family that has a savings of 30,000 Yuan after subtracting the normal living consumption from the annual gross income:

1. *Plan A*. With this money (30,000 Yuan) as a down payment, the family receives a loan of 70,000 Yuan and plans to pay the principal and interest within five years and pay less than 20,000 Yuan per year. In this way, the family can buy a car worth 100,000 Yuan.
2. *Plan B*. With this money (30,000 Yuan) as a down payment, the family borrows 270,000 Yuan and intends to pay the principal and interest within ten years and pay the principal and interest of 60,000 Yuan per year. In this way, the family can buy a house worth 300,000 Yuan.

From the analysis of the two plans, it can be seen that plan A is more suitable for the family, because such excessive consumption does not affect normal life, and provides enjoyment of the convenience brought by the car to the family in advance. However, plan B is not suitable for the family. Although this kind of excessive consumption allows them to buy valuable property, it requires the whole family to live frugally, severely affecting their normal family life. Excessive consumption contributes to national economic development, facilitating family life and the economic development of the whole society. However, excessive consumption is conditional. Otherwise, reckless consumption by borrowing is sure to have an impact on regular personal and family life. There may be a perspective in society that encourages excessive consumption, but an individual and family must have the consumption consciousness of making ends meet. We cannot pursue excessive consumption blindly, and we should be especially alert to excessive consumption by means of debt.

Case study

A family has three members and the joint income of husband and wife is 10,000 Yuan per month. They have the following expenditure:

1. It is used for house loans of 450,000 Yuan with the down payment of 150,000. It takes 30 years to pay off the loans. Each year 15,000 Yuan is paid on the loan with the annual interest rate 6 PCT and the sum of principal and interest per year is 42,000 Yuan. Subtracting 42,000 Yuan from the annual income of 120,000 Yuan leaves 78,000 Yuan.
2. 28,000 Yuan is left after subtracting 5,000 Yuan for the household living consumption per month. In China, this level of consumption belongs to the middle and upper levels.
3. By means of a loan, the family buys a car worth 30,000–40,000 Yuan to use for transport.

This premature consumption by the family is based on certain income and reasonable arrangements for the enjoyment of consumption. Any premature consumption of an individual and household with a fixed income and subsistence assurance can contribute greatly to economic development. Banks and securities companies should refuse to give loans for the purchase of consumption items to families without a fixed income through legal and administrative measures, so as to prevent financial and economic crisis. Any action of increasing consumption loans or relaxing financial instruments and business activities for profits should be strictly prohibited, so that financial and economic crisis can be avoided.

Personal household consumption and lifecycle consumption and financing

Personal household living consumption has a close relationship with the perimeter law of lifecycle. The amount of wealth a family creates when it is economically active determines its living level at present and in future. The pattern of a family's wealth consumption is also influenced by religion, culture, and custom. In China, for a long time, a considerable number of families were affected by the deep-rooted concept that raising a child was insurance for the senior. A couple of reproductive age is faced with a sandwich situation at the time of creating wealth. Most wealth is spent on children and the elderly, with little left specifically for pension funds or insurance.

Since the founding of China, this situation has changed. Although some countries in the world provide certain social security for infants, young people, and seniors, exclusive state social security to protect the growth consumption of infants and young people and security living consumption is not enough. Even the economically developed United States cannot foresee social security difficulties. Therefore, individual household consumption should follow the rule of the life cycle. In the period of creating consumption, we should manage finances reasonably and make them value-added. For example, by means of depositing, buying insurance, or purchasing security funds, the growth and education consumption of the younger generation is ensured, and the living consumption level of seniors who have lost the ability to work is guaranteed, thereby allowing them to be happy in life.

Personal household consumption and the consumption of weddings and funerals

Weddings

Marriage is very vital in human life and cannot be taken lightly, so a wedding becomes a large family expense. It is natural to receive good wishes from relatives and friends at such a blissful event. However, some families pursue a luxurious wedding exceeding personal household consumption power, which is unnecessary. A happy marriage does not lie in luxurious or frugal wedding, but in the true love between the couple. The celebration of marriage without affecting the normal life consumption is justifiable. If the celebration of a wedding with loans and luxurious consumption brings difficulties for the after-wedding life, this demonstrates irrational consumption behavior. A simple wedding does not mean there is no happy life, and a luxurious wedding cannot guarantee a happy family.

Funerals

Looking after parents is a national and family virtue. We should care for their material living consumption and spiritual enjoyment of parents in their lifetime, which can make them feel happy. The loss of loved parents is very painful for the living. A funeral in memory of a dead relative is the representation of personal feeling and national custom and culture. A funeral should be simple, to reflect social civilization progress. In memory of guard soldier Zhang Side, Chairman Mao Zedong said:

> No matter who dies in our troops, either a soldier or cook, as long as he has done some useful work, we have to hold the funeral and open the memorial meeting. This should become a system that should also be adopted by villagers. When a villager dies, we should open a memorial meeting to express our grief, thereby uniting the whole people.

Therefore, the entire community should respect the aged and love the young, hold simple funerals, and get rid of the customs of a luxurious burial. Moreover, it is not advocated to use luxurious burial of parents after their deaths just for show, instead of true love and respect during their lifetime.

Personal household consumption and social mutual help

Household living consumption is closely related to relatives, neighbors, and friends. There is a saying, 'To give roses to others as a gift, will leave lingering fragrance in your hand.' In other words, helping people in need will make one happy. Mutual help between people is a social morality and virtue. In case of difficulty in living consumption, social members, relatives, and friends should provide funds or material help, which is humane behavior and one source of social security funds.

Household consumption and deposit

When the living consumption of a person and their family is above the well-off level, they might spend their money in one of two ways. If there is a national social security system, they can spend money and enjoy living consumption, resulting in reduced household deposits. If there is no adequate social security or no social security, they have to spend money on individual and family living consumption, generally resulting in increasing savings. For example, in the United States, Germany, and other countries, as there is relatively good social security, people have a strong awareness of expenditure on household income and living consumption, and premature consumption. In rural China in the 20th century, with imperfect social security, the average family's income usually only allowed them to live frugally. Thus, savings and deposits increase the rate of consumption funds.

Enjoying excessive consumption encourages national socio-economic development, and frugal living consumption – savings and deposits – can also make a great contribution to national economic development. Developing countries that need capital to develop obtain this capital from the state's tax revenue, the profits of state-owned enterprises, and national savings, or else seek outside help and attract foreign capital and technology to make an investment in their country. The development of the three consumptions keeps meeting the increasing consumption demand for material and spiritual culture.

In summary, we have an analysis of the sources of individual household income (consumption fund) from different social systems. It can be seen that the consumption fund of a family is greatly influenced by the country's policy of wealth distribution. Household living consumption is analyzed comprehensively from nine aspects of the Engel coefficient, which is a measure of household living standards and wealth, and closely related to financial management and living consumption.

The Chinese have a saying: 'Clothing or eating cannot make you poor, but insufficient planning will make you poor', which means that a person or a family should plan for income and have planning objectives. Only by making arrangements for living consumption can a person or families become wealthy and keep on developing. The importance of family living consumption and financial management is that it can raise the living consumption level, household income, and consumption that are closely linked with economic development. They also affect the development of the consumption chain and the overall national development, and are also influenced by the market rules of macro-economic control.

Abstemious consumption is very important, particularly in developing countries during the economic development, which could give countries more economic development funds.

We also clearly see that individual household living consumption is the core of the three consumptions. Without human living consumption, there would not be social consumption and production consumption. Individual household living consumption is the main consumption of social overall consumption. In addition to individual household consumption, there is also collective living consumption. Humans will not exist without human living consumption. So, meeting the growing consumption demand on material and spiritual culture and paying attention to the wealth management of individual household income and living consumption are fundamental to the development of the three consumptions.

18

Enterprise leadership management under China's national conditions

China has its own national conditions. Leadership management under China's national conditions has the general characteristics of other countries around the world, and its own specific characteristics. Leadership management under China's national conditions will be discussed in this chapter.

Section 1 Enterprise management under China's national conditions

The object and purpose of management

Leadership management is an integrated and systematic structure with different levels. Leaders are also managed. The object of management involves people, property, and materials. Both macro management and micro management focus on people. Management begins with 'pulling an ox by the nose' – the most important element – people. If you can manage people, everything else becomes easy.

The ultimate purpose of management is to realize the enterprise's objective. During this process the enterprise will achieve high output with low investment, and obtain the highest economic, social, and business benefits.

Six types of leadership management

The Charter of Anshan Iron and Steel Plant

The Charter of Anshan Iron and Steel Plant is the conclusion of the work report of Anshan Iron and Steel Plant made by Mao Zedong. It is also the general rule of the enterprise management of Anshan Iron and Steel Plant. The Charter is built on 'two participations, one reform, and three combinations', by which Mao Zedong summarized the experience of Anshan Iron and Steel Plant. 'Two participations' means that officers participate in labor and workers participate in management; 'one reform' means reforming unreasonable production processes and regulations to plug loopholes in production and management; 'three combinations' means the management system with the combination of administrative managers, technical managers, and workers. It is of practical and historic significance to re-advocate and develop the Charter of Anshan Iron and Steel Plant.

Three honesties, four strictures, and four samenesses

Daqing Oil Field advocated three honesties, four strictnesses, and four samenesses. The 'three honesties' are being honest, speaking honestly, and acting honestly. The 'four strictures' are strict organization, discipline, requirements, and attitude. The 'four samenesses' are being the same with the leader present or absent, with and without the inspector, with good weather and bad weather, and in the day and at night.

Preciseness, prudence, carefulness, confidentiality, and firmness

'Preciseness' is being precise; 'prudence' is being cautious; 'carefulness' is taking great care and paying attention to detail; 'confidentiality' is keeping work secret; 'firmness' is acting firmly and without soft-heartedness. The leader of a country should follow these characteristics strictly and follow regulations instead of breaking them, which could encourage other people to do the same.

Four ways of being perfect

There are four qualities in management that can ensure the completion of a management task: perfect mind, perfect business, perfect work-style, and perfect management. One has a 'perfect mind' if one loves our country, the people, and the Party. To have a 'perfect business' one learns whatever one does in theory and practice. To have a 'perfect work-style' one is practical in everything one does and follows rules and instructions strictly. 'Perfect management' is the having the best management style for managing and mobilizing people, inspecting, studying, reporting, establishing models, punishing the backward, and encouraging the people stuck in the middle.

Kind-hearted management and cold-hearted management

In management, the special person does not exist and is not allowed to exist. Everyone serves as a link and a part, and will be replaced if they make a mistake. Therefore, management does not involve personal emotion or any distinction between the close and the distant.

Though management does not involve personal emotion, we all have flesh and blood and emotion after work. In daily life, we care for each other like brothers and sisters. Therefore, the leader will criticize and care about personnel as if they were their parents. Cold-heartedness does not means being unkind in daily life but in work.

Whatever we do, we will begin with the national condition of China. The biggest characteristic of the Chinese national condition is the leadership of the Communist Party, so we must adjust the relationship between strengthening the leadership of the Party and strengthening management.

Eight aspects of leadership management

These are eight aspects of leadership management:

1. *Making the best of computers for management.* There has been an information explosion throughout the world. The wide application of computers in various productive fields has improved labor productivity enormously. The computer has been widely popularized and applied to management, greatly promoting modern industrial production, social economic development, and high-tech productivity. Productivity cannot be improved to the highest level without making full use of computers, and contemporary industries must manage computers in order to develop.
2. *Supervision and restriction.* Management is a behavioral standard in the operation process. 'Supervision and restriction' is the management of management, in which managers are supervised and restricted. The task of supervising and restricting personnel is to supervise every management personnel and management organization and to prevent them from making any mistake, realizing the objectives of management as much as possible.
3. *Legal management.* As a society governed by law, the market economy society will be managed by law to guarantee the development of the economy legally. Practice has proved that legal management has a huge effect on protecting and promoting economic development. In order to ensure orderly movement, fair and legal competition in the market, and everybody's rights, legal means will be applied.

4. *Centralized and decentralized leadership management.* On the whole, enterprise management can be divided into two modes: centralized management and decentralized management. Generally speaking, large and relatively large enterprises usually combine centralized management and decentralized management; in relatively small enterprises or in the pioneering stage of an enterprise, centralized management is usually carried out; when an enterprise has developed to a certain stage, decentralized management is employed.
5. *Objective management and detailed management.* Objective management involves determining and breaking down the annual overall plan of an enterprise and committing it to every member, so all members can realize the same objective. Objective management is divided into long-term objectives, medium-term objectives, and short-term objectives. Objectives are formulated scientifically, with multiple levels. Once formulated, they are broken down and detailed. Objectives of the enterprise become objectives for the staff of the enterprise, for which they will work. Therefore, we need to divide and break down all objectives to get specific objectives for every company, department, and person. The sense of responsibility of every department and person cannot be formed without detailed objectives. During the process of objective management and detailed management, every detailed objective will be finally provided with a day of implementation, and during the practice process, any unreasonable objective will be perfected and adjusted to be reasonable. The enterprise should review, improve, and revise its yearly project every half a year.
6. *Fixed number management and piecework management.* Fixed number management and piecework management are two main means to detail management. Piecework management is usually used for countable work in factories. The operation of piecework management is simple, but quality should be emphasized. For uncountable work, fixed number management is usually applied. It is difficult to operate fixed number management. For the examination of the workload, efforts will be made to 'use fewer people, award more, and increase salaries'. The method can better mobilize the enthusiasm of personnel and prevent laziness.
7. *Macro management and micro management.* Macro management is overall planning and decision-making. An enterprise evolving towards a standardized and modern organization will first succeed in macro management, and macro management must first adapt to the needs of the transnational company and large movements of the world economy.

The manager of a modern industrial and commercial enterprise will consider whether overall planning of the enterprise can be controlled; how to establish the organization; the support of international finance; the most advanced equipment and communication tools in the world; and international law and the specific law of the country. Micro management involves specific, practical, and single operation. Every microscopic decision will be realized by a microscopic operation. Macro management is a bare outline without the normal operation of micro management or micro-economic benefit. There can be no macro-level success unless specific micro level needs are realized. Therefore, attention will be paid to micro management and macro management, and macro management is the dominant element.

8. *Multi-layer graded accounting management.* 'Multi-layer graded accounting management' means that the parent company is responsible for overall accounting management, while every subsidiary has its own accounting management. In addition, one-way accounting management can be carried out. Multi-level accounting classification increases personnel's sense of responsibility when in charge of financial management. While implementing the multi-level classification of accounting, rights, liabilities, and benefits will all be provided, so salaries and bonuses will be distributed according to the performance of financial management. Good performance will be rewarded, and bad performance will be penalized.

Section 2 Leadership management development effectiveness

We run an enterprise with the purpose of acquiring benefits to the largest extent. Benefits can be divided into development benefits and management benefits. We can acquire benefit from both the high-speed development of the enterprise and the scientific and strict enterprise management, and the two are complementary to each other, and neither will be neglected.

Emphasize balance and balance emphasis

Emphasizing balance and balancing emphasis are two aspects of the development and management of an enterprise. The purpose of development is emphasizing, while the purpose of management is balancing. During the high-speed development of the enterprise, balance is realized through management, and development is emphasized in balanced management. The two repeat the process again and again with a dynamic movement, making the enterprise develop healthily and steadily. Balance and emphasis, the same as management and development, are complementary to each other and dialectically unified with each other. It is wrong to neglect either party. The enterprise will strengthen management during development, realizing development benefit and management benefit.

The hen-raising perspective and new product development in an enterprise

The fundamental purpose of developing an enterprise is to pursue benefits and to increase profits. In this sense, it has something in common with raising hens. The purpose of raising hens is to make hens lay more eggs. It is difficult to make hens lay more eggs, make the enterprise create more benefit, profit and tax with low cost, and to acquire maximum interest with minimum investment.

Anyone who is familiar with raising hens knows that a hen is rarely raised for more than three years, or it will be un-remunerative and the 'benefit principle' of raising hens will be violated. While guiding and studying enterprise development in accordance with the law of cost and benefit in raising hens, we can easily come to the conclusion that the enterprise will continuously release new high-tech products to increase the after-effect, or the enterprise cannot remain invincible.

Problems in economic development of middle and small cities

The economic development of middle and small Chinese cities is not balanced at all. Through summarizing and analyzing, we discover the following factors:

1. Government and enterprise administrators have mistakenly understood the basic law of market economy development.
2. In fierce market competition, they fail to emphasize development and management benefits, strengthen management in development, and accelerate growth via management.

3. Enterprises do not pay sufficient attention to new technical products and scientific research, and cannot develop new products in time, resulting in insufficient after-effects and competitive power in the market.
4. Government leaders and functional departments do not have sufficient understanding of the issues above. Government has not realized that it will serve the enterprises, and governmental work mechanisms are not in step and do not coordinate with enterprise development.
5. The force of cultivating the tax source is insufficient, and phenomena like killing the goose that lays the golden egg happen now and then.
6. Some leaders do not study the economy and solve practical problems in economic development.

In order to solve these problems, specific efforts can be made as follows:

1. Use educational institutions such as party colleges and cadre schools to hold various study classes and training classes frequently and invite experts and scholars to give lectures, learn, and discuss basic economic laws concerning the health competition and economic development of the socialist market economy, so as to enhance government and enterprise leaders' competence to control the market economy.
2. Government and functional departments at various levels should change their work-style and function, strengthen service consciousness, and overcome bureaucracy.
3. The major leader of the enterprise should concentrate on the economy, measure economic development with time and energy, and pay attention to the technological development of new products.
4. Actively support enterprises and carefully cultivate tax source.
5. Reinforce public security and maintain social stability, providing a looser and better 'soft environment' for the healthy development of the enterprise. Optimize and standardize the 'hard environment' of investment, and accelerate infrastructure construction.
6. If the secretary of the municipal party committee, the mayor, the secretary, and the factory manager of the enterprise can discover the correct method for the city and the enterprise, establish and perfect an operation mechanism suitable for economic development, then the development of the city and the enterprise will be suited to each other and promoted. They are the parties to promote economic development.

Section 3 Three forces and leadership management

Material force

'Material force' is the force used by an enterprise to satisfy personnel's material demands through reasonable material interest distribution, so as to encourage personnel, mobilize their enthusiasm and initiative, and arouse their creativity. The core of material force is stimulating the enthusiasm of personnel through the distribution of material interest.

How to provide material force

There are four stages:

1. Combine the development objective of the enterprise and the development objective of the individual employee.
2. Break down the objective and the task. The objective of the enterprise will be transformed into a post objective, and it will be broken down and provided for a specific post and person.
3. Define a post responsibility system, realizing the close connection of responsibility, right, and interest while centering on interest.
4. Inspect and control work to guarantee the implementation of responsibility, rights, and interests.

Spiritual force

Spiritual force is used by an enterprise to satisfy the spiritual demand to arouse the enthusiasm and creativity of personnel by spiritually encouraging means such as enterprise philosophy education, ideological and political work, and commendations.

How to provide spiritual force

There are three stages:

1. Analyze and study the spiritual needs of the enterprise's personnel, achieving a well-defined mental objective while working.
2. Reflect personnel's spiritual needs in the enterprise objective and enterprise philosophy.

3. Satisfy personnel's spiritual needs on various levels through various means of spiritual encouraging.

Guiding personnel to establish a lofty view of spiritual demand

While giving play to spiritual force managers guide and educate personnel to train and help them establish lofty spiritual demands. They keep carrying out ideological and political work in depth. They should make use of words, such as praise and compliments, methods, and art to stimulate spiritual enthusiasm. Relying mainly on spirit with materials as subsidiaries, the initiative of staff and their family members is aroused and the information is transmitted.

Information force

Information is a symbol to represent the existence and change of everything in the objective world that can be known and perceived by people. 'Informational force' is the acting force to realize the enterprise objective by connecting the enterprise, the external environment, and every function, link, and member of the enterprise.

Mode of information transfer

Information transfer inside and outside an enterprise is realized through certain channels, which can be oral or written, such as telephone, telegraph, and the internet.

Direction of information flow

There are three main directions of information flow in an enterprise: from top to bottom, from bottom to top, and as a lateral cross flow. This is the same with the information flow between the enterprise and the outside.

The generation and function of informational force

While giving play to informational force, information acts on the leader's mind and hence influences the enterprise's decision-making and behavior. In order to make correct decisions, the leader first collects information widely. Information collecting is the precondition and basis of releasing informational force, so the process is of great importance. Once collected, information is screened. Information that is highly valuable for decision-making is reserved, the rest is deleted. The function of informational force is directly represented in the power of the model. Through the comprehensive application of the principle 'emphasis–balance, balance–emphasis', the leader constantly learns from the model, by comparing, learning, catching-up, helping, and surpassing to promote the progress of the work.

The use of informational force is restricted because the information that any decision relies on is incomplete and distorted. Any decision should be made under the precondition that the decision maker grasps a certain amount of information. However, in practice, the decision maker cannot grasp all information, and the process of decision-making is inevitably influenced by the subjective preferences of the decision maker. Therefore, the function of information force can only be relatively exerted.

The relationship between material force, spiritual force, and informational force

The three forces are complementary to and dependent on one another. As the basis of spiritual force and informational force, material force is the most important acting force, and spiritual force and informational force should be exerted on the basis of material force. The maximum material force should not be exerted without the coordination of spiritual force and informational force, and informational force should not be exerted without the support of informational force.

There are also differences between the three forces. Material force is the primary acting force. Spiritual force is more than material force sometimes, but it cannot be separate from material force in the final analysis. Influencing the decision-making of leaders exerts information action. Some information reflecting the action of material force and spiritual force is shown by spiritual force through leaders' decision-making.

The objectives of the three forces

These are the objectives of the three forces:

1. In the long-term objective, informational force is primary, spiritual force is secondary, and material force is seldom involved.
2. In the mid-term objective, spiritual force and informational force are still dominant, while material force is auxiliary. In the pattern of the

motion of the three forces, the function of the three forces is exerted by encouraging spiritual force.

3. In the short-term objective, material force is primary, spiritual force is secondary, and informational force is tertiary. The function of material force must be fully exerted to stimulate the enthusiasm and creativity of personnel, and then the function of spiritual force is exerted to satisfy and arouse personnel's spirit. Informational force feeds back the information related to the realization of material force and spiritual force to the decision maker, and then the decision maker carries out corresponding adjustments based on the information, ensuring the normal and maximum exertion of the function of the three forces.

The law of three motives

We can see from the analysis above that the three motives – material motive force, spiritual motive force and informational motive force – are the decisive forces for enterprise development. The three motives are not abstract or immeasurable. A brainy entrepreneur will always pay attention to the existence of the three motives and grasp the relationship between them and their variable of corresponding elements. Only then can he or she actually grasp the inherent law of three motives, exerting more value of the three motives.

The power and value of each motive force are regular, and every motive force and corresponding elements are related in a certain proportion. Material force and management and the profit rate are related: the more scientific management is and the higher the profit rate is, the bigger the material force will be, forming a proportional relationship. On the contrary, a reversely proportional relationship may be formed.

Spiritual force, culture connotation, and culture transformation are also proportionately related. The more advanced and practical the enterprise culture is and the more common the transformation from culture to personnel philosophy, the bigger the spiritual force will be, forming a proportional relationship. On the contrary, reversely proportional relationship may also be formed.

Informational force and the period of information capturing, the accuracy of information, and the degree of information transformation are related with corresponding proportion. The shorter and more timely information capturing is, the more accurate and reliable the information, and the quicker and more thorough the transformation from information to action, the bigger the informational force will be, forming a proportional relationship. On the contrary, a reversely proportional relationship may also be formed.

It will be noted that every one of the three motives is relatively dependent and has a huge effect on the development of the enterprise. However, the three motives are related to and dependent on one another and transform into one another. Therefore, a brainy entrepreneur must research their relationship, grasp their transformation law, and finally turn the three motives into the integral force for enterprise development.

The value of the three motives can be presented in this formula:

$$M = P - V$$
$$M = P - V$$

M stands for surplus value, P stands for total revenue, and V stands for total expense.

It can be seen from the formula that enterprise benefit – surplus value – is the difference between total revenue and total expense.

However, it is not so simple. During the process of production, if production efficiency (material force) is increased through scientific management and technical improvement, and personnel's mental outlook is changed and their working enthusiasm is stimulated (spiritual force is increased) through popularizing and spreading the enterprise culture, and the enterprise can grasp more comprehensive and accurate market trends (informational force is increased) through information capturing and transforming, then the three motives can play a comprehensive part during the process of enterprise development and create a huge composite force for enterprise development.

The formula can be stated as follows:

$$M1 = P1 - V1$$
$$M1 = P1 - V1$$

M1 stands for surplus value, P1 stands for total revenue, and V1 stands for total expense.

It will be noted that the surplus value at the moment has acted on the three motives. Generally speaking, it is much bigger than the first surplus value. Therefore, the result and speed of enterprise development are finally tested and determined by the three motives. Hence we come to the conclusion that the three motives are not superficial but effective and necessary for enterprise development. Once the law of the three motives is grasped, enterprise management will be more effective, enterprise cohesion will be more powerful, and the enterprise will continuously develop and stay invincible when there is fierce market competition.

Section 4 The political quality of enterprise leaders

Lenin once said: 'Politics is the concentrated expression of economy.' Deng Xiaoping said: 'Economic development is the most important manifestation of politics.' The sayings show that politics and economy are inseparable.

Politics, economy, and enterprises

Politics is the concentrated manifestation of economy, while economy is the basis of politics. Politics serves economy. The quality of the economic base determines that of politics. Politics under certain circumstances serves enterprises as well. Politics that are in conformity with the laws of productivity development promote progress and the development of economy, otherwise they will inhibit development. The corruption of politics necessarily brings about the recession of the economy, and the improvement in politics will lead to economic development. The so-called progress of politics means following economic laws.

Politics and the state machine

Politics, the soul of the state machine, determines the nature of the state machine, protects and serves the economic base, provides service for the cultural progress of the whole society, protects national interests, maintains a high degree of unity and solidarity, and safeguards the security of the people and the stability and unity of society. Politics is realized by means of ideology, law, and a strict state machine.

Politics and the political parties and the parties

Politics has class differences, and politics under a certain circumstance represents interests in that specific social condition. In modern society politics and the regime are generally reflected by political parties. A political party takes advantage of rights and powers by taking control of the regime, and serves the people under its leadership, and in the meanwhile checks all powers that are against its control. China is under the people's domestic dictatorship led by China's Communist Party – the Communist Party in our country stands for the proletariat and all peoples, while other parties only participate in politics instead of competing for power.

Politics, democracy, and freedom

Politics, democracy, and freedom are complementary aspects to one another. Democracy and freedom belong to politics, serve politics, and are the means of politics. Democracy and freedom are relative, and there is no absolute democracy or freedom. Politics contains democracy and freedom. The maturity level and quality of a nation, the maturity level of different classes, the actual condition of economic development, and the stability and unity of society determine the proportion of democracy and freedom. What our country adopts is political democracy – a people's democratic dictatorship led by Communist Party of China.

Politics, news, art, and literature

News organs, such as newspapers, radio stations, TV stations, and news agencies, are mouthpieces of parties and states. The stronger the quality of arts and literature, the more appealing they get. Therefore, the more meaningful education becomes. Literature is certain to serve a certain regime and politics.

Politics, class, distribution, and life

Politics belongs to a certain class and stands for the interests of a certain class. Through its organ of power, it transfers, organizes, and protects all producers and people having a life, and at the same time fights crimes to make sure of a stable and unified society and to protect the nation from danger. Living consumption and distribution are closely related and determined by the contribution to society and methods of demand, which in the meantime is determined by the regime.

Politics, belief, religion, and morals

Belief, religion, and morals are in the same scope of the superstructure. Belief and religion are protected and taken advantage of if they are not against national policies, otherwise, they are inhibited. Religion can also serve politics and be employed by politics. Morals are the sum of the norms of behaviors that adjust relationships between people and between individuals and society. But morals are at the same time built to a certain degree on the basis of the materials of society and serve class and the whole society as well.

Political reign and control

Politics takes responsibility for safeguarding social culture, economy, people's lives, and the stability and solidarity of the whole society, the protection of which entails a high degree of reign and control. Control means management, which is suitable for an enterprise, so is also true of a state. In the process of controlling a country, premier control has to be grasped. There has to be a whole set of compulsory and non-compulsory social control systems, including systems of politics, economy, law, religion, and morals.

How to enhance political caliber

These are ways to enhance political calibre:

1. *Work hard on theories*. Learn Marxism, Mao Zedong's Thought and De Xiaoping's Theories, improve political caliber, enhance political sensitivity, and have good knowledge of the Party's opinions and their mutual relations. If we want to improve our political caliber, we have to start from the bottom – from political cultivation, which entails learning the related works of Marxism.
2. *Hold on to principles*. Pay adequate attention to principles and various complex relations, and while sticking to principles, learn to handle problems in the most effective and inoffensive way.
3. *Hold on to beliefs, and enhance good manners*. If people do not have faith, they will not be firm, especially when faced with ups and downs. In the process of great setbacks and disasters, people will be diverted

from following a righteous course. In a complex society, relations between people can be very contradictory. If we cannot cultivate ourselves well, we are apt to get stuck in contradictions. If we do not have adequate perseverance, then we will not develop.

4. *Pay adequate attention to flexibility.* If there is only a sense of principles but no flexibility, we will become dogmatic, which mainly derives from being unfamiliar with dialectics or with the cause-and-effect relationship of things. Flexibility serves principles, and it is a means to an end.
5. *Grasp policy and strategy.* Policy is basic, and strategy is a means to an end, which is a process of doing great things and the assurance of success.
6. *Overcome pride and arrogance.* This is necessary for success; without it we will fail.

Political caliber that employees of Sanzhu group should have

These are qualities employees of Sanzhu group should have:

1. *Love of the party, love of country, and love of the nation.* Never say words against our party, country, or nation; do no things against our party, country or nation. Become aware of the consistency of interests between working for Sanzhu and working for country and the nation.
2. *Love of individual study and self-discipline.* Employees of Sanzhu will form a habit of love of study and of diligence in thinking, and strengthen their self-discipline.
3. Respect for the government, respect for leaders, and strive actively for leadership in the company.
4. *Integrity above all things.* They will be faithful to the Party, country, nation, company, and comrades. The development and consolidation of enterprises entails credits.
5. *Ability to integrate with groups.* If a man is detached from the group, in spite of having lots of caliber, he will be powerless. If a man has great leadership skills and lots of caliber, but he has no people to lead, he will not make his leadership come true. Therefore, it is necessary to become integrated into groups and to possess team spirit.
6. *Ability to discharge responsibilities to help develop the national economy of China.* Developing economy is just a means to an end – making China prosperous, having a thriving national economy, and doing what is best for China and for the party.

Section 5 Enterprise culture management

In the early 1980s, the research of enterprise culture first rose in the United States. Enterprise culture involves the values of a company, which determine its behavior norms, enterprise tenets, and action model. Enterprise culture is defined in various ways. My understanding is as follows. Enterprise culture is the unique values and spirit of an enterprise in the context of certain political, economic, and social cultural backgrounds gradually generated and growing during long-term production and operation. The behavior norms, moral criteria, tenets, work-styles of the enterprise are generated on that, and the operating consciousness, operating ideas, and operating strategy of the enterprise are generated on that.

Enterprise culture is of great importance to enterprise development. In modern enterprises, enterprise culture is mainly relied on to mobilize the enthusiasm of personnel and to increase the cohesion and centralism of the enterprise. Enterprise culture is the basis for enterprise survival, the motive force for enterprise development, the norm of behavior, and the core for success.

Sanzhu culture

Revolutionary, traditional, and modern enterprise culture is discussed using Sanzhu culture as an example.

Sanzhu culture came into being between the later 1980s and middle 1990s, although some ideas and enterprise tenets had been put forward in early 1980. In 1997, the enterprise culture of Sanzhu was mature.

Revolutionary Sanzhu culture

We connect the good tradition of the Party and a modern enterprise management system and connect the struggle objective and the current task of the Party and the development objective of the enterprise, realizing the inheritance and development of revolutionary culture. First of all, we will stick to the guidance of Marxism-Leninism, Maoism, especially Deng Xiaoping's theory of building socialism with Chinese characteristics, and the leadership of the Communist Party. Such is the basic political and ideological line of the development of Sanzhu Company. Next, we will persist in building socialist culture and ethics and carry out ideological and political work in depth. Third, we will inherit and carry forward the Party's good tradition and success in leading economic building for several decades, which mainly involves the Charter of Anshan Iron and Steel Plant (two participations, one reform, and three combinations), and three honesties, four strictures, and four samenesses.

Traditional Sanzhu culture

The conception of 'enterprise culture' is introduced from abroad, but its simple content has been included in the traditional Chinese culture for a long time. Confucian culture can be fused with modern economic development to a certain degree, and some values in Confucian culture have promoted the development of economy. We have absorbed and learned that the best features of some contents of traditional culture are beneficial to modern enterprise development, especially the ethics of loyalty, filial piety, courtesy, justice, and benevolence in Confucian culture, legalist culture, and Taoist culture, initially forming some moral criteria and behavior norms in Sanzhu enterprise culture.

Modern Sanzhu culture

The modernity of Sanzhu culture is mainly reflected in its absorbing and learning the best features of Western culture. We have learnt some successful management modes and management systems of Western transnational companies and combined them with the basic condition of China to form a set of modern enterprise systems with Chinese characteristics. We are now consciousness of the following aspects of modern enterprise operation and management: management, high technology, market development, competition, 'everything centering on consumption', legislation, reform and innovation, respect for rules and subjective initiative, and kind-hearted and cold-hearted management concepts as the guiding ideas for team building.

Dedication is the core of Sanzhu enterprise culture

The values of Sanzhu culture are 'dedication' to the Party, China, and the nation. Sanzhu enterprise is a component of socialist enterprise. Our mission is to be the 'head horse' in the forefront of the times, and to make greater contributions to the revitalizing of the Chinese economy.

The enterprise tenet of Sanzhu Company

The enterprise comes from society, serves society, contributes to society, and returns to society; this is also the extension of the enterprise's spirit of 'dedication'.

Doing the duty of ordinary people for the revitalization of the Chinese national economy is the banner of Sanzhu culture: 'Doing the duty of ordinary people for the revitalizing of Chinese national economy' is our banner and slogan. We struggle, fight, and dedicate ourselves with only one purpose – to realize 'national revival and Chinese mightiness'. National revival is related to every Chinese person.

Six spirit styles and three work styles

'Six spirit styles and three work styles' is our enterprise spirit. In involves the spirit of painstaking efforts; the spirit of economy; the spirit of professional dedication; the spirit of love for the Party, China, and the nation; the spirit of solidifying and friendship for progress; the spirit of national self-respect, self-renewal, and self-regard; and the work style of practical, quick, and strict enforcement; of preciseness, prudence, carefulness, confidentiality and firmness; and of enduring hard work and hardships.

Put people first and make the best of people

'Putting people first' can be done in the following ways:

- by respecting, caring for, and loving people
- by emphasizing the realization of the self-value of every employee, and realizing the self-development of everyone during the process of company development
- by recommending whoever has talent and using people based on their talent; whoever is able will work, while whoever is not able will be laid off
- by emphasizing the education and training of talents and the enhancement of their quality
- by selecting, training, and using people properly according to their ability, noting their talents.

This is the joint value pursued by Sanzhu staff: 'You and I meet challenges together, stand at the front and run to the other side, experiencing pain and happiness.' The sentence not only represents the aspirations of Sanzhu staff, but also the true feelings of Sanzhu staff to selflessly contribute to the revitalizing of Chinese national economy.

Section 6 China marketing team building outline

The standards of establishing the team with strong will and principle

Four strict elements

These are four strict elements:

1. *A close knit organization.* The upper organization is close knit, and the upper levels are connected closely with the lower ones. The lowest one consists of two men, with one of them as the first command; or consists of three men, with one of them as the first command and the organization of grade level.
2. *Strict discipline.* All of the behavior of the team (behavior against discipline) must be carried out according to the concrete rules of praise and punishment.
3. *Strict requirements.* The company must have regulations to abide by, ensure that lawbreakers are prosecuted, and act strictly according to the regulations and rules.
4. *Strict attitude.* Everyone is equal before the regulations and rules, and people who violate the regulations and rules must be punished severely and cannot be punished slightly because of their contribution.

Four excellences

These are four excellences:

1. *Be excellent in ideology.* Love the country and identify with the culture and idea of Sanzhu Group, which is the spirit of action and accept and abide by the regulations and rules of Sanzhu Group. Combine the task of accomplishing the enterprise objective with realization of one's own life value and strive for excellence.
2. *Be excellent in business.* Be proficient in business, technique, and skills, and work with high efficiency.
3. *Be excellent in management.* Manage the team and population with modern methods, and carry out effective evaluation management that is systematic, standardized, institutionalized, and digitized. Use 'three motives' to motivate everyone's enthusiasm and to achieve high efficiency and high benefit.

4. *Be excellent in behavior.* The behavioral style of leadership is to have the subordinates follow you, instead of following the subordinates in times of need, and be the first to bear hardships and rush to the front lines, endure hardships and work hard, and fight together with the team. Pay attention to decorum and politeness, respect others, be honest to others, and do not be conceited or rash. Form the habit of obeying orders as one's nature, carry out orders firmly, and carry out work creatively. Be brave enough to offer leaders advice and carry out orders firmly even when the advice is not accepted.

Central attraction of the team

Emphasize the effect of material

To establish itself the team needs strict discipline as a guarantee, but there must be the target for which the team strives and the common benefits of achieving the targets. The targets and benefits are the central attraction to establish the team, so the team must correctly set the targets in different stages, which connects with benefits. The benefits must be feasible and fulfilled, especially for the lower staff.

Establish a strong team centered on the first commander

These are ways of establishing a team centered on the first commander:

1. The leader of the team is the first commander who is both brave and resourceful and a professional assistant who is cooperative and responsible for one section.
2. Carry out the work and fulfill the task firmly.
3. Use 'four strict elements' and 'four excellences' as standards to carry out strict management.
4. Be just and strict with oneself, and manage and praise and punish with regulations and rules.
5. Carry out work correctly:
   - Unify the thoughts, convey correct advice, educate inferiors, and collect advice in a democratic way.
   - Use the method of planning first and then carrying out. Work out plans and strategies and then gain a decisive victory.
   - Use the rule of emphasizing balance to solve the contradiction between development and management. Use the rule to cultivate a model, set up

a model, generalize the method, expand the experience, and promote the overall development (the principle of shepherd theory).

- Adopt training to ensure the quality of the team and to adapt to the needs of accomplishing the tasks.
- Solve the principal contradiction and then the ordinary ones. Learn the methods of playing the piano, which is vivid and dramatic, free and easy, and bittersweet.

6. Insist on appointing staff according to their abilities and talent:
   - Select and employ staff according to their abilities, and afford enough space to put their abilities to use. Encourage them to learn from practice, and vice versa, and to learn all their lives to achieve great success.
   - Take care of the work, lives, and families (divide the responsibility according to different levels) of subordinates, and offer timely help when it is needed; it is especially important to give care to them when they are in trouble or ill.
   - Place people with special capabilities so as to tolerate all types of experts and achieve a great success. The career of reconstructing Sanzhu Group will be successful.

7. The first command must fully develop the abilities of assistants and inferiors and the subjective initiative of the first command of the department:
   - Courageously transfer power to assistants to let them develop work creatively. The first command must take the respective responsibility for the inferior's faults.
   - Approves the achievements and success of inferiors and offer them timely help and support when they are in trouble. Do not blame them except for matters of principle, and ridiculing and contempt are not allowed.
   - Grant the first command of the department the corresponding power related to the needs of the work; ask what is needed in the provinces; and carry out the system of giving different levels' management responsibility.
   - Praise staff to motivate their enthusiasm.

8. Unify thoughts with the culture and ideas that are the soul of the enterprise. As to education of culture and ideas, carry out systematic hard management; manage civilization, life, and behavior. Feel grateful for the education of parents, the Communist Party, our country, the

enterprise, and the help and support of friends to establish harmonious work and interpersonal and social relationships in order:

- to establish the team with 'nine demands and nine prohibitions'
- to be a collective hero and not an individualistic hero
- to emphasize the team instead of individuals
- to be democratic under the centralized power and unity and abandon the freedom of anarchism
- to have the sense of organization and discipline, and abandon non-organizational activities
- to be of one heart and one mind instead of disengaged
- to manage in line and not to interfere with others' work
- to be strict, tight, careful, close, and firm instead of being weak, lazy, and loose
- to employ people according to their abilities instead of their relations
- to make friends instead of enemies extensively.

Establishing the team is the most important activity. All of us must regard establishing the team with four strict elements as a priority and a chance to allow one to succeed and achieve a great career. Be a master of shaping oneself. If the self-improvement of the leader group and all the staff has advanced enough, the reconstruction of Sanzhu Group will be successful. The success of Sanzhu Group is the success of your self-improvement and self-shaping. Let us move ahead hand in hand and create brilliant achievements.

Section 7 Quality of leaders and managers (Sanzhu Company as an example)

Managers must strengthen the cultivation of quality in every aspect so as to adapt to changing situations and achieve good results. In this way the organization or company can continually achieve success and remain invincible in the more complex and increasingly competitive market.

Managers should persist in relearning

Persisting in relearning is necessary for keeping pace with the time. We are transferring from a planned economy to a market economy and integrating with the world. International market economy has a history of several centuries and has accumulated rich experiences, while we have known little or nothing at all about it. Therefore, we have to learn and understand market economic theory and accumulate experience and knowledge as quickly as possible. In addition, the development of modern science and technology changes with each passing day.

Persisting in relearning helps to widen thoughts and reduce faults in work. Relearning helps us unify philosophy and understanding to form the correct concept of Sanzhu. It is naïve to think that you can know Sanzhu Company. The company was not formed in a day but has been constantly reinforced based on practice. The Sanzhu concept was not formed in a day. You may not understand it though you learn it, and you may be not able to put the concept into practice though you understand it. Therefore, it is necessary to repeat learning and unify our mind in the Sanzhu Spirit.

Persisting in relearning helps to understand the culture and tenets of Sanzhu Company as Sanzhu Company is a micro world that has its own culture and tenets. In order to understand and accept it, we must learn management philosophy, dialectics, contradiction theory, and practice theory.

To be the one obtaining Tao rather than losing Tao

When handling various relationships in society and among employees, managers should adhere to morals, moral principles, and reason of 'Tao'. Strengthening the ideological education of employees is one of the most important parts of management. Employees are taught to be modest and keep in mind that a just cause gains great support, and an unjust cause finds little support.

So, we should stay modest and discreet, never be conceited or rash, and hold on to justice, which guarantees a healthy development of the business. Especially when an enterprise develops rapidly, these virtues cannot be ignored. Research carefully, keep on the alert, and bear crisis awareness in mind. Research the laws of crisis, and be able to handle accidental crises. Try to be modest, but at the same time do not be afraid of discharging your responsibilities so as to conduct work with preciseness, prudence, carefulness, confidentiality, and firmness.

A manager should be able to tolerate people. As a manager, one must have a big heart and tolerate people from different places across the world with different personalities; tolerate even more those who raised objections about you and were proved to be wrong.

Good managers, even if they are geniuses or well rounded, will not accomplish feats all by themselves. One should draw on the wisdom, will, and power of millions of people together and strive for a shared goal. A good manager should be tolerant of others' disrespect, of others' faults, and of others inability to correct their mistakes. Being modest and open to others' opinions is a virtue of a good leader. Consequently, a manager should be tolerant of people's shortcomings in addition to appreciating talent. We are not supposed to deny everything based on someone's minor faults. No man is perfect, and no gold is entirely pure. Only when you can tolerate the shortcomings of someone can you gather more talent.

Cultivating the self

The first in command should aim towards 'four excellences'. In a team of cadres, the first in command is of particular importance. Whether the qualities of the first in command are excellent determines the level of the whole team as well as the ups and downs of an enterprise. These are the four excellences for a manager:

1. *Excellence in ideology*. The manager should have the right ideas and values, be loyal to the enterprise, become fully aware of the properties of the enterprise, and correctly handle the interests of individuals and enterprises.
2. *Excellence in style*. Style is invisible. It can be transformed into great power. A leader establishes a good style. There is a saying in China, 'Just as grass sways at the mercy of the wind, so soldiers do whatever the general tells them to do.' This suggests that the performance of a unit is not determined by the masses, but by the leader. If leaders are soft and lazy, how can they lead an excellent, hard-working, and united team? In the meantime, a leader should be strict with subordinates. If you've got good style, you should strive to be a good leader of the team according to your style, and improve your style in practice.
3. *Excellence in business*. Leaders must possess a high level of business caliber. So a leader has to study hard to find out about marketing and our products. You know things that are not familiar to others, and you can do things that cannot be accomplished by others. Only in this way can your employees admire you and can work be done perfectly.
4. *Excellence in management*. Learn how to manage Sanzhu so as to ensure that Sanzhu develops smoothly and healthily and gets somewhere in the future. First, learn management knowledge of our own; second, refer to books related to management abroad.

We have to study hard and are prepared to be efficient managers. We have to learn, learn to do things well, or do better. A manager with high caliber needs to be highly experienced, but one has to set a goal to be a good manager. With such a goal, you will study diligently in a way that is different from when you don't have a goal like this.

Improve confidence and perform work creatively

Good managers are adept in finding the laws of things. Each kind of work has its internal laws as well as the laws of its connection to the outside world. Be adept in employing the experience of advanced units, compare it with your unfinished work, and find universal laws. Knowledge inspires us to generate new opinions and approaches, which is called the work of creativity. Under the guidance of general laws and theories, you will find new laws and figure out working methods of creativity, which in turn guide your work and help you make progress in research.

It is not easy to be the first in command. Managers must impose 'strictness' and the 'four excellences' (see Section 6).

Improve leadership knowledge, inspiration, and decision-making ability

Leadership determines the direction of team development, and the first in command is the main decision-maker. Scientific decision-making is made, verified, and generalized through understanding and using large amounts of data. We should listen to people's views, and carefully analyze the information. There is an old saying, 'Everyone has a sledgehammer and the final word is made by only one sledgehammer.' Different decisions have different results. Thus, perception, inspiration, and decision-making are required. While making a decision, the first thing to do is thinking. Faced with a number of market research data, different statements, and different views, what one needs is thinking. The process of thinking is related to personal knowledge, wisdom, and character. In particular, knowledge and wisdom have close ties with innate human sensitivity and the brain's thinking capacity.

The process of thinking involves the brain's processing function of thinking. After that information processing is over, results come out. The last result is creative thinking, namely inspiration. That 'ideas come out with frowned brows' is not accidental. It is the same with invention, which is connected with everyone's talent, knowledge, experience, and inspiration. So-called talent is the brain's processing capacity. Each person may reach different conclusions from the same material, because there are differences in subjective experience and knowledge, and the talent and capacity of brain processing.

The innovation of inspiration is instantaneous and is the origin of knowledge. In Christianity it is believed that knowledge and inspiration are from God. From the materialistic point of view, it is not God; instead, it comes out through our brain's processing of information and materials. With innovation combined with us, our work is decided. The leaders of various departments should be like this. As long as one is in charge of a part of work, one has rights and responsibilities. Therefore, savvy is put into epistemology, which is the fourth stage of the epistemology of human history.

Until now, the development of human epistemology has experienced four stages. The first stage is that Plato puts idea into epistemology; the second stage is the heart of Kant taken into the epistemology; the third stage is the practice of Marxism taken into epistemology. Putting knowledge into epistemology can guide mankind to create more inventions and consumer products of material and spiritual culture to meet the people's consumption needs. No knowledge, no invention; no knowledge, no innovation. Every progress is attributed to knowledge and inspiration, which requires us to improve knowledge, inspiration, and perception. Since we know the law, we can consciously cultivate and improve ourselves. It is not hard to improve knowledge, inspiration, and the decision-making capacity. As long as we are people with thinking, carefulness, and diligence, we will improve knowledge and inspiration.

Knowledge and inspiration does not exclusively belong to leaders. All inventors and technical innovators are the result of knowledge, inspiration, and thinking. The way of cultivation for a person is to make more observations, analysis, and acquire more data and learning, and dare to put forward new ideas. We should not be hesitant. As long as we have ideas, we should have a try, and it is easy to spark a burst of inspiration in the process of trying. A leader should gather a good wealth of resources for the job, and absorb significant wisdom from colleagues. Based on their own knowledge, wisdom and lessons, leaders inspire a form of thinking and perception and can be inspired in decision-making. Therefore, leadership decisions are closely linked with leadership knowledge and inspiration, and should be informed by specific practices.

Frustration, suffering, and passion

Frustration, suffering, and passion are unavoidable in the journey of life. Someone concluded that the chance of smooth going to rough going is two to eight. The 80% of frustration and suffering does not mean that unhappy things are always with us. So this setback and suffering go along with human growth, and anyone who has major accomplishments must go through a lot of hardships and setbacks. If nothing is done, there will be no hardships and setbacks, and no error. The more one does, the more errors one will make, the faster one's enterprise can develop, and the more problems there exist. This is a law and formula.

Frustration and suffering are bad and good. The so-called 'everything goes well' is just a hope. On the one hand, hardships are bad and no one wants to have hardships; on the other hand, hardships can train a person, cultivate people, and make people mature. Human growth is also subject to such a stage. Those who are successful must forge ahead and take the lead in the crowd, which can cause them to be surrounded by contradictions and more hardships. It is common to face difficulties and stumble, and this is frustrating and causes suffering. But we cannot be defeated by a setback or hardship. If we give up our goals, we shall not become winners. Actually there is no road in this world that is not made by people's walking. Hence, it is harder for people to take a road that none has taken, and one will learn more lessons. The more lessons one learns, the stronger one's ability to bear the stress, and the more experience one gets. Therefore, all these hardships and lessons are treasures. The more experience and lessons one learns, the easier one creates success and the faster one grows.

In order to create success, one must face setbacks and hardships. So the people who want to make success must be mentally prepared for the process in which passion is necessary. One cannot be successful if one is defeated by a hardship. The right attitude should be that the more setbacks and hardships, the stronger one becomes. We should regard setbacks as a grindstone and a training opportunity.

Passion is the first and most important element for our innovation and success. The road for the progress and comeback of Sanzhu is filled with difficulties. The road twists and turns with a bright future. No matter what kind of difficulties we face, we must dare to overcome them. Since our bright future is ahead, gossip is a matter of indifference. We should adhere to our own road and no matter what others say, we should keep an 'indifferent' attitude. If one faces difficulties in society with an 'indifferent' attitude, one will be able to succeed. Therefore, we shall not be successful unless we have the passion to pursue our careers and good attitudes towards setbacks, difficulties, and hardships. And success makes it easier to deal with suffering and setbacks.

Characteristics of successful managers

These are characteristics of successful managers:

1. *Being adept in business*. If one wants to lead everyone to start a market, one has to know about various methods and strategies of starting a market and learn in-depth knowledge of all aspects.
2. *Being able to unite most comrades to work together*. What one is able to do is limited, so only through the wisdom and talent of everyone that moves towards a shared goal and is united together can working efficiency be enhanced.
3. *Possessing an enterprising spirit*. What one wants others to do has to be done by oneself first. Practice what you preach, and set a good example.
4. *Being good at collecting the wisdom of crowds*. Learn from others around you and from your subordinates. Collect the wisdom of crowds to pool wisdom; summarize theory to guide others.
5. *Firmly carrying out the spirits prescribed by the superior*. Carry out activities prescribed by the superior; no dogma or hegemony is allowed. For projects and proposals, branches and working offices of the headquarters must be managed in a firm way.
6. *Stimulating enthusiasm and initiative of employees*. Explore the strengths of employees and bring them into full play. Be good at analyzing and seeing other people's advantages and make use of them well.
7. *Being strict with employees and loving them*. The first in command should care for every employee in life and work to make them voluntarily coordinate with your work; at the same time be strict with them.
8. *Having the courage to conduct criticism and self-criticism*. Do things righteously and raise opinions directly, do not cheat behind others' backs. Do not be afraid to lose face at a time of self-criticism or to degrade yourself, for there is no such thing as a perfect man. Whoever can be self-critical is respected.
9. *Unifying personnel's ideology*. Organize personnel to study. First, employees learn by themselves. Second, learn the knowledge in documents and newspapers and periodicals from headquarters. Unite employees so that everyone strives for the shared goal.

10. *Holding on to the financial system.* Also comply with financial and economic discipline.
11. *Promoting employees' interests.* Only by exercising the enterprise management concept of the company can the enthusiasm and initiative of staff be stimulated. And only by representing the fundamental interests of staff can you be trusted by all employees.
12. *Grasping principal contradictions.* Start from principal contradictions and grip them tightly. Focus attention on the main point at the right time until success comes.
13. *Learning to array troops for economic battles in a scientific way.* By reasonable division of labor, command is fulfilled and work is performed smoothly. Troops should be arrayed in a scientific way according to the actual situation. We should have a compact organization, rigid discipline, strict requirements, and a serious attitude.
14. *Being capable of making decisions.* When leaders are sure about some issue after thoughtful consideration, they ought to come up with leading opinions and try to make everyone else agree with them so that all people want to carry out what they demand. On the other hand, when leaders are not so sure about a certain issue, they should bring it up to others for discussion, collect good and correct ideas from them, and then make decisions and examine the effect via the feedback loop.
15. *Inspecting and give directions to work.* After work is assigned, the first in command will inspect work often to help managers sum up experience, carry forward accomplishments, help the ones that lag behind, and correct mistakes. There are three ways to inspect work: regularly, according to statements, by conducting spot checks.
16. *Learning to 'play the piano'.* There are different priorities at different periods, so learn to distinguish priorities from activities that are less important, and attach more attention to each priority. But focusing on priorities does not mean they are the only things that should be attended to, but that priorities are considered more important. At a certain time, other work is carried out complementary to those priorities so that all aspects of work are taken into consideration.
17. *Maintaining good public relations.* The first in command has to deal with public relations well, making friends with modesty and honesty, and approaching and resorting to others for help.
18. *Showing the correct attitude towards employees.* The first in command, takes responsibility for being an instructor to impart management concepts and business modes to employees. The first in command

should show generosity by not noticing trivial matters, but be good at seeing other people's merits: ignore disadvantages and employ advantages. In addition, the first in command ought to be strict with employees, treating them according to the principles of the 'four strict elements', and at the same time care for and be considerate towards them.

19. *Proceeding from reality*. Be practical, quick, strict, precise, prudent, careful, confidential, and firm.

Use the six-step work method and three formulas to achieve results

This is the six-step work method:

- Formulate the objective and task.
- Formulate the standard requirements of the objective and task.
- Define the person responsible for completing the task.
- Set the time required for the objective and task.
- Specify the discipline of rewarding and punishing for task.
- Examine, summarize experience and lessons, and implement the reward and punishment system.

These are three formulas to achieve results:

- clear assigned task: no examination and reward and punishment = zero (result)
- clear assigned task: with examination and without reward and punishment = bad(result)
- clear assigned task: with examination and reward and punishment = excellent (result)

Section 8 The philosophy of professional managers in China

Professional managers require:

- stage and responsibility
- a wage and bonus accepted by both enterprise and manager
- rights, including chief rights and specific rights
- responsibilities (definite objectives and tasks and responsibilities).

Professional managers must be committed to enterprise, shareholders, and the principles of action. According to the accredited rights from enterprise, the professional manager formulates management of his own enterprise. With the guideline and specific management rules as requirements, the manager provides business profits for shareholders and ensures the added value of capitals.

The behavior philosophy of professional managers

A successful and excellent professional manager should persist in transforming three motives – material, spiritual and informational – to policies so as to stimulate creativeness, enthusiasm and sense of responsibility of personnel:

1. Our objective and task is to realize two benefits, social benefit and business benefit, to maximize shareholders' profits and obtain their satisfaction.
2. Be people-oriented. Talents are the most important treasure rather than simple costs. Leaders and personnel should enhance communication to break down various structural barriers and solve contradictions.
3. The blueprint for success, improvement, and development of personnel should be designed to help them realize their ideal and wishes.
4. When selecting talents, we should have priority over the inside talents with the outside talents as auxiliary.
5. Transform the three motives to policies to stimulate personnel's enthusiasm.
6. Staff share achievements together.
7. Provide stable income and social security for staff.
8. Implement an administrative decentralization system and hierarchical decentralization system. Everyone has responsibilities and rights. Everyone is the owner of enterprise.
9. Leaders at all levels should be good at organizing and using the wisdom of personnel. By combining wisdom and thinking (brain's processing) the leader is inspired to act on policies.
10. Encourage other leaders and personnel to make them grow and have success.
11. Persist in 'two participations, one reform, and three combinations' (see Chapter 13, Section 2). The staffs participate in management; leaders should go to the grassroots level to look into, study, discover problems, and then solve problems. Moreover, leaders should reform unreasonable

regulations and technology, and encourage personnel to grow and be successful. In this way, leadership bureaucracy can be avoided.

12. Train each staff to strive to be a manager.
13. Operate with the requirements of the six-step work method and three working formula.
14. Make an effort to go public and let staff be shareholders.
15. Simplify procedures and reduce documentation and directives.
16. Retain performance achievements, accumulate personnel files, and leave no file with any fault.
17. Be people-oriented and put staff first. Leaders and personnel at all levels should have self-esteem, self-love, self-evaluation, and self-positioning.
18. Leaders at all levels should not advocate adherence to provisions from the upper level. Knowledge and inspiration should be encouraged in order to work with creative thinking.
19. Be professional, become experts, and continuously improve personnel's professional skills.
20. Leaders and personnel should strengthen communication to break down various obstacles of organizational structure and solve contradictions.
21. Encourage and foster the mutual care and support among staff to make them have confidence and a sense of pride.
22. Make employees aware of the market. The highest interest is the corporate interests and staff should not live on the enterprise while helping others secretly.
23. Integrate all enterprise assets and resources, and make full rational use of the means of production and internal and external human resources.
24. Adhere to market ability and strictly prohibit overproduction, overstocking, and disuse of products.
25. Adhere to prominence–balance, balance – prominence business development and management philosophy.
26. Adhere to the independent business units at all levels; assess job efficiency and effectiveness by setting quotas.
27. Control the building of infrastructure and monitor and assess returns on investment.
28. All staff participate in management and economic accounting.
29. Develop patent products and products with new technology. This is the driving force for enterprise development.
30. Strengthen financial management, cash management, and benefit budget management. Everyone has a benefit indicator.

These 30 are methods for professional managers to realize objectives and tasks. Only proper methods can ensure the accomplishment of objectives and tasks. Once the objectives and tasks are identified, the fundamental responsibilities of leadership are to discover and solve problems, unify the understanding of all staff, mobilize knowledge and inspiration of all staff, and carry out creative work.

Section 9 Conclusion

Thirty years ago, I made consumption the subject of my long-time tracking research. In my long observation and study of Chinese economy and the operation of the world economy, I deeply recognize that consumption has been the original power behind almost all social activities since the beginning of humanity. And the role that consumption plays in economic and society development is not only huge, but also permanent. I conclude that consumption is the power source of social civilization progress; consumption creates all the social wealth; it is consumption that creates all things.

Based on this concept and from the view of history, reality and future, I studied the whole development process of human productive consumption, research productive consumption, and social consumption, and expounded the position, function, and significance of consumption in economics, even the whole of social life, and on this basis, created a systematic theory of consumption.

In this book, I discussed much about the issue of consumption. However, consumption is an old topic, and I summarized and analyzed various old and new schools of thought on consumption at home and abroad, aiming at absorbing their essence. I believe the theories of former generations can be summed up in four words: learning, succession, development, and innovation. Whether ancient theories or contemporary theories, I hold an attitude of study and make contributions based on the study of former generations. My academic purpose is to achieve the goal of overhauling thoroughly and correcting the original by tracing to the source.

The study results crystallize my 30-year endeavor, which also exposes a clear-cut principle that consumption is a huge discipline. We cannot finish this work within one day. It calls for long-term hard work. In the macro perspective, I am confident that my study results may boost virtuous social operation and enhance the healthy development of social civilization and progress, which has universal meaning. In the micro perspective, it may help human beings live a more sensible life. However, these theories have not been state or nation specific. Therefore, they should be combined with the actual condition of each country or nation. Only in this way can the efficiency of the theory be displayed to the largest extent.

In the introduction, I outlined 14 main academic innovations which cohere in my 30 years of painstaking effort, and especially emphasize the following content.

One of my contributions is endowing consumption with a lofty academic position and bringing up the new classification of the three main consumptions. During the very long development process of living consumption, human beings gradually created productive consumption, social consumption, and then science and research productive consumption. The living consumption is the origin, core, and power source of the three main consumptions.

Driven by their metabolism, human beings obtain materials from the natural world and then create new desires and needs, as well as new materials and spiritual and cultural products; the sum of this consumption process is human consumption. This process comprises micro consumption and macro consumption, which are embodied in the movement process of the micro-consumption chain and macro-consumption chain.

Many academic issues haven't been studied deeply owing to limitations of time, knowledge level, energy, and so on. No theory can contain everything and no research can fully expose truth; nor does my study. Not avoiding problems is as important as not avoiding the contradiction of reality. As long as you look directly at it, you can face up to it, look into it, and develop it. For instance, though the macro control of the economy brought a more integrated system, the model for regulation and control hasn't been set up completely; though consumption leadership management science put forward some theories, it hasn't been a complete theoretic system; and though consumption social productivity brought up 15 elements, because of the restriction of the length of the article, some deeper related issues haven't been unfolded further. In addition the relations between consumption levels and production levels, the mutual adaptation mechanism of production structure and consumption structure, the issue of specific features and implementation of consumption-led economy, the problems of controlling and leading social public consumption and consumer groups under the conditions of the market economy, national administration consumption models and so on are also illustrated generally but lack deeper and intensive study.

The existence of these issues should be discussed further in a systematic way. I am confident that I will make more significant contributions in the near future. Centering on those issues, I am ready to conduct extensive communication and discussion with scholars worldwide.

My study in the future will be focused on branch theories on consumptions capable of forming an independent theoretical system. At present, I am involved in writing two books. One of them is *Leadership Management Science*, which discusses consumption, including a series of concrete theories on the macro, medium, and micro levels of consumption philosophy, in the third volume. I hope that this book may become a work on new theories with a sense of innovation.

The other work is *Productivity Science of Consumption Society*, which is the productivity formed by three important consumptions in the whole consumption society. During the process of living consumption, human beings create production consumption, social consumption, and today's scientific research and production consumption. Therefore, to a certain extent, *Consumption and Management* is a work of discussing the productivity of consumption society. I put this issue in the second chapter of the book. Because of the limits of size, I cannot fully discuss all contents related to this issue. Therefore, in *Productivity Science of Consumption Society*, I intend to fully discuss every aspect related to the issue of the productivity of consumption society. I expect this work to be available on the market in May 2012.

In this way, all my study results are presented to readers in three books: *Consumption and Management* (three volumes), *Consumption and Management* (a refined and re-edited version of the former three volumes), *Leadership Management Science* and *Productivity Science of Consumption Society*.

Readers of my works are divided into four groups: academic researchers, theoretical educators, state administrators, enterprise managers, and marketing personnel. Academic study needs new theoretical innovation; theoretical education needs new thoughts and new theories that conform to the developing situation development; state administration needs theories guiding social operations from a macro and micro perspective; state administrators and marketing personnel need the support of more operative theories. Besides, there are specific discussions on family consumption and financing, which offer a correct guiding sense for each family.

Postscript

After 30 years, with nine revisions, I have finished this book and unloaded a heavy burden in my heart.

After *Consumption and Management* was published, several hundred of the media made related reports at different times. In less than a year, the reaction in society was beyond my expectation. Many readers found it time-consuming to finish the three volumes of *Consumption and Management*, nearly 1,500,000 words, so an abridged version was required. Some professionals also think the abridged *On Consumption* has a positive meaning for readers to get the whole contents of the book in a relatively short time. I took advice and created a bridged version. Meanwhile, when reprinting, I added two articles: 'Financial Crisis and Theorists' Responsibility', delivered in *People's Forum*, and 'New Ages Calling New Theory', delivered in *People's Forum* and *China Daily* by Honorary Researcher and Professor Dai Yuanchen with China Academy of Social Sciences.

The abbreviated version changed 'Economic Science of Consumption Society' in the original into 'Systematic Theories on Consumption Science', and *On Consumption* into *General Theory of Consumption*. In addition, some contents in some chapters of the original version are slightly revised, added to, and refined.

My research on consumption theory began from the initial stages of reform and opening up in China. My first work was *Consumption and Economic Laws*, in 1982. In my research, I have found living consumption, social consumption, and production consumption, the three important consumptions, are the natural law for economic development.

The economic base determines targets of production and gives birth to basic economic laws. National interference on the market free adjusting law of merchandise exchange gives birth to macro adjusting market economic laws. Interference of the socialist state-owned economic base on the market free adjusting law of merchandise exchange gives birth to socialist macro-adjusting market economic laws. It is the basic content of my research on consumption theories. In 1984, I wrote *Consumption is the Traction Force of Market Competition* and *Consumption and Surplus Value Law*. Then I wrote articles like 'Several Thoughts on Accelerating Development of Consumption Social Productivity' and 'The Target of Reform is to Develop Consumption Social Productivity' and posted them to state leaders and related departments with the hope of supplying some references for their work. These articles were later published by Chinese Economy Publishing House and Central Party School Publishing House in 1995 and 1997. Afterwards, I suspended writing due to busy work.

In December 1996, I finished the first draft of *Consumption and Management* in 22 parts during the period I was in hospital in Beijing. The draft comprehensively analyzed the law of how human consumption affects economic circle spiral development; the relationship between consumption and the progress of social civilization; the relationship between consumption and social wealth; the relationship between nature, productivity, production relations, research and production; the relationship between consumption creating demands and demands reacting to consumption, and so on. This article was published in the first volume of *Economic Macrocosm* in 1997 and was included in my anthology. At that time, my research on consumption theories moved into a new phase. In the new century, I began systematically to research the primary structure of *Consumption and Management* and arrange articles about my learning and working practices guided by consumption theories for many years.

From September 2006 to March 2008, I spent one and a half years completely modifying the entire book and complementing it with some new materials such as the spirits of the Seventeenth National Congress of the Communist Party of China and some new conclusions from recent academic research.

My research mainly follows the principle theories of philosophy, economy, sociology, and management. I used mainly used social statistics methods, literature comparison methods, probability sampling methods, case-study approaches, and interview and computer analysis. Therefore, no matter what the basic theories or methodology, this book is not only an economic work but also a synthesis of many subjects. It is the reason why I locate it as consumption social economics.

Many friends have offered sincere support and help during the formation of *Consumption and Management*. Several times, Professor Liu Haifan organized a panel of experts to discuss my theories, offering affirmative support and encouragement; having read my *Collections of Thesis*, Honorary Researcher and Professor Dai Yuanchen with China Academy of

Social Sciences suggested I publish a book and write the preface personally; Researcher and Professor Li Xinsheng with China Academy of Social Sciences in Shandong and his colleagues edited and trimmed this book greatly, adding flavor to my theoretical works. The following comrades have offered lots of valuable suggestions and comments during my theoretical creation: Professor Zhao Jinghua, Dean of School of Government Management of Central University of Finance & Economics; Professor Wang Jifu, Dean of School of Business Administration of US Houston University; and Lifelong Professor Ms Linda, Director of Economics Study Room of School of Business Administration of US Houston University.

The great educationalist Han Yu in the Tang Dynasty said: 'Since no one is born omniscient, who can claim to have no doubts? If one has doubts and is not willing to learn from a teacher, his doubts will never be resolved.' He advocated, 'Where there is the doctrine, there is my teacher.' Actually, where there is doctrine, there is a teacher. During the course of writing this book, I saw everyone who gave me enlightenment as my teacher. Not only scholars mentioned above are my teachers, but also authors of works, papers, and articles I have read are my teachers. My superiors are my teachers; my underlings are my teachers; my relatives, including my juniors are my teacher; even competitors I have met in the market are my teachers as well. Their knowledge, opinions, and good qualities in certain aspects bring to me enlightenment on conducting myself, on working and researching. For many years, I encouraged myself in the spirit, 'One should be fond of learning and not feel ashamed to ask and learn of his inferiors.' If I have some improvement in 30 years, it has a certain relationship to the tuition the teachers above gave me. In the future, I still will make virtuous people my teachers to persevere in cultivating my morality and researching.

I am grateful for my deceased wife Song Xiechen here. She was great. When I began to study consumption theories at the juncture of 1970s and 1980s, I was crazily addicted to it, even someone jokingly calling me 'Neuropathy'. She undertook all the housework, which offered me enough time to learn and create. When I abruptly delivered some articles regarded as radical at that time, she still stood by me and always supported me without any regret. The pressure that ordinary people cannot imagine overwhelmed her body and took away her health.

Of course, here I will express my special thanks to my current wife Feng Shuqin. She is both a virtuous wife and a competent assistant in my work. With her participation, I re-lighted my passion to create since I stopped writing ten years ago, which opened a new milestone stage of my theory research. With her wonderful grammatical knowledge, she did many important editions and adaptation for my theory. Study and discussion became an important part of our life. Without her, *Consumption and Management* couldn't be brought out at the time of my seventieth birthday. It is the child of both of us and also a gift for the 30th anniversary of reform and opening up of China.

Although I am 73 years old, my gumption does not decline. The sentence 'people who are 70 years old are rare from ancientness' should go into a historical museum. This sentence was written by famous poet Du Fu in Tang Dynasty in 798, when the average age of people only was 48. A thousand years have passed, living conditions for human beings have had enormous changes, and 70 years old is no longer the symbol of life's limitation. The World Health Organization proposes a new concept called healthy horizon to analyze the life phases of human beings: youth is life's preparatory phase; middle age is life's protecting phase; agedness is life's quality phase. It is said that life is like a long river, from a streamlet in its upper reaches to the turbulent waves of its middle reaches to capacious oceans. The upper reaches are beautiful childhood; the middle reaches are ponderous middle age; the lower reaches are massive agedness. For aged people, they are peaceful, tolerated, and erudite, with a great extent of knowledge and accumulated experience. It can be seen that it is a great time for researching.

I consider that happiness in life does not come entirely from purpose and results, but from the course of struggling. For everybody, the most important thing is not to enjoy ready-made results but to mobilize their power to exploit and pursue for the future. I set 70 as a new starting point for me to keep the first power by using strong will and to mobilize the second power by using sense and intelligence. So I need to say here that *Consumption and Management* is not the end of my study, but a beginning of a more meaningful, difficult, and challenging new journey.

When I stopped writing, the rays of the morning sunshine had just appeared on Qianfo Mountain outside my window. In the season from cold to return a warm of chilly spring, I feel a little warm and relaxed in my heart. I suddenly remember a quatrain of Mr. Zang Kejia, whose title is 'Old Cattle': 'There is water and mud in every farmland, spading husbandry from east to west. Old cattle also understand the preciousness of a goodly period; it will be hard work without scourging.' I seem like the old cattle ceaselessly cultivating on farmland. 'Working hard without scourging' is the real thought in my mind.

References

Borden, Neil H. (1965) 'The Concept of the Marketing Mix', in G. Schertz, *Science in Marketing*, Chichester, Wiley.

Dean, J. (1950) 'Pricing Policies for New Products', *Harvard Business Review,* November.

Deng, X (2006) *Selected Writings of Deng Xiaoping*, Peking: People's Publishing House.

Duesenberry, J. S. (1949) *Income, Saving and the Theory of Consumer Behavior*, Cambridge, Mass.: Harvard University Press.

Engels, F. (1972) *The Origin of the Family, Private Property and the State*, New York: Lawrence & Wishart.

Fayol, H. (1916) [1963] *General and Industrial Management*, translated from the French edition (Dunod) by Constance Storrs, London: Pitman.

Friedman, M. (1957) *A Theory of the Consumption Function*, Princeton: Princeton University Press.

Glazer, W. (1969) 'Marketing's Changing Social Relationships', *Journal of Marketing*, Vol. 33, No. 1.

Guan, Zhong (1998) *Guanzi: Political, Economic, and Philosophical Essays from Early China: A Study and Translation*, edited by W. Allyn Rickett, Princeton: Princeton University Press.

Guangyuang, Yu (1985) *On Social Science Research*, n.p.: Sichuan People's Publishing House.

Howard, J. A. and Sheth, J. N. (1969) *The Theory of Buyer Behavior*, New York: Wiley.

Keynes, J. M. (1936) *The General Theory of Employment, Interest and Money*, n.p.: Palgrave Macmillan.

Kotler, P. and Levy, S. J. (1971) 'Demarketing, Yes, Demarketing', *Harvard Business Review*, Vol. 49.

Kotler, P. and Levy, S. J. (1969) 'Broadening the Concept of Marketing', *Journal of Marketing*, Vol. 33.

Levitt, T. (1960) 'Marketing Myopia', *Harvard Business Review*, July–August.

Levitt, T. (1965) 'Exploit the Product Life Cycle', *Harvard Business Review*, November–December.

Mandeville, B. (1714) [1924], *The Fable of the Bees: or Private Vices, Publick Benefits*, edited by F. B. Kaye, Oxford: Oxford University Press.

Mao, Z. D. (1957) 'On the Correct Handling of the Contradictions among the People', speech, www.marxists.org/reference/archive/mao/selected-works/volume-5/mswv5_58.htm.

Mao, Z. D. (1987) Collected Works of Mao Tse-tung, Peking: *Foreign Languages Press.*

Marx, K. (1867) *Capital: Critique of Political Economy*, n.p.: Verlag von Otto Meisner.

McCarthy, E. J. (1960) *Principles of Marketing*, n.p.: Irwin Publishing.

Modigliani, Franco (1970) 'The Life-cycle Hypothesis and Intercountry Differences in the Saving Ratio' in W. A. Eltis, M. F. G. Scott, and J. N. Wolfe, eds, *Induction, Growth, and Trade: Essays in Honour of Sir Roy Harrod*, Oxford: Oxford University Press.

Modigliani, Franco (1975) 'The Life-cycle Hypothesis of Saving Twenty Years Later', in Michael Parkin, ed., *Contemporary Issues in Economics*, Manchester: Manchester University Press.

Modigliani, Franco (1976) 'Life-cycle, Individual Thrift, and the Wealth of Nations', *American Economic Review*, Vol. 76, No. 3.

Morgan L. H. (1877) *Ancient Society or Researches in the Lines of Human Progress from Savagery through Barbarism to Civilization*, n.p.: MacMillan and Co.

Petty, W. (1662) *A Treatise of Taxes and Contributions*, London: Angel in Cornhill.

Samuelson, P. A. (1948) *Economics: An Introductory Analysis*, McGraw-Hill.

Say, Jean-Baptiste (1803) *Traité d'économie politique*, translated from the 4th edition of the French *A Treatise on Political Economy* by C. R. Prinsep, Philadelphia: Lippincott, Grambo & Co.

Smith, Adam (1977) [1776] *An Inquiry into the Nature and Causes of the Wealth of Nations*, Chicago: University of Chicago Press.

Smith, Adam (2009) [1817] *The Theory of Moral Sentiments*, introduced by Amartya Sen, edited with notes by Ryan Patrick Hanley, New York: Penguin.

Smith, W. (1956) 'Product Differentiation and Market Segmentation as Alternative Marketing Strategies', *Journal of Marketing*, July.

Taylor, Frederick Winslow (1911) *The Principle of Scientific Management*, New York: Harper.

Toffler, A. (1970) *Future Shock*, n.p.: Random House.

Zaltman, G. and Kotler, P. (1971) 'Marketing: An Approach to Planned Social Change', *Journal of Marketing*, July.